Hanns Eisler

A Miscellany

compiled and edited by

David Blake

harwood academic publishers

Australia • Austria • China • France • Germany • India • Japan
Luxembourg • Malaysia • Netherlands • Russia • Singapore
Switzerland • Thailand • United Kingdom • United States

3 Boulevard Royal
L-2449 Luxembourg

Cover illustration: Hanns Eisler in Berlin, 1958.

British Library Cataloguing in Publication Data
Hanns Eisler: Miscellany. – (Contemporary
Music Studies, ISSN 0891-5415; Vol. 9)
I. Blake, David II. Series
780.92

ISBN 3-7186-5573-X (hardback)
ISBN 3-7186-5575-6 (paperback)

For Steffy
with affection and gratitude

CONTENTS

INTRODUCTION TO THE SERIES

The rapid expansion and diversification of contemporary music is explored in this international series of books for contemporary musicians. Leading experts and practitioners present composition today in all aspects — its techniques, aesthetics and technology, and its relationships with other disciplines and currents of thought — as well as using the series to communicate actual musical materials.

The series also features monographs on significant twentieth-century composers not extensively documented in the existing literature.

NIGEL OSBORNE

Eisler at Valley Cottage near New York in 1938.

INTRODUCTION

'I do beg you to bloom, Mr. Tree; don't forget, it is Spring! Are you on strike because of the awful gloom in this yard? Surely you're not so unreasonable as to be dreaming of green forests. May I request that you adapt to the situation? Perhaps you think it superfluous to bloom in our times – what place have young, tender leaves on the barricades? In that you wouldn't be at all wrong, Mr. Tree. But don't forget: it is Spring!'

When the first plans for this book were made, Europe, and indeed the world, was a very different place. History will in due course judge the upheavals of 1989 to be comparable in significance to those of two hundred years earlier, and the fall of the Berlin Wall will be adorned with as much mystique and legend as the storming of the Bastille. For the last thirteen years of his life, Hanns Eisler lived in a country which, today, no longer exists, a country dominated and regulated by a power which also no longer exists. The political system upon which both were based and the ideology which Eisler believed in and fought for has been almost completely discredited. It might be argued that, in a musical climate in which, increasingly, the technology is the message, the market-place is the arbiter and, once again, the 'new religiosity' is gaining strength, the appearance of this book is ill-timed. Fortunately, the world remains a diverse place, the times are 'damned interesting' and Eisler's own words of 1927, quoted above, can still apply.

There is no doubt that a proper evaluation of Eisler's work and achievement has been hampered by the fact of his having occupied two seemingly contradictory spheres of activity. In the West, our easy acceptance of the concept of a mainstream of music and the powerful arguments for a logical line of development from the classics to one specific area of twentieth-century music, argued so persuasively by Schoenberg himself, by Webern (in *The Path to the New Music*) and by subsequent music historians, has led us to take interest only in Eisler the Schoenberg pupil. Wherever his work can be related to a known and well-studied repertoire, be it atonal piano sonata or serial quintet, then the criteria seem to exist for judgements to be made. Put against this, however, a contrary view, challenge the concept of a 'path', point to some contradictions, face up to the fragmented nature of our musical life, and Eisler's passionate commitment to the creation of an alternative music culture on behalf of an excluded, 'disenfranchised' class of working people becomes not only more comprehensible, but worthy of respect and study. This study must, however, be made with a proper historical perspective. Such attitudes as were shown by the GDR administration and intellectuals towards his serial compositions must be fought against. The details of the grotesque *Johann Faustus* affair, as described in Chapter 15, involving many distinguished names, which left him saddened and creatively debilitated, are a warning against the making of judgements based either on inflexible dogma or uninformed prejudice.

The breaking away from the Schoenberg ethos was painful and distressing for Eisler, but the strength of conviction which made it necessary gave rise very soon to music which was arguably more individual, more original and more useful than the beautifully imagined and crafted earlier pieces already being performed at concerts of the ISCM and other festivals. Eisler's consummate compositional technique is evident in everything he wrote and makes the choral symphony, the chamber cantata, the *Lied*, the theatre music, the tonal and serial film music and the marching song equally worthy of close study and repeated hearing.

No artist's work can be properly appreciated without an overview of his whole output. I am, therefore, all too conscious that this book, the first on Eisler to be conceived and published in English, is presented to a readership for whom it is still, more than thirty years after its subject's death, difficult to obtain the music, the writings and the recordings. One can only hope the position will improve.

From the start it was obvious that it would not be possible to do justice to all aspects of Eisler's enormous and diverse output. The shape of the book began to suggest itself more clearly once I had decided that its core would be a translation of the *Johann Faustus* libretto, one of the most substantial creative acts of the composer's life. The chapters discuss the music more or less chronologically and a balance of critical analysis, historical survey and aesthetic argument has been attempted. Some of Eisler's own articles and extracts from the conversations recorded towards the end of his life are included in order to demonstrate the liveliness of his intellect and the strength of his personality. Although Mayer's article on Eisler's relationship with Adorno dates from 1977, I know of no better or more recent analysis of a subject too important to be ignored. From my own point of view, the greatest surprise arose from my closer examination of the early compositions, those pre-dating the studies with Schoenberg. These are so much better than I had suspected that my overall view of him underwent a subtle shift.

Eisler led such an interesting life, rarely far away from vital artistic and political activity, surrounded by some of the great figures of the time, that study of him provides a valuable insight into the complexities of our century. The Western musician's antipathy towards the putting of the lofty art of music at the service of social and political needs is neither logical nor tenable. Eisler's concept of *'angewandte Musik'* – applied music – in our age of media-dominated information and entertainment, makes ever greater sense. It certainly makes no sense, for badly defined, vaguely felt and uninformed reasons, to ignore so much music which is so brilliantly entertaining, so witty, so tuneful, so profound, so stimulating. One important factor must, however, be faced. As Goldschmidt says, whoever requires only to be lulled by music, whoever is too indolent to think, will find Eisler too uncomfortable, too provocative. Like Beethoven, Eisler demands an active listener, an intelligent, alert participant in the musical performance. If you try to use his music as wallpaper, it could drive you mad!

David Blake

ACKNOWLEDGEMENTS

I am greatly indebted to Frau Stephanie Eisler for her warm encouragement and help throughout my work on this book; also for her generous permission to reproduce material from the Eisler Archive in Berlin and all music which was published in the former GDR. I am grateful also to Universal Edition AG Vienna, for their kind permission to quote from several of Eisler's early works and Webern's Opp. 3 and 12; to Deutscher Verlag, Leipzig, for permission to translate the *Johann Faustus* libretto, to Suhrkamp Verlag, Frankfurt am Main, for permission to quote the numerous Brecht texts, and to Methuen, London for permission to make translations of them.

On the occasions of my researches in the Eisler Archive, I have been given invaluable help and advice as well as comfortable facilities by the extremely knowledgeable secretary Frau Helgard Rienäcker and I thank her warmly. Throughout, I have relied on the wisdom and knowledge of my dear friend Georg Knepler to whom I have turned on countless occasions for advice ranging from matters of principle to footling details. His response has been unfailingly interested, helpful and patient. It gives me special pleasure that his article provides the overall summing-up of Eisler's work in the book.

All unattributed translations are mine.

LIST OF PLATES

(Between pp. 257 and 259)

To write a systematic study of the composer Hanns Eisler is, I think, very difficult. One risks building a cage. When it is finished, the bird has flown.

Harry Goldschmidt

1

"I DON'T GIVE A DAMN ABOUT THIS SPRING" - HANNS EISLER'S MOVE TO BERLIN

Eberhardt Klemm

Hanns Eisler, born in Leipzig in 1898, moved in 1901 with his parents and brother and sister via Brünn to Vienna. One can guess that the parents were not very happy in Vienna. His mother, a butcher's daughter, to whom Hanns was closer than to his father, came from Leipzig; his father, the Austrian scholar Rudolf Eisler, had studied and obtained his doctorate there (with Wilhelm Wundt). Even after his return to Vienna, Rudolf Eisler remained tied to Leipzig. He took over the editing there of a 'philosophical/sociological series' for a publisher much respected at that time, Dr Werner Klinkhardt; for this series he wrote (among other things) the *Grundlagen der Philosophie des Geisteslebens* [Foundations of the philosophy of the spiritual life] (1908) and translated from the French (Gustave le Bon, Alfred Fouillée). Incidentally, he remained true to the thinking of his teacher, writing *Wilhelm Wundts Philosophie und Psychologie. In ihren Grundlehren dargestellt* [Wilhelm Wundt's Philosophy and Psychology. An outline of its basic teachings] (1902). With the Austrian Marxist Max Adler he founded the Vienna Sociological Society in 1907. Later, under the influence of syncretism, he turned his attention to critical problems of cognition. His abiding achievement, however, is his philosophical-lexical works. Although an academic thinker and writer, he never had an academic career. In Vienna, Rudolf Eisler remained an outsider — doubtless also because he was a Jew. His philosophy could hardly be linked to social conditions in Austria; his books betray nothing of the spirit of *fin de siécle* Vienna. One can conclude that his parents' household did not help Hanns Eisler to form any very strong bond with Vienna.

After the First World War, Hanns Eisler seems to have been virtually homeless. The tie to his parents' house was loosened; he lived in barracks with others who had returned from the war, and had scarcely the money to buy himself civilian clothes. In the autumn of 1919 — Eisler was now twenty one years old — he began to study with Arnold Schoenberg; a year later he married. The study with Schoenberg must have given the difficult and also obstinate student a boost: he worked in the Society for Private Musical Performances founded by Schoenberg at that time, and he was allowed to accompany his teacher on trips. Eisler was not amongst the most diligent students, and the strict discipline of the 'classical' instruction may not always have appealed to him. Yet his musical thoughts flowed very quickly. Soon after concluding his studies with Schoenberg, his First Piano Sonata — the first of his works to carry an opus number — was premiered on 10 April 1923, in Prague). In October 1924 he was first acknowledged as a composer in the Viennese journal *Musikblätter des Anbruch*; six months later he received the Art Prize of the city of Vienna.

One would presume that Eisler was content. But the opposite is the case. He was indeed convinced that he could become a good composer, yet he already recognized that he would then have to accept the notion of working for a minority, and in virtual isolation. Although he was a prizewinner, his works were hardly played in Vienna; the premieres took place mostly at international music festivals governed by distinct cliques. Eisler's hatred for bourgeois musical life could no longer be hidden. A sense of surfeit (including surfeit of life — the artistic preoccupation with death cannot be overlooked), the desire to experience something new, and certainly, also, the desire to produce something more useful and significant, may have decided him — in 1925 — to leave Vienna.

Many causes probably contributed to the decision to resettle in Berlin. Eisler knew the city: Schoenberg had already taken him there on one occasion. At the same time (September 1925), Schoenberg himself had been called, as the successor to Ferruccio Busoni, to lead a masterclass in composition at the Prussian Academy of Arts. Despite their differences in outlook, Eisler had a great love for his teacher, and was not the only one who again and again — and even later — sought the company of this man.

Moreover, Eisler's brother and sister had already lived for a long time in Berlin. Both of them — Elfriede (born 1895) and Gerhart (born 1896) — had become politically active quite early, while still in Vienna. Elfriede Friedländer — somewhat later she used the maiden name of her mother, (Ruth) Fischer — was a founder of the KPÖ, the Communist Party of Austria. While still in Vienna she published a booklet entitled *Sexualethik des Kommunismus* [The Sexual Ethics of Communism]. When she went to Berlin early in 1919 and a year later became a member of the Communist Party of Germany (KPD), her rapid political rise began. She became Secretary of the regional leadership of Berlin-

Brandenburg, and was soon — together with Arkadi Maslow and Werner Scholem — at the head of the Party. As a consequence of her ultra-left, sectarian politics, she was forced to leave the Politbüro at the end of 1925; a year later she was expelled from the KPD. But on 12 July 1925, on the opening day of the tenth party conference, she gave a speech in connection with a theatre presentation, the historical revue *Trotz alledem*! [In spite of all that!], for which Erwin Piscator (director), Edmund Meisel (composer and conductor) and John Heartfield (set designer) were jointly responsible. Whether Eisler was already living in Berlin at this point, or whether he moved there only in September of that year, we do not know. And very little is known about the relationship between the composer and his sister. It is understandable that he said nothing on this subject in the published conversations with Hans Bunge and Nathan Notowicz: in any case, he was not asked about these matters. One can assume that the high political standing of his sister, her activity and intelligence, must have impressed the younger brother. Hanns, unlike his brother, had not broken with her. Even during the first years of emigration (in Paris), he supported her financially, as one can deduce from some of Eisler's letters to Brecht.

One cannot doubt the great influence that his brother Gerhart, two years older, had upon Hanns. In 1965, three years after the composer's death, Notowicz also recorded a conversation with Gerhart Eisler. Concerning the period after the war, when Gerhart was active as an agitator in the KPD, he said: "It was a hectic time. We believed every day in revolution throughout the whole of Europe. Every minute that we were not working as revolutionaries, as agitators, as journalists, we considered wasted. My brother was a part of myself." Hanns Eisler's first years in Berlin are still relatively obscure. At first he appears to have led a kind of 'coffee-house existence' (Walter Benjamin describes such coffee-houses in his *Berliner Chronik*); Schoenberg alludes to this in a letter to Eisler of 10 March 1926. He must also have made an attempt to gain a foothold at a conservatory — evidently without success; at least he can only have been active as a teacher for a very short time. Yet there are no grounds whatever for thinking that he was stagnant as a composer. Shortly after his arrival in Berlin — this has not previously been mentioned in research on Eisler — he had obviously seen the *Frankfurter Zeitung* of 16 August 1925, in which Walter Benjamin reported on a 'collection of Frankfurt children's rhymes' and reproduced, among others , the satirical rhymes *Meine Mutter wird Soldat* [My mother's become a soldier] and *Mariechen, du dummes Viehchen* [Little Marie, you stupid little thing]. Eisler set both texts; they are part of the cycle published later under the title *Zeitungsausschnitte* [Newspaper Cuttings] Op. 11, which was still addressed to a bourgeois public, but effectively signalled Eisler's departure from the usual type of concert lyricism. The songs were then premiered — with some success — at a concert of the Berlin branch of the International Society for New Music (on 11 December 1927, by Margot Hinnenberg-Lefèbre, to whom they are dedicated).

Eisler's dissatisfaction with his position as a bourgeois composer grows and comes to a head in a forceful, controversial exchange of letters with Schoenberg. Even in 1924 he hit out at Schoenberg's esotericism, and dealt more playfully than seriously with the newly-developed twelve-note technique (in *Palmström*, Op. 5). Now to Schoenberg he even expressed doubts about the possibilities of this process of composition: "Modern music bores me, it doesn't interest me, some of it I even hate and despise. Actually I want nothing to do with what is 'modern'. As far as possible, I avoid hearing or reading it. (Sadly, I must also include my own works of recent years.) [. . .] Also, I understand nothing (except superficialities) of twelve-note technique and twelve-note music. But I am enthusiastic about your twelve-note works (for example the Piano Suite [Op. 25]) and have studied them in the greatest detail." (Undated letter to Schoenberg, before 10 March 1926.)

Eisler was still expressing his hatred for everything conventional, particularly for 'the modern', even for his own situation in Berlin, in very private ways. In the autumn of 1926 — after trips to Vienna and Paris — he wrote perhaps his strangest work: the *Tagebuch des Hanns Eisler. Eine Kantate für Frauenterzett, Tenor, Geige und Klavier* [Diary of Hanns Eisler. A cantata for female trio, tenor, violin and piano], Op. 9, dedicated to his Viennese friend Erwin Ratz. The composer's texts, some mocking and ironic, some carping, allude clearly to Schoenberg. That the two of them, Eisler and Schoenberg, lived in the same city, is commented on in this way: 'It is impossible to be completely alone in a strange city. If there are two of you, you can enjoy yourself much better'. The disagreement with his teacher, in itself perhaps inevitable, was triggered by a piece of gossip that goes back to a train journey with Schoenberg's teacher and brother-in-law Alexander Zemlinsky. In Opus 9, it says: 'Travelling cannot be pleasant, if you travel alone.' Eisler's self-hatred is given voice in the following line: 'If you're a stupid, bad bourgeois lad, how hateful everything is!' Yet in the third part of the cycle one hears the following lines: 'Dear child, don't be so downcast! Don't be so content with your sorrow; don't talk so much of your suffering in such damned interesting times! At this point, one hears in the piano the beginning of the *Internationale,* then the words: 'Be alert! Eyes open, not shut! Otherwise we'll cover you up with manuscript paper today!' Here the famous fourths motif from Schoenberg's Chamber Symphony Op. 9 (!) is quoted suggestively.

Precisely because much about Eisler's first years in Berlin is still unknown, all available sources must be utilized. This has not yet really been done with regard to an Eisler sketchbook found amongst the belongings of the musicologist Erwin Ratz, who died in 1973; this is currently kept in the Hanns Eisler Archive in Berlin (EA 215/65–94). The notebook, 13.0 cm by 16.1 cm in size, consisting of forty pages, of which twenty-nine have been written on, was very probably used by Eisler in 1928. For long stretches it is so hurriedly written that publication is for the time being out of the question. Nevertheless a brief, more legible section of text was reproduced in the Appendix (Addenda) of Eisler's writings (*Musik und Politik,* III/3 p. 27 Leipzig 1983), and it has been possible to decipher a few others (though not entirely satisfactorily) in connection with the present article. The entries in this notebook are composed of fragments of songs, musical sketches, texts and drafts of songs, roughly sketched essays and other written notes (such as addresses, arrival times, etc.). Without exception they reflect the new experiences in Berlin, and they allow one to recognize a contradictory spirit whose rejection of his bourgeois past was certainly not without difficulties. On page 74, Eisler has written a text (last line illegible), that reads like a mockery of his own love life:[1]

> *'Monologue of the unhappy lover*
> *(small build, big ears, bald)*
> *"At the most, a roof tile flies towards me, but no woman flies towards me."*
> *We must indeed be conquerors. If Napoleon had been as handsome as Valentino, he would never have conquered the village of Einsiedel [near Vienna]. But he was small and ugly, yellow as an ape. [. . .]'*

Another of his own experiences — a journey at night through the streets of Berlin — is reflected in these lines (p. 91):

> *'Drunken taxi-ride (lower rate)*
> *Life's taxi-meter shows a double rate*
> *We're travelling fast; insanely fast, the whole world is lopsided.*
> *Like telegraph poles, the women are posted on the streets.*
> *O soft, exciting wall, made of smiles, flesh and blood.'*

---

[1] See Fig. 1.1 p. 10

The following text (pp. 71–73) strikes different notes – it was presumably meant to be set to music. It is closely linked to the Berlin tenements and their courtyards:

> *'I don't give a damn about this Spring*
> *I spit on this Spring*
> *[. . .]*
> *Is there anything as stifling as this Spring in an air-well?*
> *The rats blink in the sun. And the tubercular man spits in the sunshine!*
> *And the conveniences smell overpowering*
> *Frozen in winter, the filth blossoms*
> *This Spring air makes one drunk as alcohol does; you vomit; You vomit on this earth, that hopes to renew itself. The stabilization of temperature differences drives us to despair. As long as, in the flowerbeds, instead of flowers, no hand-grenades bloom, usable even in their tenderest blossoming, we vomit, we shit on a Spring in which one needs less coal but more composure, in order not to commit the most ultra-left stupidity, [. . .]'*

In Berlin, from 1927 onwards, Eisler continued those labours – half literary, half concerned with music theory – begun in Vienna. Admittedly, they now have a completely different emphasis. These critical pieces and *feuilletons* written for the periodical *Rote Fahne* [Red Flag] are distinguished from everything else that one could read at that time by their nonchalance and their utterly disrespectful tone. Whether Eisler is discussing Krenek's *Jonny spielt auf*, Hindemith's *Cardillac*, Debussy's *Pélléas et Mélisande* or Wolf's *Corregidor*, his comments are almost always dominated by epithets like 'mushy', 'boring', 'superfluous', 'remote from the working class'. And Eisler in his disparagement makes no exception of older music, as reviews of Gounod's *Le Médecin malgré lui* or Verdi's *Luisa Miller* show. The so-called renaissances of Handel and Gluck, which began during the Weimar Republic, he considered to be sheer 'literary hack-work'. Fundamentally, there was only one composer of the past for Eisler, in whose work nothing was to be quibbled over and to whom the rising classes, the proletariat, should devote themselves completely: Beethoven. He was also the subject of Eisler's first contribution of any kind to the workers' press, written on the occasion of the hundredth anniversary of Beethoven's death.

Eisler, who had been friendly with Georg Grosz and John Heartfield since the first years in Berlin, was therefore aesthetically close to the radicals of the left. Their rejection of all bourgeois art corresponded to his rejection of the symphony, which he identified as the 'world view symphony', and described as that *Reich* or 'empire' of music 'where the boundless expression of personality is so highly paid'. Such views may also reflect some influence of his sister Ruth Fischer — who, when she expressed herself on matters of art, always did so from a radical leftist viewpoint — for example, taking a stand against the views of Gertrud Alexander, leading literary critic of the *Rote Fahne* in the early years of the Weimar Republic, whose neo-classical position was allied to that of Georg Lukács.

There are also, in any case, striking inconsistencies in this early theoretical thinking of Eisler's. On the one hand, for example, we have the statement that the coming '"social revolution" will eclipse the musical production of recent years like an ink-blot'. On the other hand, Eisler makes it clear that the new socialist musical culture must reach back to Schoenberg (who himself of course also belongs to that 'musical production of recent years'), and must do so because the '"genius Schoenberg" has accomplished extraordinary things' — so Eisler expresses it — 'as a revolutionary of form'.

The sketchbook was also obviously used by Eisler for writing down thoughts which then play a role in his *feuilletons*. Hence on one occasion (p. 92): 'On: Romanticism, the "new objectivity", music for fun (Spielfreudigkeit), new Romanticism.' All things of which Eisler thought none too highly! It was also intended to become a 'contribution to the natural history of the conceptual confusion of musicians'. And he remarked on this topic: 'One should say nothing against catchphrases. They annihilate ones own opinions so beautifully, they place us in the situation of taking a position on things we don't understand, as if we were precisely informed about them; thus catchphrases have an important social function: they spare us the process of thinking.'

On three pages of the sketchbook (pp. 83–85), there is a song fully worked out. Not for the first time the text takes its cue from suicide, in order sarcastically to raise the issues of social injustice — specifically, unemployment:

'And the suicide whispers:
Man, have a good rest.
When misery makes you melancholy,
Make your house dark.
Have a kip,
Till the end begins.
Say once again,
After a thousand years,
Till the wages are more generous,
Till the wages really are more generous.'

The score of this song consists of one system for the singing voice and two systems for the piano accompaniment; the ending of the piano part is lacking, i.e. it is merely indicated. From a musical point of view, 'And the suicide whispers' belongs with the *Zeitungsausschnitte*, Op. 11 of 1925 and 1926. Clearly, however, it is meant to be neither comic or ironic; rather, it sounds darker, more 'Schoenbergian' as it were. It is difficult to discern a tonality — it is an 'expanded' one.

The Berlin sketchbook contains yet another series of examples of Eisler's encounters with reality and the not uncomplicated changes in his consciousness. One finds Berlin addresses of assembly rooms (undoubtedly those of the Communist Party) and dates; one page describes the events of a street fight. On two others one recognizes the beginning of a part of the theatre music for Lion Feuchtwanger's Warren Hastings piece, *Calcutta, 4 May,* into which a Brecht text set to music by Eisler (*Ballade vom Soldaten*) also found its way, and which had its premiere on 12 June 1928 at the Berlin Staatstheater. On another page (p. 87) one can just follow the genesis of an Eisler text (it is almost illegible), of which at least one line — 'That means turning away from reality' — later became part of the first of the *Vier Stücke für gemischten Chor* [Four Pieces for Mixed Choir], Op. 13. The piece — a set of choral variations — bears the title *Vorspruch* [Preamble] and was composed in July 1928 (and published by Universal Edition in Vienna). The line cited is in the third variation, and from it a powerful conclusion is drawn, a now-famous motto, which could serve as a summary of Eisler's entire creative achievement. The full text of this passage runs: 'That means: turning away from reality. That means: turning away from the challenge of the day. That means: turning away from our struggle! Our singing, too, must be a struggle!' Although this very passage has an incomparable, compelling momentum, satire and parody (parody of bourgeois choral works about feelings and nature) still predominate in these Opus 13 pieces; this and indeed other choral works composed by Eisler during this year 'were an attack on the out-moded and false style of the choral societies, on the *petit bourgeois* choral practices which also ruled in the German workers' singing society, and even on the mentality of many workers, who valued their emotions more highly than they did understanding' (Klemm, *Hanns Eisler*, Berlin 1973). Eisler, who in 1928 became a teacher at the Marxist Workers' School in Berlin and made the cause of the proletariat his own cause, took the decisive step as a composer when, at the end of 1927, he became the pianist of the Communist agitprop troupe *Das Rote Sprachrohr* [The Red Megaphone], led by the actor and director Maxim Vallentin. A few months later, he wrote for this troupe an entrance song, the unison choral song *Wir sind das Rote Sprachrohr,* whose first notes are actually written on a page of our sketchbook (p. 78).

Succinct, hard-hitting and simple, yet full of art and fantasy: these words describe the songs which now emerged, and the distinctive style of Eisler's militant music, soon to be fully mature. This music is the product of a man standing in for the proletariat; it is simultaneously an expression of the German workers' struggle at that time: it is inconceivable that any German city other than Berlin could have been the birthplace of such music. Barely three years had passed between Eisler's move to Berlin in 1925 and the notes and jottings in the sketchbook we have brought to light. This time was difficult for Eisler. He had to fight, like every worker, for his material existence, as well as for his artistic identity. Even the sketchbook, apparently used in the first half of 1928, mirrors the contradictions in Eisler's mental attitudes, the complicated process of a change in consciousness. This process was not yet concluded when he began working for the *Rote Fahne* and the Marxist Workers' School, but it did in the end allow Eisler to become the man that history records: the first German socialist composer.

Translated by Karin von Abrams

Published in the original German in *Sinn und Form* XXXIX Heft 3 1987.

Fig. 1.1 Page 74 from Eisler's 1928 notebook. For a translation see Klemm, p. 5

2

THE EARLY MUSIC

David Blake

Eisler's collected writings fill three substantial volumes and he was engaged in two lengthy and wide-ranging series of conversations, by Nathan Notowicz in 1958 and by Hans Bunge between 1958 and 1961. It is therefore surprising and disappointing that we know so little about his early years. The Eisler scholar Manfred Grabs, who was director of the Eisler Archive from 1965 to 1984, collated all the existing documentation (the most fruitful of the sources is the first of the conversations with Notowicz) and contributed an invaluable article to the *Arbeitsheft* entitled *Hanns Eisler today* published by the GDR Academy of the Arts in 1974.[1]

It is convenient to divide the output of Eisler's first twenty-five years or so into the following groups:

1. The earliest works mentioned, but which have not survived.
2. Works from the war years, composed in the trenches, in hospitals and sanatoria.
3. The outpouring of songs for 'Muschi' from 1918 to early 1919.
4. 'The preparation for Schoenberg' 1919.
5. Studies with Schoenberg (and Webern) 1919–23.
6. Opus 1, March 1922, onwards.

Eisler's philosopher father was a keen music lover. He worked mostly at home and after long hours at his desk liked to relax by playing the piano and singing. His wife also sang. Such domestic music-making was presumably spasmodic since we know that the family budget did not run to having a piano permanently in the home, still less to music lessons for the three children. It seems that the six-year-old Hanns composed a little piano piece for his grandmother's birthday, but the

---

[1] All Eisler scholars and enthusiasts owe Manfred Grabs an enormous debt of gratitude. His research in several areas of Eisler's activity is invaluable. The *Handbuch*, a monument of meticulous, scholarly work is indispensable.

next mention of composition relates to the 'Gymnasium' years. When, in later life, Eisler was asked who his first teacher was, he replied 'myself'. He taught himself from such books as he could lay hands on, trying out his pieces on pianos in the houses of his schoolfriends, whose mothers were 'condescending, but not unfriendly'. Through the door they will have heard songs, a piano sonata and a piano trio. When he was eleven he wrote incidental music for Gerhart Hauptmann's play *Hanneles Himmelfahrt* and also in 1913 or 1914 what he himself described as 'a bombastic so-called symphonic poem' on a subject drawn from the work of Jens Peter Jacobsen (poet of the *Songs of Gurre*, set by Schoenberg in 1900–1901). No trace of any of these has survived.

In 1916 Eisler was called up and went to serve in a Hungarian regiment of the Austrian army. Wounded and hospitalized several times, he in some way contrived to compose. He tells of a large-scale oratorio *Gegen den Krieg*, dating from the summer of 1917, the sketches for which seem to have been destroyed by a fire in a dug-out. Also dated 'August 1917, in the field' is the earliest surviving manuscript — *Dumpfe Trommel and berauschtes Gong* — two songs for voice and piano. The first, for tenor, is a setting of words from the Chinese *Book of Songs, The tired soldier*; the second, *The red and white rose*, of a poem by Li Tai Po, both in translations by Klabund.[2] These songs are remarkable for several reasons. They are by a composer who had still to receive any formal musical training, either privately or in a musical institution; they were composed in what can only be imagined as the most difficult and inauspicious circumstances: they exhibit not only great imagination but impressive technique and awareness, not only of the music of the classics and the nineteenth century, but of trends in the early years of the twentieth century. Doubtless, had he subsequently thought them worthy of public performance, he would have revised the notation (the 'spelling' suggests a rather hazy attitude to functional harmony) and improved some details in the counterpoint, but both songs cannot be dismissed as insignificant and clumsy. Ex. 2.1

Later in 1917 came the *Galgenlieder* (Gallows Songs), subtitled 'Grotesques', six settings of texts by Christian Morgenstern, a poet to whom he returned in 1924 for his Opus 5.

---

[2] Klabund — Alfred Henschke 1890–1928. Poet, dramatist, novelist and translator from Chinese, Japanese and Persian. The first to create a popular awareness of Eastern literature in German-speaking countries, he was involved in the Munich Spartacus uprising of 1919 and imprisoned. Married to the actress Carola Neher.
'*Dumpfe Trommel und berauschtes Gong*' pub. 1915.
'*Die Geisha O-sen*' pub. 1918.

Ex. 2.1 The beginning of *'Die rote unde die weisse Rose'*. August 1917

From these two works we can observe Eisler's responses to the horrific circumstances which surrounded him. In the one he chooses texts which comment on these horrors or, in *Gegen den Krieg* makes plans to write them himself. In the other, he protects himself by retreating into parody, grotesquerie and wit in a way not dissimilar to what was to become a Brechtian distancing. Morgenstern (1871–1914), a writer himself who encompassed the extremes of profound philosopher, (student of Nietzsche, Schopenhauer, Kierkegaard and Rudolf Steiner) and creator in parodistic, comic verse of the immortal figures of Palmström and Korf, seemed an ideal source of texts for the young Eisler, in whom the capacity for wit, parody and outbursts of ironic laughter was already so strong. Eisler could well have chosen any of the seventy-six poems of Morgenstern's *Galgenlieder* cycle, published in 1905. Their appeal to him must have been immediate. In his explanation of how his 'Gallows Songs' came about, Morgenstern describes them as a *'Weltanschauung'* (a way of viewing the world). In them is expressed the 'scrupulous freedom of the excluded, the dematerialized'; a gallows brother is in transition from man to universe; from the gallows hill, he sees the world differently and sees things that others do not. Did Eisler feel, as he sketched these miniatures in Field Hospital No. 808, that he saw the world differently to others; that already, with his schoolboy reading of the Marxist classics and the discussions he'd had with his brother and sister, he was in a position to view the world critically?

These settings are full of felicitous things and although the idiom is not yet unmistakeable Eisler (unfair to expect it), there are many hints of what were to become distinctive Eisler fingerprints. With hindsight, it's not surprising that they are elicited by the humorous and grotesque rather than the deeply felt and lyrical. The musical ideas are sharply characterized and the variety of musical-dramatic gesture is apt and witty — that is to say, the squarely tonal lyric ideas are ironically juxtaposed with the abruptly disruptive and chromatically disorientating. Most impressive is that the six songs do work as a cycle. The overall shaping and sequence of events is satisfyingly varied. The tongue-in-cheek lyricism, which makes reference to Hugo Wolf at his most arch and Mahler at his most sophisticatedly innocent (the pseudo-chorale of the second song, *Die beiden Flaschen*, is strongly suggestive of the Finale of Mahler's Fourth Symphony), is balanced against the grotesque gestures and ironically overdone word-painting in a way which belies the composer's youth and inexperience. The last song, *Der Würfel* (The Dice), is an almost nightmare vision. Marked *Quasi Rezitativ*, the theme in the cello register nags away at the 'dominant' low A, which is made tonally ambiguous by an E flat and a B flat approached by whole tones. With an accompaniment suggestive of a bass drum, the effect is of a highly equivocal send-up of a Mahler dead march. Ex. 2.2

This is offset by an episode in clear D major (to the words 'I'll be as bright as a carbuncle, as soon as you've got off me') which, with its mock naivety and Straussian coloratura, sounds comically daft. Ex. 2.3

In April and May 1918 in a convalescent home in Weidlingau, near Vienna, Eisler set two more Morgenstern poems, those paired together as *Die Mausefalle* (The Mousetrap). To the voice and piano, he adds a violin in order to respond with a *'Nachtmusik'* to the lines — 'It is night and the stars are twinkling. Palmström makes music in the darkness.' The idiom is similar to the earlier songs but with more chromaticism and a somewhat higher level of dissonance.

Ex. 2.2 *Der Würfel.* No. 6 of *Galgenlieder,* 1917

In the summer of 1918, whilst on two months convalescence leave in Vienna (he was finally demobilized from the army in November), Eisler shared a flat with a girl-friend, Irma Friedemann – 'Muschi', a schoolteacher who was able to alleviate his poverty somewhat. She rented a piano and accompanied him in the numerous songs he wrote and sang for her in a voice which was already the high and wheezy one we know from the recordings of the fifties. Some forty of these songs were donated in 1965 to the Berlin Eisler Archive by Irma Friedemann, then living in the USA. It is difficult to know whether, had these works still been in his possession, Eisler would have held them back from performance or publication.

All the works in Irma Friedemann's possession were dedicated to her, often fulsomely and with evident deep affection. We cannot know what scores other dedicatees might have been presented with. Given the

Ex. 2.3 *Der Würfel*

rate of composition, often at least one song a day, there is no reason to doubt that what we have is only a fraction of the total output. The most extended piece we have from the Friedemann collection is the cycle of five settings of ancient Japanese lyrics for alto and chamber orchestra, the *Gesang des Abgeschiedenen*. The approach here is not grotesque, but more conventionally expressive, with a sweet, melancholy lyricism which is rare in Eisler. Could it be that he was wanting to see how 'romantically lovely' he could be, even to the extent of 'impressionistic' orchestral colourings? Perhaps this was more to Muschi's taste. Did she have to score-read them?! Even in the lyricism, there is a hint of the future, particularly the GDR years — *Das Vorbild* perhaps: no sentimentality but sheer 'songfulness'. The instrumentation is notably assured, the textures blending convincingly and naturally. The interplay of motives between voice and instruments, the contrapuntal interest in the orchestra and the fresh and lively response to the text, all exhibit considerable skill. Stylistically the cycle lacks individuality and Eisler is clearly responding to influences, which, although they don't blatantly signal themselves, underpin the aesthetic stance of the work — Mahler, Wolf, Strauss and early Schoenberg.

The poets which Eisler chose to set were, presumably, those he read frequently. Apart from the obviously much-loved Morgenstern, he shows a penchant for classical oriental poetry, Rilke, Tagore and, less predictably, Trakl. There are two Eichendorff settings; others like Nietzsche, Büchner and the sixteenth century Johann Fischart are used only once, as are the little known contemporaries Theodor Kramer and Gustav Falke. The Tagore setting *Lass aller Spannung der Freude* (Let all the tension of joy die away in my song) also dates from what must have been the passionate summer of 1918. This has a romantic sweep and enthusiasm, swinging along in 3/4 and C minor in an almost overblown way, the piano writing suggestive or Brahms or Strauss, although the abrupt ending, lacking a conventional cadence and properly rounded-off phrase is unthinkable from Brahms. Several other songs of this time clearly did not convince their composer — *O nimm mir dies geringe Wissen, Ich pflückte deine Blume, Es war im Mai.* This seems to be confirmed by the messy state of the manuscripts. Not so the lovely Rilke setting for alto and string trio *Wenn es nur einmal,* written towards the end of that year, in which the motivic working is so consistent that the trio almost functions independently.

In 1919, Eisler began his studies, without fees, with Schoenberg. He had heard Schoenberg conduct the Opus 9 Chamber Symphony in 1917 and had been profoundly impressed, but 'musically not at all shocked.'[3] We do not know what else he may have heard or seen — the hint of the *Gurrelieder* in the song *Dunkler Tropfe* of January 1919 may be of no significance. The few works which survive from the period 1919 to the First Piano Sonata of 1923 give clear evidence of a stricter application to specific compositional problems and tasks. The close study of Brahms required of all Schoenberg pupils gave rise, probably in 1921, to the folk-song setting *Ich hab die Nacht geträumet,* a technically very assured piece of Brahms pastiche. It consists of four strophes in which the tune is presented without alteration and the piano accompaniment is, appropriately, a set of variations. In these Eisler has captured several Brahms essentials, in the harmony, rhythmic detail and keyboard style.[4]

---

[3] Notowicz Conversations p. 34.

[4] In a letter to Schoenberg written jointly with Karl Rankl in July 1921, Eisler reports that he is studying Brahms and learning much about harmony and piano writing. See Stuckenschmidt pp. 274–5.

It is interesting to compare Eisler's position in 1919 with that of an older Schoenberg pupil, Alban Berg, who began his studies, (also without fee!) in 1904, and was also accepted on the basis of a number of songs. Schoenberg observed that Berg seemed incapable of writing anything but songs, the accompaniments of which were also song-like and that he lacked all ability to invent an instrumental theme. His studies, therefore, were directed towards the classics and Brahms with emphasis on the invention of plastic themes susceptible to development, variation and contrapuntal working. Eisler's case was not so extreme. Although his output too had been predominantly vocal, his accompaniments, whether for piano or instrumental ensemble showed ample evidence of an already advanced ability for thematic and motivic work, contrapuntal development and a happy interpenetration of vocal and instrumental material. For him, it was more a question of increased rigour, sharper focus and an intense course of listening and study to expand his inadequate knowledge of history and musical repertoire.

The only purely instrumental music to survive from this time is the *Fünf Klavierstücke* and a *Scherzo* for string trio. The piano pieces, although collected into a group and recorded in 1973, date from different times — numbers one and two from 1918 and the remainder from around 1922. In comparison with the vocal music they are less striking. The 4 × 4 bars of No.1, *Allegro moderato*, show Eisler attempting new ways of approaching traditional procedures, but the only way of excusing the heavy cadences of bars eight and twelve is to attribute Morgenstern irony to them. Such interest as has the second, *Walzer*, derives from the grotesquerie of its gesture, although harmonically it is more adventurous. The fact that the *Allegretto, Moderato* and *Andante* of 1922 are all also sixteen bars long makes it obvious that these are exercises, probably set by Schoenberg with a specific brief. Although all five pieces might serve quite suitably as themes for variations, significantly, in the later three, the element of internal variation is much greater. In the *Allegretto*, the four-bar *Nachsatz* is a variant of the *Vordersatz*. Bars 9 to 12 (pp *mit Humor*, fff *grell*) divide into two bars plus a two-bar variant and bars 13 to 16 repeat bars 5 to 9. The idiom is now more chromatic, pointing up the incongruity of the fully tonal C minor cadences at both half-way point and end. Ex. 2.4

The manuscript of the *Scherzo* for trio is dated 26 August 1920, although just after the Da Capo direction at the end of the Trio Section, there is written 6.1.1918. Here again, formal squareness and chromaticism are set against sudden outbursts and cadences which surprise by their unequivocal diatonicism. Parody is again present. One suspects

Ex. 2.4

that, once again, Eisler is taking refuge behind irony and (self?) mockery. On the evidence of entries in his diary [5] beginning in August 1921, Eisler was prey to great changes of mood, suffered extreme depressions and used the diary to indulge in self pity, self mockery, bitter irony and sarcasm. One entry reads: 'I am very alone, no one knows me. Not even myself. When I play hide-and-seek, it's called a pose. When I make jokes, I'm really funny.' A little further on: 'I won't live to be old. Unfortunately. But the few things I've done will remain. 12 July 1922.' Eisler confesses (to himself only, or posterity too?) that he's writing the diary because he can't work. 'May this book of impotence never be filled.' Well-known as the 'naughty' member of Schoenberg's circle, Eisler's frustrations are obvious: 'Schoenberg has one thing in common with Napoleon — he suffers only blockheads in his circle. If someone clever is included, it's only because he considers him foolish.'[6] Or 'There are (not) also talented idiots, who can express the nothing they have in them quite smoothly and stirringly.' Not unrelated to this is: 'I'm slowly coming to the opinion that it isn't good to study composition with Schopenhauer. (Not even with Kant and certainly not with Hegel). One could easily become a Marxist from it.'[7]

Two songs, both dated 5 September 1920 are of interest because of their extreme brevity. *Bitte an den Hund,* to a text translated from the Japanese, lasts forty seconds; *Rondell,* to words by Trakl lasts fifty. We know that when Schoenberg was away, Eisler received lessons from Webern and we will later observe the indebtedness of the Opus 2 cycle, dedicated to Webern, composed two years later. One might conjecture that these two earlier songs were the first projected numbers of a cycle and later rejected: or that Eisler was composing songs in this laconic vein and only early in 1923 decided on which six to use for Opus 2. It is odd that, given their quality, they did not find a place in another publishable work.

[5] The *Wiener Tagebuch* was discovered in the estate of Eisler's close friend of that time, the musicologist Erwin Ratz 1898–1973. In *Schriften, Addenda* pp. 10–21.

[6] Schoenberg's timetable of his teaching schedule and the names of his pupils in 1919 is reproduced in Stuckenschmidt pp. 256–7.

[7] The diary is deserving of detailed study and 'analysis'. Even its scurrilities are inspired. See pp. 62–4.

The first work to be given an opus number was the Piano Sonata, the manuscript of which has 5–9 III 1922 at the end of the first movement and, after the third, FINIS March 1922. This latter date could be mistaken and might be 1923, for we know from Berg's letter to his wife dated 29 March 1923 that Eisler's playing of the first two movements took place on that same day:

> *'First there was an Italian and then Eisler, who later on played his piano sonata. A very nice piece, which Schoenberg will immediately get performed in Prague (through Steuermann). . . . . .Schoenberg is now in his 'punters' mood again, backing Eisler's sonata in Prague almost without reflection, and recommending it to Hertzka, although the third movement isn't even finished yet.'*

Schoenberg's positive response may well have given Eisler the confidence to believe that he was ready in general to put his works before the public. The four *Klavierstücke* Op. 3 probably also date from 1923 and the *Divertimento* for wind quintet Op. 4 is from May that year.

Comparison of Eisler's Opus 2 songs with Webern's five George songs Opus 3 of 1907–8 reveal a clear influence on the twenty-four-year-old student. It is perhaps not surprising that Eisler's 'model' should have been this early set. Webern's output was never great and, since the outbreak of the war, he had produced only four works, all sets of songs of enormous concentration, complexity and density, exhibiting an almost manic obsession with achieving a consistent dodecaphony.[8] His Opus 3 songs, although economical, brief and highly chromatic use abundant parallel thirds (relating closely to the choral George setting Opus 2), do not avoid octave doublings or octave transpositions (cf. Op. 3 No. 4 bar 10), set the texts syllabically, absolutely without melismas and have a strong emphasis on *Klangreiz*. The *Four Songs* Op. 12 of 1915–17 and the orchestral set Opus 13 of 1914–18 were also presumably known to Eisler and their texts would have been attractive to him, including as they do Goethe, Kraus, Trakl and Li Tai Po translated by Bethge.[9]

The extent of the younger man's indebtedness is clear. In the first two bars of the first song, in a tempo of *leicht bewegte* ♩. the piano, p *zart*, sings a line which begins with a four-note whole-tone collection and ends with a chromatic one, all with octave displacements. The phrase ends with a five-note chord, ppp: Ex. 2.5

---

[8] Opp. 12, 13, 14 and 15.

[9] Hans Bethge 1876–1946. Like Klabund, a specialist in translations of Eastern texts, preponderantly short epigrammatic poetry. Best known as translator of texts used by Mahler for *Das Lied von der Erde*.

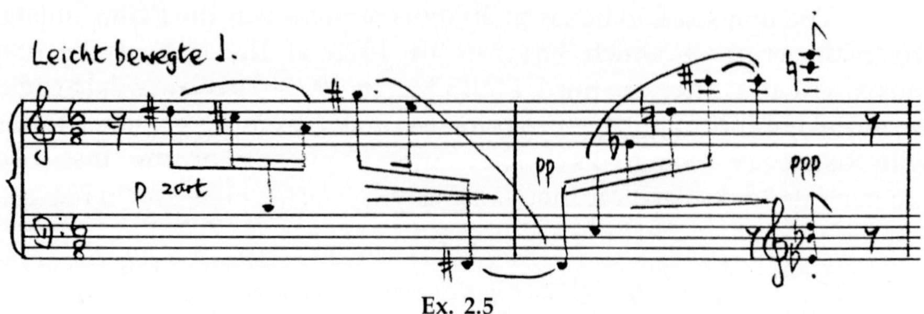

Ex. 2.5

Webern's Opus 3 No. 1, marked *zart bewegt*, begins with a ppp chord: Ex. 2.6

Ex. 2.6

and in the left hand in bars 6 and 7 there are two chromatic collections of five and three notes: Ex. 2.7

Ex. 2.7 Webern. No. 1 of *Fünf Lieder* Op. 3

The right hand thirds of these bars relate to Eisler's bar 4 sonority. The regular collision in Webern of a semitone with one or other notes of the third is also part of Eisler's technique. The extent to which Webern exploited this procedure, as well as the building of chords symmetrically or by the multiple leading-note voice-leading used by

Schoenberg as early as 1899, is well-known. Indeed, by July 1922, when he completed the second and fourth of the *Fünf Geistliche Lieder* Op. 15, his preoccupation with using this as a means of achieving a consistently high level of dissonance and avoiding all suggestions of tonality was total. Eisler never reached such a position.[10]

The choice of Matthius Claudius' poem *Ein Wiegenlied bei Mondschein zu singen*[11] and the charm and grace of Eisler's setting irresistibly calls to mind Webern's ravishing treatment of the folksong *Der Tag ist vergangen* as his Opus 12 No.1. The following phrases: Ex. 2.8, 2.9

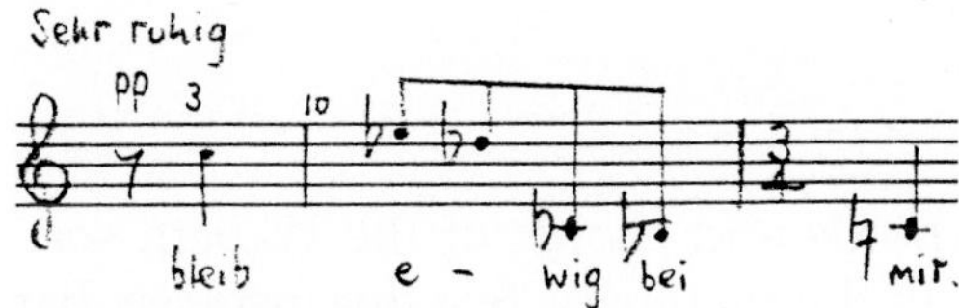

Ex. 2.8 Webern Op.12 No. 1

Ex. 2.9 Eisler Op.2 No. 1

are related in just the same way as is Eisler's variation of his own initial motive in the second Claudius setting of Opus 2, *Ach, es ist so dunkel*: Ex. 2.10, 2.11

In this second song, although the semitone relationships are frequent, they do not predominate. A more traditional interplay of dissonances seems to be in operation — a progression of major sevenths

[10] The first two songs of Opus 2 are dated 28 and 29 November 1922. These together with the third, make up the *Drei kleine Lieder* which Eisler dedicated to Schoenberg *'in höchster Verehrung'* the following Christmas. The manuscript is in the Schoenberg Archive in Los Angeles. We can assume that the remaining three songs were composed early in 1923.

[11] Matthias Claudius 1740–1815. Collected works pub. 1882. It is significant, in the light of Eisler's future *'Entgipsung'* technique (see p. 213 and p. 426) that only two of the poem's twelve verses are used.

Ex. 2.10 Eisler Op.2 No. 2

Ex. 2.11 Eisler Op.2 No. 2

and ninths chords, whole-tone chords and chords of the Webern sort, these last used as the most tense in the hierarchy. See, for instance, bar 2 second chord and bar 4 second quaver: Ex. 2.12

Ex. 2.12

Eisler obviously has no worries about octaves — in bars 5, 7, 8 and 9 — or about progressions with tonal connotations — bar 8 — although in the pianist's cadence (not the singer's; she has started the next phrase), he is careful to include a minor ninth. The piano texture of bars 6–9 of No.2 is reminiscent of Schoenberg's third little piano piece Opus 19.

The compositional assurance, strong musical characterization and the confident handling of an atonal idiom in both a warmly expressive and witty way is equally evident in the two piano works of this time — the Sonata and the *Klavierstücke*. The former begins with a handful of fingerprints — a minor third plus a major seventh, a trichord of perfect fourths, a semitone trill and two major thirds a semitone apart. The arpeggio in bar 3 includes an augmented triad, the triads in bar 4 are successively whole-tone and superimposed augmented and perfect fourths, and the cadence chord is B flat$^{7-9}$ arrived at with a ritenuto. Ex. 2.13

Sonate.

Ex. 2.13

All these constituents are instantly recognisable features of the chromatic 'expressionist' language of Schoenberg and his two senior pupils. This much could have been written by a talented pasticheur. Where Eisler shows how profoundly he had absorbed the lessons in composition he had received is in bars 9 to 18. What begins as a counterstatement of the opening two bars is extended to four, bar 14 is inserted as a recall of the texture of bars 7 and 8, and bar 15 begins as in bar 10 with quaver displacements and develops differently again.

The *Gesangsperiode* arrives in bar 23 and is brusquely interrupted after only three bars. Its second attempt to sing results in an *accelerando* and an outburst *mit grosser Kraft*, succeeded in its turn by a *pianissimo* cadence theme. The forty-one-bar exposition is repeated — a double sequence of extreme contrasts of gesture, dynamics, texture and phrase-length, all things we associate with the Second Viennese School. In Eisler's hands the palette is handled with wit, vivacity and a dash of grotesquerie, steering clear of the overripeness which threatens enjoyment of an earlier Opus 1 piano sonata.

Eisler satisfies his master's pedagogic demands for variation forms by casting his Intermezzo as a passacaglia, which involves fourteen statements of a four-bar ground bass organised as a ternary structure.

This is a superbly economical movement with melodic memorability and sufficient inner variation to offset the calculatedly more relaxed rate of incident and degree of contrast. The ending is typical. The strong G minor of the ground bass with its sffz E flat at mid-point and cadence by means of a flat supertonic, Ex. 2.14

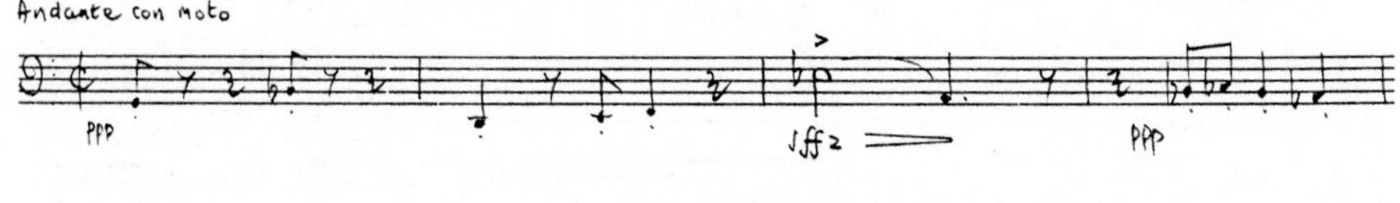

Ex. 2.14

is swept away in five bars of nervous collapse in which the previous B flat — A flat is made to serve as dominant to an E flat inflected by its flat supertonic. Even this is questioned by a sub-mediant C flat — wonderful imagination and fantasy! Ex. 2.15

The finale we know to have been composed very quickly after Schoenberg's approval had been won. Another sonata form with exposition repeat, it is a logical and appropriate conclusion, capitalizing on procedures already used, making reference to the earlier movements,

Ex. 2.15 Sonata Op.1. 2nd movement conclusion

twice starting tongue-in-cheek *fugati* and generally taking an ironic look at the histrionic potential of the chosen idiom. Possible evidence of his already wry attitude to this is his decision to end all three movements on E flat — in the case of the Intermezzo, as we have seen, by hook or crook.

The four pieces of Opus 3 explore the same idiom and keyboard style. The first has a delightful *fugato* with stretto, the third employs textures which reappear repeatedly in Eisler's later works, motivic material is common to all of them and the fourth sums up in a similarly exaggerated way to the Sonata's finale.

In all three of these works, one waits almost in vain for unequivocal consonance. Eisler seems uninterested in using triads in the 'new' way available to Schoenberg in the 'new aesthetic' of the *Book of the Hanging Gardens*. The only diatonic chord on which the ear is allowed briefly to focus is found in the last of the songs, where, in the setting of Klabund's line *Ich habe nie vermeint mich selber zu erkennen*, (I have never presumed to understand myself — a typical *Tagebuch* entry!) the word '*selber*' is accompanied by a first inversion E major chord!

The first sketches for Schoenberg's *Wind Quintet* Op. 26 are dated 14 April 1923. The finale was completed on 26 July 1924. It may be that Eisler's knowledge of Schoenberg's work on it gave him the idea to write for such an ensemble. Nothing could be more different from the master's enormous 'symphony' than the Opus 4 *Divertimento*, in two movements lasting only eight minutes.[12] A quirky Andante is followed by a theme, six variations and coda. The horn has the last say in a cadenza slightly suggestive of a short trip down the Rhine.

---

[12] The first sketches suggest a minuet was intended as middle movement. The first movement of Opus 7 is a minuet.

We know from Eisler's letter to Schoenberg of March 1926 that he felt some enthusiasm for the twelve-note works, mentioning in particular the *Suite* Op. 25. His own first attempt at serialism is subtitled 'Studies on twelve-note rows' and came about as a result of a suggestion from the master. Schoenberg was concerned that, for all its atmosphere and power, *Pierrot Lunaire*, lasting only some thirty minutes, could not stand alone in a concert programme. He proposed that Eisler write a piece using similar forces with which to precede it.[13]

Composed early in 1924, the Schoenberg models for its serial technique could therefore have been:

i the Waltz, dated 14 March 1923 from the *Five Piano Pieces* Op. 23.
ii the Petrarch Sonnet of the *Serenade* Op. 24.
iii the *Suite for Piano* Op. 25 — movements composed variously between July 1921 and March 1923.
iv less likely — the *Wind Quintet*.

Eisler's feelings about this invitation must have been mixed; firstly, deep pleasure at the confidence shown in him — clear proof of Schoenberg's opinion of his talent; secondly, some discomfiture at having to create something which could sit convincingly alongside a masterwork which seemed to bring into focus his growing personal dilemma. What was during this period beginning to define itself more and more clearly was the contradiction between his respect, even reverence, comparable to that felt by Berg and Webern, for Schoenberg's musical intelligence, knowledge, technique, creativity and stature, and a distancing from the imaginative world it inhabited. He later described the Giraud/Hartleben texts of *Pierrot* as *'alberne Provinzdämonik'* — simple-minded parochial *diablerie* — whilst playing tribute to the work's musical innovations — 'wonderful chamber music.'

---

[13] The only evidence I have for this is Eisler's telling me so in 1961. In the *Wiener Tagebuch* there is an entry (see p. 62) showing that the idea for such a piece dates back probably to the end of 1921. *Pierrot Lunaire* was performed at the last concert of the Society for Private Musical Performances on 5 December 1921, which Eisler surely attended.

He solved the diplomatic problem by retreating into humour and inevitably reverted for his texts to the ironies of Morgenstern, even re-using one of the poems of the 1917 cycle. Eisler's bare five minutes of music hardly solved the concert planning problem but they do provide an upbeat and a foil to the seminal twentieth century masterpiece. The clarinet is not required to double bass clarinet and most sensibly, in view of the cataclysmic uses Schoenberg puts it to (e.g. in *Die Kreuze*), Eisler dispenses with the piano.

The published score (UE, Vienna 1926) has the subtitle 'Studies on twelve-note rows.' Later the 'Studies' became 'Parodies.' [14] What are we to understand by this? Parodies of what? Of numbers from *Pierrot Lunaire*? Of serial composition? Or is it simply a reference to the use of parodistic texts? Is Eisler offering Morgenstern's brillance as a parody, a send-up of Hartleben's embarrassments? The first suggestions are hardly likely for diplomatic reasons, the last unconvincing, since it places the responsibility on Morgenstern, not an original thing to do and no reason to change the subtitle. It's a pity we have no comment on this marvellous work from Schoenberg. He, too, must have had mixed feelings — approval, one assumes, of Eisler's imagination and compositional skill; but also a puzzled queasiness about what it did to an audience's perception of his own nightmarish monster. Although that had been conceived in a 'light, ironical, satirical tone', the cumulative effect of the twenty-one poems and the superabundance of musical invention lavished upon them is at the opposite extreme of 'light'. It was the horrors of fascist Germany which evoked from Eisler expressive extremes, not the introverted reflections of an artist about his own identity, however self-mocking. The level at which Morgenstern and Eisler pose such questions is truly ironic and much funnier. In *Palmström,* there is no blood from consumption or impaled limbs, moths are replaced by a startled sparrow, Gallows brother's song is one of Spring, not of a whore who pierces his brain with a needle and the moon *doesn't* shine on the cheerful little wallpaper flower.

With regard to the delivery of the vocal line, Eisler adopts Schoenberg's approach. Whether he was able to interpret the directions for the performance of *Sprechstimme* as given in the score of *Pierrot* better than anyone else is not known. His own vocal line is notated similarly (with crosses through the note stems) and it is freely composed i.e. not part of the serial organization. Of course, the voice in *Pierrot* is

---

[14] I'm not sure when. *Parodien* appears in the score as published in Volume 6 of the *Lieder und Kantaten* 1962.

also free, albeit closely related motivically and rhythmically to the instrumental parts. In No.17, *Parodie,* it becomes part of the imitative counterpoint, but in No.18, *Mondfleck,* it ranges freely, albeit sympathetically to the ensemble. Otherwise, it is only on occasions that Schoenberg chooses to alert the listener to a motivic relationship, most obviously and atmospherically with the sung *'verschwiegen'* of No.8, *Nacht.* It was not in Schoenberg's make-up in 1921 to write merely approximate pitches in a chamber work of this density and intensity, even when requiring them to be so quickly distorted or quitted (*verlassen*). In the more tonal idiom of the 'Summer Wind' melodrama in part three of the *Gurrelieder,* the pitches make harmonic sense and *could* be sung. The delivery of the text in the *Ode to Napoleon* (1942) by a 'reciter' and in *A Survivor from Warsaw* (1947) by a 'narrator' is not *Sprechstimme.* It is quite different and a suitably different notation is employed.

Eisler's voice part is also fully 'composed'. The relationship between voice and instruments is more crucial because instead of Schoenberg's free (and, it must be said, sometimes puzzling) chromaticism, here we have serialism. Thus the anomaly occurs that if the fundamental purpose of serialism is to ensure unity, then the inclusion of a contrapuntal line excluded from it will destroy that unity. Significantly, in the last number, *Couplet von der Tapetenblume*[15], Eisler changes the notation to ♪ and gives the direction 'to be delivered as in a cabaret, half singing.' This more precise pitching of the notes leads to the voice's adoption into the serial working. By inference then, the vocal delivery in the other numbers should be *very* free and thereby less disunifying! Given the diversity of approaches to Schoenberg's *Vorwort* over the last eight years, this is a problem which need not detain us.

Eisler's first 'attempt' at serialism is simultaneously straightforward and subtle — straightforward in that he uses the basic set almost exclusively; just occasionally a retrograde form, or part of one, is employed. The monotony this could result in provokes the subtlety. Behind the considerable freedom of note-ordering, there is a sort of segmentation technique. The text for the first setting, *Venus Palmström,* is as follows:

Palmström wünscht sich manchmal aufzulösen,
wie ein Salz in einem Glase Wasser,
so nach Sonnenuntergang besonders.
Möchte ruhen so bis Sonnenaufgang

---

[15] Morgenstern's title is simply *'Tapetenblume.'*

> *und dann wieder aus dem Wassersteigen –*
> *Venus – Palmström – Anadyomene . . .*[16]

The row is:

Ex. 2.16

Beginning with a homage to Schoenberg (A-S (E flat)), this is clearly a melodic inspiration, elegantly shaped and expressive of Palmström's daydreamings. Ex. 2.17

Ex. 2.17

Intervallically it is not very rich; apart from the tritone and minor third, it consists only of major and minor seconds and their inversions. Yet Eisler cunningly creates contrapuntal textures, accompaniment figures, four-part homophonic sonorities and *grazioso* lightness in only sixteen bars. Ex. 2.18

---

[16] Palmström sometimes wishes he could dissolve
like salt in a glass of water,
Especially after sunset.
He'd like to rest like that until sunrise
And then rise up out of the water again:
Venus Palmström Anadyomene!

*) = A(rnold) S(chönberg)

Ex. 2.18

rit. - - - Breit
- gang und dann wie - der aus dem Was - ser stei - gen: Ve - nus
Flatterzunge
(natürlich)
pp
mf
am Steg
pesante
Palm - ström An - a - dy - o - me - ne!
p
pizz.
4 for O and R
Tempo I
rit.
arco
pizz.

Ex. 2.18 (cont'd)

The second number, *Notturno*, is most certainly a parody of *Pierrot Lunaire*. Rapid, soft and spooky like its No.11, *Galgenlied*, Palmström's terror is healthily normal by comparison with Pierrot's.

Palmström takes paper from his drawer.
And spreads it artistically round the room.

And after he's made pellets out of it.
And spread it artistically, and at night.

And spread the pellets thus (at night),
so that, when he suddenly awakes in the night,

so that, when he awakes in the night, he hears
the pellets rustle and a secret terror
strikes him (so that in the night a secret terror
strikes him) of the spectre of wrapping-paper-pellets. . .

The complications of a parodistic, ironic response to the 'light, ironic' begin to grow! Since these pieces are also studies, Eisler uses different rows in each, once again showing no regard for unity. The rows are not related in any significant way, but do share certain segments which Eisler obviously likes. Ex. 2.19

No. 4 uses again the poem he set in 1917 but with an entirely different approach. Spring is hinted at by the opening gesture and perhaps the flute twitterings of bars 4 and 5 are Spring-like, but the only

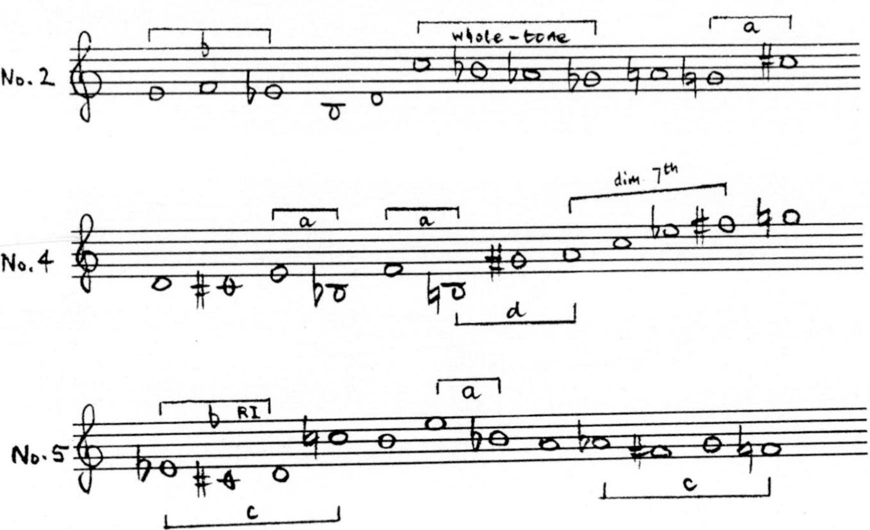

Ex. 2.19

suggestion of a song comes at bar 8, when the *'Hälmlein'* (the little shoot) 'sways back and forth in the wind. It is to me as if I were he who I yet no longer am. . . .' Ex. 2.20

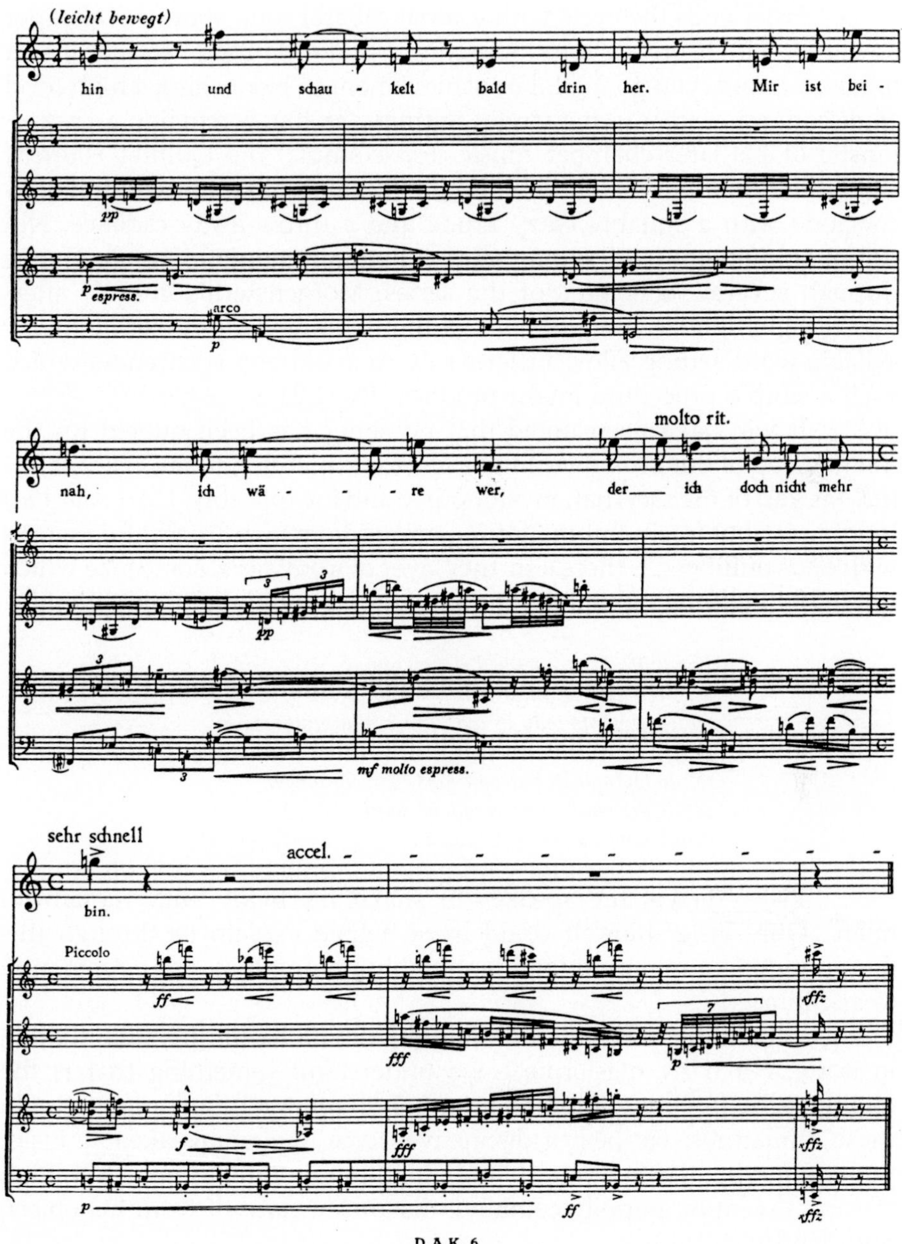

Ex. 2.20 *Palmström.* Bars 8–16 of *Galgenbruders Frühlingslied*

The song is emphatically dismissed with a grotesquerie which was refined over the years to become the typical Eisler ending, a Heine-like kick-in-the-teeth to make you reflect on or even analyse previous lyric beauty (cf. *Speisekammer, An eine Stadt*).[17]

Eisler ends the cycle with a serial cabaret song about a wallpaper flower which cheerfully repeats itself all round the room, so that if you follow it round, you go mad. His achievement in reconciling a high level of dissonance with a scherzando lightness of touch remains a characteristic of his later chamber music, for example, the Quintet *Fourteen ways of describing rain* and the *Violin Sonata.* Here the string players conclude with a suitably crazy Etude and a throw-away cadence. Not unlike in Schoenberg's setting of the Petrarch sonnet, the voice runs through several statements of the series. Morgenstern's lines of alternating eight and seven syllables and the three deviations from a totally syllabic word-setting allow Eisler easily to avoid any squareness which such a simple procedure might produce. Ex. 2.21

It will have been noted that no series has been quoted for the middle song of this sequence. I have found no mention in the Eisler literature (as yet) of the fact that, mysteriously and inexplicably, *L'Art pour l'art* is not serial, but freely chromatic in a similar idiom to the earlier four works with opus numbers. Is there a further layer of irony here, some joke which reveals his growing distaste for the art work for art's sake?

The fluttering of a startled sparrow
inspires Korf to an artistic creation,
which consists only of looks, airs and gestures.
People come with cameras,
to photograph it; but von Korf 'can no longer
recall the work,' can recall no work
concerning an 'excited sparrow.'

Eisler directs the speaker to shake his head 'with thoughtful mien'. Only Eisler himself could have helped explain us through this dense thicket of relationships. Regrettably no one took the opportunity to ask him.

Palmström is Eisler's first masterpiece, albeit a tiny one written in irony. For if by masterpiece we understand something that is the totally successful realization of an original concept, then such it is. In these miniatures, we hear a distinctive voice, the unmistakeable Eisler personality in which wit, charm, quirkiness, intelligence and high musical invention happily combine, distancing himself from his object, not identifying with it.

---

[17] See Hennenberg in *Sammelbände zur Musikgeschichte der DDR* Band 2.

*) Als Couplet, wie im Kabarett vorzutragen; halb singend.

Ex. 2.21

im Main und Mon - den - schein, auf je - der der vier
accel.
etwas ruhiger
Wän - de. Du siehst mich nim - mer -
p
fp
rit.
stringendo
dar ge - nung, so weit du blickst im Stüb - chen, und folgst du mir

Ex. 2.21 (cont'd)

Tempo
— per Rös - sel-sprung, wirst du ver-rückt, mein Lieb - chen!
molto accel.
a tempo

Ex. 2.21 (cont'd)

The *Duo* for violin and cello Op. 7 is, like the *Wind Quintet*, a two-movement *divertimento*. Dating from July 1924, it reverts to a freely chromatic idiom. It was written for Rudolf Kolisch, leader of the Kolisch Quartet[18] and Schoenberg's son-in-law, and the quartet's cellist Joachim Stutchewski. It is a virtuoso piece which makes great demands on the players' technique and musicianship. The first movement, *Tempo di Menuetto*, begins with a lazy grace, quickly disturbed by lively enthusiasm then allowed to droop into a slow waltz, in a simple, easy-going rondo form. The second movement recalls the mood and gesture of the finale to Opus 1 and contrives to quote the scherzo theme of Schoenberg's Opus 9 with wit and naturalness. The humour is at its most beguiling in the furore of the last sixteen bars where well-worn gestures from 'classical' music are overwhelmed by spoof expressionism.

The circumstances of Eisler's move to Berlin in 1925 are discussed by Eberhardt Klemm in Chapter One of this book. The atmosphere within the tightly-knit group of Schoenberg pupils must surely have begun to be oppressive to him. The master demanded unswerving, (unquestioning even) loyalty, which, in general, he received. Whenever bad feeling arose, we know what pain it caused — with Berg *a propos* of his clarinet pieces Opus 5 in 1913, with Webern with regard to his personal career plans in 1918. Eisler was in awe of Schoenberg, but not in fear, and as his political thinking developed, as his doubts gathered about the music he almost inevitably wrote in this united group (united against Viennese conservatism, hostile critics and alternative views about modern music), the quarrel with Schoenberg drew nearer. He had always been the awkward, argumentative one in the class, whose non-conformity and bad behaviour tested Schoenberg's store of paternal tolerance.

When a performance in Berlin of his Opus 1 Sonata by a Schnabel pupil, Else Kraus, was well received, the attraction of the capital, the leading musical centre of the German-speaking countries as well as the hub of the working-class movement, was irresistible. He got a post at the Klindworth-Scharwenka Conservatory and was asked by Artur Schnabel to write new piano music for his pupils. The Second

[18] Founded in 1924 as the Viennese String Quartet.

Piano Sonata was the immediate response. Early sketches date from 1924, but one sketch page exists with the date 25.10.25, Berlin. Cast in the form of a theme and fourteen variations and thus playing continuously, the sonata is a rather grim and often manic scherzo. The clearly defined tripartite shape of the theme, when later expanded by phrase extension, gives the impression of scherzo-trio-scherzo within itself. When Eisler treats the first three variations as such a shape, the result is:

	Var. 1			*Var. 2*	*Var. 3*
	Scherzo	*Trio*	*Scherzo*	*Trio*	*Scherzo–inverted*
	a b a		a b	a b a b a b	a b a c a
no. of bars	4 7 4	9	4 3	6 3 5 6 5 7	4 7 4 9 4+4

Tiny *scherzo* or *Lied* forms pervade the whole work. Characteristics of the series are emphasised and made clearly perceptible and the nagging motif of repeated notes in many rhythmic variants

acts as an obvious signpost, both in mid-variation and as a link at cadences.

The way in which serial technique is used has not developed significantly since *Palmström*. Eisler is more concerned to create audibly related motivic shapes than to adhere strictly to pitch orders, so that if anything he is composing more freely within his self-imposed discipline. Unlike Opus 5, the sonata, 330 bars long (but lasting only eight and a half minutes) is based on one series, untransposed. A few retrograde forms appear and leading out of the use, in bars 8 and 9 of the theme, of the inverted row, variations three, nine and thirteen are composed from it. The row and its inversion are: Ex. 2.22

Ex. 2.22

A numbering of the pitches in the theme illustrates how straightforward Eisler's approach is, as well as showing freedoms taken and typical anomalies.

Ex. 2.23

Harmonically, emphasis is placed on the two seventh chords supplied by 4 3 5 and 8 6 7, first heard in bar 2. The major-minor triad created by 3 8 6 7 (bar 6) is distinctive when simultaneous but a little weak when not, as in bar 26. This is not to suggest that triads are avoided, but most are fleeting and unaccented. That provided by 3 6 7 appears as cadential relaxation in two positions in bars 53, 61 and 72. The requirements of a set of variations — diversity of character and mood, audibility of 'variational logic', avoidance of 'bittiness', cumulative power, are reconciled with the choice of Sonata as a title by a judicious grouping and overall timing of the events. The scheme is:

Theme	*dark and percussive*	
Vars. 1–3	*Scherzo — poco presto*	
Var. 4	*slow movement —*	*larghetto*
Var. 5		*allegretto*
Var. 6		*andante alternating with presto*
Vars. 7–8		*allegro deciso*
Vars. 9–10		*marziale*
Var. 11	*quasi Waltz*	
Var. 12	*calm {suddenly energetic} Quasi Finale*	
Var. 13	*{still energetic }*	
Var. 14	*Coda — reprise of theme*	

The description above of this work as a grim scherzo is prompted by the predominantly dark 'scoring', the frequent use of martellato attack, jazzy syncopations[19] and the fact that (again!) Eisler treads the fine line between seriousness and ironic joking. Ex. 2.24

When the pounding fierceness reaches to extremes in bars 288–314, the excess results in an almost grandiose climax, an harmonically astringent and rhythmically focussing 'resolution' in bars 319–326 of the final variation Coda.

If we compare Opus 6 with the two earlier piano works, it is obvious how the textures are sparer and the harmony fresher. The superabundance of thirds and sixths is gone, augmented triads and melodic formulations based on them are reduced and there is much two-part writing. The primary effect of serialism was, then, to clear the

[19] I was not entirely confident of this suggestion of 'jazziness' with regard to the passage in Variation 12, bars 288–299, until, reading the autograph score in the Eisler Archive, I found, to my astonishment, interleaved between variations 6 and 7, a one-page sketch for a piano piece called *Jazz der Idiosynkrasisters*. It is not very good, peters out after fifteen bars and is firmly crossed out.

Ex. 2.24 2nd. Sonata Op. 6, variation 12

air and enhance the clarity.[20] This tendency persists into the altogether delightful *Klavierstücke* Op. 8 which were probably also composed as a result of Schnabel's request, in the autumn of 1925. In the four which are serial (Nos. 1, 3, 5 and 7), Eisler manipulates the series so as to produce consonant diatonic-sounding harmony and spare, dissonant textures of great subtlety. The remaining pieces are freely chromatic and one might well question Eisler's intention in alternating them in this way.[21] Doubtless the mix pleased him, not only to tease his young performers and their audience, but to test his own ability to achieve a unified group in a diverse way. One does feel that here, albeit in a lightweight piece of modest pretentions, he has cast off the shadows of his mentors and is putting into practice something more personal of himself, is on a different path, is breathing different air — of *this* planet!

The first piece, 'to be played very lightly and gently', is a charming scherzando complement to the dark scherzo of only a few weeks earlier.[22] The melodic material relates closely to previous ideas: Ex. 2.25

---

[20] The published score (*Breitkopf und Härtel*) has many errors. The following errata list may prove useful.

bar		
bar	24	RH G sharp A should be demisemiquavers
	29	LH treble clef
	35	middle part B quaver, G flat
	78	RH chord, ledger line missing — B flat E G
	84	LH chord, G sharp missing, i.e. A E sharp G sharp
	132	RH bass clef (133 treble clef stet)
	139	RH chord E flat F *natural* B
	201	LH ledger line missing — chord C sharp F D
		RH fourth beat, *D* natural not B natural
	207	middle part B flat tied over
	226	RH C sharp quaver
	231	LH third beat D C. I'm suspicious of the D. It could be A
	261	LH F *natural*
	292	LH first note F sharp
	296	LH F sharp tied over
	309	RH G probably tied over (Not in autograph)
	317	RH A sharp not flat
	323	RH last chord F natural not sharp

[21] Schoenberg's Opp. 23 and 24 are, of course, precedents.
Berg's *Lyric Suite*, which also juxtaposes the serial and non-serial, even within a movement, was not composed until 1926. Unlike Berg, who was moving towards the complete adoption of his very personal serialism, Eisler was already moving away.

[22] For this section on Opus 8, I have lightly plundered my article *Mein Lehrer Hanns Eisler* in the *Sinn und Form Sonderheft* of 1964.

Ex. 2.25

The second is forceful and abrupt, with sudden changes of mood and much variety of tone colour. The row is heard at the outset as a six-part chord and then the simultaneous melodic statement of the remaining six notes in counterpoint with the retrograde of them: Ex. 2.26

Ex. 2.26

Eisler uses the four basic forms. Since two of the four segments form triads Ex. 2.27

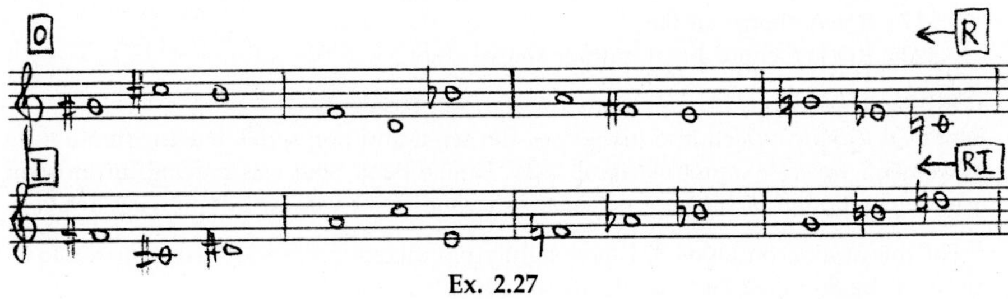

Ex. 2.27

material readily available to the less sophisticated listener is created: Ex. 2.28

Ex. 2.28 Op.8 No. 2

As before, he changes the note order, particularly within each segment and produces a store of consonant chords: Ex. 2.29

Ex. 2.29

A little episode at bar 39 results: Ex. 2.30

Ex. 2.30 Op.8 No. 2

Number three is a transparent set of four variations on a theme, with coda. Although not serial, the variation technique is the result of 'serial thinking' . Number six is something of a self-portrait — it has nervous haste, wit and humour, vivacity, elegance, brevity, surprises, the hint of Eisler marches still to come. With art and cunning he writes serially to avoid Schoenbergian *Trauer, Verzweiflung, Hysterie* and *Schmerz;* and we already know that Schoenberg's 'grotesque' is not Eisler's. Ex. 2.31

Ex. 2.31 Op.8 No. 6

Ex. 2.31 Op.8 No. 6 (cont'd)

On page 4, Klemm refers to the Opus 9 *Tagebuch* as Eisler's strangest or most remarkable ('*merkwürdigstes*') work. It is without doubt his most self-centred, commenting on specific incidents in his life and directing all his Morgenstern-style mockery at himself. Called 'a little cantata' and lasting about seventeen minutes, its sequence of events and the choice of forces is unique. The texts are his own.

Part 1 Motto – unaccompanied soprano, mezzo, alto.
'Yes, yes, the old man is right! It is impossible to be completely alone in a strange city. If there are two of you, you can enjoy yourself much better!'
Theme and five variations – solo violin
Rain – soprano, tenor, piano
'The whole world is a cold douche ......it drips on my bald pate.'
Intermezzo 1 – piano
In the bathroom – unacc. soprano, mezzo, alto; coda for piano.
'When you sit in a hot bath, life is easy.'

Part 2 Introduction – piano solo, violin solo, piano solo
Rest – unaccompanied soprano, mezzo, alto; coda for violin
'A little rest does no harm, I say to my own face, smiling. We are cannibals of love! Ah, how sad that is!
Intermezzo 2 – piano
Depression – tenor, piano
'If you're a stupid, bad, bourgeois lad, how hateful everything is! When some day I go to my eternal rest, cover me up with manuscript paper!'

Part 3 Good advice – soprano, piano
'Dear child, don't be so downcast. . .don't talk so much of your suffering in such damned interesting times. Be alert! Eyes open, not shut! Otherwise we'll cover you with manuscript paper today!
Observation on travel – unacc. soprano, mezzo, alto; coda for piano. 'Travelling cannot be pleasant, if you travel alone. As you sit down in the train, life, unfortunately, begins.[23]
Forward and Backward Look – pot-pourri. Soprano, tenor, piano. 'In three and a half years, we'll know better if it's possible to be alone in a strange city; if the world is a cold douche and life really

[23] This is surely a reference to the train journey during which Eisler expressed his feelings about modern music to Zemlinsky. This was reported to Schoenberg and led to the unpleasant and painful row. It should not be forgotten that Schoenberg and his wife had moved to Berlin in January 1926. Schoenberg's letters to Eisler (Nos. 91 and 92 in the English edition pub. Faber 1964) date from the following March. Thus at the time of the *Tagebuch*'s composition, August to November the same year (whilst on the move; the score has Paris-Vienna-Berlin), Schoenberg and Eisler were again in the same city. See p. 442–3 for Knepler's comments on the quarrel.

> *so awful. Let's hope we're not as old as the hills, shrivelled up and icy cold!'*

Eisler indulges himself completely, even in the way the resources are so wastefully used — the violinist is redundant from half-way through, the tenor sings only three times. The least Eisler could have done is to allow everyone's involvement in the concluding *pot-pourri*. However the piece is determinedly eccentric and for Eisler so obviously a 'one-off' written whilst 'in a mood', that such quibbles seem irrelevant. There is no use of serialism, although the violin variations, like those of Opus 8 No. 3, show the influence of serial thinking in the way they adhere closely to nodal notes of the theme. The vocal trios are freely imitative, the word-setting predominantly syllabic and the formal shapes simple ternary or rondo-like. Triads and use of whole tones are frequent. The little piano link to the last number gives the flavour: Ex. 2.32

Ex. 2.32 *Tagebuch* Op. 9

For all his self-indulgence, Eisler maintains his ironic detachment, his distanced objectivity (he was too intelligent to do otherwise). Even in the movement called *Depression*, the music, whilst using mostly 'minor' harmonies, doesn't whine or become self-pitying. The process of simplification, the 'cleaning' of the harmony and textures continues and more and more tonal suggestions occur. The last bar is a typical Eisler gesture.[24] Ex. 2.33

Klemm has mentioned (page 5) the quotation jokes — the juxtaposition of the *Internationale* and the fourths theme of Schoenberg's Opus 9. A more abstruse joke lies in Eisler's counterpoint to the upwards striding fourths — a descending whole-tone scale, demonstrating, surely, his awareness of the very crux of the musical-dialectical argument of the 'old man's' symphony, the battle for a tonal outcome between the 'negative' forces of fourths harmony and whole-tone harmony. Ex. 2.34

---

[24] See p. 36.

Ex. 2.33 *Tagebuch* Op. 9

Ex. 2.34 *Tagebuch* Op. 9

This weird piece was followed by another unusual one, the *Zeitungsausschnitte* (Newspaper cuttings) Op. 11. In fact, only two of the ten songs are what the title implies. Having presumed to use the word masterpiece of *Palmström*, I dare again here, of a work which is both a climax to Eisler's 'first period' and a transition to the next. From now on, his involvement with workers choirs (already in 1925, he had flexed his muscles with the three male voice choruses Opus 10),[25] with the agitprop group *Das rote Sprachrohr* (The Red Megaphone) and collaboration with Robert Gilbert, Walter Mehring, Ernst Busch and, in 1930, Bertolt Brecht, takes over.

The fourth song is dated 18 September 1925; numbers two and three, September 1926; the remainder were probably written early in 1927. The choice of texts represents a significant step away from art poetry. Not one song is a setting of poetry of any sort at all but is, seemingly, a disparate collection of odds and ends lacking any unity or *raison d'etre*. But Eisler has ordered and set them with intelligence and cunning — the sequence has variety, surprises, even incongruities but convinces through the strength of the musical sensibility. Consider the texts as listed:

1. *Mariechen*. The text was described by Adorno, in his review of the cycle's premiere in the *Musikblätter des Anbruch* 1929, as 'a pre-war hit song in a sadistic children's variant.' Other sources could be the French song *Mariette* and a Berlin children's rhyme.
2. *Kinderlied aus dem Wedding* — precisely that, a children's song from the Berlin district of *Wedding*.
3. *Liebeslied eines Kleinbürgermädchens — Heiratsannonce*. Love-song of a petit-bourgeois girl.
8. *Liebeslied eines Grundbesitzers — Heiratsannonce*. Love-song of a landowner.
   Both of these are actual newspaper personal column marriage advertisements.
4. *Kriegslied eines Kindes*. Child's battle song, from the Great War.
5. *Die Sünde* — Sin
6. *Mutter und Vater* — Mother and Father } *Aus einer Enquête*
7. *Der Tod* — Death
   These three texts are taken from answers by junior school children to a provincial education authority's examination paper on 'The Meaning of Words.'
9. *Predigt des Feldkuraten* — The Field-Curate's Sermon. A slightly shortened and altered passage from Hasek's *Svejk*.[26]

---

[25] To Heine poems which he freely adapted to his needs. See Betz 'Hanns Eisler — Political Musician' 1982 p. 53–7 and Drew, Tempo 161/2 p. 26–27 for more about these choruses. I have taken the view that they belong more properly to the next phase of his career and have not dealt with them here.

[26] The passage occurs on p. 448 of the English translation by Cecil Parrott pub. Penguin books 1973

10. *Frühlingsrede* — Speech in Spring to a tree in the rear courtyard. Text by Eisler.

It is important for performers and listeners to be clear about the stance, the *Gest* of this cycle. Not one of the songs requires the vocal delivery or interpretative approach appropriate to the Romantic *Lieder* repertoire, or to Schoenberg's Opp. 8, 10 and 15, to Berg's Opus 2, to Webern's Opp. 3, 8, 12 and 13, or even to Eisler's own Opus 2. Numerous warnings appear in the score. No.2 is to be sung 'coarsely', both love-songs should be delivered 'lightly, without parody, humour or wit,' and the curate is a coarse, rough fellow. Most of all, all high seriousness and tragic intensity must be avoided when singing an eight-year-old's thoughts on sin and death, even when, in 'Mother and Father', the bread-winner comes home late and 'we all have to be quiet, or he beats us!' Eisler has *composed into* these songs the compassion and wit. By standing back to observe the human emotion the texts reflect, the loneliness, the childish innocence and experience, the curate's savagery, we find the effect is emotionally purer, without the inflated bombast of Romantic and post-Romantic music which Eisler loathed so much. Thirty years later, he was still demonstrating to conservatoire-trained *Lieder* and opera singers the desirability of a simple and straightforward delivery of the text, of the power and persuasiveness of a modest, non-heroic, 'epic' stance.[27]

Although not all written in one burst, the harmonic language and the vocal lines are consistent and the cycle is unified by a recurring *Leitmotiv* of falling semitones. In its most obvious and simple form, it begins the *Kriegslied*, suggesting that when he continued work a year later, Eisler consciously developed the idea: Ex. 2.35

Ex. 2.35

The motive, with its text, recurs as a refrain three times in this song. In the third song it appears in the piano thus: Ex. 2.36

[27] See the Sixth conversation with Bunge p. 417 ff.

Ex. 2.36

and twice more in the last five bars: Ex. 2.37

Ex. 2.37

In the first song it has a *scherzando* lilt: Ex. 2.38

Ex. 2.38

and in number six, the vocal line decorates it: Ex. 2.39

Ex. 2.39

It is given a mordant, almost sneering character in number nine, with 'popular' parallel sliding chords: Ex. 2.40

Ex. 2.40

In bars 11–12 of the landowner's love-song, Eisler indulges in the first of his mockings of Wagner by inverting the motive to produce a Tristan quote to the words 'Am a widower of thirty-four, a wealthy landowner with a child — the child needs a good mother, myself a good wife.'[28]

The chosen musical idiom has just the flexibility needed for word-painting of gentle humour and feeling. For instance, reference in No. 1 to 'the German Men's choir, which sings you a pretty little song', allows a parody not of his own, rather difficult Opus 10, but of the sentimental repertoire he mocks in the first of the *Four Pieces for chorus* of 1928 — 'How lovely it is in this green wood, where echoes resound.' In *Der Tod,* his already extensive experience of musical irony produces some suitably touching harmony, avoiding exaggeration, for 'Then you go over to a better hereafter, when you die.' Ex. 2.41

[28] In October 1936, in London, he perpetrated a more extreme joke at Wagner's expense by quoting the same Tristan 'motif of longing' (this time with the harmonies) in his setting of Brecht's *Kuppellied* (Song of the Madam), in the music to *Die Rundköpfe und die Spitzköpfe.* There the words are: 'Money makes you sexy, as experience tells us.' In 1961, for the Paris production of *Schweyk im zweiten Weltkrieg,* he composed the three scenes 'In den höheren Regionen'. In the first, after Hitler's words 'when tormented by sleeplessness, I ask myself, how does the Little Man in Europe view me?', the motif is played literally by four cellos (although the sequential continuation is at a different pitch). Eisler may well have had in his mind's eye the celebrated photograph of the Führer and his fellow gangsters at a Wagner performance (Die Meistersinger?). See Chapter 13 p. 206.

Ex. 2.41 Op.11 No. 7 *Der Tod*

In No. 8, the quote from *Tristan*, the work generally held responsible for the demise of the tonal system, is followed by a device which was at the very heart of that system — the circle of fifths. 'I seek understanding, sincere spiritual life, not wealth.' Ex. 2.42

In the final song, in which Eisler sets his own words as a sort of personal *envoi*, the inverted motif is followed, in bar 5 by a varied form of Example 2.36. The song is one of his Heine-like double-edged statements, beginning with a gentle, pastoral six-eight but incorporating two outbursts and an uncompromising end, typical of so many cadences to come.

'I do beg you to bloom. Mr. Tree; don't forget, it is Spring! Are you on strike because of the awful gloom in this yard? Surely you're not so unreasonable as to be dreaming of green forests. May I request that you adapt to the situation? Perhaps you think it superfluous to bloom in our times — what place have young, tender leaves on the barricades? In that you wouldn't be at all wrong, Mr. Tree. But don't forget: it is Spring! Ex. 2.43

There are two more songs which were originally intended for inclusion, possibly following No.3. Just as Nos. 5–7 are a sub-group under the title *Aus einer Enquête*, these have the title *Lustige Ecke*

Ex. 2.42 Op.11 No. 8 *Liebeslied eines Grundbesitzers*

Frühlingsrede an einen Baum im Hinterhaushof

Ex. 2.43 Op.11 No. 10

Ex. 2.43 Op.11 No. 10 (cont'd)

(Cheerful Corner). Eisler must have thought either that they would make the cycle too lengthy or that the texts were unsuitable. Perhaps he was right! The first, *Noblesse oblige* translates: 'What do I hear, Herr Graf! Your son has become a business agent! Yes! Now he visits his clients on horseback!' The second, *Der kleine Kohn*, depends on an untranslateable pun; 'Little Kohn comes out of school and his father asks — what have you learnt today? Today we learnt that the Lord God is a sieve. That's impossible! Think again, more clearly. Yes, father, I got it wrong. God is a ladle! (*Schöpfer* = ladle/creator).

Of the *Zeitungsausschnitte*, Eisler himself said:

'They are lyrical. But the lyricism has, to some extent, been damaged by the war. It is no longer a Schubertian lyricism. It has, so to speak, pale cheeks and is in a strange condition, although everything is still in order — the scrupulous piano accompaniment and the nice tune. But the Devil only knows, someone has distorted things a bit. It wasn't me, of course.'[29]

The years spanned by *Dumpfe Trommel und berauschtes Gong* and the *Zeitungsausschnitte*, 1916–1927, during which Eisler grew from being an eighteen-year-old aspirant experiencing the traumas of war to a fully-fledged professional musician suffering the traumas of manhood were those we normally consider to be a human being's 'formative' years; when experiences and ideas, study and experiment, love and despair, mistakes and successes all contribute fundamentally and crucially to the mature personality which results. By the age of twenty-nine, Eisler had run the full gamut. They had been rich years in every respect. He had been in close contact with one of the greatest pedagogues in musical history; he had read, argued and travelled; he had suffered physical injury and privation, had loved and had deep depressions. He had performed and taught and the close Schoenberg circle had been offset by his conducting of workers' choirs. He had married, his father had died. His works were receiving public performance and critical recognition and his historical knowledge of music had become extensive. The *Rote Fahne* reviews listed by Klemm (page 6) and the two articles of 1928 included in this book show what justified confidence he had in his

[29] Notowicz conversations pp. 51–3.

ability to view the contemporary world from a critical perspective. He had made the painful break away from Schoenberg. He had applied for membership of the German Communist Party.

The next step was to find a working environment, to write and make music with people of similar political and aesthetic persuasions, with the same artistic objectives. The move would necessarily be a radical one.

Wiener Tagebuch

Translation of passage (*Schriften*. Addenda pp. 12–13) of the autograph diary reproduced opposite.

God!, women are good-hearted. They can undress down to the last vest for a man. (Words of a cynic: X has thoroughly revived me with his description of his hopeless situation.)
A cynic: . . . It would have been very tedious if X had not cheered me up with a description of his hopeless situation.
(If) She: you have robbed me of my virtue.
He: I have had the honour. [also, Goodbye. Ed.]
When a woman extends a little finger to you, you must kiss her breast.
[German proverb: When you extend a finger to the Devil, he takes your whole hand. Ed.]
Very alone. The old flat is full of dust. Everything very empty.
Behind me lie, with a sort of bitterness (the) 8 days of festivities.
Flight from the self. Surrender to a great person. [i.e. H.E. Ed.]
Fear of the future. Unreal existence.
Grotesques, for voice and chamber orchestra (in form of variations) Fl. Cl. string quintet w[ith] l[ight] r[ecitation] Harm[onium]. [Three letters unreadable]

1. Palmström sometimes wishes he could dissolve.
2. 2 Funnels wander through the night.
3. P. takes paper from his drawer.

Many only view life so badly because they look down their noses at it. Evening. Cigarette, liqueur: (Creme de Mocca) no (wife) woman (Thank God). After work, it's good to rest. (O) most proper triviality, most blessed trifles [backside-wisdom]. (It sits so comfortably, this excellent backside-wisdom, that it's already got haemorrhoids.)
That one still thinks about work with a liqueur and cigarettes nearby is absolute proof of the existence of God. Sine coitu(m)s vita(m) est dulc(e). [Without union, life is sweet] O my old Latin professor (or was he young), you seem only to have taught me Latin so that I don't have to say coarse things in German. You classical philologist, nationalist; 'We won't want any judges; said the Lord and threw sulphur over Sodom and Gomorrha. Death is like having a cold, you go atishoo and experience great relief.

Herrgott!, sind die Frauen gutherzig. Das letzte Hemd können sie sich für einen Mann ausziehn

---

~~Worte eines Zynikers: X hat mich durch dann die Schilderung seiner trostlosen Lage ordentlich aufgeheitert.~~

Ein Zyniker: ... Es wäre sehr langweilig gewesen, wenn mich nicht X durch die Schilderung seiner trostlosen Lage aufgeheitert hätte.

... ~~Wenn~~ Sie: Du hast mir meine Jugend ~~ge~~ geraubt
Er: Ich habe die Ehre.

Wenn ~~man~~ einem eine Frau ~~an~~ den kleinen Finger reicht so nimmt man sie auf die Brust ~~Arme~~

Sehr allein. Die alte Wohnung liegt voll Staub. Alles sehr leer. Hinter mir liegen mit einer Art Verbitterung die 8 fehlenden Tage

---

Flucht vor dem Leben. Hingabe an eine große Person. Angst vor der Zukunft. Wiedersehen.

Grotesken. für eine Singstimme und Kammerorchester (In Variationenform.) Fl. Cl. Streichquintett m. P. R. Harm. 40 m.

1. Palmström wünscht sich manchmal aufzulösen.
2. 2 Trichter wandeln durch die Nacht
3. P. nimmt Papier aus seinem Schranke

Mancher sieht das Leben nur so schlecht ~~an~~ weil er es über die Schulter anschaut

---

(~~kleine~~ Werk ~~Prosa~~ Entsai: 2 ...)

Abends. Zigarette, Liquer: (Creme de Mocca). Nach getaner Arbeit ist gut ruhen, o wahrste Trivialität, beglückendste Afterweisheit. (Sie sitzt so gut, daß sie schon Hämorrhoiden hat diese brave Afterweisheit.)

Daß man neben Liquer und Zigarette überhaupt noch an Arbeit denkt, ist geradezu ein Beweis für das Dasein Gottes.

Sine coitu vita est dulcissima. O mein alter Lateinprofessor (oder war es ein jüngerer), du scheinst mir nur Latein gelernt zu haben, damit ich Schweinereien nicht auf deutsch sagen muß (du klassischer Philologe, Nationalist;

„Wir wären kein Richter Rauben" sagte der Herrgott und schüttete Schwefel auf Sodom und Gomorrha.

Das Sterben ist wie wenn man Schnupfen hat man macht Hatschi und d. spürt eine große Erleichterung.

3

ON THE SITUATION IN MODERN MUSIC

Hanns Eisler

For those gathered dutifully round the bed, the death-rattle of a dying man is so boring that they fall asleep. But their snores sound so like the death-rattle that it is difficult to ascertain who is actually dying. Such is the relationship between bourgeois society and modern music.

Of course, music is a remarkable art. Its muse has a bodily defect. She lacks both legs and so cannot stand or walk on earth. She is forced, by means of a pair of extremely dilapidated wings, to move in 'higher regions'. But now up there too, there is inconvenience from the aeroplanes and the smoke from the factories, and radio listeners curse the disturbance and static. But the somewhat disabled muse flutters bravely on and, in spite of everything, assists a multitude of people to produce a host of questionable things; questionable because they have almost nothing to do with anybody, not even those who produce them; questionable because mostly they aren't worth the question.

Meanwhile her previously much less esteemed sister, light music (that is, music which, in contrast to the serious, one may converse to) has attracted some notice. She conquers everyone, is at home everywhere and serves a more real purpose — for dancing and love-making — and is well on the way to driving her sister off to heaven.

What on earth! Whoever goes to heaven must have died! That sounds like poetry, but is only the desperate cry of the musician of today who refuses to be deceived about the awful isolation of his art, for whom it is not enough to produce work after work purely for the sake of producing, who strives for something more vital because it concerns everyone and is therefore alive in everyone, to whom it is repugnant to procure ever more refined pleasure for just a few gourmets.

Every development of recent years results consciously or unconsciously from a knowledge of this. For example: the new classicism (as if the imitation of a past style could restore the social structure which gave rise to it), the mechanization of music (as if music in today's society could become more generally valid if performed or created by machines), the new renaissance in religious music (the prerequisite for which must be a renaissance in religiosity)[1] and so on.

Also the turning away from the Romantics can be attributed to all this. It was discovered that the feelings of a single individual were no longer sufficient to express something generally more valid and so what was wanted was 'absolute' music-making, without emotion, without expression, just a game with notes.

At last a quite simple recipe was found — take elements of light music, mix them with the 'serious', add a bit of new classicism and carefully pour over a drop of religiosity. Result — we hear the same jazz as in the night club, only somewhat more stylized and badly made.

All these fashions show, however, to what extent the isolation has led to confusion — and to rootlessness, a sign of how far the social crisis is beginning to take effect in music as well.

In addition there is a quantity of typical manifestations of decay. In no other time has craftsmanship been at such a low level in terms of knowledge and ability. In no other time was pure incompetence and the most uncultivated dilettantism celebrated with such orgies. Whether it's a question of tonal or atonal works, the overall picture is one of disintegration: incompetence to express a thought precisely, be it ever so banal, inadequate harmony, voice leading etc.

There is one artist who already in 1910, in his *Harmonielehre,*[2] recognised that a deterioration in craftsmanship had begun — Arnold Schoenberg. His new theory, 'composition with twelve notes', based on his new conception of tonality, tries to place craft and knowledge on a healthier footing. This cannot be praised enough, for in music, perhaps more than in any other art, all intellectual problems are connected with problems of the technique of composition.

The picture is the same in musicology. New methods which have for a long time been used in the other arts are completely lacking. There is for example no sociology of music (apart from a relatively short essay by Max Weber[3]) and even the best minds, who really do have something

---

[1] In his *Rote Fahne* article of January 1928 entitled *The new religiosity in music,* Eisler refers, amongst others to Stravinsky's *Requiem,* by which he can only mean the *Paternoster* of 1926, Honegger's *King David,* Hindemith's *Das Marienleben* and a Latin Mass by Otto Klemperer.

[2] The *Harmonielehre* was published in 1911.

[3] *Die rationalen und soziologischen Grundlagen der Musik* Munich 1921.

to say, like Paul Bekker[4] and Adolf Weissmann,[5] at best transfer the new idealistic philosophy (the Phenomenology of Husserl) on to music. On the other hand the incidence is growing of mere compendia in bulky volumes or muddled phraseology which feeds itself on catchwords and is not in a position to say anything halfway to the point.

This bewilderment in private and public opinion, this ignorance of craftsmanship, this incapacity for acceptance by more than a few stands in the most blatant contradiction to a music business which has taken on ever greater dimensions since the war and is already making a considerable noise. There is, for example, in Germany an immense number of modern music societies who put on many concerts, admittedly to empty seats and almost behind closed doors. The big music festivals have become virtual stock exchanges where the value of a work is taxed and agreements for the coming season are concluded. But all this noise is made as if in a vacuum flask; not a sound will be heard. An aimless industriousness celebrates orgies of inbreeding with absolutely no interest or participation from the public.

Of course some young composers are no longer conforming. They are making efforts to be properly up-to-date, more or less renouncing absolute music and turning to the theatre. But as soon as their music is involved with words and action, then we see all the more clearly how completely out-of-date these young composers are. Only recently we found on a German opera stage a whole range of ingenious devices, a railway engine, car, film camera, radio etc. which, we are assured, because of their usefulness caused a great stir.[6]

We shouldn't joke about it though. It is at least something and if these young composers work hard, perhaps they'll notice one day that the earth is populated by people not theatre props and if they work even

---

[4] Paul Bekker 1882–1937. German writer with a special interest in opera. He supported many German composers.

[5] Adolf Weissmann 1887–1929. German musicologist.

[6] In Eisler's review of Ernst Krenek's *Jonny spielt auf* (text by the composer) in *Die Rote Fahne* of 19 October 1927, the following passage occurs:

'When, in the next scenes, a car and even a railway engine appear on the stage, it doesn't get any more interesting, for in the car sits Max the composer, who sings mournful sentimentalities, which he could have delivered without the car. . . . Basically a really unsuccessful libretto. The opera, in spite of fashionable infusions, is the same old *petit-bourgeois* pap as most operas by modern composers.'

The first performance had taken place in Leipzig on 10 February. It was enormously successful. Krenek was twenty-six.

harder, perhaps they'll notice later on that these people are not one homogeneous mass, but are divided into classes and that they are participants in what appears to be the most gigantic social struggle in the history of mankind. The musician, who loves his art and for whom it is an absolute necessity, will recognize with horror the total isolation of his art. But it is essential that he does recognize it and isn't taken in by this busy, incestuous music industry.

Now if someone comes up and says: Fine, that's all quite right, but what are we to do? Where are we to go? One cannot adopt a frivolous optimism and shout: To pot! That certainly sounds very nice but is just a bit inadequate. Perhaps one could advise him in this way. Step out of your intellectual isolation and interest yourself in everything, not just the night club and sport (for which you haven't had much interest anyway). Don't forget that the machines exist solely to satisfy the needs of people. If, while composing, you open the window, remember that the noise in the street doesn't create itself but is made by people. Try hard for a while to abstain from bombastic symphonies, played-out chamber music and esoteric songs. Choose texts and subjects of interest to as many people as possible.

Try really to understand your own time, but don't get caught up in mere externals. Discover people, the real people, discover everyday life for your art, then perhaps *you'll* be rediscovered.

Published in an earlier version under the title *Über moderne Musik* in Die Rote Fahne 15 October 1927. This later version probably dates from late 1928. In *Schriften* 1924–1948 p. 88 ff.

4

ON THE BOURGEOIS CONCERT BUSINESS

Hanns Eisler

So many advertisements for concerts. They hang in the subway stations. They're stuck to the advertising hoardings, to the fences around building sites. They fill two to three pages in the Sunday editions of the big bourgeois papers: orchestral concerts, violin recitals, piano recitals, vocal concerts, evenings of new music, string quartet societies. Every evening six to ten concerts. The music critics run about until their feet are flat and their shoe leather gone.

The musical hunger of the bourgeoisie? The artistic hunger of the broader, more numerous masses? A golden age of musical life? All a con.

At the overwhelming majority of these events there is no audience. The few people one can find there — relatives of the artists, professional colleagues, critics and the concert agent — are all on complimentary tickets, and they take off their coats backstage, to save the cloakroom fee. All of this is played out in the complete absence of any audience.

Who pays the cost of the venue, of the printing of tickets and programmes? Who pays the high rates for advertising, who rents the orchestra? The artist. Yes indeed, the artist, who is filled with such wide-eyed, devotional enthusiasm for pure art, wishes to know nothing of politics, complains about being misunderstood and is a well-dressed, well-brought-up man from a good family, which pays thousands of marks for the education of its offspring. (E.g. an hour's private lesson with a great, leading pianist: 100 marks. Five hours must be paid for in advance at the start of instruction.)

Who earns anything from this? The concert agencies, who take over the arrangements for such an event, the newspapers, who are well paid for the concert advertisements, the owners of concert halls.

But the newspapers get their own back. They have engaged two to three critics, who must attend all these concerts. So if one gives a concert that costs, say, 1000 marks, then one finds, some days later, according to the usual procedure, the 'review'. It usually runs as follows: "Herr X or Fräulein Y played Chopin in very gifted fashion. Yet the final refinement of touch was lacking. A talent capable of development, which one would like to encounter more often."

The artist collects these reviews. That happens courtesy of a newspaper clippings bureau, which thus also benefits from this business. If one has a number of such more or less good reviews, one hopes to get one or more of the very few regular symphony concerts which artists can pay for, because these concerts, relics of the good old days, have a fixed number of subscriptions and the orchestras are the permanent orchestras of the city and provincial opera houses.

But even with such occasional engagements (and there are very few who manage to get these) an artist cannot support himself. The business forces him to give new concerts again and again, so that his name does not fall into oblivion, and so that again and again he receives new 'good reviews'.

This kind of art business reveals like no other the relationship between art and capital. The basic principle of bourgeois idealism about art, the independence of art from the political and economic situation of society, has today already begun to falter. Like a poison, Marxism has undermined the views on art held by the 'leftist' bourgeoisie. But the basic principle: that everyone can become an artist, every artistic gift can win through (see, for example, the worker poets: Gorky, Jack London, Alfons Petzold, Kurt Kläber), if only it is strong enough, is still held to be sacrosanct today, even by the 'leftist' bourgeoisie. Applied to music and to the special character of its business, this basic premise is ridiculous. It is crude and glib.

In music, only someone who is socially well-placed can achieve anything. A virtuoso can only be of bourgeois extraction. Even if he comes from a *petit bourgeois* milieu, he brings along with him at least the smooth, soft, supple hands without which the career of a virtuoso becomes an impossibility; he brings with him at least the ideology of art which enables him to find this kind of existence meaningful. The son of a member of the proletariat has never yet become a virtuoso, a composer, a conductor. All great artists, if they have come poor into the world, come from the families of musicians. But the fewest have come from oppressed, *petit bourgeois* circumstances, and that is almost exclusively the composers. This again strengthens the class solidarity of the bourgeoisie: patrons, stipends, prizes, free places in the state institutions for musical education. Even the *petit bourgeois* family which is badly placed in social terms will sacrifice everything for the musical education of a talent; the son won't have to go to work at the age of fourteen. Just knowing that someone is musically gifted presupposes a particular economic situation.

The pressure to enter the musical profession has been increasing for years. The dissatisfaction which the best elements of the young bourgeoisie feel with regard to the bourgeois professions (office-worker, clerk, etc.) drives them in flocks into the field of music, where the uninhibited living-out of the personality is so highly paid. Musicians are increasingly recruited from better circles, which are more highly placed socially. And what remains for the son of Stresemann, except to become a composer?

And Prince Joachim of Prussia? The young Werner F. von Siemens would also like to become a conductor, and rather than directing the works of Siemens prefers to direct the works of Mozart. The regular concerts of the Berlin Symphony Orchestra are paid for by Franz von Mendelssohn, president of the Chamber of Commerce, for the conductor of these concerts is his son-in-law. And all these sons of factory-owners and bankers, who compose or conduct, play piano and violin with such genius. *The proletariat pays for all of this!* They have to sweat so that these chaps can make pure art.

In Russia, since 1917, this kind of music business has vanished. — When will this happen in Germany?

Translated by Karin von Abrams
Die Rote Fahne 15 April 1928.
In *Schriften* 1924–1948 p. 74 ff.

5

MY FATHER

Georg Eisler

A long time ago Elias Canetti asked me how I got on with my father. When I pointed out that Hanns Eisler had been dead for a dozen years, he answered that he did know this, but nevertheless wanted to learn from me how I got on with my father. 'Very well,' I replied, and Canetti assured me that the relationship with my father would be still better in the future.

In the first-year class at the elementary school in the *Schöngasse* in District 2 in Vienna, the senior master (whose name I have forgotten but whom I remember well) remarked: 'I hear your father is a great Communist.' 'He is a great composer,' I answered, for although I was still very young, the timely recognition of traps had already been taught me at home.

During my childhood, I saw my father rarely and at irregular intervals. My parents' separation, which from my point of view occurred relatively early, was partly to blame for this, but above all it was due to the events of the time. The meetings in Vienna are particularly clear in my memory. Visits together to the *Café Museum,* where Hanns Eisler met his friends from the Schoenberg circle. Because my mother was a singer and a pianist, I spent a significant part of my childhood in a circle of musicians, whose specialized language was familiar to me from an early age. The second circle that surrounded me, partially overlapping with the first, was that of leftist, largely Communist, intellectuals, for my parents were firmly bound to both of these groups. My father was for a long time perceptible to me primarily through his reflection in his friends. That this picture of Hanns Eisler was transmitted intact over many long years — without distortions or the kind of indistinctness caused by the times, albeit somewhat diffused — I owe first of all to my mother, who also ensured that our correspondence did not break off during the decade of exile and war — so that I had to learn early to communicate my thoughts in writing.

Representative of the relatively few friends to whom my father remained close throughout his life, Erwin Ratz springs to mind. He was the sorrowful part of what was (viewed from the outside) a truly comical duo which he formed with Hanns Eisler. Ratz was melancholy and sometimes frantic, Eisler effervescent and expansive. The former was to be proved right in his eminently pessimistic view of the world. During the time of the thousand-year *Reich*, this prophet of the world's demise not only saved human lives, but also hid Eisler scores and manuscripts (likewise a very dangerous thing to do) under the ever-decreasing sacks of flour in the cellars of his bakery; for Ratz was not only a student of Schoenberg and a musicologist, but also a baker.

Then there was Mildner, musical expert and agronomist of a *solkhoz* in the Caucasus; he was to vanish in 1938, never to be seen again. And the beaming Ernst Busch, in the hot summer of 1936, in the *Hotel Moskva*, rehearsing my father's songs. He sat, dressed only in a towel, next to Hauska the pianist, and ordered a great jug of cold *kvas* to be brought to the room for me.

These, then, were the friends, who were for the most part very well disposed towards me, the son. I myself also appeared pre-programmed for a career as a musican, even a composer. At a proper distance from my father, naturally. It was generally established, with satisfaction, that I was indeed very musical; my quick understanding and my youthful compositions seemed to point in that direction. In Vienna I saw Eisler conduct choruses from the *Massnahme* and the *Mutter* — concerts whose musical and political content were received stormily and very emotionally. Seeing my father in this aspect of his work remained an essential element of my image of him. As an interpreter of his own music, he was — this was repeatedly confirmed — unique: the singer with the clapped-out, barely audible voice, the anti-virtuoso pianist, is today still a yardstick for all those who want to perform his work. I also saw him extract the utmost in skill from rather mediocre musicians. At the same time he was always a man of great, almost ritual politeness and gratitude towards the interpreters of his music. For many years this music remained for me the thing that bound me to my father. I knew it very well, knew how to play the piano variations, at least the easier ones, decently. But above all, the songs were sung by my mother in numerous concerts and naturally, before that, rehearsed in our apartments, strewn over half of Europe; I knew them by heart from the time I was small.

As a painter, which I have since become, I often reflect on life in a musical family: the piano-playing and the singing from the next room, the frequent chamber music (today one would say: 'everything live') signify for me the submerged world of childhood. In this world my father, whether present or not, represented the focal point and the person decisive for all relationships. He was both the guiding principle and the sound barrier which one had to penetrate. In this world of childhood, the friends of my parents are illuminated again and again in snapshots: Ratz, Polnauer, Webern, Steuermann. . . all of them, without exception, involved with music. Apart from early visits to museums, painting remained a peripheral thing (at roughly the same time the five-year-old was taken to his first *Zauberflöte*, remembered to this day). The only painter with whom my father had a close relationship was Georg Grosz. Thus it was, primarily, an acoustic and not a visual home, broadened by (so it appeared to me) a vast number of books. One wall of books followed another. Hanns Eisler and I each spent years of our respective childhoods in the shadow of the bookshelves of my grandfather, his father, the philosopher Rudolf Eisler. It was a fortress of books, which I had to leave when I was still very young, but to which my father, for his part, owed a considerable part of his amazing philosophical and literary education. Naturally there were also new political and literary books at that time, amongst which those of the Malik Verlag, above all, remain in my memory, chiefly because of the bindings and book jackets by John Heartfield, whose name was familiar to me even at a very tender age. As childhood reading I had Auguste Lazar's Comintern fairy tale *Tante Sally Bleistift in Amerika* and (in German translation) the Robin Hood novel *Arrows against Barons* by Geoffrey Trease.

One thing that has remained vivid in my memory is a visit with Eisler to a coffee-house garden in the *Prater* in early 1935. Hitler was already in power in Germany, Eisler's Berlin apartment long ago abandoned, and he himself was travelling through Europe; to Denmark to see Brecht, to Paris, Moscow, to London for film work and then also to New York. He wanted to give me something for my seventh birthday. In the arcades of the railway viaduct in the *Prater* there was a toy shop, and there a great wish of mine was fulfilled: a Diana air rifle, from then on the terror of our visitors and one that left visible traces on the door-frames.

The following years of emigration and war were years without my father, in which the divorce of my parents was only one of many weighty events. Survival was made easier by the fact that mother and son crossed the borders more easily than larger families, and formed the most compact unit for escape. The written contact with my father was not broken off during this time. After the outbreak of the war, efforts were undertaken to send me to him in the USA. He had already found a school place for me, but the increasing danger of an Atlantic crossing led my mother to decide that I should remain in England. So for more than a decade we had only the exchange of letters.

Eisler's music constituted another kind of bond. I could soon play his songs by heart; the instrumental music — the easier piano variations, so far as I know the ones dedicated to me — I knew only superficially.

The habit many of his friends had of seeing me first of all as Hanns's son amazingly produced no complexes in me. That murderous period had little time left over for such things. Perhaps it would have been different for me in this respect if I had grown up with my father. When (admittedly in the course of these same contemporary events) a few comrades and friends believed all too readily rumours that Eisler had changed sides politically, I (at that time fourteen years old) felt attacked and dismayed, and like my mother attempted to take a stand against these rumours.

Then there were the Hollywood films, for which Eisler had composed the music, events which again and again prompted joyful comments in my letters; and in the art cinemas the old avant-garde films with his music. Music was often the chief subject of our letters.

When I began my art studies, my father did not react at all enthusiastically, and asked whether my artistic leanings could not be combined with a serious career, possibly architecture, which would earn me a living. One could surely not live by painting alone; he knew that from numerous cases.

A further subject of our letters was the period after the war. I, who had intended from the beginning to return to Vienna, wanted to know from my father whether he too thought of returning home. He appeared to avoid this question — only later did he make clear to me that he was thinking of a return to Vienna, but in the meantime wished to remain longer in Hollywood, where he had friends and a good deal of work.

Twelve years were to pass before I again faced him. I was now twenty years old, and his departure from the Californian paradise had been hastened thanks to the House Un-American Activities Committee. What his courageous appearance before this body, one of whose members was the future president Nixon, really cost him, became clear to me only long after his death, as I in Los Angeles, like Hamlet, pursued my father's ghost.

Eisler's return to his home city was a return to the Vienna of the Cold War. Asked by an American journalist soon after his arrival about his political views, he answered: 'I'm not interested in politics, politics are interested in me.' The encounter in 1948 with the city, still suffering from serious war-damage and divided into four sectors, and the people, for the most part just as badly damaged, caused him to alternate between joy at seeing it again, and depression. The latter mood could hardly fail to appear, as despite several attempts, no possibility arose for him to resume his teaching at the Academy or at the Conservatory — being Communist and a student of Schoenberg, he inevitably overstepped the limit of tolerance habitually shown here by those with cultural power, not a few of them relics of the immediate past.

Our conversations during this time of re-acquaintance often revolved around the USA (Eisler was never to see it again), object of unexpressed love and frequently expressed hatred. Added to this were greater difficulties in acclimatizing to the ravaged condition of post-war Europe, above all where his artistic work was concerned — which in Austria, apart from the various cultural events of the Communist Party, found virtually no audience.

As far as his appearance was concerned, my father had hardly changed in all those years; not only memory but also our many photographs served to confirm this.

The fourteen years that remained to us until his death formed the temporal frame of a changeable, often very intense father-son relationship, its venue alternating between Vienna and Berlin, where from 1950 onwards he spent a considerable part of each year.

Individual remarks that have stuck particularly in my memory (concerning those countries ruled by the system termed 'real existing socialism'): 'Here everything is deceptive, except appearances' or 'Dear Georg, capitalism too has its dark sides.' Hanns Eisler owed his reputation as an uncommonly witty, jolly person to this kind of quick, concise, biting humour — even today his *aperçus* are still in circulation around the world and in several languages.

At the same time, these fireworks of wit overlay (as I could perceive) a rather melancholy, indeed a vulnerable nature, which he was able successfully to conceal.

Phases of increased creativity: I watched him in Berlin, composing — while doing the instrumentation he could simultaneously read the newspaper lying on the piano. And still, almost every evening, he was the brilliant focus of richly intelligent gatherings. In contrast to this, the dark, very sad times, in which he achieved nothing new. Hanns Eisler's attitude to my own artistic works was ambivalent; he would hardly be drawn into a conversation about painting. 'What you say about your painting doesn't interest me, what interests me is what others say about it. (Ultimately, he was interested in the first detailed reviews of my works.) As a partner in conversation on musical topics, by contrast, I was listened to quite readily. And he told me much about Schoenberg, also with didactic intent, in order to demonstrate to me the process of teaching.

Sometimes, not often, but then very seriously, there were rows. Yet my visits to his little house in Niederschönhausen always passed harmoniously. I have a particularly wonderful memory of an evening in Brecht's strange spartan-luxurious home in Berlin. To observe the two friends together was fascinating.

In 1962, at the start of the year whose end Hanns Eisler would not live to see, the performance of the *Deutsche Sinfonie* took place in the BBC's main studio in Maida Vale, in London. Afterwards there were many drinks and friends in a nearby pub. As I congratulated my father on his great success, he suddenly became serious, waved it away. 'It comes too late.'

Only a few of his old friends are still alive. The friends of his music become more and more numerous, and for a composer too this is what matters.

Over the years, I, in quite different circumstances, have sought out almost all the stations of his life, and I realize again and again how near to me he is in that foreign country — and receive again and again his message: how one should live with and from one's art, even in dark times.

Translated by Karin von Abrams
Published as *Intervalle* in *Skizzen — Schriften und Zeichnungen*
Compress Verlag, Vienna 1990

6

DIE MASSNAHME: THE VANISHING LEHRSTÜCK

John Willett

So far as we know (which is not such a very long way) Eisler and Brecht probably came across one another in 1927. This was the year when Hindemith's *Neue Musik* festival at Baden-Baden featured mini-operas, of which one was the Brecht-Weill *'Songspiel' Mahagonny*. Hindemith's own brief music-theatre palindrome *Hin und Zurück* to Marcellus Schiffer's text was also given, as, more marginally, was Eisler's *Tagebuch*. The same summer Brecht joined the 'dramaturgical collective' at Piscator's West End theatre while Eisler began working with the Young Communist agitprop group *Das rote Sprachrohr*, the alarmingly-named Red Megaphone. Brecht was not yet a committed communist (though Piscator was). Eisler's signature tune for his group *Wir sind das rote Sprachrohr* was primitive, to say the least. But his brother and sister were leading Communists, and he had applied to join their party the previous year.

1928 was the year of the *Threepenny Opera*, Brecht's great and unexpected success with Kurt Weill, after which he abandoned work with Piscator in favour of his new interest in different kinds of music theatre, in particular the cantata-like *'Lehrstück'* form, on which he started working with Weill and Hindemith. On his recommendation, it seems, Weill had provided the incidental music for three plays he was concerned with — one by his mentor Lion Feuchtwanger, one for Piscator by the Austrian journalist Leo Lania, which included the devastating 'shell' song, and his own *Man equals Man* whose music is alas lost. For Feuchtwanger's *Warren Hastings* play, on which Brecht collaborated the same year, Eisler set the poet's Kipling-style *Song of the Soldier*. Then in 1929 both Brecht and Piscator had failures — the former the gangster play *Happy End* with Weill, the latter Walter Mehring's *The Merchant of Berlin* with music by Eisler. One of the actor/singers in this was Ernst Busch, who had also been in the *Threepenny Opera*. From then on he became a central figure in the Eisler-Brecht collaboration: in their

Berlin communist works, in their emigration of the 1930s (when he sang with Eisler in the USSR and Republican Spain), and again after the Second World War.

It would be a mistake to think that Brecht wanted to work exclusively with any one composer, but Weill and Eisler never really became friends. Nor however were they poles apart — not even politically, though thanks to today's Weill lobby it tends to be assumed that they were. Their divergence starts from common points of interest — in new theatre music, in jazz, in clarity of statement, in the poetry of Brecht and in the socio-musical concerns being promoted by Hindemith — and at the centre of it all were Arthur Waley's translation of *The No Plays of Japan* which had been published in 1921. These austere and tightly condensed dramas were brought, during the run of *The Three-penny Opera*, to Elisabeth Hauptmann, Brecht's English-speaking aide who had collaborated with him and Weill on that work, and she translated several, including notably *Taniko* or *The Valley-Hurling*, whose text she published in a theatre magazine. Weill, who had been looking for a libretto to set as a 'school opera' for the 1930 *Neue Musik* festival, suggested using this, and Brecht went over it making small revisions. Almost simultaneously — or anyway, overlappingly — he decided to make a 'counter-play' together with Eisler.

Weill's extremely successful work was *Der Jasager*, He Who Says Yes, and Brecht was disturbed by its reception as a model of religious traditionalism and suicidal self-sacrifice, a relic from feudal times. This was all the more so when he heard that it was the reactionary critics who liked it and the provinces that wished to perform it. Accordingly he organized a production in a Berlin school as a result of which the young performers called for a different ending, with the boy victim rejecting his traditional obligations and becoming *He Who Says No*. Brecht then wrote the new version. 'The two little plays should if possible never be performed separately', says a note to the dual texts. This was something of a mystification, since it was never actually carried out in Brecht's lifetime except in a small New York production by the Living Theatre; for Weill never altered his setting to fit any but the very first version of the text (which was the closest to Waley's); nor is there anything in Brecht's published letters to suggest that he asked Weill to do so. Weill did however know about the proposed 'counter-play' with Eisler, since it was intended to be a kind of unidentical twin, to be performed at the same *Neue Musik* festival. And when the festival committee, including Hindemith, barred its performance on the grounds of 'formal inferiority of the text' — in other words, its political message — he lined up with

Brecht and Eisler and insisted that *Der Jasager* too should be taken out of the festival and be separately performed at a Berlin teaching institute.

Eisler's work on the 'counter-play', *Die Massnahme*, represents the closest collaboration by any composer on the actual structure and text of one of Brecht's music theatre works. He functioned for Brecht, so he later said, as 'the messenger of the working class' — in other words, of the communist movement. What exactly this meant was never spelt out, but one aspect certainly was the resituating of the *Taniko* theme in modern China as the story of a Comintern mission, based apparently on the experiences of Eisler's brother. Gerhart Eisler had been a leading member of the German Communist Party, initially with his sister Ruth Fischer as one of the Left tendency before spring 1923, then as an ally of Brandler and Thalheimer, leading Rightists, against Stalin's man, the non-intellectual Thälmann. Following the Right's defeat in 1928 he was summoned to Moscow and put to work for the Comintern, specializing, it seems, in Chinese affairs. As a secret agent he took part in the Canton commune, then later, disguised as a Dutch business man, became political adviser to the Red unions in Shanghai. Apparently his first-hand reports of this experience with an international team of agitators — Besso Lominadze was its best known member — became fascinating material for the new work, which Brecht termed a *Konkretisierung*, or actualization, of *Der Jasager*. The boy becomes the Young Comrade (in an early fragment he is still called *der Knabe*) and his offence is a romantic enthusiasm for the World Revolution that leads him more than once to risk the lives of the whole team. Deliberately or coincidentally, the theme ties in with Lenin's pamphlet *Left wing Communism, an infantile disorder*, which appeared in German in April 1930, just before the first version of the text was ready.

The other new contribution from the 'working class' was Eisler's concentration on the workers' choral movement with which he (like Scherchen, Webern, Horenstein and Karl Rankl) had become involved. As Manfred Nössig points out in his new edition of the text, all previous experiments with the *Lehrstück* form had originated in such middle class efforts to reform the media and the arts as the *Neue Musik* festivals, works for radio and the movement for new music in the schools. In these too the essence of the new form was that it should not merely teach laymen the pleasure of making music together (Hindemith's '*Gemeinschaftsmusik*') but also convey an ethical or political message for absorption by the performers. But in so far as Eisler's singers were working class amateurs, organized in a predominantly left wing association at a time of increasing political tension, the didactic element now became more markedly agitational. Clearly he approached this task with the Bach Passions in mind; thus he told his interviewer Hans Bunge (of the Brecht-Archive) towards the end of his life that the recitatives of the Evangelist in the *St John Passion* were for him and Brecht the model of how to set a report — of what they and Kurt Weill called 'gestic music'.[1] At the same time he must have been thinking of the simplicity of the great chorales; there were performances of *Die Massnahme* where the audience too were expected to join in, to judge from the projection of the texts. Of all the composers who were attracted by Brecht's irregular broken verse, it was he to whom Brecht allowed most freedom to cut and change it. And this was because of his sure ear for words, quite as much on any political account.

The result is an extraordinarily powerful work, in which words, music and staging combine equally in a single hour-long thrust. There is the dialogue of the four agitators as they act out the short episodes in prose or irregular verse, there are the tenor solos — recitatives or jazz numbers, sung not by the actor Busch, who had only a speaking part, but by trained singers such as Wirl or Topitz — there is a speech chorus leading into a canon, there are switches of rôle among the actors, there is rhythmic speech. Not much of this sounds quite like Bach, yet the affiliation is clearly there, along with a comparable sense of declaration of faith, something to which a number of Communist critics objected as being 'idealist' (in Lenin's sense). These objectors were not all steel-headed Socialist Realists by any means, and it is true that one of Brecht's main preoccupations in all four of the first *Lehrstücke* (including the 'school opera') was religious rather than Marxist in origin. This was the concept of *'Einverständnis'* as seen in the conscious self-risk and self-sacrifice of the aviators in the first two plays and of the youths in the second. To be *einverstanden* is a common German expression for agreement, consent, approval, acquiescence, but in Brecht's use of the noun the tacit stress is on the *Verstand* (reason, *ratio*) element, meaning that, to him at least, the agreement is not a passive one so much as the product of logical thought. And what actually interests him is not just the process but the self-denial that is part of the terrible decision.

So the reception of this piece in Germany during the last two years of the Weimar Republic was a divided, contradictory one even within the extreme left. On the one hand its performance by a committed body of players (unobtrusively including Eisler himself in the chorus at the première and Brecht as the Young Comrade in the single

---

[1] Conversations with Bunge p. 67 [Ed.]

recording) made an overwhelming impact on many listeners, while its songs became central to the worker-singers' movement; it is still a great work, a monument to that tragic and fascinating time. On the other hand the consensus of the party ideologists — led by Kurella, Keméný, Bihajli–Merin — was that for various doctrinal reasons, some of which were borne in mind in subsequent revisions, it misrepresented the Party's policy and was politically amateurish, originating in the authors' book-reading rather than in any practical experience of revolutionary activity. Whether this possibly concerted campaign of objections was enough to explain the rather gingerly treatment of the play by right-thinking Communists from then on seems doubtful. The *Kulturpolitiker* (that lamentable category of people) were always slightly nervous of Brecht; Eisler's sister and brother were now both outside the Party pale; and the work's oriental element, at once formal and thematic, was considered by traditionalist pundits like Georg Lukács to be a mistaken diversion from the correct path.

Nevertheless the remaining months before Hitler became Chancellor saw the Brecht-Eisler collaboration pursued further, at first along very similar lines. So in summer 1931 they worked together in the collective which made the unique Communist film *Kuhle Wampe* (including their most famous *Kampflied*, the 'Solidarity Song' sung by Ernst Busch and a large chorus). The same autumn they provided songs for Busch and others to perform in a 'Red Revue' in mid-November, and began work with the writer Günther Weisenborn on *Die Mutter*, a play mixing *Lehrstück* and agitprop forms, which was staged in January in a simple and transportable set; this started out with only nine songs in a minimal orchestration, but had much of the simplicity and force of *Die Massnahme*, and once again included Busch and Helene Weigel among its performers. In spring 1932 the film, which had had trouble with the German censorship, was given its première in Moscow, with Brecht and the director Slatan Dudow attending. Eisler seems to have missed this, but arrived to work on Joris Ivens's film about the new Soviet city of Magnitogorsk, becoming linked thereafter with its co-writer Tretiakov, and possibly also Brecht, in an inconclusive plan for an opera on the *Aufbau des neuen Menschen* — the Construction of the New Man — for the Leningrad Opera. Tretiakov, their best and closest Soviet contact, was about to prepare a volume of translations of three Brecht plays, including *Die Massnahme*, for eventual publication in Moscow.

All this activity is a sign that, whatever misgivings the German Communists might feel about Brecht's orthodoxy, he and Eisler had reason to treat those as secondary compared with the encouragement being given by the Russians just when the cultural reaction in Germany was reaching a climax. That November Eisler took part in the Moscow meeting of the International Revolutionary Theatre Organization which then regrouped itself as MORT, part of a new set of Comintern cultural secretariats covering also the visual and literary arts. An International Music Bureau was one of its offshoots, and Eisler was at once appointed to the latter's committee. This newly-activated network was for a short while influential in the spread of what became a Popular-Front (or anti-fascist) culture flourishing in many parts of Europe, Australia and the USA during the rest of the 1930s: the French *Association d'Ecrivains et Artistes Révolutionnaires,* for instance, with its magazine *Commune* , the British Unity Theatre and Workers' Music Association, the Artists' International Association, the WPA Art projects in the USA and so on.

Though several such examples of the generally 'progressive' Thirties arts movements are now studied as contributions to the world's cultural history, little seems to have been done subsequently to link and relate them, let alone to consider them as part of a coherent policy. And this may well be due to the suppression of the central secretariats during the Soviet purges, along with the mysterious disgrace and death of the German Comintern member Willi Muenzenberg whose organizing ability they (like the Mezhrabpom film company for whom Eisler and Ivens worked) appeared to reflect.

So long as there was a cultural International of this kind — and its aesthetically pluralist influence persisted well after its heads had been lopped off — the Stalinist values of Socialist Realism were not yet absolutely stifling even inside the USSR. Externally, Piscator as head of MORT could open the organization's arms to avant-garde theatre provided it was opposed to Hitler: to the French Surrealists, for instance. Unity Theatre could begin welcoming professionals, while Eisler could justify, and perhaps hope officially to promote, the new compositional techniques (notably those of the Second Viennese School) as being unacceptable to fascism and contrary to *kitsch*. In 1934 Tretiakov's volume of three Brecht plays appeared; the next year Brecht paid a two month visit to Moscow at Piscator's invitation; Eisler for his part became president of the International Music Bureau. This, according to his own account, was when he visited Gorky (along with Romain Rolland), playing him three of the songs from *Die Mutter,* which the old man apparently liked. And probably it was then too that Brecht was commissioned to write a *Lehrstück* for the Red Army, and joined in planning the *Lenin Requiem* for the State Music publishers for the twentieth anniversary of the Revolution. Likewise the unaccompanied choral theme and variations *Gegen den Krieg* may have originated in the same year, when Brecht first conceived the anti-Nazi epigrams that made it up. Both these last works used dodecaphonic techniques, as also did the *Deutsche Sinfonie,* again to Brecht texts, which Eisler started working on that spring.

All of which now seems the height of slightly manic optimism. For within a few months Pravda had made its notorious attack on Shostakovitch's *Lady Macbeth of Mtsensk* ('A Mess instead of Music'), and the campaign for Stalin's quasi-Nazi standards of Socialist Realism had been launched. None of the new Brecht-Eisler works got performed in Russia: the *Lehrstück Die Horatier und die Kuriatier* because Eisler never wrote the music, the others seemingly because Moscow now fought shy of them, while the composer's Western supporters only wanted his easier works. So what of *Die Massnahme,* which surely comes under this head? Like *Saint Joan of the Stockyards* and *The Mother,* the other two Brecht plays introduced by Tretiakov, it was never performed in the USSR, and so far as we know this is still the case. There were a number of performances in German cities before Hitler came to power in January 1933, as well as one in Vienna by a 'proletarian theatre' directed by Hans Vogel, where the young Socialist Bruno Kreisky, later to be Austria's Chancellor, sang in the chorus. But with Hitler's assimilation of Austria and the German-speaking parts of Czechoslovakia all likely outlets became blocked before the Second World War. There was a small-scale performance under the title *The Expedient* at the Westminster Theatre in London in 1936 with Alan Bush conducting an amateur chorus from the London Labour Choral Union, while individual songs from this and *The Mother* were performed elsewhere via the WMA. There had also been rehearsals in late 1935 for a New York performance by a group led by Lee Strasberg, whom Brecht had met through Piscator in Moscow earlier that year. Following the failure of the New York production of *The Mother,* Brecht evidently took part in these, writing to Strasberg just before returning to Europe that he much regretted their interruption 'for political reasons'.

The Third Reich collapsed in May 1945 with the unconditional surrender of the German armies. At that time, Eisler, Brecht and also Kurt Weill were all living in the United States. *Die Massnahme,* so far as we know, had not been performed again, though neither of the collaborators had formally banned it. By then however the Eislers' sister Ruth Fischer, a former leader of the German Communist Party, convinced that her brothers were trying to have her assassinated by the Russian secret police, had told Hanns Eisler that she would defend herself 'thoroughly'. One consequence of her denunciation of them to the FBI was their summoning of Eisler, followed by Brecht, to testify before the House Committee on Un-American Activities, where a crude translation of the play under the title *The Rule (or Doctrine) /Drill* was cited as evidence of their ruthlessness. Repeated in Fischer's book *Stalin and German Communism* (in a chapter called 'Bert Brecht, Minstrel of the GPU') it led, via a much-quoted article of 1952 by Herbert Lüthy in the CIA-financed *Der Monat*, to their work's further interpretation as an attempt to justify Stalin's purging of the old Bolsheviks four years and more after its composition. From then on, throughout the period of the Cold War, it would be unauthorisedly staged as an example of Stalinist brutality, nearly always without Eisler's music.

Eventually Brecht decided, with Eisler's agreement, formally to stop this, writing to the Swedish director Paul Patera in the last months of his life to say that –

> *'Die Massnahme' was not written for an audience but exclusively for the instruction of the performers. In my experience, public performances of it inspire nothing but moral qualms, usually of the cheapest sort. Accordingly I have not let anyone perform the play for a long while.*

– after which Volume V of his collected *Stücke*, comprising the last of the *Lehrstücke*, was followed by a note to say that the term *Lehrstück* . . .

> *applies only to plays that teach something to the performers, and accordingly need no audience.*
> *The playwright has repeatedly turned down proposed performances of Die Massnahme, since only the actor playing the Young Comrade can learn from the play in question, and even he only if he has played one of the Agitators and sung in the Control Chorus.*

This not entirely convincing statement has been repeated to would-be producers for the past thirty-three years, and the effect has been odd. In many parts of the world, starting with Sweden and the production planned by Patera, directors have gone ahead without permission, or with permission solely from the translator, often interpreting the play in exactly the manner most feared by Brecht and ignoring the music (which was never contractually tied to the text as was the case with the same writer's works with Weill). The Brecht heirs – that is his three surviving children – have put up with this without actually stopping such productions though inflexibly turning down more straightforward requests from East and West Germany, the USSR, all the former Soviet bloc and the majority of other countries. Only in the English-speaking world has the ban been relaxed, and even then it has not been simple to get the Eisler Estate's advisors to allow the publishers to provide copies of the music; moreover there was for a time a strong resistance in North America to any performance of Eisler's work, which even today is disgracefully little known there. Nor has it been possible for the holders of the music rights to change the ban — not so much because Eisler, in giving his agreement, had no idea that it was to continue indefinitely, but because it is legally possible to detach his music and use other settings or none. In short, even the Berliner Ensemble itself has never been able to perform *Die Massnahme*, and when Manfred Wekwerth, its last artistic director under the old regime, along with Isot Kilian, a party member from an old Communist family, wished to stage the play at the State Theatre Directors' School, their request was turned down by the heirs. And yet it was Wekwerth who in August 1956 asked Brecht to name a play that in his view embodied the right form for the future. 'The answer', he writes, 'came like a pistol shot: *Die Massnahme*.' That was within days of Brecht's death.

The reasons given in the first place for prohibiting this major Eisler--Brecht work have always seemed to me hypocritical. Probably no human being has ever fulfilled the condition of playing the Young Comrade and another Agitator and singing in the chorus, and I for one have seen no record of any performance of a *Lehrstück* — rehearsals apart — that was meant not to have an audience; moreover the surviving photographs of *Die Massnahme* show an audience present. Eisler himself in 1934 (in a piece called "History of the German workers' movement from 1848') wrote of it as a 'political *Lehrstück*' from which 'not only the audience but also the performers' were to learn revolutionary conduct. The fact clearly is that Brecht didn't want to voice his genuine political reasons for not wanting it used for Cold War propaganda — which he was perfectly entitled to prevent if he could — and therefore devised this bit of bullshit for the deception not only of the growing body of *Lehrstück* theorists but also, as it turned out, his own legatees. It was a failure from the start, since anybody seriously wishing to misuse the work in that way went ahead and did so with impunity; indeed the American title *The Measures Taken* now commonly conveys the idea of a play about the Moscow trials, without music. Unfortunately the heirs, that is to say a crucial section of them, have been unwilling to recognize this, or to admit that the play has other more important aspects, or that the Cold War is not what it was thirty-five years ago, or even, as the author himself said in relation to *Der Jasager*, that one has to think afresh in every fresh situation. Over much of the globe they have virtually suppressed the work.

In London in 1987, following laborious discussions with the Brecht agents, Universal Edition, the Eisler heirs and others, there were two performances in the Almeida Festival. These were given in English (mine) under Robert Ziegler (conductor), Stephen Unwin (director) and the title *The Decision* and may well have constituted the first authentic production for fifty years or more. Admittedly they coincided with the British General Election by whose result Mrs. Thatcher was returned to power, but they did not seem to be received as political propaganda one way or another, rather as a profound experience, painful but deeply moving, an eye-opener to many and instructive to some, at least, as a reminder of the blazing commitment of the best German Communists just before Hitler took over. These performances were not a political undertaking so much as an attempt to reinstate a great work after half a hundred years of silence; performers and audience together were exploring a turning-point in 1930–33 where the history of our own time was decided and a music-theatrical peak attained that has not been touched since. Some of us certainly were left of centre — to the point even of having doubted if the work should be performed at all — but such orientation was not a criterion for taking part, and our splendid tenor Philip Doghan actually told me that if the Election was won by Labour he was going to leave England. As for the critics, most papers treated this as a musical work and saw Eisler's Schoenbergian past as more interesting than his supposed un-American activities. Rather a limited view.

It would be good to think that his production, together with the ensuing broadcast, cracked the top of some kind of egg. For a work of such original grandeur rises well above all normal considerations of political topicality to express a climate of feeling, an artistic attitude that gives unusual strength and coherence to music theatre or indeed any multi-media work. Whatever ones attitude to the immediate subject — in this case a surely wrongful killing in an extreme situation — one catches a rare sense of purpose and a massive simplicity that are not common in the arts of our own time. This means that we are now far enough removed from the events described to view them with detachment — with Brecht's *'Verfremdung'*, in fact — so that ideological niceties like the occasional Lenin quotation seem less relevant than in the old Cold War days. In that respect it is indeed a case of 'back to Bach' : you don't have to agree with the story or the argument to be bowled over by the quality of their expression; in much the same way the great Passions and cantatas are not exclusively for religious believers but can be a repeated revelation to us all. And this is also what Eisler and Brecht managed to achieve in a desperate time. The first lesson, then, of this 'teaching piece' is that there can be no inhibitions about re-examining and re-experiencing such works; they are both impressive and instructive, whether you agree with their intentions or not. And secondly, for those who have the privilege of deciding such matters, it is a crime to block access to a masterpiece, and never more so than when it is somebody else's and represents a summit in his work.

7

THE INVIGORATING EFFECT OF MUSIC? MAKING MUSIC ABOUT MUSIC IN BRECHT AND EISLER'S 'SONG OF THE INVIGORATING EFFECT OF MONEY.'

Gerd Rienäcker

Lied von der Belebenden Wirkung
des Geldes

1

Niedrig gilt das Geld auf dieser Erden
Und doch ist sie, wenn es mangelt, kalt
Und sie kann sehr gastlich werden
Plötzlich durch des Gelds Gewalt.
Eben war noch alles voll Beschwerden
Jetzt is alles golden überhaucht
Was gefroren hat, das sonnt sich
Jeder hat das, was er braucht!
Rosig färbt der Horizont sich
Blicket hinan: der Schornstein raucht!
Ja, da schaut sich alles gleich ganz anders an.
Voller schlägt das Herz. Der Blick wird weiter.
Reichlich ist das Mahl. Flott sind die Kleider.
Und der Mann ist jetzt ein andrer Mann.

2

Ach, sie gehen alle in die Irre
Die da glauben, daß am Geld nichts liegt.
Aus der Fruchtbarkeit wird Dürre
Wenn der gute Strom versiegt.
Jeder schreit nach was und nimmt es, wo er's kriegt.
Eben war noch alles nicht so schwer.
Wer nicht grade Hunger hat, verträgt sich.
Jetzt ist alles herz- und liebeleer.
Vater, Mutter, Brüder: alles schlägt sich!
Sehet: der Schornstein, er raucht nicht mehr!
Überall dicke Luft, die uns gar nicht gefällt.
Alles voller Haß und voller Neider.
Keiner will mehr Pferd sein, jeder Reiter
Und die Welt ist eine kalte Welt.

3

So ist's auch mit allem Guten und Großen.
Es verkümmert rasch in dieser Welt
Denn mit leerem Magen und mit bloßen
Füßen ist man nicht auf Größe eingestellt.
Man will nicht das Gute, sondern Geld.
Und man ist von Kleinmut angehaucht.
Aber wenn der Gute etwas Geld hat
Hat er, was er doch zum Gutsein braucht.
Wer sich schon auf Untat eingestellt hat
Blicke hinan: der Schornstein raucht!
Ja, da glaubt man wieder an das menschliche Geschlecht.
Edel sei der Mensch, gut und so weiter.
Die Gesinnung wächst. Sie war geschwächt.
Fester wird das Herz. Der Blick wird breiter.
Man erkennt, was Pferd ist und was Reiter.
Und so wird das Recht erst wieder Recht.

Money is generally considered to be a rather vulgar thing, yet when it is lacking, this earth is a cold place. But then, it can suddenly become very hospitable through the power of money. Certainly, without it, all was hardship. Now all is golden. What was frozen is now sunlit — everyone has what he needs! The outlook is rosy. Look up; the chimney is smoking! Yes, all at once everything looks quite different. Hearts are full, the horizon is wide, meals are ample, clothes are smart. And the man is now another man.

All who think money has no importance are wrong. When it ceases to flow freely fruitfulness becomes sterility. Everyone sets to and gets what he can. Things still aren't all that difficult — whoever isn't downright hungry can put up with things. But life is now heartless and loveless. Father, mother, brother — all are fighting each other! See! The chimney is no longer smoking. The air is thick and unpleasant, hatred and envy everwhere. Noone wants to be the horse any more, everyone the rider — and the world is a cold world.

So it is with everything good and great. Things die off quickly in this world, for with empty bellies and bare feet, people aren't in the right frame of mind for greatness. They want money, not goodness. They feel dejected. But when the good man has some money, then he has what he needs for security. You, who've already geared yourselves for crime, look up. The chimney is smoking! Yes, there they believe once more in the human race. People are noble, good and so on. The conviction grows. It had weakened. Hearts grow stronger, horizons broaden. Men recognise who is the horse and who is the rider. And so right is once again right.

Money warms a cold world, makes people 'noble, good and so on', it straightens out their relationships — so says a judge, and he does so with good reason: he has just experienced that very same invigorating effect of money, so long as he dances to the tune of the new masters, who give or promise him bread, dignity and a secure life. What else these new masters bestow upon mankind, how they came by their power and what comes of it, we are told in Brecht's parable *Die Rundköpfe und die Spitzköpfe*, 'The Round-heads and the Pointed-heads,' a play which seeks to reduce the processes of German National Socialism, right at the outset of that barbarism, to concepts, that is to say, by means of stories. Hanns Eisler composes the music and he does this with complete understanding i.e., he records 'the events behind the events'[1], as a commentator, not an illustrator of what is presented. The 'Song of the invigorating effect of money' is a commentary on everything. What follows is about that, or more precisely, about one peculiar feature: the making of music about music as the music-making about social concerns which have *become* music.[2]

I

There is a striking divergence between the musical worlds which the song draws on and which are pointedly kept apart in the various sections: a *quasi-toccata* and prelude as instrumental introduction, displaced and made alien by jazz instrumentation, a slow waltz tending towards *valse triste* in the first and third main verses, and a toccata-quick march as a refrain.

What is incorporated here has long been commonplace — music which is in both fundamentals and details, second-hand, laden with significance that has meanwhile become worn-out; worn-out like the musical vocabulary itself, fit only for sale in a junk shop for a few coppers. And so the inventory of events is to be commented on second-hand too, as events that are equally second-hand, whose base qualities can be seen at second if not first glance. Meanwhile communal life is (or seems to be?) ruled by these base qualities; indeed it is reduced to the cheapest exchange value, to the copper coins, now cheap, which formerly might have been high and holy, exchangeable at your pleasure; what to each person was unmistakeable is, or seems to be, irreplaceable. C major, once a symbol of serene, sunny, simple relationships and situations, radiant C major, both before and after Berg's opera *Wozzeck*, has been transformed into a faded stuck-on transfer of former times. And what shines now is only the copper coin; that's what glints in

[1] One of Brecht's basic concepts.

[2] A reference to Adorno's clear-sighted words on the socialising of the musical material (cf. T. W. Adorno *Philosophie der Musik*).

Wozzeck's hand when he holds out his meagre earnings.[3] *Ländler* and waltz, even the *valse triste*, once at home in the rich interiors of the nobility and bourgeoisie or on village dance-floors, have been cheapened to the *'Immerzu, immerzu'*[4] of the wretched in order to drown out the unbearable.

In Mahler and Berg, these forms bear the scars of misery, of the wretched for whom, to echo Brecht, it is not possible to reflect on where they come from or where they are going — unless such reflections lead to madness, to the murder of the wrong person! In the tavern, Wozzeck's misery will only increase, Marie's no less, for the Drum Major, a 'fourth-hand' Don Giovanni seduces her — *'Immerzu, immerzu.' Ländler*, waltzes and chorales, together with all those musical forms which take shape around them, all lead to such misery.[5]

According to Brecht, the orange of the operetta should be for sale[6], and he praises the honesty, at least, of such saleability, in order to pull down the pseudo-philosophical ornaments which the lofty genre of opera offers as a defence against this very saleability. In this defence the vocabulary which, half a century before, kept the musical world in breathless suspense, has become cheap — the so-called Tristan chord perhaps, chromatic progressions in general, mediant shifts through the circle of fifths for the purpose of 'hotting things up' (in Eugen d'Albert's *Tiefland*, amongst others). And what excited bourgeois salons in the first three decades of the nineteenth century were configurations of heightened expressivity — Chopin's *Preludes* or Field's character pieces — any café pianist now can repeat them *ad infinitum*; sighing suspensions in long notes mixed with repeated chords in quavers gradually falling chromatically, the wrenching effect of broken diminished fifths and minor seconds that for Chopin, and Mozart, denoted piercing pain[7], archaic plagal cadences (brought back in the late or even middle nineteenth century, not least by Brahms); all have been discarded, have gone to the dogs or to the junk shop. But even there they retain their power, as captivating as conjuring tricks. To include these in a new

---

[3] *Wozzeck* — Alban Berg. Act 2 Scene 1.

[4] *Wozzeck* — Act 2 Scene 4. Marie unwittingly dances past Wozzeck singing *'Immerzu, immerzu'* (On, on).

[5] Cf. Gerd Rienäcker, *Brings nit zsam* — Notes on the tavern scene in Berg's *Wozzeck*, in *Georg-Büchner-Studien*, Berlin 1988 p. 227 ff.

[6] During his years in Augsburg.

[7] But this is the vocabulary quoted — and slyly reflected — by Eisler.

compositon could mean to capitulate. On the other hand to reject them means the denial of points of reference. But accepting them, not in a mindless, but in a considered way guarantees sensible music-making and sensible discourse which allow insights into the whole, and not just the aesthetic whole: provided that what is included, what is reflected upon succeeds in regaining that strangeness which, when heard, invites the listener to wonder what it stands for or might stand for. Whatever is usual, all-too-usual, must be converted into the unusual i.e., made alien[8], by introducing gaps and breaks, by reorderings, by thwarting the expected just at the moment of fulfilment, by procedures which are foreign, or seem to be, to the material, so that the vocabulary is wrenched out of what is usual — while, at the same time, not being wholly foreign or external to the material, because relationships can only be made to dance to tunes played in their own proper way.[9]

It is inconsistencies, peculiarities and distortions as such, not gaps and breaks in themselves which surprise the listener or make him think, but then only those which get close analytically to the essential quality of what is being used. They therefore have something in common, not in *un*common, with it, which above all makes it possible to get below the surface. This is actually what analysis is and therefore what analytical composing is too, and it only comes about on the basis of a highly developed capacity for musical or musically related discourse. Such a discourse is then on several levels. Eisler, in composing stage music, has to have at his command the subtleties of a compositional idiom dating from the early eighteenth century onwards as well as the no less highly developed light music of around the twenties, which had long since incorporated jazz from over the Atlantic. What he fits together has been diverging for a long time — and yet bridges between one element and another exist. How else could they be combined?! But the breaches between co-existing elements can be composed with by a man who knows how to handle the immense contradictions surrounding music, by a dialectician who has not yet sacrificed his profession to the empty phrase. He will have to formulate how others debase dialectics. From this comes Eisler's life-long condemnation of stupidity in (and outside of) music.[10]

---

[8] Here is not the place to go into the principles of Brecht's theory of *Verfremdung*, still less its numerous sources!

[9] Thus Karl Marx in the *Grundrissen der politischen Ökonomie*.

[10] The abysmal tragedy of this statement is only obvious today — obvious also is the devaluation of Eisler!

II

There is a striking divergence between the types of music which are linked together in the opening bars of the quasi-prelude. Half-direct quotations are but the tips of icebergs. The first bars of Chopin's E minor Prelude gleam through – repeated quaver chords, a chromatically descending bass, sustained sighing figures, many times repeated and inflected by the chromaticism, and with a sinking down which sudden quasi-cadence leaps try to counter, adjustments between the top part and the layer of chords such that the obligations of each level are lost in the process.

Lied von der belebenden Wirkung des Geldes

(Bertolt Brecht)

Ex. 7.1

15
Und sie kann sehr gastlich wer - den plötzlich durch des Geld's Ge_walt.
20
E_ben war noch al_les voll Beschwer_den, jetzt ist al_les gol_den ü_ber_haucht.
25
Was ge_fro_ren hat, das sonnt sich. Je_der hat das, was er braucht!
poco rit.
Molto pesante
30
Ro_sig färbt der Ho_ri_zont sich. Blik_ket hin_an: der Schornstein raucht!
pp
(pp)

Ex. 7.1 (cont'd)

Ex. 7.1 (cont'd)

There is no 'melody-line' as such and the chords gradually offer up their carefully concealed polyphony! Yet both levels obey the downwards pull, reminders what's more of quasi-archaic chaconne basses etc. Of course, all this is combined slowly, with expressive touch, with a slight right hand rubato, while the left hand imperturbably plays its repeated quavers, giving, in the process, expression to the emerging polyphony.[11]

But Eisler's quasi-prelude is not slow, not to be played *con sentimento*. Instead it is *allegretto*, the repeated chords are staccato and

[11] Rienäcker, obviously, refers here to the piano reduction. The original scoring is for flute, two clarinets, two saxophones, two trumpets, trombone, percussion, banjo, piano and bass. [Ed.]

the obligatory sighing suspensions, chromatic descents and repeated chords don't fit in with the intended effect. The song opens without preparation with a semiquaver figure which, by its sudden upward leap, overaccentuates the following minim, the sighing sustained note growing as it sustains. Two descending steps of a minor second are countered by a new upwards leap and so each phrase unites downward and upward movement, the small step and the unprepared large leap. Gradually other equally familiar gestures establish themselves — a falling diminished fifth and minor second, a rising diminished fifth and so on. Such configurations are legion in music history, familiar not only from the time of Mozart's late concert arias. If Eisler adopts them and follows their logic i.e., their tendency to fall, he upsets the equilibrium of the constituent elements. The bass by no means tries to provide a counter-movement to the top line, as would be the case with Mozart, but the overall downwards movement is made absolute and so whatever hopefully offers itself for sequential treatment is cast off. The damaged equilibrium braces itself, also shifting harmonically and this is the more important since the adopted vocabulary promises otherwise, the preservation of balance in fact. We hear the progression from tonic minor to dominant, to the neapolitan, to secondary dominants, almost into the plagal with secondary subdominants etc. certainly with confusion over the destination! For it is not F minor which is finally arrived at — B flat minor blocks the way. Mind you, Eisler uses keys and trusted routes between them in order to put pitfalls in the way. And whatever he chooses to use still has the dull gleam of the worn-out. The turning of what was formerly affecting into something utterly cheap is communicated with a gesture rather like a slightly contemptuous movement of the hand, with no further elaboration. The unceasing staccato quavers become a bad dream, they beat on your skull and are transformed into a quick-stepping march, like people in a twenties silent film. Bustle is their watchword and bustle is what this is all about: 'The chimney is smoking!' Feeling borrowed from Chopin or Mozart is turned into toccata and quick march, it gets overwound and at the same time is tamed and disciplined — both the feeling and the overwinding! Yet in all this oppressive rules of unity are preserved, not least the stolid two-, four-and eight-bar phrases which falter only toward the end, rituals of tonality prey to many misfortunes. And the slight gesture of the hand, the initial idea, is unwilling to stop without passing on some of its characteristics — certainly the bustle, the running which involuntarily copes with interruptions, the almost machine-like music, as if quoted from a Rossini Finale and, even if only for a moment, the *musica mechanica* of the pseudo-baroque, so massively reproduced in the twenties — all levelled out into a cheap pattern.

Eisler's idiomatic borrowings and procedures contribute to this, only it is all made thematic i.e., 'reflected'; it is reduced to the characteristics of an aggressive, hammering music-making, to the elegance of a slap delivered with a flick of the hand. Such are Eisler's songs and music for the stage since the late twenties. It is, however, thanks to the unity of the stylistically diverging elements that this pattern constitutes only *one* level of music-making — there is more to it than stupidity.

Everywhere it is a question of the spring in the rhythm — as if every beat sprang upwards, recoiling almost by itself; *'das Einfache, das schwer zu machen ist.'*[12]

III

No less cryptic is the *valse triste* of the main verse. The swaying pendulum of the bass, the correctness of the harmony whose fullness leaves nothing to be desired, the antiphony between the voice and the top line of the accompaniment which becomes almost imitative, filling out the gaps in the vocal line, the languishing suspensions immediately resolved, rotating figures everywhere and suspensions at the end of each two-bar phrase; these and other elements are promises and recognizable as such. Yet they all appear strange. The pendulum of the bass tries its hand at fifths and fourths, but these are so shaped that the hoped-for key does not materialize: B flat-E flat-A flat-D flat. But the progression B flat to D flat is in no way unfamiliar. It's just that the tonalities we've set our sights on are obliterated by the prevalence of the minor mode, while the assertive plagal phrases are forced to yield. Both tendencies become insistent together with intensified longing; both prove to be out of joint. There is not one cadence which doesn't elicit strange mixtures of sound, no key progression without residue, no chord which isn't too much of a good thing. But also there is a clash between the technical rules — the obligatory ones of counterpoint, overemphasized in the fragmented *cantus firmus* of the instrumental top line, the thematic connections in the bass lines, or more exactly the reference to connections as well as to the quasi-*basso continuo* (as though neo-baroque strictness, not to say stiffness, had to offset the sentiment referred to!). Yet it is precisely the insignia of these sentiments which play into the hands of the stiffness — they are masks and mask-like they convey the quality of dissolution as

---

[12] The quotation is from the *Lob des Kommunismus* of Brecht's *Lehrstück Die Mutter* with music by Eisler. 'It is the simple thing, that's so hard to do. [Ed.]

well as their iron-hard cohesion. Various masks overlap — are they interchangeable?

It is obvious from the very first bars of the vocal declamation that whatever begins to flow moves as in a bed of concrete. The emotion created by the turn to the minor and the subsequent sighing suspensions which accompany *'auf dieser Erden'*, 'on earth', a universally popular phrase with obvious biblical overtones, is countered by the music, by declamation in quavers indifferent to any nuances, unless the singer introduces them. Changes of accent, correctly responding to the stress of the words, at once get into thickets of at first hardly noticeable and then more insistent distortions. However, these distortions are applied even to traditional hierarchies of ordinary verbal sentences i.e., it is no longer, as would expect *gástlich werden* but *gastlich werdén*: everything, was not still *voll Beschwerden* but *voll Beschwerden* (*full* of hardship).

In the same way, Brecht's verbal promises boast of golden times and rosy outlooks, where, however, the prosaic chimney is smoking — calling forth a whispered, prayerful *pianissimo* and an accompaniment of full chords.

Transient, at times cheap, everything in this pseudo-romantic inventory is like dross. The *valse triste* is marked Andante, not Adagio, and is strangely domesticated; the refrain wishes to know nothing about it, verbally or musically. Instead the toccata and march confine the promised broad vision into a tiny format, in the bonds of a hasty delivery in quavers which stops quite abruptly. At once it is clear what is inherent in this briskness — 'martiality', presented in the ornamental way girls are seen in a chorus line.

Consequently the march-toccata, the quick march, bears a variety of 'messages.' One verse later, the required or promised vision is followed by 'the air is thick', the combining of hatred and envy, the damaging of an established social hierarchy, the fear of the others which turns into marching. The one can be exchanged for the other: abundance and want, prosperity and its opposite, the broad vision and the narrow, nobility of soul *und so weiter* and malice, abundance and emptiness. Not interchangeable though are the mechanisms, the machineries which drive all this and makes them interchangeable; but not interchangeable are the gestures of hectic activity which only *seem* to turn into something pleasant, the cry of 'Work, work!' with which capitalism to this day causes man to bleed to death in an unremitting race round the clock.

To make this the central issue however makes other layers more obvious — melodic turn shapes, which would or could be cantilena, only they have lost their *legato* and quiet, sigh figures, the screwing together of diminished fifth and rising minor second (here amputated, admittedly!), dammed-up chromaticism, a powerful background polyphony which gradually expands and as a result of which other instrumental voices come to the fore. More and more shared qualities emerge between the *valse triste* and the march-toccata — in motivic substance, types of variation (transformed by Eisler's adoption of twelve-note technique) and the jazz influence on the instrumental performance style.

It is however thanks to the overall cohesion that the adopted material is reflected, indeed compositionally analysed, according to measures of what is proper or strange, looking at what is used and who is the user, that bridges exist between different things and the utmost transparency governs both structure and methods. 'One should compose honestly', Eisler used to say in his last years, often enough to the anger and astonishment of verbose colleagues. Occasionally he'd found fault with the compositions of others. Was it to silence with technique those fellows whose aesthetic and, even more, political bigotry and unscrupulousness he knew all about?

To compose honestly entailed stretching the concept way beyond the purely musical. It also entailed thinking about necessary changes to normal practice as well as about preserving compositional potency within what was altered functionally; and also therefore the consideration of the relationships between structure and function precisely at those moments when they rapidly drift apart. There are bound to be disjunctions in such considerations, even more so in the multiplicity of results. He who takes up the fight against stupidity can at a certain point succumb to it — in the cantata *Du grosses Wir*[13] perhaps — but even that momentary succumbing provokes so urgent thinking about music (and not only music!), about art (and not only art). So one talks about the invigorating effect of music not only to correlate Eisler's profound exorcisms of the dead with everything which is invigorating and at the same time deadening dross, but to make it quite clear that 'reflected' music-making really does contribute to the reviving of deadened relationships — in other words, it could be made to dance, still, or now more than ever!

[13] Part three of the cantata *Mitte des Jahrhunderts* for soprano, chorus and orchestra. Text by Johannes R. Becher. 1950. [Ed.]

8

EISLER'S SERIALISM: CONCEPTS AND METHODS

Tim Howell

I

Hindsight and history, the perspective of time, condition our response to music of a previous generation. Although, in varying degrees, this has always been the case, it is especially pertinent in relation to music of our own century where the rate of change in terms of compositional technique has been so quickly and directly mirrored by that of musical criticism. It is particularly difficult to stand aside from developments in music theory when considering the work of a serial composer but important to do so if the perspective of today is not to distort the achievements of the past. By now, some may view the development of twentieth-century music as partially characterized by the failure of serialism to gain little more than a passing credence in the overall scheme of things; the possibility that the note-row would offer atonal music the equivalent organizational potential of the diatonic scale in a tonal context, proved not untrue but remarkably short-lived in relation to the tonal system. Additionally, early serial compositions can today appear somewhat lacking in sophistication given the perspective of total serialism which, in turn, may have inspired current preoccupations with mathematical systems and processes (magic squares, pitch matrices and the like), even though all of this is increasingly viewed as merely one type of approach amongst many.

Early developments in serial technique are conveniently exemplified by the trinity of the Second Viennese School whose variety of technique and range of style serve as a catalogue of achievement which critical orthodoxy views as mainstream in an age of neat, historical packaging. The works of Schoenberg, Berg and Webern have been dissected and analyzed just about as much as those of their Classical counterparts with the parallel effect of codifying compositional technique into generalized theory. Thus, nineteenth-century theorists arrived at their ubiquitous delineation of classical-period sonata form, which has preconditioned the response of many generations of music students, by elevating the lowest common denominators of a richly varied idiom to a level which became dangerously misleading. It is ironic that the music which readily fits this formal mould tends to be that of the 'lesser' composers of the period (Hummel and Spohr, for instance) who, in turn, are largely ignored because they do not conform to the mainstream. These formal theories offer little that is useful in our understanding of the masterpieces of the time which, after all, are partially defined as such because of the individuality we find in the works of Haydn, Mozart and Beethoven. Attitudes towards the Second Viennese School are directly analogous. This music provided the perfect diet for the insatiable appetite of a new discipline of analysis since the composer's need for method and the analyst's desire for accountability went directly hand in hand. Once, however, the overwhelming appeal of 'note-counting' as somehow constituting 'analysis' had been overcome, the music theory of the 1960s quickly revealed underlying rules, common practices and arithmetical niceties which were neatly codified into dictionary definitions. Equally neatly, other pupils of Schoenberg, the so-called 'lesser' composers of the day (such as Dallapiccola, Sessions, Gerhard), were ignored in the all-the-more extreme reductionism of the twentieth century and composers offering differing, if not distinct, dodecaphonic techniques are seen as standing outside 'common practice' serial method.

Hanns Eisler occupies exactly this position, for many complex reasons an outsider, yet his importance in the still-to-be-written history of serialism should not be overlooked. He is a particularly intriguing figure in this context, both embracing and rejecting Schoenberg's aesthetic of a new music in an abrupt change of emphasis towards a directly popular idiom which is almost as remarkable as Stravinsky's late adoption of serial method and certainly no less idiosyncratic. Such a coexistence of extremes of attitude, both intellectual and popularist, assigns to Eisler a unique place in the annals of musical history and whilst the political reasons which underline this stance remain beyond the scope of the present discussion, a composer so concerned about his function in society yet later returning to an apparent serial élitism merits special attention. With music that is so crucially reflective of its time, it is important that any examination of Eisler's serial technique is sensitive to that context. For the purpose of considering his serial method in detail it was necessary to select one work in order to give a focus for such a study. The piece needed to be a mature composition, to take account of the earlier shift in emphasis away from serial technique and also sufficiently small-scale to be practicable for detailed investigation.

Therefore, given Eisler's awareness of the social context for which he was writing, it was not surprising to discover that an appropriate example existed within the genre of chamber music. The String Quartet of 1938 fulfilled all these requirements. It is in two movements, *Variationen* and *Finale,* and is based throughout on one twelve-note series.

II

Since analysis seeks to rationalize the compositional means which engender particular effects, a thorough investigation of inherent characteristics within the pre-compositional series is an important starting-point. In the present context, this may be broadened by considering the nature and construction of the row in comparison with examples taken from an earlier piece to ascertain characteristic features and compositional potential from these abstract structures. Towards this end, Example 8.1 juxtaposes the row from the Quartet with two others taken from the *Klavierstücke,* Opus 8, of 1925.

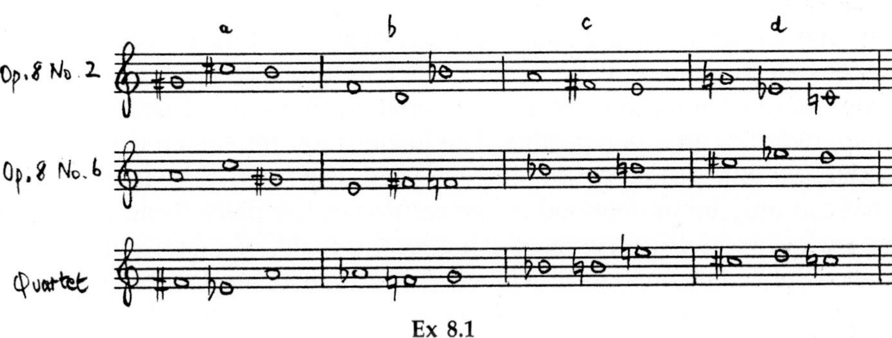

Ex 8.1

Both of the Opus 8 series are characterized by a strong degree of internal symmetry with close correspondences between alternate pairs of trichords. Analytically, the most direct way of illustrating this symmetry would be to reduce this succession of four trichords to prime-form pitch-class sets applying the set-theoretic criteria of Allen Forte. Whilst this shows clearly the symmetrical relationships, revealing the pattern:

[0,2,5] [0,3,7] [0,2,5] [0.3.7] for Op.8 No.2 and
[0,1,4] [0,1,2] [0,1,4] [0,1,2] for Op.8 No.6,

such a reductive approach, with its reliance on inversional equivalence, removes any individual aspects of interval succession which are so important to the character of the series. In the case of Op.8 No.2, it is perhaps better to explain that trichord (c) is a permutation of (a) in terms of interval content with both containing a minor third and a whole tone within a perfect-fourth span (hence, [0,2,5]). Further symmetry arises from their common whole-tone descents of C#-B and F#-E. More closely symmetrical is the relationship between trichords (b) and (d) which are both triads, a whole tone apart, but representing the equivalent degree of permutation in the reversal of major-/minor-third intervals: (b) is a major triad, (d) a minor one. (Although this may seem a rather ponderous way of illustrating internal symmetries, particularly given the presence of triads, it demonstrates the working of Set Theory and provides a model for later, more complex, row forms.)

Both the internal symmetry and the tonal implications of this construct are highly characteristic of Eisler's early serial style and these simple, small-scale pieces exploit these features in an extremely economical manner. Also typical is the way in which the series is not treated strictly, in the Schoenbergian sense, since the literal order of events, particularly within a segment, is also subject to variation technique. This interest in preserving content rather than order, the use, for example of one hexachord from a given row-form independently from its twelve-note context, already distinguishes Eisler's attitude to serial composition from that of his teacher, whilst the tonal implications of this source-set help underline that perspective. The justification for such a departure in serial ordering (assuming one were needed) is governed by musical logic that can only be understood in the context of the piece itself, as part of its surface motivic processes. Such a local scheme of organization exists outside of serial concerns at a level which the listener directly perceives, suggesting that for Eisler the series was a pre-compositional construct: it is the inherent characteristics, rather than the row in itself, which are to be made audible to the listener. Whilst this approach may present extra difficulties and even frustrations for the analyst, it must be emphasized that being able to account for every note in a serial piece is an obsession of the present and not a preoccupation of the past.

Comparably symmetrical, but without obvious tonal implications, is the series of Op.8 No.6 shown in Example 8.1. Once again, trichordal partitioning is useful, revealing that (a) and (c), with their particularly characteristic emphasis on major-/minor-third cells, are inversionally related. Trichords (b) and (d), chromatically infilling a whole-tone interval, are related in terms of transposition, significantly involving the distance of a minor third. The nature of the correspondences between alternate trichord groups (due to inversion and transposition) is directly related to those governing the row of Op.8 No.2 and, moreover, it is a prominent interval *within* trichords (a) and (c), which conditions the interval of transposition *between* trichords (b) and (d) in both cases: the whole tone in Op.8 No.2 and the minor third in Op.8 No.6. The conclusion emerging from these early examples concerns not only the carefully calculated construction of these series but demonstrates that the process involved in forming a source-set for subsequent variation is, itself, the product of variation. From the outset, the series is constructed from motivic principles and its inherently organic nature will be reflected in, or indeed will condition, the progress of the piece itself.

The effect of all this allows us to consider the nature of Eisler's preoccupations at this early stage of his career. Whilst any student, even today, attempting serial composition will be drawn to the advantages of using a row that contains internal symmetries, their significance for Eisler should not be underestimated. Although such correspondences permit easily gathered analytical niceties, more importantly they generate compositional relationships, in that some kind of unity, beneath the surface motivic processes, is bound to emerge due to the purposefully limited number of discrete intervallic shapes to be manipulated. Thus the divergence from strict serial ordering can be seen to arise from necessity — if sufficient variety is to be created — or, alternatively, it allows a composer whose technique involves motivic workings of local, imitative logic, full reign in exercising contrapuntal freedom, without destroying something of the uniformity of sonority which the background of the series will always provide. That uniformity may, of course, become something of a limitation regarding the establishment of patterns of tension and release and this, in turn, could necessitate deviation from the strict, twelve-note ordering of events. Additionally, an interest in aspects of harmonic thinking not completely divorced from the diatonic system (possibly to generate those effects outlined above) can quite naturally emerge, since absolute equality between members of the chromatic scale will cease to exist. The temptation to be critical of these preoccupations should be resisted, since a lack of serial strictness in the ordering of events is not necessarily a negative feature. So long as the ordered arrangement of the prime form somehow governs musical events in a consistent and logical manner, then ambiguities and licences can be taken without any detrimental effect. To this end, Eisler can be seen to embrace the principle of Schoenberg's method, though as something to be considerably modified in practice.

III

Returning to Example 8.1, the row of the String Quartet, written some thirteen years (and much tonal music) later, differs considerably from the examples taken from Opus 8. Trichordal partitioning and comparison suggest little in the way of symmetry which, perhaps, makes set theory more relevant, revealing the prime forms of:

[0,3,6]	*[0,1,3]*	*[0,1,6]*	*[0,1,2]*
(a)	*(b)*	*(c)*	*(d)*

Despite such drastic reduction and inversional equivalence (or maybe because of it), only basic correspondences emerge: (a) and (c) both contain a tritone, (b) and (d) a semitone and major second; (a) and (b) have minor thirds, (c) and (d), semitones. Although surprisingly little of interest can be deduced so far, it is important to emphasize the differences with the Opus 8 models both in the lack of symmetry (in terms of recurrent interval patterns) and tonal implications, (whilst noting that these two features are conceptually related). Despite the consistency in analytical approach, it is important to resist drawing significant conclusions — for instance that the mature serial writing of Eisler appears to reject significant features of his early works — on such little information. Certainly the logic behind the construction of this series is more complex than that of Opus 8 which, in turn, demands wider terms of reference in analytical approach. Suppose we partition the series in a different manner and consider each hexachord; with each six-note group confined within the compass of tritone, perhaps something of the sought-after symmetry may emerge? Reduction to prime form gives the sequence [0,1,2,3,4,6] in both cases, which, given the governing role of the tritone, is not so very remarkable. Example 8.2, however, lists the content of each hexachord in ascending chromatic order and the placing of whole-tone intervals reveals some sense of large-scale symmetry in terms of content:

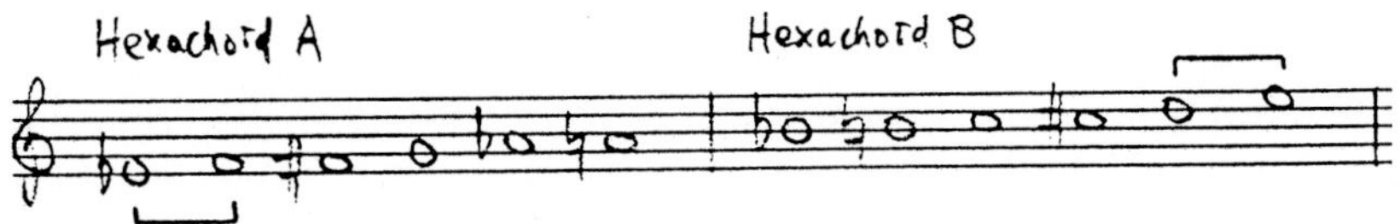

Ex. 8.2

Whilst such analytical symmetry is reassuring, its compositional significance is limited, since this observation relies entirely on chromatic content and not on serial ordering. Nevertheless, the decision by Eisler to arrange the series so that each hexachord is confined within its smallest registral compass (the tritone) may be of interest not least because it suggests that the composer, quite literally, views serialism as a rationalization of the total chromatic: the compass of each half of the chromatic scale defines the register of each half of the series. Additionally, with correspondences involving symmetry occuring at the hexachordal level, then combinatoriality must ensue. Indeed, this is the case and Example 8.3 shows P^0 and I^7 to be hexachordally combinatorial in the 'traditional' Schoenbergian manner, whilst the interval of a perfect fifth which forms this transpositional relationship not only results in the same pattern inversionally (that is, between I^0 and P^5) but intimates latent tonal properties to which the associations of the perfect fifth give rise. Ex. 8.3

Ex. 8.3

In fact, latent is the operative word here since Eisler chooses *not* to use any transpositions whatsoever within the entire work so that this particular compositional property is never explored — but more of that in due course. Meanwhile, if we consider the inversional relationship that Eisler does explore, between P^0 and I^0 (i.e, without recourse to transposition), then relevant latent symmetry does emerge. Ex. 8.4

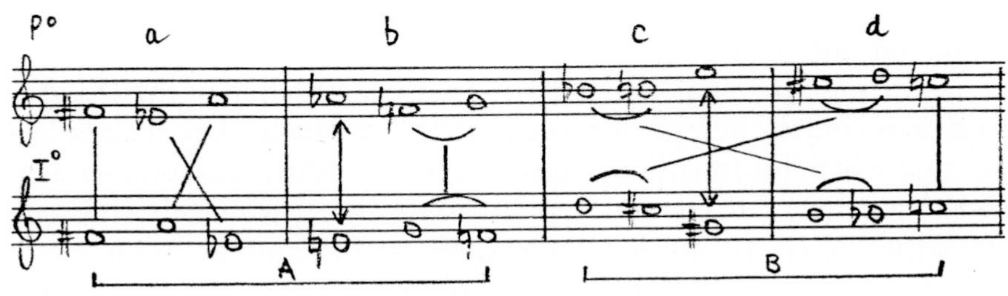

Ex. 8.4

Example 8.4, which compares these two set-forms, reveals the highest possible level of invariance (other than complete combinatoriality) with five, out of the six, members recurring significantly between *adjacent* hexachords. Thus, hexachords A from each of P^0 and I^0 swop Ab/E (reversed, of course, in hexachords B) and this highlighting of a major-third interval may well be important given its complete absence within the interval succession of the prime-form series. Trichordal partitioning reveals a sequence of correspondences concerning pitch-class content of initially three-, then two-note, groups. These invariant elements may be summarised, in relation to Example 8.4, as follows:

P^0 (a) and I^0 (a): same content, different order, due to symmetry of intervals;
P^0 (b) and I^0 (b): same whole-tone element (F–G), reverse order;
P^0 (c) and I^0 (d): same semitone element (B–Bb), reverse order;
P^0 (d) and I^0 (c): same semitone element (C#–D), reverse order;

The large-scale symmetry of the series as a whole, its overall span of a tritone (F#-C) reflecting internal registral concerns, ensures that the last notes of P^0 and I^0 are the same. This, given the lack of transpositional variants in favour of cyclic permutation, allows certain ambiguities to be explored, notably with regard to retrograde forms; the last note of P^0 = the first of RI^0. Perhaps, rather like the issue of hexachordal combinatoriality, this is the time to mention one idiosyncracy concerning discrepancies between serial order and compositional practice. Although the ordering shown in Example 8.4, with I^0 ending on C is correct, Eisler chooses to reverse the position of its last two notes — consistently throughout the piece — so that I^0 ends C-Bb (*not* Bb-C). Whilst speculation as to the reasons behind this may encompass illusiveness, ineptitude or even inaccuracy on the composer's part, the effect is to ensure that RI^0 does, in fact, begin in a distinct manner; after all, there are only four discrete serial forms employed throughout the work and R^0 will begin with C in any case. Nevertheless, the close invariant parallels between the opening three-note figures of P^0 and I^0 are clearly preserved and, as a result, something of the ensuing ambiguity of set-form identity is explored during the piece.

By now, we come to realize that the construction of the Quartet's series does contain internal symmetry, but at a much more distant level than that which informed the earlier examples. Although commendably subtle, this may be compositionally irrelevant, given the way such symmetries have manifested themselves so far, though some of the properties listed above will certainly contribute to a general sense of background unity. In terms of the surface of the piece, however, it is the presence of symmetrical relationships within the actual ordering of the series which would be most significant regarding any literal compositional potential of the row. Trichordal correspondences between P^0 and I^0 forms lead us, full circle, to reconsider partitioning the series into three-note groups, but in a slightly different manner. Ex. 8.5

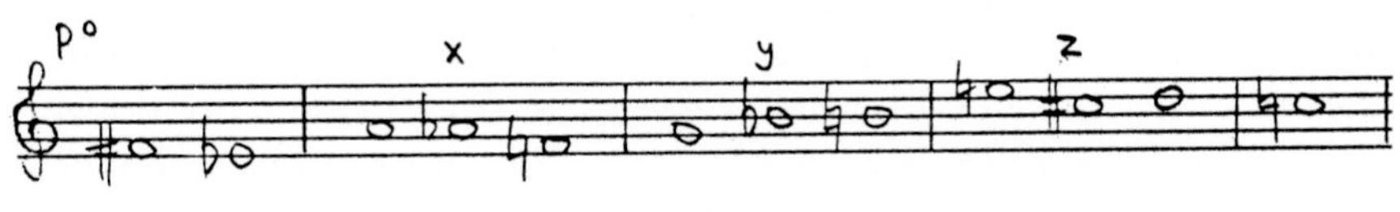

Ex. 8.5

Example 8.5 suggests that, embedded within this prime form, are three recurrent, motivic shapes presented in a way which, though more subtle than that of Opus 8, offers an equivalent degree of invariance. Segmenting the series from its third element, significantly after the initial, generative, minor-third interval, reveals three cells; each of these contains the highly characteristic minor-third plus semitone shape. Whilst (x) and (y) are inversionally related (directly analogous to (a) and (c) from Op.8 No.6 in Example 8.1), (z) is a permutation comprising the descending minor third from (x) and the ascending semitone from (y); as a result the interval content is compressed within an overall span of a minor third and (z) is a kind of epigram in this respect. As a result of partitioning in this way, the last note of the series, C, is isolated, though Eisler's preoccupation with permutational serialism suggests that it is not too contrived to link it with the (similarly isolated) first two notes of the row. This final — or perhaps initial (?) — trichord (C-F#-Eb) comprising a tritone/minor-third complex encapsulates the most significant invariant properties within the row-forms of this piece. A symmetrical division of the octave, or total chromatic, available here from order numbers 12, 1, 2, 3 (C, F#, Eb, A) is the ultimate clue to the background symmetry behind the construction of this series. Whilst such preoccupations remain essentially consistent over the long gap between Opus 8 and the Quartet, the subtlety with which these elements are incorporated here intimates something of a new-found maturity in Eisler's serial precomposition.

Equally consistent is Eisler's limitation of the number of row-forms employed in the piece, though it may appear surprising, given an obvious maturity of approach, to find that this attitude remains. Our associations with such an apparently restrictive practice are confined to 'early' serial works of Schoenberg where our knowledge of his later method allows us to view this approach as merely the simple origins of an increasingly sophisticated methodology. In the Quartet, the self-imposed restriction to four row-forms, that is, the exclusion of any transpositions of the set, can be viewed as highly characteristic of Eisler's serialism and the possible rationale behind this, together with some assessment of its effect, deserves comment. Whilst the rejection of transpositional combinatorial relationships could incur censure from the purist, or at least be cited by the analyst as a compositional opportunity missed, it is worth reflecting upon its potential effect in relation to actual reality. Combinatoriality offers an integral, systematic means of achieving both consistency and variation between pairs of sets since content is preserved yet order is changed within a given hexachord. But variation in order yet invariance in content can be created by other means and the properties of recurrent, three-note cells particular to the Quartet series can generate an analogous effect. The crucial difference, and one that offers a significant clue to Eisler's individual interests in the system, is that his cellular invariance relies on intervallic correspondences rather than pitch-class relationships. Indeed the most plausible and musically relevant reason for the re-ordering of I^0 and RI^0 forms, is the literal preservation of those shapes (in distinction to P^0 and R^0) which it engenders. Ex. 8.6

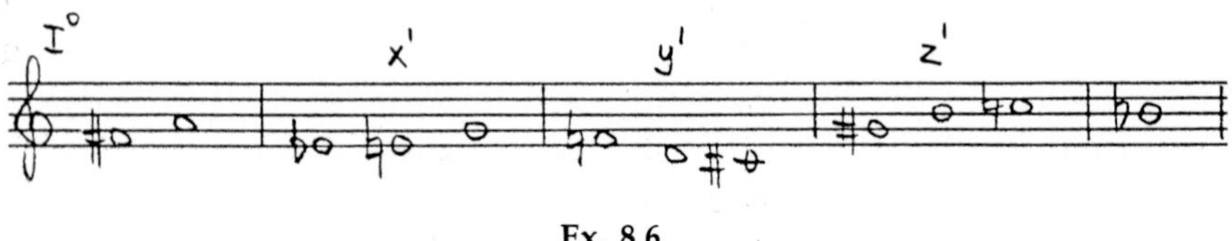

Ex. 8.6

Example 8.6 partitions the consistently re-ordered (12–11) I^0 into trichords (in the same way as Example 8.5 segmented P^0) and the corresponding figures, (x'), (y') and (z') *all* comprise cells of a major third encompassing a minor-third interval; (z') stands as an inversion (rather than the permutation of (z) within P^0) and, moreover, the remaining trichord, Bb, F#, A has the same interval content. (The irony here, of course, is that although this observation satisfies analytical curiosity as to why this reordering takes place, it still begs the question as to why the prime form did not end C-D in the first place!) However, the crucial premise concerns an interest in invariance that is fundamentally motivic;

it is not merely the product of variation but is an organic process, since it is intervallic shape, rather than pitch-class content, which is being manipulated. The compositional effect finds direct analogy in contrapuntal, tonal music and it is from this concept, rather than from directly diatonic references incorporated within the series itself, that any vestige of tonal preoccupations emerges. Such an approach has all the advantages of Schoenbergian, pre-serial method (Op.11 No.1, for example, offers a possible parallel) whilst, at the same time, drawing upon the large-scale unifying mechanisms that the background of genuinely twelve-note serialism can provide. It is concern for this all-important, underlying unity which helps explain Eisler's confining his serial choice to the four basic row-forms; transposition would increase diversity to a level that could possibly undermine this and there is, in fact, sufficient variety available — essentially from contrapuntal rather than directly serial means — to render unnecessary the use of transposed forms. From this perspective, their absence may be viewed as a positive attribute and not a shortcoming, since it arises from reasons of compositional integrity rather than serial pragmatism. Also, by limiting the complexity of the dodecaphony, the work's pitch sonority is more easily grasped.

Such considerations of the inherent compositional potential of the Quartet's series have provided speculative deductions regarding Eisler's serial method. The next stage in this investigation is to measure these analytical theories against musical practice and the purpose of this lengthy overview is to orientate the analyst, reader and, above all, the listener through this critical process. An immediate consequence already is that any exhaustive (not to say, exhausting) note-count of the work is unnecessary, given Eisler's conviction that rigid adherence to strict serial ordering is not a prerequisite of his compositional practice, since invariant motivic shapes offer a compensatory effect. It is an investigation into individual, contextual and musical logic in relation to serial methodology that should condition our approach to this piece. Nevertheless, for ease of reference, the four row-forms employed (with the ordering of I and RI as defined by the composer) are listed in Example 8.7.

Ex. 8.7

IV

The title, *'Variationen'*, given to the first movement of the Quartet immediately suggests a correspondence between compositional method and formal outline. Nevertheless, despite the obvious attractions of such a fundamental relationship between foreground process and background product, a series of variations where each element contains a variation of the series, could result in a piece which is highly fragmentary. It is Eisler's preoccupation with using the series merely as a starting-point from which to generate an essentially organic compositional technique which counteracts that potential for epigrammatic short-circuiting. Consequently, his motivic process creates a sense of large-scale continuity and contrast, the latter articulated by means of tempo variations and textural concerns, which give rise to patterns of tension and release associated with an overall formal scheme. As a result, whilst it is possible to observe surface events in terms of a set of variations, it is their grouping into larger formal sections which gives a structural sense to the movement as a whole. With such a formal scheme in mind, especially as this is uppermost in the listener's recall of an overall shape, it is possible to proceed by investigating how these essentially traditional, larger patterns are created in relation to the controlling function of the series; fundamentally, this concerns the balance between musical practice and compositional theory.

The first part of the movement is in three sections where two passages of contrasting material are linked by a transition. Defined by means of tempo and texture, there is some feeling of proportion in that the opening paragraph, comprising the first twenty bars, is balanced by a transition (*etwas drängend*) of the same length; this leads to new material (*rascher als Tempo I*) from bar 41. Given the organic nature of the way events are ordered within this movement, it is worth considering these opening sequences in some detail because of the generative potential of the material and its consequences for later events. The first twenty bars can be divided into three phrases of 8 + 4 + 8 bars. Each is characterised by its own texture (melodic, harmonic, contrapuntal, respectively) which, in turn, accounts for the differing ways in which the series is distributed. The opening eight bars, shown in Example 8.8, give the prime form of the row followed by its retrograde yet, despite the obvious directness of these serial statements, their character is of interest. Ex. 8.8

Ex. 8.8

It is by no means trivial to note that the row is initially presented as a fundamentally melodic concept with a strong rhythmic contour which, given the parallels between bars 1 and 3, suggests a question and answer effect. Moreover, the ensuing retrograde form maintains that characteristic, in effect providing an answering phrase at the four-bar level due to its contour and, above all, the consistent rhythmic pattern. Such concerns for shape and balance result in a simple statement of material as would traditionally initiate a set of variations, whilst, in serial terms, a close aural connection between prime and retrograde forms is made at the outset. This is an important feature since, theoretically, it is always the P/R relationship that is the most difficult to perceive aurally unless the series is highly symmetrical. Already, from the outset, the principle is established that relatedness of events is to be achieved by musical, rather than serial, means.

Example 8.9 shows the link of the next four bars which immediately contrasts with the directness of the opening in its reordered presentations of two statements of P^0. Strict serial ordering has been modified here in favour of textural and, above all, harmonic issues. Whilst the minor-/major-third characteristic of the row is emphasized in the repetition patterns given to the violins in bars 9–10 (which are varied

Ex. 8.9

and slightly compressed in bars 11–12) the A pedal in the cello suggests tonal possibilities. The supporting viola C#, the A-major 7th sonority of bar 10, the absence of D♮ there and its delayed (displaced) appearance in bar 12, all support momentary diatonic allusions. Tonal potential aside, the important feature here, which is to be significant in other passages within the movement, is the principle that local harmonic logic, instead of strict twelve-note ordering, will condition events. Bars 13–20, shown in Example 8.10, provide the conclusion to this first section in their contrapuntal presentation of P and R forms of the series. Ex. 8.10

Ex. 8.10

With minimal alteration, the viola statement of P directly follows the rhythmic pattern of its original format (see Example 8.8) whilst its continuation, using the retrograde form from bar 15, simplifies that contour. At this stage in the movement, serial technique and contrapuntal texture are presented by the simplest of means with the cello mirroring the viola in terms of row-forms (R, then P), reflected in the counterpoint by way of local imitative effects arising from the prominence of major-/minor-third cells. Ex. 8.11

Ex. 8.11

The passage from bars 21–40 shown in Example 8.11, whilst clearly continuing smaller-scale variation processes, has the larger effect of suggesting a transitional function. In a general sense, whilst the opening passage is one of *statement* of material (in three clearly-delineated stages), this paragraph concerns its *development* in that there is an increase in tension and a sense of almost 'directed' motion towards bars 40–41, where a passage of statement involving contrasting material ensues. With this larger function in mind, it becomes possible to rationalize the serial processes at work, noting the correspondence between heightened musical tension and departure from strict, twelve-note ordering. Since this is the first of such developmental passages in the movement, the extent of these serial licences is, quite logically, limited and the governing function of the background series remains clearly discernible. Example 8.11 shows the section in question and, apart from the tempo change, the most immediate means by which motion is generated is from the rhythmic, ostinato-like figure of the second violin. To the purist, such pitch-class repetitions may be viewed as contradicting accepted serial theory, whilst in practice the underlying identity of the retrograde form of the row remains intact with the symmetrical patterning of repeated notes (D-E-G-A) giving an all-important sense of direction, even at this early stage. Although this may appear to be deflected by the quaver statement of I^0 in bar 25 (the first appearance of this row-form) the large-scale placing of the ostinato figure (and its continuation using the inversion) which the cello begins in bar 26, continues the overall sense of movement. Against this more motoric strand in the texture, melodic presentations of the prime-form model occur. Initially, the cello statement from bar 21 pursues earlier characteristics by adopting, though gradually simplifying, the rhythmic contour of its entry at bar 13 (see Example 8.10). Subsequent melodic statements of the prime form (violin bar 25, viola, bar 26) augment note values so that the stasis of their dotted minims sets into relief the driving force of the surrounding material.

In a passage that relies so much on rhythmic configurations and contrapuntal activity to generate its transitional function, it is not surprising that motivic relationships condition the heightening of tension from bar 30. The three figures listed in Example 8.12 have some degree of gestural similarity in terms of basic contour and compass and each contains recurrent intervals: semitone, minor third and perfect fifth. An important compositional principle and one which is highly characteristic of Eisler's approach emerges here since, although these figures can be accounted for in serial terms — (a) is from RI^0, (b) from I^0 and (c)

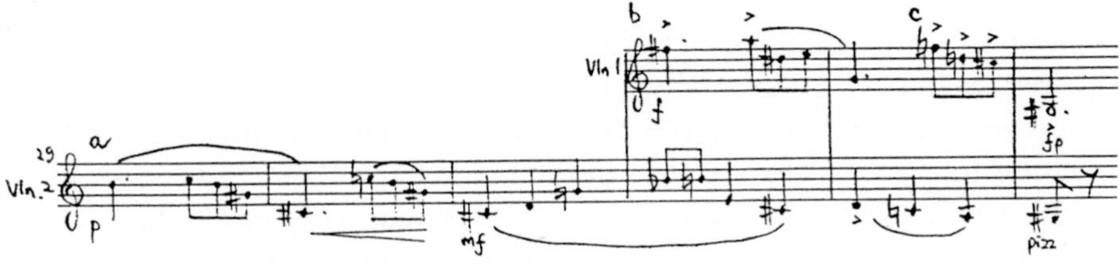

Ex. 8.12

is its continuation — they are far more easily understood in terms of local, motivic logic. Their serial origins, particularly as this involves fragments from different row-forms, is less important to our aural perceptions than the consistency of musical gesture which informs this sequence of events. Thereafter, the texture collapses with the solo viola entries of bars 36 and 38 (using I and RI row-forms, respectively) contrasting with the highly arresting nature of intervening chords in an abrupt juxtaposition of the horizontal and vertical. Again, in a corresponding manner to the motivic process described above, these harmonies can be accounted for in serial terms yet they have their own *raison d'être*. Thus, although these chords partition the prime-form series (the first comprising five elements, the second its remaining seven pitch-classes), the musical logic behind these events arises from their major-/minor-third (and chromatic) emphasis which is carefully spaced in order to control levels of dissonance, with the second event forming an intensification of the first. Above all, their arresting nature is precisely that: the function of these chords is to bring the transition to a highly dramatic conclusion.

V

From an analytical perspective, offering a detailed account of these opening bars is important for reasons of comprehensiveness which counteract any criticisms of preconceptions which could arise from a more selective approach. In terms of serialism, this detail is important too since Eisler's modification of strictly dodecaphonic practice could suggest a corresponding lack of rigour on the composer's part if at least one stretch of music was not considered in terms of twelve-note orderings. However, to pursue analytical enquiry at this level would become self-defeating because the sheer quantity of information would cease to clarify any assessment of musical effect and compositional technique which analysis seeks to rationalize, essentially by weighing one against the other. Additionally, as certain aspects of Eisler's method have emerged from this survey of events, strict serial ordering has, in itself, become less important to our understanding of this music than other compositional characteristics. Already, at a relatively early stage in the movement, elements of texture, harmony, counterpoint and motivic workings inform the progress of the piece in a manner comparable to many works, whether serial or not. They form part of a well-developed and adroitly judged technique which is almost independent of serial organization — though, crucially, not completely so. Whilst the remainder of this discussion needs to address that balance, between serial concepts and compositional method, so far it appears that the row imparts a sense of background unity by limiting the number of shapes being manipulated; it provides a systematic means of exercising control and restraint.

Whilst the progress of the surface of this music can be understood in this essentially traditional way, it is significant that events are grouped in order to articulate larger formal patterns. Already, a balance between statement and development, stability and instability, is discernible which, although operating apparently independently from serial concepts, is inextricably linked with them in terms of the considered equilibrium between strict and modified twelve-note orderings. The overall design has analogies with sonata-form architecture though this, like the serialism that ultimately engenders it, proves to be an abstract principle which is considerably modified in practice. It seems, therefore, logical and appropriate to allow this formal scheme to provide the framework for subsequent analytical observations which, in deference to both musical and literary concerns, can proceed in a more selective and economical manner. The focus now should involve an exploration of Eisler's compositional technique both on its own terms and in relation to its serial background.

The passage from bar 41–72 constitutes a 'second group' in effect and subdivides, according to tempo change and a gradual return to more familiar shapes, from bar 55. This subdivision is also conditioned, to a certain extent, by serial concerns in that the first part explores motivic inter-relationships between prime and inverted row-forms, whilst the second stage correspondingly involves the retrograde and retrograde-inversion. Since traditionally, and indeed in this context, a significant characteristic of a 'second group' involves contrast, then the question regarding Eisler's limiting his choice of rows, in the absence of any transposed versions, inevitably arises. Although it would appear that within his own terms of reference transposition would provoke too great a contrast in that it would represent a threat to a sense of underlying unity, given such wholesale diversity, this deliberate restrictiveness is not a limitation; Eisler has sufficient means at his disposal to be able to generate a strong sense of contrast whilst maintaining a feeling of continuous development of material. Although both P and I forms of the row were present during the preceding transitional passage, no aspect of their motivic invariance had been explored at that stage. Example 8.13 presents the opening bars of this passage where strongly imitative writing between the cello (I^0) and first violin (P^0) allows motivic identities to emerge clearly; nothing is predictable though, since the repetition of the cello F#-A motive reverses the sense of imitation so that it proves to be the cello which follows the violin and not the other way around.

Ex. 8.13

Eisler pays careful attention to registral detail so that the sense of inversion operates on different levels involving contour (ascending/ descending minor thirds) and intervals (major seventh/minor second, major sixth/minor third, perfect fourth/fifth and so on). All this is clarified, or complicated, depending on the aural skill of the listener, by a third line in this counterpoint: the second violin has a version of P^0

occurring canonically 1½ bars later than its model. Imitation thus occurs on different timescales but definite motivic identity emerges. Thus, when I^0 and P^0 are re-presented in a further variant, though with identical rhythms, as two phrases in the same voice (see Example 8.14), their close correspondences in terms of interval content are more readily perceived.

Ex. 8.14

Part of the thinking behind this continuous development of material seems to be the idea of making motivic relationships as clear as possible from the outset so that as events progress, and consequently move further away from their model, some sense of identity is still understood. Thus the four subsequent shapes in the first violin between bars 49–52 (see Example 8.15) due to their common gesture, (that is, register, rhythm, articulation) can be heard as a logical succession of related events despite a lack of precise intervallic or pitch-class correspondences. Initially then, it is a serial process, such as inversion, that conditions motivic identity whilst subsequent relationships emerge in terms of general shape, essentially independent from their generative row-forms.

Example 8.15 can be rationalized in terms of parts of P^0 and RI^0 but the selectivity and note repetitions involved are the product of local motivic thought which extends beyond strictly serial practice. With such concern for aural accountability and with due deference to an overriding control of serialism, it is probably not insignificant that beneath these gestures is a clear statement of the prime form (see Example 8.15) though its distribution (five elements clearly articulated by the second violin, with these and the remaining seven provided by the first violin and cello) is equally typical in its idiosyncracy. Similarly, during the second part of this passage, from the Tempo I at bar 55, familiar landmarks return in order to orientate the listener by way of unifying shapes that underpin surface variety. Thus, although the melodic line from bar 59 (shown in Example 8.16) can be explained in terms of the last ten elements of I^0, aurally its rhythmic shape and gesture recall the opening theme with that clear recollection for the listener becoming a reality given the immediate return of the ostinato figure from the

Ex. 8.15

transition (compare bar 62 with bar 21) later adopted by the cello, which even its new guise of RI^0 cannot undermine.

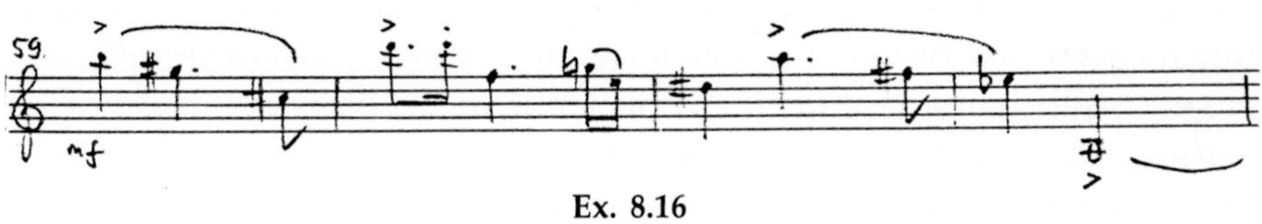

Ex. 8.16

By this stage in the movement, the invariant qualities existing between pairs of row-forms have conditioned its contrapuntal, motivic workings and, although Eisler takes a certain licence regarding strict ordering of events, the governing role of the series is still operational. The next section of music, with its controlled increase in tension, suggests analogies with developmental processes of sonata-form thinking. This lengthy passage, bars 73–106, shown in Example 8.17, constitutes the most dense sequence of musical events in the entire work and the calculated instability it engenders coincides with considerable freedom in the distribution of row forms. The logic behind these events comes from local motivic development and contrapuntal relationships pursuing the technique described above but with heightened independence from complete twelve-note identity. It is this passage, more than any other, that departs most directly from accepted principles of serial organization. Though this might evoke censure from the purist and certainly places considerable demands on both listener and analyst, the justification for such a potentially radical position raises interesting issues. In the context, leaving aside serial theory in favour of compositional practice, with a full exploration of conventional serial relationships having been achieved (given the lack of transposed row-forms) any further variation of this material will, almost of necessity, involve the actual re-ordering of serial elements. Whilst this may be viewed as an extension of traditional serial practice, many would see it as a regressive step since it apparently threatens the large-scale structural purpose of Schoenberg's method. The mosaic effect of the early stages of this passage is difficult to rationalize beyond a very localized continuous development process with abrupt gestural contrasts, and these appear to undermine an overall sense of direction that twelve-note ordering can impart. Texture plays a significant role in this effect due to contrast between simultaneous levels of activity, closely imitative motivic statements and the arresting result of more homophonic organization. It is this diversity of surface presentation informed by its own local musical logic which creates 'developmental' tension.

While critics might, with some justification, object to such a fundamental undermining of Schoenbergian practice, perhaps a different perspective is required in order to understand Eisler's thinking in this respect. The progress of events at this crucial stage of the piece is, paradoxically, closely reminiscent of Schoenberg. Not, of course, of his mature, serial works but rather of those earlier miniatures which rely on local, motivic development and which the same critics admire, given the hindsight of an emerging dodecaphony, in terms of cellular serialism. The shortcomings of this technique were clear to Schoenberg for precisely that reason — the inability to evolve large-scale structure — yet it is exactly this effect which Eisler seeks to explore at a particular stage within a serially organized composition. From the twelve-note 'chaos' of this interlude of carefully calculated musical tension, close observation suggests the continued presence, though at a much more distant level, of identifiable, yet varied, row-forms. Ultimately, a case can be made that, given the internal motivic characteristics of the background series, this construct does govern the progress of surface contrapuntal activity, though much less directly than elsewhere in the piece.

73
frisch (den Triolen Zeit lassen) 𝅗𝅥 = 96
(begleitend)
pizz.
75
cresc.
77
arco
79
82
energico
vorwärts!
pizz.
arco
stacc.
85

Ex. 8.17

Ex. 8.17 (cont'd)

The increase in musical tension that Eisler achieves requires control and eventually resolution if it is to be effective. Thus, there are two significant landmarks, after this disruption of serial identity, which contribute to a feeling of 'return'. Example 8.18 shows the textural resolution of the passage from bar 107 though this, significantly, is still subject to an increase in tempo. The cello isolates the main opening motive of P^0 in a clearly audible fashion which, with a full version from bar 111 in conjunction with the first violin statement of I^0, almost feels like a false recapitulation. Subsequent events follow serial orderings much more closely and there is a substantial emphasis on *retrograde* forms (both R and RI) as the means of directing events towards a moment of return. Despite all the surface diversity of motivic variation and development which appears to dominate this considerable stretch of music, the background logic of the series does seem to control events on the larger scale.

Ex. 8.18

Thereafter, whilst the sense of return and its attendant stability is clearly felt, this passage is no mere carbon copy of the opening of the piece – but then the movement is, after all, a set of variations. It is almost as if nothing can ever be the same again after the frenetic outburst of the previous section. The initial distribution of the prime-form series, from bar 141, places emphasis on certain intervals due to repetition patterns. Whilst the opening theme of the work clearly returns in the second violin in bar 164, it is one internal motivic shape (see Example 8.19 bar 178, cello) that dominates the end of the movement. Both large-scale serial and local motivic organization condition the progress of these final bars, significantly drawing together both levels of the compositional process, so carefully juxtaposed and balanced elsewhere in the piece, in this concluding passage.

Ex. 8.19

VI

With the analytical focus directed towards compositional method, there is little that needs to be said about the organization and progress of the *Finale* to the Quartet since, in terms of technique, it offers no new departures. It is, in a sense, a continuation of the set of variations. Perhaps then it is sufficient to give one final music example, showing the opening theme of the movement, as this immediately illustrates how with the same series Eisler is able to generate further variety and a highly dissimilar effect. Example 8.20 shows the initial, eight-bar theme, fashioned from prime and retrograde row-forms, and the totally different character of this music in comparison with the first movement stands as testimony to the composer's ingenuity in manipulating material. (The reference to Mozart's D major Quartet, K.499, is surely intentional.) At the same time, these opening gestures encapsulate the musically contrasting, yet serially complementary, mood of this *Finale*, giving a balanced, two-movement structure to the work as a whole.

Ex. 8.20

The fundamental issue which characterizes Eisler's use of serialism concerns a balance between strictness and freedom which is highly personal and wholly idiosyncratic. A broader context suggests that this was an area of serial theory in which the composer consciously experimented, providing a variety of solutions to this particular problem over a range of pieces. Thus, at one end of the spectrum there are examples where Eisler adheres faithfully to ordered row-forms and the vocal movements of the chamber cantatas provide good examples of this, with *Die römische Kantate* as perhaps the most exemplary in this respect. Elsewhere, in addition to early works which explore a balance between serial and tonal organization, are mature pieces, which contain a mixture of strictly ordered row-forms and freely organized motivic workings. The *Vierzehn Arten den Regen zu beschreiben* provides a good example. The response to a text in the former instance and the control of the strictly compartmentalized variation form of the latter may, at least to some extent, explain these differing attitudes towards the rigour of serial technique.

The String Quartet therefore occupies a central place within this range of serial thinking and may be held up as an apposite and wholly representative example of Eisler's method from which various conclusions may be drawn. The balance between strictness and freedom can and has been justified within the specific context of this piece, though obviously such an issue has external ramifications regarding serialism in itself. Reviewing the given context, whilst the inherent tension arising from densely worked motivic processes can be explained within the overall form of the first movement, those early stages of the 'development' section (from bar 73) are problematic for both listener and analyst. Any attempt to segment this music into discrete motivic shapes with a view to grouping them into larger categories, that is to discern underlying patterns that would provide direction to an otherwise momentary sense of logic, has proved futile. Although, in context, derivation from well established serial patterns can be adumbrated, the effect certainly lacks larger level coherence and this would appear to contradict some very fundamental principles upon which the serial method was founded.

The recurring issue here concerns the use of transposed versions of the series. The paradox is clear: the greater variety that transposition would engender (appropriate for a development section) appears to threaten Eisler's personal view of unity, yet the compositional solution employed (with its notably short-circuiting effect) seems to pose the same problem. Conceptually the solution is an obvious one: transposition which produces combinatoriality. Here the composer can preserve fundamental pitch relationships with the serial model, that is, a larger-scale sense of unity, by way of a logically achieved variation in its ordering which has a totally different effect from the wholesale shift in pitch levels which transposition alone would engender. It is, of course, unclear as to what Eisler's views on this aspect of compositional theory were, though he surely must have been aware of Schoenberg's experiments in this area, and the complete lack of transposed row-forms remains a fundamental characteristic of Eisler's method. Nevertheless, employing one pair of combinatorially related row-forms would provide the requisite sense of 'development' whilst at the same time drawing upon the larger scale structural ramifications of complete twelve-note orderings. Eisler's cellular serialism is an undoubtedly interesting and ingenious solution and elsewhere in the piece this kind of motivic invariance provides analogous effects to those outlined above. However, for the particular passage in question, transpositional invariance may have resulted in a more satisfactory way forward.

Schoenberg's development of serial method offered a compositional theory which has fundamental parallels with that of the tonal system in so far as it provided a means of generating music operating on differing but related structural levels. Although most of its analysis has concentrated on foreground (note counting) and background (formal outlines) levels and there is a noticeable lack of discussion about middleground patterning, its presence is perceived by analyst and listener and is of crucial importance to the system as a whole. Eisler's individual adaption of his teacher's method has many advantages, not least of which is the limited control he allows the underlying series to impose on otherwise musical decisions. The freedoms he therefore allows have very positive effects for the listener in terms of how approachable and appealing a given melody or contrapuntal passage can become as a result of manipulating strictly twelve-note rotation. For example, the phobia that note repetitions could, at a stroke (perhaps it is two strokes!), undermine the whole method by inferring tonal allegiances has been proved nonsensical. The Quartet is atonal music but much of its textural character arises from this simplest of devices. However, the crucial point about Eisler's serialism in relation to Schoenberg's that arises from all this, concerns the apparent absence of any middleground level. The Quartet is fundamentally a linear piece, motivic, melodic, contrapuntal; the role of simultaneity in terms of larger level harmonic patterning is negligible. It is, therefore, significant that at moments equivalent to directed harmonic motion in a tonal composition, transitional passages for example, note repetitions are used to create ostinato-like, motoric strands (often in conjunction with a tempo change) in order to generate this effect. Unlike examples in Schoenberg's music, such passages of musical tension (arising from an essentially harmonic phenomenon) are not created by serial means.

This absence of a middleground level of organization may evoke censure from critics concerned about the limited application of serial methodology that Eisler chose to apply. However, this limitation may be viewed as something of a strength regarding just how approachable this serial music may be for the listener. By restricting the complexity of the dodecaphony, the consistency of sonority is perhaps more readily grasped than in Schoenbergian examples and the emphasis on linear processes makes the progress of events more easily understood. Thus the musical impact is much more immediate and direct than that arising from more complex serial works. The use of a set of variations as the product of serial method, resulting in a direct correspondance between form and content, produces a sequence of events which is clearly intelligible on a purely instinctive, musical level without recourse to an academic understanding of technical processes, since the motivic organization makes this musically self-explanatory. With a composition which relies so heavily on the generative potential of its opening material, problems may arise should the listener not find the initial gestures of sufficient appeal; however, the musical clarity arising from the serial directness and simplicity of these opening statements, may well compensate for any such reservations. Similarly, the textural density of the central section, with its lack of easily perceptible serial organization, can be understood in terms of larger-scale patterns of tension and release which govern the work as a whole and can be instinctively grasped by the listener. Whilst all these features combine to produce a serial piece that is notably approachable and immediately appealing, it is this very immediacy, given an absence of deeper structural levels, which could well become problematic upon repeated hearings. Nevertheless, the balance between intellectual technique and directness of expression remains an intriguing aspect of Eisler's individuality and one which will continue to arouse interest for analyst and listener alike.

Despite all the theoretical advantages of Schoenberg's method, his solution to the problem of generating large-scale atonal music was relatively short-lived. The irony here seems to arise from the very strictness on which that system relies which, for many, became far too restrictive. Eisler's search for freedom and balance within well-defined but purposefully limited boundaries of serial organization can ultimately be viewed as constituting quite a progressive stance. The relative simplicity of his method, its apparent lack of sophistication in the light of later theoretical developments concerning deeper structural levels can, after all, be seen in a very positive light; perhaps if others had sought these freedoms of approach instead of pursuing increasingly mathematical solutions, 'serial' composition may have had a wider appeal to both composer and listener alike. When the history of serialism is finally written, the works of Eisler with all their apparent idiosyncracies (or, hopefully, because of them) will assume that significant place which, for all too long, seems to have been overlooked.

9

EISLER AND ADORNO

Günter Mayer

The following text dates from the year 1977 — a time when socialist societies seemed quite unthreatened in their existence and development. It was a time when many people in the East (and in the West) — the author being amongst these, as was Hanns Eisler during his lifetime — were convinced that here a new social order was taking shape, a historic alternative to capitalist society, containing within it the potential to achieve the great aims of the real democratic, socialist-revolutionary movement despite any amount of set-backs, mistakes and sacrifices.

Hanns Eisler was always well aware of the immense difficulties of this self-contradictory process which was after all by no means supported from the capitalist side. On the contrary! In 1953 he noted in his diary: "It is terrible to view the birth pangs of a new social order. What courage, talent, discipline, heroism, what intense work, what intelligence and what stupidity! Huge successes undermined by unspeakable mistakes".[1] We have now had to witness the inability of the leaders and citizens of 'real-socialist' countries to build either on what had already been achieved or on the desired social alternative or historical perspective. As we have in the meantime recognized, the conditions — both objective and subjective — were not yet ready for this. The forces within could not hold their own against the functioning capitalist world, let alone retain and develop their appeal for the mass of the people — an appeal which they had during the new beginnings after the two world wars.

Adorno's sceptical and distanced attitude towards politics of a revolutionary nature was closer to the truth than his then critics — including Eisler — could or would see: the capitalist, alienated, 'totally administrated' world is triumphant internationally and has until now not produced a single viable idea to counter the "Tellurian catastrophe" (Adorno). Alternative forces, which could at least hold in check the

---

[1] H. Eisler, *Tagesaufzeichnungen*, in *Musik und Politik, Schriften* 1948–1962, Leipzig 1982, p. 265.

spiralling existential crisis for the whole of humanity, have not yet been able to form or develop effectively. The future is utterly uncertain, because previously valid convictions and standards have proved to be highly relative and limited in their application.

Does this now mean that in his basically pessimistic attitude — with its resultant criticism of politics and culture as well as in his negative judgement of Hanns Eisler — Adorno is right retrospectively and Eisler's criticism of Adorno now invalid?

The problem is not, in my opinion, as simple as that. Above all, it must be remembered that the cause which Eisler stood up for had a chance of succeeding. The stabilizing of the socialist states, presupposing that their internal weaknesses and contradictions would be overcome, was a real possibility. Although the terms 'progress', 'the emancipation of the masses' and 'historical perspective' can no longer be thought of as they once were, this does not necessarily mean that the future is without potential and that the final decline is inevitable.

New consideration and intensive discussion on the basis of sober analysis of the situation as it appears must now be addressed to the question of a new concept of society, music and music-culture in the context of post-modern relativisations — in the meantime fashionably pluralistic and uncommitted — as well as in the context of competing paradigms. In these discussions about the possibilities of reasonable action neither Adorno nor Eisler can simply be unquestioningly 'adopted'. Even recent attention to their opposed polemic could be more useful in the necessary search for new beginnings than the useless process of uncritical rehabilitation or hasty forgetting. The particular oppositional relationship between Adorno and Eisler documents a general, significant difference in reactions to the contradictory movements of the first half of the twentieth century. Like these, this relationship is part of history and thus belongs in a critical appraisal of the past — in so far as the present and the future are not seen as the indestructible negativity of the 'unchangeable'.

For this reason the 1977 text on the relationship between Adorno and Eisler has been left unaltered — as it was written and conceived then. It is thus furthermore possible for the reader to reconstruct the problems and polemics to which the author was reacting, with regard to basic questions of music theory and politics, under the reigning conditions in the GDR, in the Federal Republic of Germany and in western Europe.

General Questions: Music and Politics

For some years now the historical significance of Adorno and Eisler has been the subject of controversy. The debate concerns, on the one hand, the philosopher who was to set the aesthetic standards of the Frankfurt School and, on the other hand, the composer with socialist ideals, "the strength of whose natural gifts was equalled by his intellectual ability"[2] and whose achievement as a theoretician has only recently received proper recognition. Opinions on their work are as varied as they are numerous and in need of critical evaluation in view of their not inconsiderable influence on attitudes to the primary sources.[3] Although in what is to follow we shall concentrate on the historical context, we shall in fact be guided by present experience and the reception of Adorno and Eisler up to now, and above all by the question of the possible role of their work in the current and future theory and practice of a progressive, materialistic, dialectical concept of music and the culture relating to it. Although this can only be done in general terms here, the hope is that it will encourage a re-examination of some established value judgements – such as the 'Neo-Marxism' of Adorno's aesthetics or the invalidity of Eisler's model for a type of music which could advance the cause of socialism, or even the idea that there is simply nothing more to be learnt from Adorno.[4]

In certain respects, Adorno and Eisler maintained opposing positions despite their 'friendship dating back to 1925'.[5] In Adorno's words, "there were never any serious personal differences between

---

[2] Th.W. Adorno, Letter to Hans Bunge, 11.2.1964.

[3] Works on Adorno worthy of mention include: *Die neue Linke nach Adorno*, ed. W.F. Schoeller, Munich, 1969; O. Massin, *Adorno und die Folgen*, Neuwied/Berlin, 1970; H. Redecker, *Im Westen nichts Neues* in: *Weimarer Beiträge*, 9/1973; J. Kuczynski/W. Heise, *Bild und Begriff*, Berlin, 1975, pp 283–301; M. Jay, *Dialektische Phantasie*, Boston/Toronto 1973, Frankfurt am Main, 1976; D. Kliche, *Lukács und Adorno* in: *Weimarer Beiträge*, 7/1977.

[4] See H. Paetzold in *Neomarxistische Ästhetik*, Part 2, Düsseldorf 1974; or C. Dahlhaus, *Politische and ästhetische Kriterien der Kompositionskritik*, in: *Darmstädter Beiträge XIII*, Mainz 1973.; or: K. Boehmer, *Adorno, Musik und Gesellschaft*, in: *Die neue Linke nach Adorno*, op. cit.

[5] Th. W. Adorno/H. Eisler, *Komposition für den Film*, Munich, 1969, p. 213: new edition, Leipzig 1977. Translated as Composing for the Films, New York 1947, under Eisler's name only.

them".[6] When they saw each other for the last time in the late fifties in Frankfurt (am Main) — Eisler had arrived unannounced — they spent "an evening together, just like in the old days" although admittedly they "as though by agreement did not touch on politics".[7] It is in the basic divergence of their political views, which is at the root of important philosophical, social and music-aesthetic differences, that they represent opposing positions in the criticism of capitalism in the twentieth century.

Their assessment of the basic contradictions of musical culture, governed by the specific conditions of a society moving from late capitalism to socialism, is in many ways similar, although they reach very different conclusions. Central to this is the question of the relationship between musical and social progress, in short: the question of the relationship between music and politics.

Adorno on Eisler: a negative overall judgement

The small amount of attention which Adorno in his extensive output devotes to Eisler the composer — disregarding altogether Eisler the theoretician — is concerned directly with this relationship and contains in essence his general attitude towards political music. Through it runs his sceptical, negative evaluation of the relation between the political intention and function of music on the one hand and the relevance and authenticity of music on the other.

This can already be seen in 1929 in Adorno's review of the *Zeitungsausschnitte* Op. 11. Commenting on the negative lyrics and tone of these songs and expressing concern for Eisler's further development, he writes "that for the sake of being understood he has lowered his musical means to a new outdated level, rather than rising to the challenge of present-day music."[8] This is clearly expressed in Adorno's first major essay *Zur gesellschaftlichen Lage der Musik* (On Music in Society), his most distinctly 'left' work, published in 1932 and which he did not include in any volume of his later collected works. In it he does pay lip service to proletarian 'communal music' ('*Gemeinschaftsmusik*') as a source of propaganda and as being politically correct but at the same time claims that these productions — taken as a form of art — cannot

[6] Th. W. Adorno, Letter to Hans Bunge, 11.2.1964.

[7] Ibid.

[8] Th. W. Adorno, *Der Anbruch*, 1925/5, 20/21.

hold their own against the advanced bourgeois product, and show themselves to be a questionable mixture of the remnants of outdated bourgeois styles and forms. . . and of the remnants of advanced new music, losing through this mixture both sharpness of attack and economy on a technical and formal level."[9] Adorno, in his *Einleitung in die Musiksoziologie* (Introduction to the Sociology of Music) of 1962 and with specific reference to some 'Workers' Choruses' by Eisler, at least does not expressly repeat his ideas from 1932 on the impossibility of a music suited to the role of the proletariat, but two years later (in 1964) his old standpoint re-emerges in his use of the term 'primitive immediacy'[10] (*'primitive Unmittelbarkeit'*). In a hitherto unknown letter to Hans Bunge of 11 February 1964, Adorno writes that he is of the opinion "that in artistic questions, a political stance should not make itself apparent in primitive immediacy — and this is the very opinion which accounts for the difference between myself and poor Hanns Eisler".[11]

This sentence expresses clearly enough the generally subjective and narrow attitude of Adorno towards the composer Eisler. Adorno's writings on the far-reaching life's work of his 'friend' Eisler do not extend beyond a wary scepticism as to the future development of the young Eisler and some similarly uncommitted generalisations "about some works from the late twenties and early thirties".[12] Even among the many pieces of *'Kampfmusik'* in which Eisler established a historically quite new and modern type of revolutionary, proletarian music and which had a wide international influence, Adorno only saw 'some works' as fit for general mention. Which ones he meant by this he did not specify. He never attempted to verify his overall evaluation of Eisler's directly political works by concrete analysis. Adorno passed in silence over the rest of Eisler's work in all its breadth and variety, the works written in exile (from 1933 to 1948) and after that in the GDR up until 1962, although he knew some of it well, particularly the works composed in America. The one exception was the *Hollywooder Lieder-*

[9] Th. W. Adorno, *Zur gesellschaftlichen Lage der Musik*, in: *Zeitschrift für Sozialforschung* Jahrgang 1, Leipzig, 1932, p. 124.

[10] Th. W. Adorno, *Einleitung in die Musiksoziologie*, Frankfurt (Main), 1962, p.77.

[11] Th. W. Adorno, Letter to Hans Bunge, 11.2.1964.

[12] Th. W. Adorno, *Einleitung in die Musiksoziologie*, op.cit. p.77.

buch which was written in 1942–43 — at a time of close personal contact — and in which he showed a particular interest. In 1958 Eisler wrote about this: "At any rate the situation was that my erstwhile friend Adorno requested most earnestly that he might write the foreword when it was published. Well, I did not remind him of this the last time I saw him in Frankfurt, in order not to embarrass him. He would hardly show himself in public with me, let alone link his name with mine."[13] In the sixties it was Adorno's intention to write "something serious for once" about Eisler and to broadcast it on the radio[14] but as far as I know nothing further came of that.

Common ground: early points of contact

Adorno and Eisler's attitudes to the theory of many aesthetic, sociological and specifically musical questions were broadly similar, agreeing in numerous details. Although with differing motivation and divergent aims and intentions, both were striving early on for a philosophically and sociologically orientated theory of music beyond the normal bourgeois methods of studies in the Humanities and Musicology. Each took as a starting point — Adorno somewhat later than Eisler — the analysis of the contradictory process where music is regulated by capitalism and governed by the laws of the market.

Since the late twenties Eisler had been giving lectures on music in the *Berliner Marxistischen Arbeiterschule* (known as MASCH — Berlin Marxist Worker's College) from the standpoint of historical materialism. He led a study group on this subject until 1931 and in the same year brought together the results of this — independent of Adorno — in his first major essay *Die Erbauer einer neuen Musikkultur* (The Builders of a New Music Culture).[15] At just this time in 1932, Adorno wrote and published his first comprehensive attempt at an analysis based on dialectical and historical materialism of the 'sociological status of music'.[16] It is probable that they had discussions on this matter at the

[13] H. Eisler, *Gespräche mit Hans Bunge*, Leipzig, 1975, p. 45.

[14] Th. W. Adorno, Letter to Hans Bunge, 11.2.1964.

[15] H. Eisler, *Die Erbauer einer neuen Musikkultur*, in: *Musik und Politik, Schriften* 1924–1948, Leipzig 1973, p. 140ff. (Translated in *Hanns Eisler. A Rebel in Music).*

[16] Th. W. Adorno, *Zur gesellschaftlichen Lage der Musik*, op.cit.

time.[17] Whatever the case, these two contemporaneous pieces of work are significant examples of a new type of 'music sociology', of 'music-aesthetics'. However, despite the same methodological intention and despite much common ground, the above mentioned political divergences in sociological and art theory are already evident at this early stage.

Adorno's basic position on society and music

Adorno stresses the formal language of music governed by its material as the largely unconscious, antinomic articulation of the "duress of social conditions" ('*Not des gesellschaftlichen Zustandes*') in a capitalist monopoly, as a "hieroglyph of suffering" ('*Chiffrenschrift des Leidens*'), — as an expression from within of social contradictions and of the necessity of overcoming these.[18]

In this he shows himself to be a brilliant analyst of the experience and structure of alienation in the contradictory development of bourgeois music, its main movements and representatives — and this at a level far beyond that of contemporary hermeneutics. His immanent method using the dialectic of consciousness in the individual's response to art, showing up the pressures of capitalist alienation, has its limits when it comes to the question of the potential and actual breaking out of this alienation. According to Adorno the function of art has certain analogies with social theory. But understanding music as a symptom of society cannot replace analysis of that society, which is determined essentially through its own standards. Since Adorno does not in the end see the monopolistic capitalistic system as a "material relationship on the path to dissolution" (Marx), and since he sees absolute need and suffering from the point of view of repressed subjectivity, dialectic is reduced to the sphere of reflection on the self, to the possibility or impossibility of individual autonomy within these alien pressures. The innovative attempt to link the notion of the autonomy of art, which sees its relative autonomy as something absolute, with its materialistic,

---

[17] This is evident from statements by E. Bloch to A. Betz in Tübingen on 27.5.1973 about his connections with Eisler amongst others: "I probably first got to know him in Berlin in about 1923 in a café: there were the three of us including Adorno. At that time Adorno was still very pro-communist. . ."; See A. Betz, *Hanns Eisler, Musik einer Zeit, die sich eben bildet*, Munich, 1976. Translated as Hanns Eisler, Political Musician, Cambridge, 1982. p.261.n.55.

[18] Th. W. Adorno, *Zur gesellschaftlichen Lage der Musik*, op.cit., p. 105.

sociological aspects, thus perverts the idea of the autonomy of art as a social alternative to society. The social function of music is reduced to its material. The dialectics of developing musical material and, at the same time, changing its function for the masses are thereby out of the question as far as Adorno is concerned. His striking criticism of the ideological function of bourgeois communal and every-day music becomes something absolute. Adorno denies apodictically the positive existence of a proletarian class-consciousness, thus concluding that music appropriate to the role of the proletariat must remain incomprehensible to it.[19]

As early as 1932 there were already many problems which Adorno was unable to analyse in detail or to think through to their practical consequences: the fact that the ideological and aesthetic creation of a proletarian class-consciousness can only be thought of in the context of a highly developed class struggle; the fact that in this contradictory process a new non-bourgeois experience of reality, self-awareness and aggressive individual subjectivity would develop; furthermore the fact that, as a result, musical productivity would be created quite apart from bourgeois positions and forms of organization; lastly the fact that the idea of progress, when seen as a dialectical process of innovation and regression (*Zurücknahme*), would take on a different complexion. Adorno maintains that the results of advanced bourgeois production are "simply pushed aside" by proletarian art theory and practice; that this conforms "in a passive, one-sided manner to the state of consumer-consciousness"; and "that in this way the class-produced condition of art is being preserved, whereas its eradication is the aim of the proletarian class struggle."[20]

This false assertion leads to a negative conclusion. The only concrete alternative offered by Adorno for the practice of proletarian music to the abstractly criticized so-called 'makeshift solutions' was "that one should fit new texts to the existing melodies of common bourgeois music", by this means "altering their function dialectically"[21] — an alternative which had long been left behind by proletarian music, above all as a result of Eisler's achievements. There could be no use for this meagre product of a dialectic which was not even consistently aporetic.

---

[19] Ibid. p. 123–4.

[20] Ibid. p. 124.

[21] Ibid. p. 124.

Eisler's basic position on society and music

Eisler, on the other hand, emphasized the necessary change in the function of music. He took as his starting point the historical function of the proletariat, the unity of Marxist theories of communist politics, the real experience of the international class struggle. His analysis of the development and crisis of bourgeois music culture is by no means as detailed as Adorno's, yet is largely along the same lines. But Eisler takes as his starting point the materialistic interconnection of individuals, the relationship of the classes to each other. Thus for him, dialectic is intrinsically critical and revolutionary at one and the same time: conscious action — a means of practical intervention. Accordingly, for Eisler, the future is communism: "not a condition to be created, an ideal for reality to live up to "but rather . . . the actual movement overtaking the present".[22] The conditions for this are a result of the relevant, existing, concrete, historical prerequisites.

Unlike Adorno, Eisler pursues an analysis of the practice of workers' music and generalizes the results achieved in the 'hieroglyphs of battle': songs of the masses, political didactic pieces and choral montage. He subordinates the inheritance of the great musical tradition up to and including Schoenberg, the *'Materialrevolutionär'*,[23] to the central question of a great, new change in the function of art, which was the historical order of the day with the beginnings of the move from capitalism to socialism. All aspects of the relatively autonomous development of music, which Eisler — as does Adorno — tries to grasp in their social implications, are assessed in the wider context of the 'actual movement' (*'wirkliche Bewegung'*), from an overall historical perspective. His concept, therefore, of the function of music is at variance with that of Adorno. His concept is an alternative to bourgeois art music in its isolation from the struggles of the masses, an alternative to mass-effective bourgeois entertainment music and also to *petit-bourgeois* variants in the workers' music movement. He sees bourgeois music in all its forms as either directly or indirectly stabilizing the existing balance of power. Central to this is the demand for the transference of experiences made in the class struggle by way of new forms of production, interpretation, distribution and reception of music. Eisler's critical analysis of the traditional concert and entertainment industry monopoly

---

[22] K. Marx/F. Engels, *Die Deutsche Ideologie*, in *Marx-Engels Werke*, Vol. 3, Berlin, 1969, p. 35.

[23] H. Eisler, *Die Erbauer einer neuen Musikkultur*, op.cit. p.154.

is, at the same time, constructive. He looks for possibilities of the democratization of music culture in social upheavals, in technically transmitted mass-communication but also in the *'Materialrevolution'*. Some formulations of music-historical relations, of the functions of struggle and didactic music as strictly opposed to beauty and enjoyment, are one-sided and simplify the given contradictions. Eisler — allergic to aestheticism — operates in his theoretical reflections with contrasts with which he was obviously already well used to mediating dialectically in his aesthetic-compositional practice at that time. Even so, his first attempt at theoretical understanding proved to be fruitful and was developed through continued experience and discussion. He is not the free-floating, powerless bourgeois intellectual. His first attempt at programmatic generalization arises from the collective practice of revolutionary artists and theoreticians — in which the outlines of a new quality of proletarian art theory and of materialistic-dialectical aesthetics became evident in the twenties and early thirties: as for example in the work of Arvatov, Meyerhold, Tretjakov, Nejedly, Haba, Schulhoff, Burian, Heartfield and ultimately Lukács, Brecht and Benjamin.

In 1932 Eisler reacted to Adorno's text *On Music in Society*. He noted at the time: "Also a certain Herr Wiesengrund-Adorno, who ... took the trouble to apply 'Marxist methods' gets no further than the straight interpretation of reality without making the attempt to delve deeper into the forces which might change it. It is a strange case of mistaking dialectical materialism for dialectical mysticism and it does not suffice to replace the good God (an old man with a white beard) with the twelve-note technique!"[24]

Common ground in exile: Composing for the Films

Adorno and Eisler's achievements in theoretical writings not only exhibit parallels in the years 1931–32 and beyond — but there was also, as is known, direct cooperation. Both had gone into exile — Adorno later than Eisler — after the triumph of Hitler's Fascism in Germany and lived from 1938 until after the Second World War in the United States. In the early forties both had the chance to work on theory within the framework of research projects funded by the Rockefeller Foundation: Eisler as the leader of the Film Music Project and Adorno as the leader of the music

[24] H. Eisler, *Zur Krise der bürgerlichen Musik,* in: *Musik und Politik,* op.cit. p.188. [translated in *Hanns Eisler A Rebel in Music*]

section of the Princeton Radio Research Project.[25] Furthermore (according to Adorno's version of 1969), they had had a "deep mutual awareness" of each other for many years due to their practical and music-theoretical work and had simultaneously spent some time in Hollywood in close contact with film production.[26] The result of their cooperation was the book *Composing for the Films*.[27] Leaving aside the question raised by Adorno after Eisler's death as to their relative input to this book, there is no doubt as to the cooperation itself. The following reference to Adorno is to be found both in Eisler's version of the preface – written in 1944, long before the hysterical wave of anti-communist theory and signed only with 'Eisler' – and in the first publication of the book in New York in 1947 under Eisler's name alone: "This book is largely based on his (Adorno's) theories and formulations with regard to (later: The theories and formulations presented here evolved from cooperation with him on) general aesthetic and sociological matters as well as (to) purely musical issues!"[28]

Cooperation in this area was possible for various reasons. The overall circumstances of exile in American in conjunction with the framework of the research project set distinct limits on the further development of Marxist theories. Political activity was only possible in the cause of anti-fascism, while the expression of communist aims was quite out of the question. In addition, the research project took a broadly critical attitude to the monopoly-based culture industry, looking at the possibility, even the reality, of modern advanced music in radio and film. Thus it was both possible and necessary that the radical differences between Adorno and Eisler, between the American off-shoot of the Frankfurt Institute and the New School for Social Research[29] should remain in the background in this co-operation on the "by no means political book". They both avoided "discussing political matters".[30] A

---

[25] See Th. W. Adorno/H. Eisler, *Komposition für den Film*, p.9; also M. Jay, *Dialektik der Phantasie*, op.cit. pp. 226, 228, 231, 266. This shows that the Radio Research Project ran from 1938–39, that is to say somewhat earlier than the Film Music Project (1940–43).

[26] Th. W. Adorno/H. Eisler, *Komposition für den Film*, op.cit. p.9.

[27] H. Eisler, *Composing for the Films*, New York, 1947.

[28] H. Eisler, Preface in: *Musik und Politik*, op.cit. p. 488. This sentence is, however, deleted in the typescript; H. Eisler, *Composing for the Films*, op.cit.

[29] See M. Jay, *Dialektik der Phantasie*, op.cit. p.213.

[30] Th. W. Adorno/H. Eisler, *Komposition für den Film*, op.cit p.213.

social programme was not at issue so their common ground became more evident. This was to be seen on various levels which I can only touch on here, in order to devote more attention to one, in my opinion, significant aspect of their work.

Composing for the Films is the first important attempt at a critical analysis — it is in fact a systematic analysis — of monopoly-based capitalist mass culture as found in the film industry. Here, expert analysis of this significant part of the entertainment industry and of the use made by capitalism of the historically new qualities of art in the age of technical reproduction was carried out in the light of the ensuing altered interrelations between the various art forms, that is to say, taking into account the prevalent artistic situation as a whole. In this way the two distinctly different areas of highbrow and lowbrow music (*'E-Musik'* and *'U-Musik'*) are seen as parts of a whole. This exerts both positive and negative contradictory forces on musical development, comprising, as it does, work specialization and the rationalization of musical production according to capitalist organizational practice with the hierarchical conditions which that implies, as well as the consequent effects on the function and structure of the music itself. Adorno and Eisler take a broad overall view of 'advanced' music. Above all they agree in general terms about Schoenberg and Stravinsky as well as in their criticism of the clichés found at that time in film music. Their overall analysis results in a differentiated synthesis of the view which they both already held but had hitherto expressed independently on the way in which social history enters into and is realized in musical material. This approach made it possible to render transparent the deceptively natural quality of historical determinants in music and to understand better the inner, contradictory development of musical material in its relative autonomy and in its social mediation (*'gesellschaftliche Vermittlung'*).

Accordingly Adorno and Eisler basically agree on the dialectic of musical material defined broadly in terms of 'advanced (new) material', of 'worn-out material', of the 'historical level of musical material' and of the 'renewal of material', thus agreeing in their basic view of the changes in the structure of musical language which occurred in the avant-garde music of the early twentieth century (before the introduction of dodecaphony) — that is to say, agreeing on the level of development of compositional experience. In this, they see the composer having every musical possibility at his free and conscious disposal without regard to any existing terms of reference or to traditional conventionalized norms of musical structures. This quality of new music, its lack of convention, its subtlety, its tendency to express sudden changes, the derivation of individual musical elements from the construction of the whole, as well as its leaning towards objectivity in the sense of rational construction — these are all seen to be similar to the qualities of film, corresponding to the actual technique of the new medium of film, but having been discovered independently even before sound film had become a reality. This led to the following conclusion: "the more music is controlled by the principles of its own construction, the more manageable it will be in its application to another medium."[31] This understanding led Adorno and Eisler to a general theory of modern progressive composition. The significance of this theory has, in my opinion, not been at all fully evaluated, neither in general terms nor with respect to the different experiences which Adorno and Eisler associated with it, nor with regard to any assessment of the historical significance of Eisler's compositional achievements. What becomes apparent here as a new form of interrelation between the arts, emerging as the historical result of their autonomous development, has hardly yet been given further consideration because of the conventional separation of individual art forms.

The shared thesis of the independence of material and its working methods

This then is the theory: "If appearances really are to be believed, then music has now reached a stage at which its material and its working methods are becoming independent of one another, in the sense that the choice of material is relatively insignificant as opposed to the working method. The mode of composition has developed its own logic to the extent that it need not result any longer from its material, but that it may make use of any material to its own ends."[32]

Although Adorno and Eisler insist that in principle priority should be given to the "really new material",[33] they do at the same time see the possibility of legitimately using other, diverse materials in film music, as long as it has raised itself to the highest level of the most advanced methods of contemporary composition. At this level even

[31] Ibid. p.59.

[32] Ibid. p.117.

[33] Ibid. p.118.

traditional, out-dated, material will be open to refraction, in its expression as well as in its purely musical substance.[34]

It seems to me that this generalization formulates a qualitative change in the conditions of production, in the development of music in the early twentieth century, which signals not just changes in compositional technique in the narrower sense but in fact a fundamental change in the institution of music as a whole; a — relatively independent — consequence of the extent of socialization which had reached crisis point under the conditions of late capitalism and which was geared towards a new way of organizing both the social and musical interrelationships of individuals. Through their negative experiences in monopolist mass communication, particularly in the institution of film, Adorno and Eisler recognized, in the production, in the form in which it exists, in the distribution and the effect of even a traditional work of art in the age of its technical reproductability (*'Reproduzierbarkeit'*), qualitative changes which were also to be observed immanently in the crisis in concert music both before and parallel to the reality of sound film.

In the above theory Adorno and Eisler brought together in general terms quite divergent individual and collective experiences of this problematic situation and as a result of fundamental differences of opinion on basic questions of social analysis drew very different conclusions from it. This becomes particularly clear if one considers the theory in *Composing for the Films* concerning the "increasing irrelevance of the material" (*'Vergeichgültigung des Materials'*) — in the light of both Eisler's compositional practice up until and beyond the early forties, as well as in Adorno and Eisler's theoretical writings before and after the book.

Adorno and Eisler initially substantiate the theory in question by referring to the later 'minor' works of Schoenberg (the last chorus from Op. 35, the second movement of the 2nd Chamber Symphony, composed much later than the first movement).[35] At that time, at the beginning of the 1940's, Adorno had already completed the chapter on Schoenberg in his *Philosophy of Modern Music*, which was then published in 1949 together with the complementary chapter on Stravinsky.[36] In this book Adorno discusses the proven separation of

[34] Ibid. p.119.

[35] Ibid. pp.117–8.

[36] Th. W. Adorno, *Philosophie der neuen Musik*, first edition — Tübingen, 1949 translated — Philosophy of Modern Music. New York 1973.

material and compositional method in the work of Schoenberg in much more fundamental terms:

1 What emerged in the 'minor works' of Schoenberg's late period, where he had reached the ultimate stage in the ordering of material, had already manifested itself, both in the overlaps of his early and middle periods (*Gurrelieder, Die Glückliche Hand*) and, since the beginnings of twelve-note technique, as a general tendency towards using different compositional techniques during the same period. It appears as a tendency towards the growing indifferentiation of the material in a "long list of secondary works – arrangements or compositions which do not employ twelve-note technique, or which employ it as a means to an end, thus rendering it purely fungible", and which take on significance in the form of *'parerga'*, as compared to the "iron-clad twelve-note compositions", through their sheer quantity (the tonal works, works for commercial purposes, the orchestrations).[37] In the *Philosophy of Modern Music* particularly, Stravinsky's transition to neo-classicism and Schoenberg's transition to free atonality are seen as analogous. Although the step taken by Stravinsky may not be understood as a consequence of the inner dynamic of composition, something that is in principle comparable did take place in both cases: the "transformation of the most specifically designed and applied means into, as it were, disqualified, neutral material, severed from the original meaning of its appearance".[38]
2 Adorno emphasized as a common factor in all Schoenberg's late 'secondary works' – possibly stemming from his earlier experience of orchestrating operettas – "a more conciliatory attitude towards the public". In dialectic terms: "Inexorable music represents social truth in opposition to society. Conciliatory music recognises the right to music which, in spite of everything, is still valid even in a false society – in the very same way that a false society reproduces itself and thus by virtue of its very survival objectively establishes elements of its own truth."[39] These two claims occasionally converged as a result of the growing irrelevance of the material: "even tonality bows to the demands of total construction, and for the late Schoenberg the musical material of composition had no significance

[37] Th. W. Adorno, *Philosophie der neuen Musik,* Frankfurt (Main), 1958, p. 115.

[38] Ibid. p.190.

[39] Ibid. p. 116.

any more. An artist, for whom the compositional procedure means everything — and the material, on the other hand, nothing — is able to make use of what has disappeared and what even the enchained consciousness of the consumer still has an ear for."[40] Adorno saw the late Schoenberg as thus denouncing the sole domination of material — in itself his own idea — thereby breaking with the classical bourgeois concept of the closed art-form.[41]

3 Since Adorno and Eisler view material and compositional procedures as increasingly separating, neither identifies the use of note rows with the idea of the planned disposition of compositional elements, even with regard to Schoenberg. That has frequently been done by subsequent interpreters. The idea of planned disposition also applies to other characteristics in the development of music in the early twentieth century, in the works of Ives, Stravinsky, Bartók, Satie and others, long before the introduction of dodecaphony. In addition to this it is a known fact that Schoenberg designated the use of note rows as only one of the possible principles for ordering the new, advanced material in a new way. Furthermore it should be remembered that by the early forties Adorno had already anticipated the emancipation of music even from the twelve-note technique if its 'hibernation' was to have the chance of new spontaneity in its critical listeners.[42]

Contradictions in Adorno's Thinking

The idea of the most advanced experience of composition, of the constructive use of the available means, is kept quite general by Adorno and Eisler, thus remaining relatively undefined and ambiguous. However: in the book *Composing for the Films* this idea is applied in a positive sense even to Eisler's *Septet No 1* (*Variations on American Children's Songs*), composed under the auspices of the research project for a film with the title *The Children's Camp*, in order to show "that even with the simplest of materials. . . . . it is possible using constructive procedures to make music in a manner that is differentiated, unconventional and free".[43] Adorno accepted this admittedly not most important of Eisler's

[40] Ibid. pp. 116–7.

[41] Ibid. p. 118.

[42] Ibid. p.110–11.

[43] Th. W. Adorno/H. Eisler, *Komposition für den Film*, op.cit. p. 163.

compositions, but also accepted his most advanced twelve-note compositions which also arose from the research project: the *Chamber Symphony* and the *Quintet* Op. 70 (*Fourteen Ways of Describing Rain*) — this latter dedicated to Schoenberg on his seventieth birthday. As far as Adorno was concerned, these works of Eisler's were more or less 'unpolitical'. He accepted them, even playing them to other people. Thus Brecht notes in his 'Working Diary' in April 1942: "Heard Eisler's record with Rain lyrics at Adorno's".[44] Even in the last edition of *Composing for the Films* with which he was associated, Adorno did not distance himself from these compositions.

What he could not accept were Eisler's 'political' works — regardless of the fact that the great songs and ballads, the choruses from the *Kampfmusik* period, the famous stage music for the *Die Massnahme* and *Die Mutter,* the many film scores and suites and the orchestral works, chamber cantatas and songs written in exile — the fact that all of these were largely composed in a much more differentiated manner (than the Septet already referred to), although differentiated and unconventional by use of the simplest of material and constructive procedures: thus the same musical-technical determinants apply which Adorno took as being valid in a non-political connection. This blatant contradiction in the logic of his argument is not to be ignored. It results from Adorno's social vision, restricted by political haptephobia (*'Berührungsangst'*), rejecting broadly acceptable generalizations.

This shows itself not only in his differing estimation of various, musically wholly comparable, works of Eisler's, but also in the fact that he recognized criteria establishing the value of the work of others but does not accept that the same qualities exist in Eisler's work, although they are equally well to be found there. In 1961 for example, Adorno spoke on Winfried Zillig's *Verlaine Songs.* In this lecture, what he sees as the positive features of the extended tonality (not twelve-note) of the songs, their "economy", "lightness", their self evident quality, the fact that "the sparsest of means" achieves "the most palpable effect", and finally that Zillig's music "owes its modern aspect to the most discriminating economy within the greatest of differentiation"[45] — all this could have been found on a musical-technical level in Eisler's political compositions too and has been similarly formulated by other writers. Adorno, on the other hand, was unable to accept these qualities

---

[44] B. Brecht, *Arbeitsjournal,* Vol. 1 1938–42, Frankfurt (Main), p.424.

[45] Th. W. Adorno, *Zilligs Verlaine Lieder,* in: *Moments Musicaux,* Frankfurt (Main), 1964, pp. 143, 146.

positively, simply because of his and Eisler's political differences. He ignored them and even resisted them, that is to say, judging them negatively — as remnants, questionable stop-gaps, leftovers etc. He simply allowed this contradiction in his thinking and in his evaluation of music to stand, making barely an effort towards dialectical mediation, which, on the grounds of his premises, could not be resolved.

Eisler's reaction to the independence of material and its working methods

It has already been indicated in remarks on Eisler's compositional practice after the late twenties — particularly since the period in exile — where the simplest and most differentiated of means co-exist, that these remarks refer largely to a much broader reality and experience of music, including that of Eisler himself. Since the late twenties and the transition of music also to the position of the revolutionary proletariat, Eisler's music was an original attempt to take progressively further the existing "revolution in material" by overcoming bourgeois restrictions in the emergent, historically new, quality of music as an institution. Eisler reacted to the new autonomy of the arts and their application to other media from a socialist standpoint. This included, in his work on music theory, close collaboration with Brecht, as is clearly to be seen for example in Eisler's writings on the changed social function of music.[46] Equally, however, it included the dispute with conservative positions within the Marxist movement. This is clear from the controversy with Lukács.[47]

Thus Eisler's view of material and procedures leads him to the following conclusions: with the orientation towards progressive mass-experience from the position of a revolutionary sense of the future, new semantic-pragmatic qualities, new modes of expression and social gesture come into musical material. These are intrinsically self-contradictory expressive features which stem from a dialectical relationship with the dialectic of reality, going beyond the expression of misery and suffering as bourgeois musicians experienced and expressed it;

[46] H. Eisler, *Musik und Politik,* op.cit. p.370ff.

[47] See E. Bloch/H. Eisler, *Avantgarde-Kunst und Volksfront* and *Die Kunst zu erben,* in: *H. Eisler, Musik und Politik* op.cit. p.397ff; also G. Mayer/G. Knepler, *Hätten sich Georg Lukács und Hanns Eisler in der Mitte des Tunnels getroffen? Zur Polemik zwischen gegensätzlich Gleichgesinnten,* in: *Dialog und Kontroverse mit Georg Lukács,* Leipzig, 1975, pp.358–95. [See also Betz (1982), p. 160 ff. Ed.]

productive dissatisfaction, critical affirmation, passionate sobriety, controlled enthusiasm, illusion-free optimism — clearly defined and critically directed toward out-dated aesthetic experience: sentimentality, hysteria, tearfulness, false naivety, gullible excess, blind spontaneity, dishonest communal spirit, self-satisfaction etc. The contrast between opposing characteristics is achieved above all in the vocal, stage and film-music by the juxtaposition of action and reflection, the use of montage, alienation, commentary by means of a counterpoint of different media — all these are new elements in the process of planning a work, in the constructive use of the means.

For Eisler this implied the development of material with a new and original simplicity both for those with little experience in music and for the specialist. What has been discovered here cannot be adequately comprehended by bourgeois notions of accessibility or by "conciliation towards the public". Because Eisler had a socially based motive for a new simplicity and because he had such supreme control of the most complicated aspects of composition, he was able to be original with the simplest of means. Eisler quite rightly criticised as a metaphysical belief the idea that only the most complicated aspects could lay claim to providing an historically authentic aesthetic experience.[48] Given the divergence of material and procedures, the refraction and renewal both of old and new, in fact of largely used-up material, Eisler put the emphasis on different areas of musical practice that had an effect on the masses: international workers' fighting songs, active forms of the agitprop movement and jazz. And, in addition to this, Eisler's position with regard to the new relationship between material and procedures is characterized by his attempt at a dialectical synthesis. After the temporary holding back of complexity at the end of the twenties and in the early thirties, his compositional practice is characterized by the parallel existence of the simplest and the most complex and its differentiated, unconventional treatment within one work. Brecht referred to this as "breadth and multiplicity of a realistic style of writing." Lastly, let it simply be noted in passing that in his twelve-note compositions Eisler was composing fully aware of the 'apories' of twelve-note technique, having already observed them before Adorno. So he had drawn logical conclusions in his choice of form, preferring 'open', 'continuing' forms for developing variations.

---

[48] See H. Eisler, *Inhalt und Form* in: *Materialien zu einer Dialektik der Musik,* Leipzig, 1973, p.300ff. Also in *Schriften* 1948–62 p.501ff.

Eisler's concept of 'angewandte Musik'

All this can, however, in my opinion, only be assessed adequately within the larger context of Eisler's concept of 'applied music' as the progressive alternative to the bourgeois institution of the concert, which had hitherto been supreme but which was now experiencing a crisis. Eisler's approach to material and procedures is broadly determined by this concept of 'applied music', at least during the larger historical space of a 'period of transition'. It affected his relationship with musical genres, his attitude towards the existing and new ways of organizing the communication of music, his search for what was new in composition, interpretation and reception.

In his concept of 'applied music', Eisler was concerned with a broad alternative to the crisis in bourgeois musical culture and to the capitalist organization of mass communication. Through 'applied music', the increasing isolation and emptiness of bourgeois concert music — in itself ever more incomprehensible to the masses — was to be broken down and something new was to counter the increasingly mass-effective clichés of bourgeois entertainment music. The aim was therefore to narrow the gap between new music and progressive mass-experience. Eisler was trying to solve the perceived basic problem of a new musical culture and a new musical style by centring it on the situation and the historical perspective of the class which is most closely associated with the modern means of production, with mass production, mass political action and mass communication, that class which replaces bourgeois life forms with new forms of living and which needs a new artistic practice and theory. This is at the very heart of the concept of 'applied music'. Hanns Eisler was articulating in the sphere of music the experience of the shattering of the traditional concept of art similar to that of Arvatov at the beginning of the twenties in the Soviet Union in the programme for 'Production-Art' — experience similar to that of Brecht in the late twenties and early thirties in his *Radio Theory* and his *Threepenny Lawsuit* and similar to that of Benjamin not much later, in his works *The Author as Producer* and *The Work of Art in the Age of Technical Reproduction*.[49] All these views stemmed from the lives and struggles of the working masses seen from the standpoint of Communism.

---

[49] See B. Arvatov. *Kunst und Produktion*, Munich, 1972; B. Brecht, *Schriften zur Literatur und Kunst*, Berlin/Weimar, 1966, pp.127–47; W. Benjamin, *Lesezeichen*, Leipzig, 1970, pp.351–414.

In the same way as the above authors, Eisler also focused his observations on the quantitive and qualitative changes in the processes of art within the general context of historical development. He concluded that instrumental music and the concert as the preferred genre and dominant organizational form of bourgeois musical life had to be understood as historical phenomena, with the result also that the prevailing values in that area could only be taken on an historical level. This meant for him, in the light of reality and particularly in the light of the recent political success of mass movements in the Soviet Union, that concert music was losing its importance, while the area of music involving practical, objective activity, that is music in conjunction with words and images, was experiencing a new blossoming and would gain superiority — at least during a period of transition. It is therefore not simply chance, that instead of the traditional forms of instrumental music, Eisler clearly preferred other more highly developed or innovative forms and those which were linked to other media. He composed music for almost forty plays, over forty films and wrote hundreds of songs. The reason was obvious. A revolutionary-orientated music which was to be at the same time modern and effective for the masses could not possibly have been achieved on the road of bourgeois concert practice or reformistic or classically-orientated socialist educational programmes and by so doing arrive at a high-art music. It seemed to Eisler that the best means of creating a qualitatively new musical culture was by a joining together of the historical achievements of bourgeois concert music — which he, as a pupil of Schoenberg, could handle with ease — with the new possibilities of the means of mass communication in the production, exchange, dissemination and reception of the arts.

It was Eisler's opinion that the favoured link between music and a text and stage action made possible a new clarity and simplicity, enabling the broad masses of musically inexperienced listeners — who were in fact crucial in the musical culture of the emergent working classes — to grasp more easily the sense of even complex, unfamiliar modern music. In this context the ubiquitous clichés of bourgeois entertainment music and worn-out musical turns of phrase could, with the developed compositional technique, be 'broken', giving them a new sense and with that a new usefulness. This means: the concert style would be 'applied' in order to put backbone into hitherto ambiguous music by linking it to subject matter of socio-historic significance, which would mean something to the masses of the workers and peasants. In this way music was to raise itself all the more easily from the private to the general, from differentiated bourgeois individualism to the individually differentiating, history-making collective of revolutionary world change, thereby drawing into itself all the arts of that craft.

This concept was no sectarian rejection of concert music forms. In fact the concrete intention was to establish the independence of music in the 'applied' genres as equal to poetry, the theatre and film, composing as far as possible so that music, without being connected with any stage action, could in its own way also gain access to the changed concert hall. This is how most of Eisler's instrumental works came into being. And that meant finding new ways to bring to the listeners new synthesised forms of change and the transformation of the traditional concert hall and concert-giving through the collective working together of revolutionary artists from different media, (resulting in choral montage, didactic pieces) — change too in traditional concert practice which would make evident "by the radicalisation of their political and musical contents the contradiction between the revolutionary intent and the concert form".[50] The concept of 'applied music' is therefore central to Eisler's thinking. It is a revolutionary political and aesthetic alternative to the *petit-bourgeois* concept of 'functional music' and 'music for fun' (*'Spielmusik'*), according to which the crisis in concert music was to be overcome by compositions specifically intended for use on all sorts of practical occasions — with the exception of progressive political ones — or by a playfulness pretending to optimism and a cosy sense of community. Eisler's concept of 'applied music' is also a revolutionary political and aesthetic alternative to the *petit-bourgeois* concept of the 'folk music movement', which transferred the concert into schools and class singing lessons with the conservative aim of using amateur music-making to rescue bourgeois music-culture by means of an escape into Nature and the past.

Divergence: late points of contact

Adorno was unable to understand or accept Eisler's theory and practice in this matter, opposed as it was in principle to his own concept. To the extent that, especially since the forties, he saw the working classes and socialism integrated into an administered world of inescapable, total alienation, blindly and inexorably bent on its own destruction, Adorno could only adopt an attitude of rejection and scorn towards socialism (in all its contradictions) and art with socialist aims. Even more than at the beginning of the thirties, he reacted without adhering to any particular

[50] H. Eisler, *Geschichte der deutschen Arbeiterbewegung von 1848* in: *Musik und Politik,* op.cit. 1924–1948 p.223.

standards. This is especially clear in Adorno's most emotional essay, *Die gegängelte Musik* ('coerced music'(?)) — in which he indirectly polemicises against Eisler.[51] In this essay he refers to the manifesto of the Second International Congress of Composers and Music Critics which had taken place in Prague in May 1948. Eisler had delivered a lecture there — immediately after his return from the United States — with the title 'The Basic Social Questions of Modern Music', which, with regard to its general analysis of modern music and the position of Schoenberg, had certain parallels with Adorno's *Philosophy of Modern Music* which appeared one year later.[52] The text of the manifesto so sharply criticised by Adorno was largely Eisler's work.[53] It was an attempt at productive criticism of the misapprehensions of the understanding and politics of music linked with the name Zhdanov, in which generally correct demands had been turned into the opposite by the wrong people using the wrong arguments and which, in addition, were forcefully put into effect.[54] Neither the overall problematic situation nor Eisler's tactical reaction can be analysed here. However, it is quite clear that Adorno, who was otherwise so concerned with exactness, attacks in *Die gegängelte Musik* a banally emotive image of horror instead of tackling the heart of the actual, complicated process. Wholly uncritically, he uses the vocabulary of the cold warriors. Whether or not he knew is uncertain, but his opponent was Hanns Eisler.

Adorno's conception of art

For Adorno the painful and despairing experience of subjective powerlessness had become the norm which made questionable any practice aimed at change. His overall perspective, consisting of stock phrases from marxist theory and terminology, is only conceivable for him as a chiliastic dream of 'reconciliation', a picture of the future that is so far from and so utterly opposed to the 'existing', that, measured against this,

[51] Th. W. Adorno, *Die gegängelte Musik* in: *Dissonanzen*, Göttingen, pp.156, 46–61.

[52] H. Eisler, *Gesellschaftliche Grundfragen der modernen Musik* in: Materialien zu einer Dialektik der Musik, op.cit. pp.181–194. See also *Schriften* 1948–62 p.13 ff. [Translated in *Hanns Eisler A Rebel in Music*]

[53] See A. Bush: "It will not be generally known that the draft of the statement which was accepted with only minor changes by congress was largely his work", in: *Sinn und Form, Sonderheft Hanns Eisler* 1964, Berlin, p.332.

[54] See also B. Brecht, *Schriften zur Literatur und Kunst*, op.cit.p.334.

any action is simply confirmation, indeed confirmation of the wrong set of conditions. And from the standpoint of a perspective of this sort, Adorno's basically idealistic concept of dialectic becomes visible. He sees it as "the ontology of false conditions". The right, preferable conditions would be free from dialectic, "neither system nor contradiction".[55] This is the old hope of the dreamed-of 'reconciliation', the longing for a lost paradise as an abstract measure for the future.

In this general context of an ideology of pessimistic resignation, autonomous art acquires the status of a — non-achievable — social alternative to society. Art, from Adorno's point of view, can only be viewed as a hermetic area of lonely reflection with a tendency to fall silent — which is without doubt only one aspect of the developments in late bourgeois art. Thus Adorno logically takes Beckett's "childlike, blood-covered, clown grimaces" for historical truth, seeing socialist realism as "childish".[56] In the late Adorno's *Aesthetic Theory*, it scarcely makes sense therefore to think in terms of dialectical representation ('*Abbildbeziehung*') and the question of realistic art is simply taboo — while what constitutes historical truth is already laid down as an immutable scheme and set of value judgements. Whoever assumes that there are no such things, at least not any more, as productive revolutionary forces or a working class, with the result that it is not possible to focus on a revolutionary subject, cannot accept the historical laws of social development and at best retains historical possibility simply as a vague picture of the future. In addition — and this is very clear in Adorno's case, — the idea of the subject is reduced, in the context of this critical theory, to that of the overwhelmed, integrated individual as victim and object. In Adorno's case this is then at the same time exaggerated into the opposite position, to that of the subject as human being trying through self-reflection to escape the universal constraint of alienation. According to Adorno, society receives the work of art through the mediation of experience which has through time become part of the material — but this is largely unconscious and indirect, rooted utterly within reality. He sets up his understanding of art as a psychogram, as a social symptom of the individual's lonely oblivion against the programme for art of Brecht, Eisler and others which, with an "art in the scientific age" was to make sense of the social context and to show it as open to change.[57] This all led to his

---

[55] Th. W. Adorno, *Negative Dialektik*, Frankfurt (Main), 1966, p.20.

[56] Th. W. Adorno, *Ästhetische Theorie*, Frankfurt (Main), 1970, p.370.

[57] Ibid. p.15.

extreme, psychoanalytical concentration on the individual subject. For Adorno the permanent truth of art is the fetishised history of the suffering of oppressed subjectivity: the active side disappears almost entirely. What is left of it is the productive construction of the individual oeuvre which reacts negatively towards society — the absolute negative — and was driven to a loss of function and communication. For Adorno mass-communication is the wholesale deception of the masses with no viable alternative.

In this sense Adorno's aesthetic is, despite its orientation towards the "fictitious totality" (*"unwahre Ganze"*), less a theoretical analysis of the historical process of art from the point of view of history and systems, than a philosophical consideration of "authentic" art "as the substance of personal experience".[58] It is, as Wolfgang Heise has said,[59] even in its negative way, the last remnant of a traditional aesthetic — indebted to Hegel and Kant. Even when analysing monopoly capitalism it is still using a system of values originally established on a pre-industrial basis, whose basic conservatism halts all dialectic. Adorno formulates this in these terms: "In an age where traditional aesthetics and contemporary art cannot be reconciled, the philosophical theory of art has no choice other than . . . . to think of disappearing categories as transitional in the certainty of their negation."[60]

The direction taken by this transition remains open for Adorno, as does the fate of the arts themselves. His attitude is one of scepticism and resignation.

Eisler on Adorno: a negative judgement

Eisler's programme for art is on the other hand open to the future, part of the revolutionary programme of action, in which the new, huge change in the function of art is seen as necessary. To move on, beyond positions viable for a given period in history, is a matter of course. This can be seen in Eisler's late conversations with Hans Bunge.[61] His programmatic statements are not without inconsistencies and contradictions. Particularly in the last period, there are contradictions in his

---

[58] Ibid. p.182.

[59] W. Heise, *Annotation zu Th. W. Adorno, Ästhetische Theorie,* in: *Referatedienst,* Berlin 1/72, p.99.

[60] Th. W. Adorno, *Ästhetische Theorie,* op.cit. p.507.

[61] H. Eisler, *Gespräche mit Hans Bunge,* op.cit. p.234ff.

theoretical statements and his own compositional practice. These cannot be analysed here. However, these failings are different from those of Adorno's and convey more productive ideas than they — although Adorno's intellectual legacy, which was "to face the disconcerted without fear and without making allowances" should not be ignored. His extreme sensitivity brings to light, particularly in aesthetic matters, much which a revolutionary self-assurance might overlook.

Despite their basic differences, Eisler respected Adorno as a significant thinker. In his *Notes on a Dialectic of Music* of 1956, he remarks that with Adorno one "never really knows what he wants", that in his case "great talent and mental demands turn into a form of cunning which is as finely crafted as a piece of fretwork".[62] Some of Eisler's later statements about Adorno are blinkered, as for example in 1958 when he holds against him a view of the development of music which he considered to be abstract and disconnected from social reality and emphasises that this is in some way bound up in social relationships.[63] Adorno had in fact never denied this. He simply had a different conception of society.

Eisler's overall judgement of Adorno and the *'Frankfurturisten'*, which he made in 1958 to Hans Bunge, goes even without detailed philosophical and theoretical analysis to the heart of the matter: they — the *'Frankfurturisten'* — view "with a kind of semi-marxism, all tendencies towards dissolution" as progressive. "But one cannot define the march towards the abyss as progress" and "these Frankfurturists, as Brecht called them, take up no real fighting stance against bourgeois society. One simply cannot be a marxist without politics. This is one of the essential experiences which everyone today must actually think through. As far as I still read the writings of the Frankfurturists today, they suffer from one basic ill: they want simply to be cleverer than the bourgeois theorists — but they do not want to fight them. Thus they become the star pupils of decline."[64]

Translated by Fiona Elliott

Given as a paper at the Adorno Symposium in Graz in 1977, published by the *Institut für Wertungsforschung* at the *Hochschule für Musik und darstellende Kunst* in Graz. Vol. 12, Graz, 1979.
Foreword 1992

---

[62] Quoted by M. Grabs, Preface to *Materialien zu einer Dialektik der Musik*, op.cit. p.17.

[63] H. Eisler, *Gespräche mit Hans Bunge*, op.cit. p.28.

[64] Ibid. p.40.

10

EISLER'S 'AN DIE NACHGEBOREN': ANOTHER CONCRETE UTOPIA

János Maróthy and Márta Batári

Ernst Bloch's concept of a 'concrete Utopia' was first applied to music by Jürg Stenzl[1] to characterize Nono's rainbows of soft and high-floating sounds as opposed to the acoustic aspects of rude reality. Such a sensing of the world may arise from the sharp contradictions of twentieth century movements of emancipation, especially when their temporary defeats inspire reflections to a point where the rest is silence (*Fragmente-Stille*) — a rich silence, though, containing even in this extremely reduced form the promises of a *condition humaine.*

Looking back now from such a point, not in anger but in deep understanding, its precedents appear in a new light. One of them is *An die Nachgeborenen,* written by both Brecht and Eisler in exile. The importance of its idea for the authors is shown by the number of variants of the poem and its musical settings.

If 'classical music' may transgress different musical space-time systems in such a way that it still continues to move in a single system, the opposite is equally possible. One may start from a point where there is no fixed musical space-time system at all; where one floats in music as well as in actual life, in an indeterminate space of the universe not to be defined by reassuring co-ordinate systems. Then, at best, the outlines of a system gradually being fixed are born *during* the piece. While the classical version gets into relation with coordinate systems c^1, c^2, etc. from among the fixed coordinates of a given C system in a way that the former are incessantly being reintegrated into the latter, simultaneously making the *outer* world *interpretable* and the *inner* world *enrichable,* the other way round we start from the state of a maximal incertitude and dissolution towards the creation of possible systems.

---

[1] Jürg Stenzl: *Luigi Nono und Cesare Pavese.* In: *Luigi Nono. Texte – Studien zu seiner Musik.* Ed. Jürg Stenzl. Zürich-Freiburg i. Br. /Atlantis/1975, pp. 409–433.

The latter version, as a matter of course, becomes typical on the ground of alienated twentieth century life-experience. *Dodecaphony* itself, namely the emancipated twelve notes of the tempered system without their inner relations, negates the musical space-time systems brought about up to then in the dimensions of tonality, genre, structure and even rhythm. There is no above and below, no key note and moving away, no 'pillar' and 'non-pillar', no A, then B and A again, no 2/4 and 6/8. This is precisely why the outer organizing force of dodecaphonic construction is needed.

Hanns Eisler's piece composed in 1937 to Brecht's poem *An die Nachgeborenen* (To Those Born Later),[1] seems to be such a twelve-note music. We quote it here as printed in Eisler's *Gesammelte Werke* Serie I, Band 16. Ex. 10.1

Ex. 10.1

[1] Svendborgergedichte. Brecht Gesammelte Gedichte Band 2, p. 724 Suhrkamp Verlag

fin-ste-ren Zeit, der ihr ent-ronnen seid.
Gingen wir doch, öf-ters als die
Schu-he die Län-der wechselnd, durch die Klassen-krie-ge, ver-zweifelt, wenn da nur Unrecht war und
nicht eilen
kei-ne Empörung.
Da-bei wußten wir doch: Auch der
etwas Zeit lassen, ruhig
Haß ge-gen die Niedrigkeit verzerrt die Zü-ge, auch der Zorn ge-gen das Unrecht macht die Stimme

Ex. 10.1 (cont'd)

vorwärts gehen, Tempo I

hei - ser. Wir, die den Bo - den be - rei - ten— woll - ten für Freundlichkeit, wir

konn - ten sel - ber nicht freundlich sein. Ihr aber, wenn

es soweit ist, daß der Mensch dem Menschen kein Wolf mehr ist, gedenket unser mit Nachsicht.

Ex. 10.1 (cont'd)

At first hearing, this floating music is hard to perceive as a movement in mutually related living musical systems. What is its basic rhythmic pattern? Where is the tonic? What is a new section and what is reprise?

Enter the musicologist to show that the piece has been structured according to the procedures of twelve-note technique, that is, its 'system' is in fact not musical but speculative. It has a basic series determining the order of the twelve notes, equal in rank, as follows: Ex. 10.2

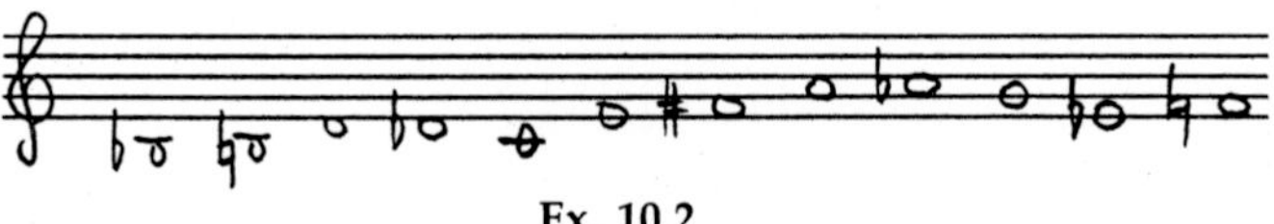

Ex. 10.2

By mere deduction, we can produce the inversion (I), retrograde (R) and retrograde inversion (RI) of this series: Ex. 10.3

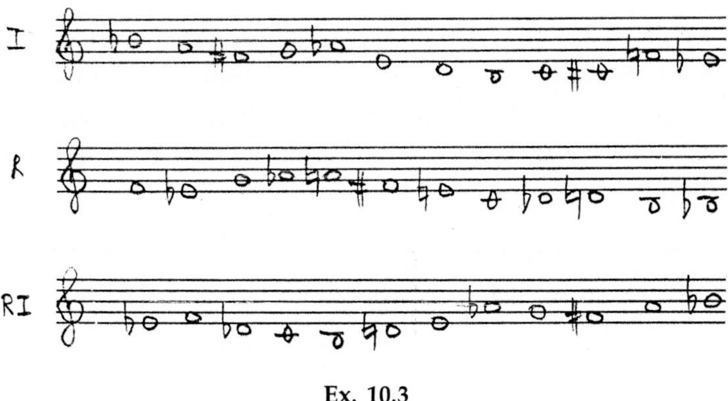

Ex. 10.3

Thus, if we examine the events occurring in Eisler's piece from the entrance of the vocal part on, the first four bars of the vocal part present the basic series and the piano bass, canon-like after half a bar, the I. The upper parts in the piano produce fragments of the basic series in unison with, or imitating, the vocal part. In bars 10-15, the vocal part repeats the basic series firstly an octave higher, then from the middle at the original pitch; the upper piano parts do the same with divided roles while the bass is already presenting the R. The RI makes its first appearance distributed in the middle parts of the piano interlude in bar 14. From bar 16, for three bars, the vocal part produces again the I, then the RI in such a way that its last two notes are cut off while a smaller fragment of it is repeated.

Here, the musicologist becomes more and more hesitant even though he takes account of the fact that the repetition of individual notes or groups of notes before continuing the series belongs to the variation possibilities of a twelve-note row, not to speak of the still more acceptable freedom of transposing the series as a whole or even one note of it (as, for example, the A flat following the E of the RI in bar 19) an octave higher or lower, thus transforming ups into downs and vice versa. At all events, Eisler avails himself of such possibilities in bars 18–21 so frequently that he almost explodes the discipline of serial method, crossing over into the motivic-repetitive-character variational space-time system of traditional music. The repeated A flat – G – E flat – F succession of the upper piano part in bars 17-20 forms an ostinato pattern of the last four notes of the basic series; the B – E – F sharp –

A passage in the upper part of the left hand is simultaneously doing the same with notes 2 6 7 8, and the D – D flat – C progression of the lower part of the right hand with only three notes, 3 4 5, of the same, while the bass sustains its first note alone as a pedal point. It is as if the continuous progress of the row, constantly developing and changing up to now, were suddenly benumbed, freezing into a motionless picture, where the individual parts are each repeating — grinding out a fragment of the basic series. Thus, the twelve-note succession is accomplished like a mosaic only:

right hand upper part:									9	10	11	12
right hand lower part:			3	4	5							
left hand upper part:		2				6	7	8				
left hand lower part:	1											

In Eisler's montage, this benumbed section is followed by a veritable explosion in the piano interlude of bars 20–21: the anapaestic rhythms bang out a furious march during a bar and a half as if they wanted irrevocably to burst the predestination of the twelve-note series. Yet, this episode itself, having started with the last notes of the previous vocal part (notes 6–10 of the RI), where the anapaests also first appeared, now to develop into a march-revolt, results in nothing but the restitution of the row. The upper part of the piano, in spite of its protests, obligingly completes the RI with the still missing notes 11 12 and, in its powerless anger with this, repeats again notes 8–10 (A flat – G – F sharp) of the RI. Meanwhile, the other parts are using chordally, march-like, the fragments or individual notes of the the series and its inversions.

So, the dramatic outburst is tamed back into the dodecaphonic order of the row. Above a sustained four-note chord in the piano, which consists, in an acquiescent manner, of the first four notes of the basic series, the vocal part obediently sings through the I, then the first five notes of the R (bars 22–26), then again the I from note 4 to the end and once more notes 1–5 of the R, with the overlap again. The listener may be surprised how the different fragments of the series and its inversions can now be transformed into the sustained serene harmonies of the piano, in contrast to the previous enraged march music.

What happens now, from bar 29, is a double consolidation. On the one hand, the serial principle is restored, so we have definitely submitted ourselves to the dodecaphonic space-time system. On the other hand, this victory of the row simultaneously represents, in terms of traditional musical morphology, a *reprise* — so that what has happened up to now is interpreted as an ABA form. Is this then a *joint* victory of two *opposing* musical space-time systems? On top of all this, the closing section from the end of bar 35 is nothing but a worded-vocalized version of the piano introduction commencing the piece. So the work as a whole assumes a palindromic form, with a mirror-like reversion of the events as if, after all the dramatic developments and in spite of all the struggling, the film were now turned backwards and so the end, led back to the beginning, would place us into an eternal circular orbit.

This pre- and postlude is already a germ of all later developments — a germ indeed, as the complete series is heard by the middle of the first bar, in the space of six quavers lasting about two seconds! The progression B – C sharp – C – E – A flat – G in the upper piano part contains notes 2 4 5 6 9 10 and the three chords of the left hand (B flat – D; F sharp – A; F – E flat) notes 1 3 7 8 11 12 of the basic series. This is immediately followed by the R, notes 1 2 of which are already provided by the F – E flat chord sustained in the left hand and note 3 by the right hand. The remaining notes continue in the right hand, with the exception of 7 and 10, which appear as an inner part. At this point, we come to a stammering repetition, which anticipates the dramatic climax of bars 19–21 and thus, the development of the piece as a whole. From the middle of bar 2, the first six notes of the I are heard in the right hand: B flat – A – F sharp – G and left hand: G sharp – E, that is, 1–4 and 5 6 respectively, but then we become entangled in note repetitions, first presenting the second half of the I: right hand B – C – E flat, that is, 8 9 12 and left hand D flat – F, that is, 10 11, then again circling like in an R of the R, thus anticipating this time the palindromic principle of the whole piece. This circling involves notes 11 10 8 counted from the rear of the R, that is notes 2 3 5 of the basic series B – D – C; meanwhile the bass firmly sustains the central note E (6 in the basic series and I; 7 in R and RI) and the upper part of the left hand sadly descends with the chromatic progression A flat (= G sharp) – G – F sharp of notes 8 9 10 of RI. Here, once again, we step over into the traditional space-time system with the falling major sixths B - D, B – D suggesting idyllic *Alphorn* calls, repeated first imploringly, then sternly, while the low A of the bass informs us of our duty at last to begin, and in an orderly way, with the B flat of the basic row. In the RI, this same note should be the ending, so the 'morning hooter' of A in the bass (11 of RI) prepares, like a dominant or leading note, for the expected B flat beginning of the basic series. (This, in fact, has not happened so far. The prelude began with B and the B flat appeared only after a hesitant quaver rest in the accompaniment).

Thus it is clear that the prelude, lasting only a few seconds, condenses the whole process of the piece not only as regards the repeated exposition of the row in all its versions but also its dramaturgy. A dramatic, almost stutteringly human exploding of the row is followed by a renewed vindication of the row's regime and a link-back with the beginning, producing a circular film with its mechanical *retour éternel*.

Similar processes take place, at a still more fundamental level, in the basic series itself. The complaining chromatics of notes 1–5 are followed by the outburst of 6-8 and then by the severity of the closing A flat – G – E flat – F, which can well be viewed as a traditional diatonic-modal cadence. This three-part shape in itself simultaneously contains three inertia systems, the order and the role of which can variously interchange by means of the inversions, partial or complete transpositions and fragmentations.

We have seen how dodecaphony, traditional form and seemingly free declamation are also constantly intercrossing in the macrostructure of the piece. In this sense, traditional music is represented not by the ABA structure alone but also by the fact that the piece is simultaneously a serial variation and a *character* variation. Thus, the series is at the same time a *subject* assuming now the character of a lament, then that of dramatic declamation, now that of a march, then that of a hymn.

In such a way, the serial principle itself attains a deep aesthetic significance. The constant presence and incessant return of notes, note relations, note progressions which arise from serial principles become an *immutable rotation*, where even a quitting is a recurrence, as existing human relationships have not yet produced the possibility of diverting it from its rails. The even quavers themselves, variously configured into bars of different sizes, produce the feeling that whatever shape these occasional associations may assume, there is nothing permanent but the raindrop-like knocking of the separate quavers. Quitting this mechanism is only possible, in the given historic moment, at the level of Utopia, by dreaming up another system of relationships, while the gloomy final A in the bass repeatedly makes us aware of the fact that, *in the existing system*, nothing but a re-rotation of the same series can follow.

Brecht's poem similarly unites the Utopia of a future with the experience of the compulsory course of the present. The Utopia is represented by his imaginary stance of contemplating his given possibilities from the angle of a happy new mankind and so what he himself can do seems still more miserable.

Here is a translation:

You who will emerge from the flood,
In which we have gone under,
Remember, when you speak of our failings,
The dark time too which you have escaped.
For we went, changing countries oftener than our shoes,
through the wars of the classes
despairing when there was only injustice and no revolt.
Yet, we knew:
Even hatred of meanness distorts the features,
Even anger against injustice makes the voice hoarse.
Oh, we who wanted to prepare the ground for friendliness
Could not ourselves be friendly.
But you, when the time comes at last
That man is a helper to man,
Think of us with forbearance.

[Trans. Ed.]

Formally, the verse moves in the metrical uncertainty of prose, where from time to time emerge, like a variety of 'perhaps', trochaic, dactylic, anapaestic and iambic patterns. At some moments, they assume a more defined verse scheme, say, a regular iambic decasyllable:

gedenkt, wenn ihr von unsern Schwächen sprecht

or an Alexandrine, the caesura of which is reinforced by an interior rhyme:

auch der finsteren Z e i t
der ihr entronnen s e i d.

Anapaestic intonations with their march-like gestures appear at the words about injustice and the lack of revolt, as if they metrically realised a semantically absent rebellion. Phonologically, however, this leads not to 'friendliness' but to still harder and harsher developments at the words about the distorting effect of even the noblest kind of fight. Phonemes like *ts*, spitting with hate, a cracking *r*, a hoarsely rattling *h* are accumulated:

Auch der Haß gegen die Niedrigkeit
verzerrt die Züge,
auch der Zorn gegen das Unrecht
macht die Stimme heiser.

Otherwise it is a palindrome, in which the dominance of *h* in the outer verses embraces the dominance of *ts* and *r* in the inner ones (*z* is pronounced as *ts* in German).

Towards the end, the shortening of verses produces a *morendo* of disappearing and submerging. The metrical accents clearly hint at a separation, a fragmentation of speech units:

Ihr aber,
wenn es so weit i s t,
daß der Mensch dem Menschen kein Wolf mehr i s t,
gedenket unser
mit Nach s i c h t.

This is a palindrome again. Gradually it expands to the middle, where the longest line presents, through the rhyme *ist*, a twofold doubling of the preceding verse – also because the number of syllables is exactly doubled. But then the two concluding verses decrease again in precisely the same measure as verses 1–2 were growing. The succession, counted in syllables, is as follows: 3 5 10 5 3.

Thus, the channels of versification and phonology interpret the message of the semantic channel in a similar way as was observed in the succession of musical events. Concrete figures emerge "on the waves of the flood" only like uncertain fragments. The process is still condensing; it leads to hard collisions, as if to a negative climax when the *equally dehumanizing* effect of the lack of revolt and of the possible form of revolt is at issue. And all is finished by a disappearance when the light of Utopian hope goes out.

Eisler's music not only realizes the *movimento* of the verse in its own medium but it also extends it to new dimensions and even counterpoints it. The principle of "always the same is haunting" arising from serial procedures, the succession of character variations meaning "in a different way but always the same", finally the thesis "beginning and end are the same" accentuate in every way the determination of prescribed compulsory trajectories as against any possible Utopian vision. All this is rhythmically reinforced by the constant raindrops of quavers, which form merely temporary configurations and the passing of time becomes abstract now and again. (A 'pendulum-clock of time', as Sabinina has characterized the last moments of Shostakovich's Fourth Symphony.)[2]

---

[2] Marina D. Sabinina. Soviet musicologist, born 1917. 'The symphonies of Dimitri Shostakovich' Moscow 1965.

Yet, another solution of Eisler's, a direct counterpoint to Brecht's verse, strengthens the aspect of a positive vision. The negative drama of the poem reaches its climax in the section beginning with *Auch der Haß...* In a strange way, Brecht's hoarse *h*-s, spitting *ts*-s, rattling *r*-s are coupled with an almost hymnic-harmonic rainbow in Eisler's music. In contrast to the harshness of bars 20–21, by bars 24–29 a process is completed, the broad sustained rhythmic values and harmonically combined serial pitches of which, connected with the regularity of six bars of 3/4 (the 'friendliness' of a slow waltz as it were), anticipate the *Freundlichkeit* mentioned by Brecht only in the subsequent section and, even there, as something unrealizable. The most interesting moment is that the almost pure harmony of E major, (coloured only by a minor seventh) being at the same time the counterpole of a tritone to the initial B flat and the middle axis of the series, appearing this time in the middle of the piece as a whole, is coupled with Brecht's most negative words: *Haß* and *Zorn* — hatred and anger!

In this way, Eisler applies the principle of a double climax: the scattered-furious negative climax of bars 18–20, immediately *preceding* the middle of the piece, and the harmonic-hymnic positive climax of bars 24–27 immediately *following* it, both reach E, the highest note in the piece. Thus, the charge - discharge process produces, in this double centre, a strange explosion, as if a rain of flowers were suddenly bursting out of gun barrels — a genuine counterpoint to the words and also to the previous music.

This, too, has been anticipated in its germ by the six bars of the prelude with the pure E major chord appearing in its third bar, that is, in its middle; and it had already been contained by the series itself, also arriving in the middle at E, the antipode of the initial B flat. The effect is heightened by the fact that this *farthest possible* point is reached *upwards* in the circle of fifths.

So this piece ranges over vast areas of the rich disorder of life, moving in many space-time systems of music history and genres. Yet, disorder is made order again and the different space-time systems are brought into mutual relation also by the fact that the whole piece, from the smallest units to the largest ones, is organized by the rhythm of a common pulsation. This "gives a rhythm to the antagonisms" and thus makes it possible to experience, in one continuous act of sensing, what could conceptually be perceived in a fragmented way only: "The World as a Whole".

This is how totality (in Lukács's sense) could be regained through its destruction — if not in life and not in political theory, yet in a world of art.

Translation by the authors

11

ARNOLD SCHOENBERG

Hanns Eisler

I do not need the Chinese proverb, 'someone who does not honour his teacher is worse than a dog', to affirm here that Schoenberg was one of the greatest composers, and not merely of the twentieth century. His mastery and originality are astonishing, his influence was and is enormous. His weaknesses are dearer to me than the virtues of many other people. One cannot conceive of the history of music without him. Decline and fall of the bourgeoisie: certainly. But what a sunset!

It should not suffice for us merely to pursue the sociology of music; it must also be expanded, through the application of the materialistic dialectic, to the inconsistent development of the musical material as well. If we do not wish to fall into a shallow, vulgarly materialistic sociologizing, we should examine the emergence and dying away, the exhaustion and renewal of musical material in the socially conditioned musical styles with their changing functions, in a 'dialectic of music'. I say this, because in the little that I have to report about Schoenberg, particular consideration will be given to this method of handling material, his characteristic compositional technique.

If in the course of this I often separate form and content for the purpose of analysis, I am only taking my cue from the peculiar quality of Schoenberg's music, in which form and content often stand in sharp contradiction to one another. To select one example of such a contradiction: in his opera *Von heute auf Morgen*, the subject, the treatment and the language correspond, approximately, to those of a mundane operetta, and a bad one at that. To accompany these banalities, Schoenberg wrote — this is one of his twelve-note works — a highly disturbing music, which suspends the fun of the operetta, makes the banality of the text ambiguous and places the whole thing in a curious light. The people in this opera who act, drink coffee and finally restore order to a tedious conflict with a tenor like a caretaker, appear through the music like the future occupants of the air-raid shelters, like the despairing souls in the destroyed cities. All of this took shape in music before its time. Schoenberg did not intend that. Yet it is not what a person intends, but what he does, that is decisive. Schoenberg wanted to write a lively opera, but thanks to the peculiar character of his compositional method and his treatment of material, what came out was a kind of domestic apocalypse. He wrote (to employ a formulation of genius by Heinrich Heine) an 'exaggerated music' ('*übertriebene Musik*'). Such contradiction between form and content is typical of Schoenberg, and we will be stressing this even more in due course. Concerning the youthful works, *die Gurrelieder,* [sic] *Verklärte Nacht* and *Pelleas und Melisande*, we should say here only that they are the proof of a young genius. Despite their dependence on Wagner and Brahms, they already have many original features and a characteristic inclination toward combination and construction in what is still a traditional technique of form and harmony. After these highly romantic excesses, after this pseudo-symphonic phase in his music, the consideration and retrospective conquest of classical forms begins with the *String Quartet* Opus 7. Yet the quartets Opus 7 and Opus 10 and the *Chamber Symphony* Opus 9 are already the last tonal compositions Schoenberg wrote up to this point. (Only at an advanced age did he find his way back to tonality in a few occasional works.) These three works are amongst the most significant achievements in all chamber music; they can stand with the classics. Originality and wealth of invention, unity of form and content, technique of construction and power of synthesis are all of the highest calibre. With the exception of the last two movements of the *String Quartet* Opus 10 in F sharp minor, the expressive characters — in other words, the contents — are in general those of good, bourgeois tradition. But there are already a few places — e.g. the *Adagio* in the *Chamber Symphony* —, in which a sorrow is audible, a brokenness of expression, which goes far beyond the range of feeling of his class, of the middle-class bourgeois.

This already sounds like decline and like a premonition of catastrophes. Unfortunately, I can go into these three important works only very briefly, and restrict myself to what is characteristic in them. In the exposition of the *Quartet* in D minor, a very well-structured theme is accompanied by a precise bass; yet in the reprise of the theme we hear the bass as a higher voice. Theme and bass are thus conceived in double counterpoint. Such a technique is uncommon in homophonic music. Certainly one finds it in the symphonic passacaglia forms, for example, in the last movement of Beethoven's *Third Symphony*, and in the last movement of the *Fourth Symphony* of Brahms. Yet something like this has hardly ever been employed in homophonic sonata movements. Now the question is, where did Schoenberg get this? Are these things arbitrary? No. Schoenberg has taken this from Beethoven's works with variations and from the *Variations on a theme of Schumann* in F sharp minor Op. 9 by Brahms.

This bass plays a large role in the whole quartet. It is restructured to form a subordinate movement, it is inverted, and rendered in many variants. We hear it in the coda, as well, transposed into the major. These small innovations are very characteristic of Schoenberg. He did not want to write anything that had only a limited significance. He despised voices which are merely decorative and give a false impression of substance. Every voice should fulfil a number of functions. It is thoughts and experiences like these that later led him to the rigorous serial technique of the twelve-note system. We find a further innovation in the third movement of the *String Quartet* in F sharp minor. It is a sung piece based on a text by Stefan George: "Deep is the sorrow that surrounds me with gloom." Now it is strange that Schoenberg forces this highly expressive and unfortunately turgid text into a variation form. The contradiction between the extremely expressive character of the piece and its fundamental construction is enormous. It is as if he wanted to curb any excess. But in curbing it, he nevertheless does allow it. In this process, the variation form is strictly adhered to. It is linked to the highly developed technique of Beethoven's *Diabelli Variations* and Brahms's Handel and Haydn variations. In this bold piece as well, Schoenberg continues to make use of the classical legacy.

In the fourth movement of the *Second String Quartet* tonality is suspended for the first time in the history of music. We hear its complete suspension, however, in the *Three Piano Pieces* Opus 11. Despite their very different structural technique, these pieces repeatedly reveal Brahmsian features, in fact those of late Brahms, for instance the Piano Intermezzi. The third piece shatters the form. It already sounds like a precursor of the monodrama *Die Erwartung* [sic] and the opera *Die glückliche Hand,* Opus 18, [but] to our ears today — at least to my own — appears in no way more radical. The thematic material is plastic, the harmony simple, the motivic relationships and the form — even the shattered one — are easily comprehensible. The expressive characters already reveal reluctance, effort, the collapse of a consistent mood and, in the third piece, virtual hysteria.

What did Schoenberg want from this new style? He wanted to express himself, and that should not be hindered by any pre-existing, worn-out material nor by any clichés. It is an extremely private, subjective music, such as very seldom occurs in the history of music. One could compare it most closely to Beethoven's last piano sonatas and string quartets.

It is astonishing that this music was written in 1908, in Vienna. In this city full of the waltzes of the inspired Johann Strauss, the bombastic symphonies of Bruckner and Mahler, in this city of operettas and the intensive cultivation of the classical legacy, Schoenberg swam against the current. His music was not cosy, it was not sublime, it did not transfigure, it did not triumph nor conquer; it had — and this was hardest of all for its listeners to grasp — a fundamental note of despair. That Schoenberg — in the period before the First World War — expressed himself in this way, that he did not conform, is a mark of his humanity and his historical merit. Long before the invention of bomber aircraft he expressed the emotions of people in air-raid shelters; he had always made it clear with his music that the world was not beautiful. In doing so, he made things hard for his listeners and himself. For who wants to hear that the world is not beautiful?

The harmony of Schoenberg's atonal period is nothing arbitrary; it arose from the musical experiences of the nineteenth century. The sounds themselves are not new. There are seventh chords, ninth chords with the inversions, augmented triads, whole-tone chords and hybrid forms. What is new is that dissonances are no longer resolved. The history of music is the history of dissonance. Once the ear, after a hundred years, had become accustomed to dissonances with their resolutions, it finally demanded dissonances without resolutions. Schoenberg was the first to make use of unresolved dissonances in his music. He came to this innovative kind of composing in a traditional way. The function of the music was unchanged. But while Brahms still turned to musical amateurs and made possible domestic music-making, Schoenberg turned to a musically educated élite. He did not know that. For him the listener was the listener, and he thought little about the class structure of bourgeois society. In bourgeòis leisure-time, however, he was an alien presence, who made impossible the cosiness, the joy in what is well known and the recognition of the familiar, the mood of Sundays and the conviviality. Schoenberg makes such extensive demands on his listeners that his music to a certain extent invalidates the bourgeois concert hall, because he makes it impossible to hear something properly on first hearing. His music is almost a *musica reservata*. He was mistrustful and uncomprehending of popular appeal and of its effect on large numbers of people. He left that to Lehár and Puccini. That was not arrogance, but rather the attitude of the highly cultivated, bourgeois specialist, who lived in a city where the most complex works of the classical legacy and of baroque music also had a relatively wide audience. One could hear well-executed chamber music in the houses of the Viennese middle class, of lawyers, doctors and engineers; one found knowledge and musical education. That was the milieu Schoenberg came from, and this educated middle class, these connoisseurs were his public, before they were annihilated.

Folk music gave Schoenberg a good deal of pleasure. His arrangements of folk songs are outstanding. He also arranged waltzes by Johann Strauss and wrote variations on the song *'Es ist ein Ros' entsprungen'*. When what he left behind is published, one will find still more. In his original works, however, he could do nothing with folk music. He considered folk music, by comparison with classical music, to be a primitive early form, which the classical composers had already assimilated in any case. And so he attached himself to the classicists. Yet one hears popular elements, and indeed Viennese ones, in the melodic structure of even his most advanced works. It sounds as though the ghosts of departed folksongs are invoked, which after all the catastrophes that one has suffered appear pale and distraught.

In the works of Schoenberg's atonal period — the *Five Orchestral Pieces*, the operas *Die Erwartung, Die Glückliche Hand, Die Herzgewächse* [sic] — not only is the predominance of dissonance a characteristic aspect, but also the dissolution of the musical form. It is a curious way of composing music; one could call it 'athematic', for there are no self-contained themes. The most significant work of this period is undoubtedly the monodrama *Die Erwartung*. Sadly, this opera is written to a very stupid text. I must here emphasize, with sorrow, that the text does not allow this music of genius to develop. In this work, there are no longer any forms familiar to us, yet it still sounds logical. This logic arises in associative ways, although there are interesting isolated melodic passages.

I consider these works of the atonal middle period to be the most significant Schoenberg wrote. But they are an isolated instance, a wonderful dead end. Eight years later, Schoenberg had composed nothing else. He knew that things couldn't go on in this way. In 1922 he discovered the method of composition based on the twelve-note series. A twelve-note series together with its inversion, its retrograde and the inversion of the retrograde, becomes the foundation of a composition. In any composition of this kind, there are no free notes, but rather all harmonic and melodic elements must be obtained from the series; in the course of this the series, once begun, must be carried through to the end. The basic series and its three associated forms can be transposed to all notes of the chromatic scale. Hence this in itself yields rich material. One need not be too alarmed at the necessity of taking the series, once begun, through to the end. In the fugue, also, it is well known that the theme, once begun, must be carried through to the end. And in three- or indeed four-part counterpoint there is just as little 'freedom' as in a serial composition. The difference, however, is that three-part and four-part counterpoint is relatively rare; they are special forms of a highly developed character. The principle of the twelve-note technique, however, is meant to apply to all kinds and genres of music. That is inconvenient and dangerous, for every genre must create its own way of writing. A mechanical, uniform method can blur the characteristic nature of the genre. Yet clear demarcation of one genre from another is necessary if we want to produce art rather than school homework or mere personal declarations. A composer must at least know which genre can tolerate the twelve-note technique. It must not be allowed to become a style, but should be simply one method among several others.

The emergence of the twelve-note technique is not historically unprecedented. Consider the development of the major and minor tonalities. As is well known, these developed out of the church modes, through a kind of selection process. The lonian and Aeolian emerged as the most practical modes – practical for musical composition. The relation between whole-and half-tone intervals in these two was best suited to the purposes of cadence and modulation. Thus they were increasingly preferred, until they gave rise to the major and minor keys. The other modes died out. Whoever wishes to polemicize against the unnaturalness of the twelve-note series – and certainly this method of composition does contain much that is unnatural – must have it pointed out to him that the concept of 'naturalness' in composed music is an extremely questionable one, for it is not a simple matter to find an abstract-natural quality in what is artfully beautiful. In tonality as well, there are a host of unnatural elements. One such element is, for example, the minor scale. In order to work out the sound character of the minor, very 'unnatural' constructions were employed. It is known that there are the harmonic, the melodic, and finally the pure sequence of the minor scale, to which the accidentals are added. There can hardly be anything more trickily contrived in any other art. Now, if the major and minor keys arose from the modes, the twelve-note technique arose from the major and minor keys in the following way.

In the nineteenth century, chromaticism increasingly undermined the diatonic system of major and minor. Tonality began to fall into disuse, until finally one finds isolated passages, as in the case of Wagner, which no longer came full circle in a balanced way, in a main key. Chromaticism finally obscured the major and minor to such a degree that a kind of anarchy arose. Schoenberg's middle period, the atonal, is characteristic of this. But the suspension of the basic keys led to the decline of musical form. It was necessary to create a new order, with which it was possible to build up forms once again. For it is in form that music finds its language and its thoughts, and without form one babbles, but one does not speak. Thus the emergence of twelve-note composition should be seen as being firmly grounded in history. Yet it contains a wealth of inconsistencies and contradictions and here even an abstract-historical foundation is of no help. First of all, there is the question of listening, and when one is dealing with music, that is the most important thing. Listening to a retrograde inversion is not everyone's cup of tea. On the other hand, it is easy for every schoolboy to write down on a piece of paper a twelve-note series and to derive from it mechanically the other three basic forms. In the process of composition, then, the basic forms written down in this way are always generated automatically. This is an unusual thing in music. Also the imagination and power of invention are no longer employed freely, but contingently. One does not invent *ab ovo,* but uses the mathematical method of permutation.

Schoenberg's infallible ear and his astonishing power of imagination are not given to everyone. And so I warn the possessors or more modest ears and a weaker imaginative power against adopting his methods mechanically. In music, unfortunately, the proverb still holds: *Quod licet Jovi, non licet bovi,* in English: what Jove can allow himself, a bull certainly cannot allow himself.

With such a method of composition, the imagination of the composer becomes one-sided; it can become impoverished. It takes ability to form a reasonable piece of music from the series which has been derived in this way. To be blunt about it: Schoenberg, together with Anton von Webern and Alban Berg, at least, succeeded in doing so.

A special problem with this technique is the harmony, which must also follow the imperative of the series. In tonal music, as is well known, one cannot harmonize a melody by adding a triad to every note. But in twelve-note music the notes of the series must be used in any harmonic progression. Such a kind of harmony brings with it the danger of seeming automatically applied but not functional and one hears such weaknesses even in the case of so eminent a master as Arnold Schoenberg, from whom we can all still learn in a critical way.

Another contradiction in the twelve-note technique is the relationship of the series to the musical form. This contradiction is the most interesting, for serial technique was introduced in order to return once more, after formlessness, to self-contained musical forms. During his twelve-note period, Schoenberg did reach back to classical forms (with one exception, the *Suite* Opus 25). That is, back to the sonata, the scherzo, the rondo, variations, the two- and three-part song form and several mixed forms. Classical forms arose out of tonality, and are scarcely to be separated from it. Obviously the contrasts between the main theme and the subsidiary group in the tonal sonata form are not merely rhythmic, melodic, metric and formal. The most important contrast is the difference in the key. The modulation from the main group to the subsidiary group, the modulations in the development and the return to the reprise provide the real tension and charm of the classical form. If we take that away, then certainly some contrasting elements still remain, but the contrasts have a mechanical effect. The development passages in a twelve-note composition do not modulate, they merely become like the ghosts of the departed, conjured up once more, yet they remain abstract, like the departed themselves, and no longer have any power that actually formally pulsates. For if one employs the twelve-note technique, why then have developments, returns and transitions, which without their tonal function have lost their characteristic meaning?

Types of accompaniment and figurations constitute a further contradiction. It is touching to hear how Schoenberg, even when employing his twelve-note technique, still repeatedly follows certain structural techniques of Beethoven and Brahms. One hears broken chords used as accompaniment. But in contrast to tonal chord fragmentations, which follow the functional harmony, the chord fragmentations in serial composition must follow the series, which in no way guarantees a functional harmonic result. Thus curious dislocations and violent departures from expectation often arise. Classical form and twelve-note technique do not tolerate one another. One must force them. The forcing of material is a thoroughly legitimate procedure. Nature is forced to become art. With the twelve-note technique, however, there is the danger that the form is fulfilled in an abstract sense, as a kind of intellectual obligation, but is no longer realized concretely. The lack of contrasts is also a danger inherent in the twelve-note technique. An exposition, because of its complex internal structure, already sounds like a development, and the development that follows it hardly distinguishes itself from what has gone before, and the reprise is audible as nothing more than a return of the exposition. In Schoenberg's works it is evident that the sonata movements are precisely the most difficult to grasp and are perhaps the most problematic. The easiest are the rondo movements, as, for example, in the *Violin Concerto* and the *Fourth String Quartet.* In Schoenberg's variation movements the theme is varied so quickly that its basic shape is soon barely recognizable. This is to some extent true of some classical variations, for example, in Bach's *Goldberg Variations,* the *Diabelli Variations* and the *Eroica Variations* of Beethoven, and the Handel and Haydn Variations of Brahms. But when the theme is very substantially varied, Bach, Beethoven and Brahms quickly return to a simple form of the variation, in order to maintain coherence. In the Schoenbergian variation movements this does not happen. And so they become pieces of music which are indeed based on a precise plan of construction, yet sound like free fantasies. A twelve-note series is however more easily permutated than varied, and so in this way, too, the danger of a lack of contrast arises.

Schoenberg expanded the range of expression of musical characters. The sensibilities of classical and romantic music, the transfiguration, the sublimity, the grace, the humour, the fighting and winning are absent. Grief becomes desolation, depression. Despair is converted to hysteria, lyricism becomes a fragmented, glassy game, humour becomes, as in *Pierrot lunaire,* grotesquerie. The fundamental tone is that of the most extreme pain. That is an enrichment of music.

I should like to consider in particular Schoenberg's vocal works. Schoenberg almost always had 'bad luck' with his texts — though one can cite one or two exceptions: the splendid chorus *Friede auf Erden,* based on the beautiful poem by Conrad Ferdinand Meyer, and *A Survivor from Warsaw,* for which he himself wrote the text.

The other texts — for the George songs, for the operas *Erwartung, Die Glückliche Hand, Von heute auf Morgen, Moses und Aron,* and *Die Jakobsleiter* — are, sadly, highly questionable. If the texts were naive, still nothing would have been lost, but Schoenberg had an unfortunate inclination towards eclectic-mystical philophizing. And this 'philosophizing' constitutes an injury to this music of genius. What a new generation will be able to make of this remains to be seen. In his opera *Die Glückliche Hand,* incidentally, real workers do appear. This is the only place in Schoenberg's works where workers are presented. I quote from the stage directions: "When the man is right at the top, he passes behind the piece of rock, moving towards the centre, stops and observes the workers reflectively. A thought seems to take shape in his mind. He breathes heavily . . .". It is a shame that the text of *Pierrot lunaire,* one of Schoenberg's most brilliant compositions, is a weak copy of Verlaine by a third-class Belgian poet, Albert Giraud, and, on top of that, translated by Otto Erich Hartleben. For Schoenberg, sadly, the choice of text was not something decisive. A text, for him, was an inducement to compose music.

Schoenberg is no less significant as a teacher and theoretician than as a composer. Today his aesthetic theories are of little use to us; but his textbook *Harmonie und Kontrapunkt* [sic] is amongst the most significant achievements of music theory since Albrechtsberger and Simon Sechter. One must have experienced how shallowly the craft of music was taught in the music high schools and conservatories in order to evaluate Schoenberg's achievement. His *Harmonielehre* has become famous. A two-volume book on counterpoint which he was working on at the time of his death has not yet been published. But it will become — and this is easy to predict — the most important handbook for teachers and students. Unfortunately he has not, so far as I know, left behind any notes of his analyses of classical music. That is regrettable. For now it is only his students who know with what great depth and originality he understood the works of Bach, Mozart, Beethoven and Schubert. It is not well known that Schoenberg was a strictly conservative teacher; he did not teach 'modern music'. Students' assignments had to be written in a verifiably tonal style."I cannot teach freedom; that is something everyone must take for himself", was his basic precept, and a storm broke over anyone who attempted to smuggle a few Schoenbergian turns of phrase into a school assignment.

A billion workers and farmers who live in countries freed of capitalism will, for the time being, be able to make nothing or very little of Schoenberg. They have other, more pressing tasks. In the field of music it is the liquidation of musical analphabetism. Only after such liquidation, and only after the most complicated classical works have become part of the popular tradition, can Schoenberg again be reintroduced as a subject of discussion. I am not without optimism concerning the result of such a discussion. How many of his works will remain alive, I do not know, but he must at least become famous as a despiser of clichés. He did not transfigure nor gloss over the social order into which he was born. He did not dress anything up. He held a mirror up to his time, his class. What one saw there was not very pretty. But it was the truth.

Translated by Karin von Abrams
Delivered as a lecture on 17 December 1954 in the *Deutsche Akademie der Künste*, Berlin GDR.
Published in *Sinn und Form* 7/1 1955. In *Schriften* 1948-1962 p. 320 ff.

12

HANNS EISLER'S 'DEUTSCHE SINFONIE'

Erik Levi

It seems paradoxical that the *Deutsche Sinfonie*, a work which Hanns Eisler considered to be one of his most important compositions, has failed to establish itself in the repertoire and has received relatively few performances in the last thirty years. Practical reasons may well have mitigated against its wider dissemination. The work has not as yet been published in its entirety[1]. Moreover, the three commercial recordings, all issued in the former German Democratic Republic, have not been widely distributed throughout Western Europe.[2] Yet this comparative inaccessibility can only provide a partial explanation as to the work's neglect. A more pertinent factor must surely be the general and somewhat narrow-minded view of Eisler which regards the composer exclusively as a miniaturist, a master of song and theatre music, but one who seemed unable to sustain ideas on a much larger scale. This notion can certainly be supported by the absence of other works of similar size, scope and emotional impact in Eisler's output. Yet such an argument fails to take account of the fact that the composer began his career at a time when the reaction against symphonic music of Mahlerian proportions was at its height. Eisler's first works were in fact conceived for small forces —

[1] Although the *Deutsche Sinfonie* is expected to be published in connection with the projected Complete Edition of his works, the present position is as follows: Movements I, II, IV, V, VII, VIII, IX are published in Volume 3 of Eisler's *Lieder und Kantaten, (Breitkopf und Härtel,* Leipzig). Movement XI is published in Volume 10 of the *Lieder und Kantaten.* The other movements remain unpublished.

[2] The three recordings are:

1 A transcription of the first performance in the *Deutsche Staatsoper,* Berlin on 24 April 1959 conducted by Walter Goehr. Nova 8 85 061–062

2 Performance with *Rundfunk-Sinfonie-Orchestra* Leipzig conducted by Adolf Fritz Guhl (26 June 1964) Eterna 8 20 481–482

3 Performance in the *Schauspielhaus* Berlin on 30 October 1987 conducted by Max Pommer Nova 8 85 281

The appearance of Thomas Phleps' major study *Hanns Eislers Deutsche Sinfonie. Ein Beitrag zur Ästhetik des Widerstands,* Kassel 1988 has not inspired further performances.

piano, voice and piano and chamber ensembles. He seemed unattracted to the idea of writing music for the conventional symphony orchestra. Indeed, the only other compositions to which Eisler gave the title of Symphony, the *Kleine Sinfonie* of 1932 and the *Kammer-Sinfonie* of 1940, perfectly illustrate his distaste for inflated romantic gestures and extravagant orchestration. In particular, the *Kleine Sinfonie*, with its spare thematic ideas and brittle instrumentation, compresses a four-movement structure into a time-span of only ten minutes.

If the *Deutsche Sinfonie* appears to stand apart in Eisler's work as a whole, it would be misleading to suggest that it is somehow untypical of its composer. Despite the fact that the score calls for large vocal and instrumental forces and that its overall structure is expansive, there is no evidence to suggest that the composer made a conscious decision to embrace the stylistic features of an earlier romantic tradition. On the contrary, the *Deutsche Sinfonie* distils some of the musical and political preoccupations which profoundly affected Eisler after his exile from Germany in 1933. Three strands of his compositional activity during this period — the writing of *agitprop* songs, cantatas and a revived interest in composing chamber music — are combined in a multi-faceted work which is unique in its conception yet wide-ranging in its emotional message.

Eisler began work on the *Deutsche Sinfonie* in March 1935 during his first visit to the United States. The initial impulse for embarking upon such a composition was the need to expose to the world the impact of Nazism upon German cultural and political life. A letter to Brecht written in July 1935 explains the composer's original intentions:

> *"..... I want to write a large symphony which will have the subtitle 'Concentration Camp Symphony'. In some passages a chorus will be used as well, although it is basicially an orchestral work. And certainly I want to use your two poems Begräbnis des Hetzers im Zinksarg [this will become the middle section of a large-scale funeral march] and An die Gefangenen in den Konzentrationslager ....."*[3]

In the event Eisler's plans became much extended in both conception and formal structure. Although he wrote three purely orchestral movements, the greater part of the work is vocal and choral. Moreover, the attack upon Nazism was expanded to incorporate a wider examina-

---

[3] Albrecht Betz, *Hanns Eisler Political Musician*, Cambridge University Press 1982 pp. 156–7.

tion of German history and by implication the relationship between fascism and capitalism.[4]

The long compositional process of the *Deutsche Sinfonie* is fully documented in Manfred Grabs's *Handbuch*[5]. Eisler completed three movements (the *Präludium, An die Kämpfer* and *In Sonnenburg*) by the end of 1936. Two of these were submitted to the jury of the International Society for Contemporary Music and were accepted for performance at the Society's annual Festival held during the Paris World Exhibition in March 1937. But a few weeks before the Festival took place, the organizers demanded the removal of Brecht's texts and requested that the vocal lines should be recast for a saxophone. Such an absurd suggestion was prompted probably because the authorities were reluctant to embarrass the Nazi regime.[6] Unfortunately, Eisler was unable to revoke this decision and the movements were withdrawn from the Festival. Yet this setback did not in fact deter the composer from proceeding with the work. Indeed, Eisler seemed if anything more committed to completing the *Deutsche Sinfonie*. Even without the prospect of immediate performance, he composed a further four movements in 1937 (*Bauernkantate, Erinnerung, Arbeiterkantate* and *Begräbnis des Hetzers im Zinksarg)*. To these he added an orchestral *Etüde* which was taken from an earlier composition, the *Suite No. 1* of 1930. After this, work on the *Deutsche Sinfonie* proceeded more fitfully. The two other purely orchestral movements, the second *Etüde* and a concluding *Allegro*, were composed over a longer period of time, the former being completed in 1939, while the latter was written in *Particell* between 1936 and 1938, and was only fully scored nine years later. Although the work was effectively finished by the time Eisler returned to Europe, the composer had to wait until 1959 for a public performance. The post-war cultural atmosphere in the German Democratic Republic had been dominated by Stalinism, and Eisler's use of dodecaphonic techniques was deemed to be 'formalist'. Under these circumstances, it is possible that the composer felt it was pragmatic to add yet another movement to the work to form a short *Epilogue*. This section, taken from a choral composition entitled *Bilder aus der Kriegsfibel* written in 1957,

---

[4] At one stage Eisler thought of calling the work the *Deutsche Misere* — the German predicament. The title *Deutsche Sinfonie* was established in 1938.

[5]. Manfred Grabs, *Hanns Eisler Kompositionen - Schriften - Literatur,* Leipzig 1984.

[6] The ban by the ISCM is particularly interesting since the Nazis had outlawed German membership of the organization (attacked in the official press as an agent of 'Jewish Bolshevism') in 1933.

stands apart from the rest of the *Deutsche Sinfonie* in not using twelve-note material. It also forms a touching retrospective conclusion to the whole composition, since it is a lament for the vanquished German soldier.

The overall structure of the *Deutsche Sinfonie* therefore, is as follows:

I *Präludium* (text by Brecht)
II *Passacaglia An die Kämpfer in den Konzentrationslagern* (To the Fighters in the Concentration Camps (Brecht)
III *Etüde I* for orchestra (*Hörfleissübung*, Radio Music — fourth movement from *Suite No. 1*)
IV *Erinnerung* (*Potsdam*) (Remembrance) (Brecht)
V *In Sonnenburg* (Brecht)
VI *Etüde II* for orchestra
VII *Begräbnis des Hetzers im Zinksarg* (Burial of the Agitator in a Zinc Coffin) (Brecht)
VIII *Bauernkantate* (Peasant Cantata) (Eisler after Silone)
A. *Missernte* (Crop failure)
B. *Sicherheit* (Certainty)
C. *Flüstergespräche (Melodram)* (Whispered conversations)
D. *Bauernliedchen* (Peasant song)
IX *Das Lied vom Klassenfeind/Arbeiterkantate* (The Song of the Class Enemy/Workers Cantata (Brecht))
X *Allegro* for orchestra
XI *Epilog (Seht unsre Söhne)* (See our sons) (Brecht)

Given the rather piecemeal evolution of the *Deutsche Sinfonie*, one might assume that the composition's overall structure is rather diffuse. Certainly, the mixture of different genres, elements of oratorio and cantata style juxtaposed with powerful marching songs and strident symphonic allegros, might superficially suggest a lack of clear direction and an absence of a unified concept. But in fact Eisler achieves unity not only through diversity, but by articulating several inter-connections between the various movements.

First of all, the work is structured as a progression from the relatively simple formal outlines of the early movements to the much greater complexity of the later ones. In addition, the major emotional weight is concentrated in the three most expansive movements which deal with the wider issues of political agitation as related to the intellectual (*Begräbnis*), the peasant, (*Bauernkantate*) and the worker (*Arbeiterkantate*). Eisler's three purely orchestral movements serve a dual purpose. They release both the in-built tension of the preceding movements and provide an apposite instrumental anticipation of what is to follow. Thus the first *Etüde* introduces an element of rhythmic energy and aggression which is subsequently utilized to telling effect in the peroration of *Erinnerung*. Similarly the rather resigned and withdrawn quality of the second *Etüde* is immediately continued in the anguished opening of *Begräbnis*. The final *Allegro* is the most highly developed orchestral movement, being cast in sonata form with a double development section. In effect, it reinforces the existing sense of a steady crescendo which is characteristic of the *Arbeiterkantate*. David Drew has pointed out another interesting feature of these three movements, namely that they form a symphony within a symphony, with the second *Etüde* combining elements of a slow movement and a scherzo.[7]

A further source of internal unity is manifested in the utilization of note rows with related intervallic properties. Thus the striking use of perfect fifth and tritone, which characterize the original row of the *Präludium*, is more or less echoed at the opening of *Erinnerung*. Ex. 12.1

Ex. 12.1

Similarly, the characteristic use of intervals of a second and a third are present in thematic material from *An die Kämpfer, In Sonnenburg* and the first *Etüde*. Ex. 12.2

Ex. 12.2

[7] David Drew, *Eisler and the Polemic Symphony,* The Listener January 1962.

Eisler's highly individual application of dodecaphonic techniques also enables the listener to grasp the major thematic material without great difficulty. Few melodic lines explore intervallic relationships which extend beyond the octave. In addition, sequential repetition of fragments of a particular note-row reinforces a distinctive rhythmic and thematic characteristic of a specific movement. Such flexibility makes it possible for the composer to integrate passages of unequivocal tonality at moments of great emotional and structural importance without disturbing the overall harmonic structure.[8] The most striking examples of this process can be seen at the trumpets' quotation of the opening notes of the *Internationale* (in D flat) in bars 81–86 of the *Präludium* in combination with the trombones' statement of the revolutionary song *Unsterbliche Opfer* (in A flat minor). Other distinctive utilizations of consonance occur at the violent E minor crescendo which accompanies the words *'Wenn sie den Führer sehn, dann stehn sie wie Wände'* in *In Sonnenburg* (bars 23–26) and at bars 26–33 (pedal E) and bars 123–124 of *Begräbnis* where a pedal first inversion of G major is sustained by the full orchestra. Ex. 12.3

Ex. 12.3

Rhythmic and textural interconnections also abound. The oppressive and sinister dotted quaver figurations of the *eroico* unison violins and violas in *An die Kämpfer* (bars 23–25 and 68–70) are developed to greater intensity throughout the following vocal movement, *Erinnerung* (cf. bars 21–27 and 40–48). Later in the work the

[8] It may indeed be argued that the quasi-tonal implications of Eisler's writing owe more to Schoenberg's earlier rather than middle period.

appearance of repeated note quintuplets (bars 153–185 of the *Bauern-kantate*), is effectively recalled in the repeated note rhythms of bars 224–245 of the *Arbeiterkantate*.

Eisler's orchestration is typically spare, with little inclination to overload textures even in passages of the greatest intensity. This economy of means is particularly evident from examining his writing for string ensemble, which rarely extends beyond four parts. At the same time, there is no lack of variety in the range of instrumental effects harnessed by the composer. His vast experience in writing incidental music for the theatre and for films is crucial in achieving an impressive juxtaposition of utterly dissimilar textures within a relatively short period. Perhaps one of the finest examples of this can be seen in *Begräbnis* where the pianissimo string writing of the opening bars is countered by a violent triple forte passage dominated by braying horns, trumpets and trombones (bars 26–32).

Just as the instrumentation is notable for its restraint, Eisler's prime concern in setting Brecht's poems is to make the words completely intelligible. There is little use of vocal melisma and the rhythmic emphasis at all times respects the metre of the text. Yet in view of the tensions which arose between Weill and Brecht when they collaborated on the *Rise and Fall of the City of Mahagonny*, it is interesting to note that Eisler did not feel the need to remain entirely faithful to the order of the original text. Most of the alterations are clearly made for musical and structural reasons. For example in the *Präludium*, Eisler uses only verses one and six of Brecht's poem *Deutschland:*

O Deutschland, bleiche Mutter!	*O Germany, pale mother!*
Wie sitzest du besudelt	*How you sit defiled*
Unter den Völkern.	*Among the peoples.*
Unter den Befleckten	*Among the polluted*
Fällst du auf.	*You stand out.*
Und dabei sehen dich alle	*And yet all see you*
Den Zipfel deines Rockes verbergen,	*hiding the hem of your skirt*
der blütig ist	*which is bloody*
Vom Blut deines	*From the blood of your*
Besten Sohnes.[9]	*Best son.*

And even these lines are compressed, partly to give the greatest impact to the subsequent entry of the full orchestra and partly to reinforce the common theme which runs throughout the work:

[9] Brecht *Gesammelte Gedichte* Band 2 pp. 487–8 *Suhrkamp Verlag.*

O Deutschland, bleiche Mutter!	*O Germany, pale mother.*
Wie bist du besudelt	*How you are besmirched with*
mit dem Blut deiner besten Söhne.	*the blood of your best sons.*

Similarly, in *Begräbnis*, Eisler removes two words from the fourth line of Brecht's first verse. He then adds the outburst *'Begrabt ihn!* from the chorus (bars 29–30) to introduce the *Quasi Marcia Funèbre* from the whole orchestra before returning to a faithful setting of Brecht's second verse. (See Ex. 12.3)

Both the *Präludium* and *An die Kämpfer in den Konzentrationslager* are broadly conceived in a ternary structure. In the *Präludium* an intense orchestral threnody frames the setting for chorus of Brecht's *Deutschland*. The opening twenty-eight bars clearly demonstrate an orthodox yet highly fruitful application of twelve-note material. Four versions of the row are presented below with the bar numbers in which they are first introduced, with some later examples of variation. Ex. 12.4

Ex. 12.4

The resulting combination enables Eisler to juxtapose dissonant harmonies with clearer implications of tonality. Ex. 12.5

Bars 10–15 introduce a sequential repetition in the violins of three notes from the inversion of the row. This oscillation between C sharp E flat and D supported by a pedal A in the bass and a wavering G and F in the violas, with its composite whole-tone flavouring, provides a crucial structural point which appears later on at bar 40 in the horns to form a bridge passage to the entrance of the chorus. Furthermore a similar pattern of three notes appears in the choral alto and bass lines. Ex. 12.6a, 12.6b

Ex. 12.5

Ex. 12.6a

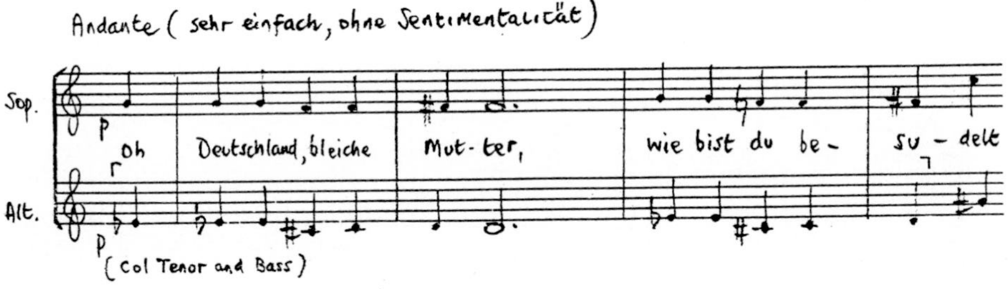

Ex. 12.6b

In contrast to the intensely polyphonic orchestral writing, the first choral entry is homophonic and is directed to be sung 'very simply and without sentimentality'. The influence of J.S. Bach is immediately apparent not only in the use of a simple chorale with its parallel thirds divested of all warmth, but later in the build-up of individual entries which emphasise the interval of a tritone which is so strong a characteristic of the row. The emotional temperature of the choral writing, at first marked piano, is suddenly intensified at the entry of the solo soprano, who provides a passionate reiteration of the first lines of the text to the original row above the general dynamic level of the chorus (bars 60–63). This produces a violent outburst from the orchestra with canonic entries of the original row marked fortissimo in the horns (from bar 65), flutes, clarinets and violins (from bar 68) and tuba and basses (from bar 74) pitted against the retrograde inversion in the bassoons, cellos and basses (from bar 69), and trumpets and trombones (from bar 72). The build-up eventually culminates in a reiteration of a two-bar phrase first heard in the movement's earlier climax (cf. bars 38–39 and bars 79–80) which pulls the music towards the C sharp pedal and the quotation of the *Internationale* and *Unsterbliche Opfer*. Ex. 12.7a and 7b

Ex. 12.7a

Ex. 12.7b

The movement ends with a pianissimo recapitulation of bars 6–10 in the strings with an extended crescendo on the oscillating three-note figure.

In *An die Kämpfer in den Konzentrationslagern* for mezzo soprano, chorus and orchestra, Eisler maintains the bleak atmosphere of the *Präludium* by paring the texture down to two parts without offering any supporting harmony. He again pays homage to Bach by casting the outer sections of the movement in the form of a relentless and obsessive passacaglia in 3/2 time — a perfect vehicle with which to convey the overriding defiance of Brecht's poem. After the relatively four-square rhythmic structure of the previous movement, some contrast is provided in the more syncopated material of the flute's first entry which recalls the style of the composer's film and theatre music. Ex. 12.8

Ex. 12.8

This syncopation is further intensified in the choral middle section where the texture veers between unison passages and bare two-part writing. Ex. 12.9

Ex. 12.9

The first *Etüde* provides a necessary release from the dramatic intensity of the previous movements. It also offers a further illustration of the directness and simplicity of Eisler's thematic material. The row stated at the outset by unison strings is quasi- tonal, suggesting a cadential pull from C to F. This theme is heard again in augmentation on the trumpets at bar 34 with the row inversion in the trombone. In the middle section (bar 56), the trumpet intones the inversion with the strings replying with the original row in march tempo. At bar 88, the row is heard in diminution on the piccolo with the inversion played on the trombone — a particularly grotesque piece of orchestration with chattering woodwind and flutter-tonguing in the second trumpet. Later, from bar 124, the original row is heard in canon on the trumpet and trombone accompanied by frenzied dactylic rhythmic patterns based on the inversion in the strings. Finally at bar 138, the row and its inversion are heard in augmentation in the first trumpet and trombone with the second trumpet counterpointing the row in quavers followed by the retrograde inversion in quavers and semiquavers. Ex. 12.10

Ex. 12.10

The next two vocal movements follow a different formal pattern in that they approach the structure of a strophic song. In *Erinnerung*, a brutal attack on the association between the state apparatus and the honouring of Germany's dead, symbolized in Brecht's mind by the alliance between President Hindenburg and Hitler, the potential inflexibility of Brecht's clearly articulated metrical pattern is broken down by interpolating more agitated material in the orchestra (bars 23–27, 40–49). Eisler builds a brief but ruthless crescendo and accelerando, developing more complex textures and thereby intensifying each succeeding verse. The climax is reached with the introduction of triplet quaver ostinati in the violins and the combination of Brecht's sixth verse in the baritone with the fifth in the female chorus (bars 66–74). Undoubtedly, the most terrifying passage of all occurs at the end where Eisler depicts the arrival of the police who 'beat the mourners to hell'. Each strand of the orchestral texture is pivoted on tritone and open fifth intervals played *sehr rasch*.

In Sonnenburg is an equally concise movement but the angular vocal lines of *Erinnerung* are replaced by a more consonant melodic style based upon a row whose final four notes form a distinctive and memorable pattern. Ex. 12.11

Ex. 12.11

Eisler's setting captures a number of the different emotions that are implied in Brecht's poem. For example, anger is conveyed in the orchestral accompaniment through the use of fierce double stops in the violins and violas punctuated by rasping flutter-tonguings in the muted trumpets and trombones (bars 1–2, 19–21 and 45–48). The cold, almost matter-of-fact, vocal line appears to reflect the bleakness of day-to-day existence in the concentration camp. A particularly telling effect occurs just before the final coda where the use of a melisma on the word *Stiefel* serves to underline the overwhelming feeling of irony in Brecht's lines *'dann hätt'es wirklich einen Nutzen wenn die Reichen den Armen die Stiefel putzen'*. (then the camp really has a purpose when the rich can polish the poor man's boots). Ex. 12.12

Ex. 12.12

Similarly, irony plays a prominent role in the double-edged sentiment of *Begräbnis des Hetzers,* whose text is based upon a fascist speech. The opening is both tense and sinister — a string threnody in which the original row is combined with its inversion in the violas, while the basses are embedded on an almost 'timeless' pedal note. Ex. 12.13

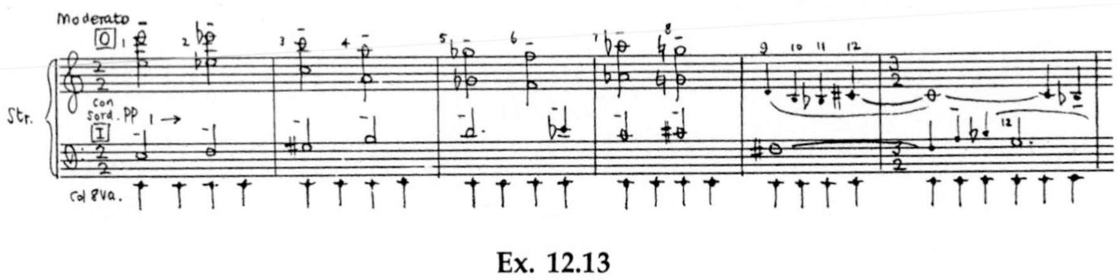

Ex. 12.13

The last three notes of the row's inversion — A, B flat and G — suggest the minor mode, especially when turned into an ostinato pattern in the timpani and basses at bars 46–50 and the coda from bars 135 to the end. Ex. 12.14

Ex. 12.14

This movement provides the most extreme contrasts of texture, tempo, dynamics, instrumentation and mood within the whole work. The first entry of the chorus is accompanied by unusually wide intervallic leaps in the upper strings (bars 24–25). These are followed by a rhythmic variation of the row's inversion over an E pedal, preparing the ground for the Funeral March patterns at bar 30. Yet this violent climax subsides to introduce a recitative-like duo between the bass soloist and a timpani ostinato (bars 46–50). At bar 60, the mood changes once again, when the mezzo soprano introduces a melodic pattern over a march rhythm that is typical of Eisler's *Massenlieder* idiom. The text, designated to be sung in a 'friendly manner', mocks the Nazi pose that a decent living wage will be achieved under conditions of oppression. Ex. 12.15

Ex. 12.15

It must be noted that Eisler achieves these disturbing emotional juxtapositions without sacrificing musical unity. In the passage quoted above, for example, the melodic line is based upon the retrograde inversion of the original row.

Eisler divides his *Bauernkantate* into four sections, each bearing a subtitle. Although the overall structure of this movement seems to be more episodic, there are perceptible connections particularly between *Missernte* and *Sicherheit*. Both carry sustained material for the chorus which features similar harmonic progressions cast in the form of a dynamic scherzo. A powerful six-bar melodic line stated at the outset by the unaccompanied bass frames this discourse much in the manner of a baroque ritornello. It is heard three times in the opening movement and appears at the end of *Sicherheit*. The most experimental and indeed remarkable writing in the whole work appears in the *Melodram*, where Eisler introduces whispered dialogue, to be spoken without expression against a background of static blocks of dissonant harmony, with the sopranos and alto sections of the chorus humming in two-part counterpoint. As this section subsides, the sense of anticipation is released in the final *Bauernliedchen*. This march begins its purposeful journey with the cellos and double basses enunciating a characteristic sequence of repeated crotchets of which the most distinctive feature is the menacing interval of a minor third. There are obviously clear echoes here of Eisler's most potent marching songs.

Because of the extended duration of the *Bauernkantate*, Eisler utilizes more transpositions of his original row than in earlier movements. This tendency is further intensified in the *Arbeiterkantate* where the structure is more clearly symphonic. In essence, the movement follows the outline of a sonata form with three telescoped recapitulations. The musical argument can be summarized as follows:

INTRODUCTION: bars 1–20. Brief orchestral Prelude which presents fragments of material to be utilized later, including a clear anticipation of the central scherzo (bars 11–15).

EXPOSITION: bars 21–169, which introduces two contrasting ideas. First, a quasi-strophic song for mezzo soprano and orchestra marked Andante con moto (bars 21–133) with a short interpolation (bars 72–82) of faster triplet material. This becomes a feature of the second idea (bars 133–169), a march for baritone and orchestra with similar instrumentation to the *Bauernliedchen*, which casts a possibly unwitting glance back to the character of the first movement of Mahler's *Sixth Symphony*.

FIRST RECAPITULATION: bars 170–245. A recapitulation of material from the song and the march. The song is heard now in the baritone followed by an accelerando and a brief allusion to the march (bars 188 – 199). The chorus enters dramatically at bar 200 over a pedal roll on the timpani. Further repetition of material from the song for both mezzo soprano and baritone culminates in a unison melisma to the words *'Und sie sollten das übrige tun'*.

DEVELOPMENT: bars 246–342. Closely knit polyphony in the chorus propels the music towards a demonic scherzo in 3/4 which features homophonic choral writing pitted against hemiola patterns in the orchestra. The scherzo recalls material presented in the *Sicherheit* section of the *Bauernkantate*.

SECOND RECAPITULATION: bars 343–413. The march material for baritone and orchestra is followed by allusions to the song at bar 377. A short orchestral bridge passage at bar 406, *sehr breit*, leads to:

CODA: bars 414–466. The climax of the movement is reached in two stages; first, a homophonic choral passage answered by lines declaimed by a speaker (bars 414–430); second, a compressed recapitulation of the song and march material, the former by the mezzo soprano and baritone, the latter by the chorus. This section reaches its culmination at the crucial words *'Und der Klassenfeind ist der Feind'* (And the class enemy *is* the enemy), (bars 456–462).

A brief orchestral peroration recalls a thematic idea stated at the very opening of the movement.

The basic row juxtaposes two harmonic fields, a chord centred around A flat contrasted with one around C, which sometimes incorporates an added sixth or seventh. Ex. 12.16

Ex. 12.16

The cadential pull towards the A flat is felt at several points in the score, for example bars 16, 65, 350, 406, 435.

Continuing the process of expansion as manifested in the *Bauerkantate*, the crowning glory of the *Deutsche Sinfonie* is the dynamic *Allegro* movement — a purely orchestral conception that utterly refutes the notion that Eisler was only able to sustain his ideas over a small time-scale. Apart from the amazing physical energy generated by the thematic material itself, perhaps its most distinctive feature is the way it seems to tie all the threads of the work into a convincing entity.

Two aspects of the *Allegro* are of particular interest. First, it should be noted that Eisler's mastery of variable tempi (four different tempo markings are delineated within the score) appears to balance structural coherence with an impression of almost spontaneous improvisation. Second, unlike all previous movements, the *Allegro's* thematic material is derived from the initial row stated at the outset of the *Präludium* — a crucial means of imposing unity on a work that could seem diffuse on first hearing. There are further implications in the way Eisler employs this original row. In the *Präludium* the tone is darkly resigned, only breaking out in angry defiance at the big orchestral climax. In the *Allegro*, however, Eisler effects an almost Lisztian transformation of the material, from darkness to light, from despair to optimism.

The overall design of the *Allegro* is striking — a sonata structure with a double exposition and development section. It begins with an introductory passage (bars 1–26) generating immense energy through syncopation of the row in a dialogue between lower and higher instruments, punctuated by violent chords from the brass and percussion. This rises to a climax through a series of four-bar phrases which culminate in a gradual accelerando of the syncopation (bars 17–19) towards a rumbling ostinato pattern in semiquavers from the lower strings. At bar 27 the horn states the first subject, a rhythmic transformation of the mournful string threnody at the opening of the *Präludium*, but now conspicuously marked *fröhlich*. Ex. 12.17

Ex. 12.17

Ten bars later the trumpet takes over the same rhythmic material, but in its inversion. There follows a lengthy accelerando in which Eisler intensifies the rhythmic potential of this theme through passages of intricate contrapuntal interplay, before the violins, spaced an octave apart in a passage of almost Brahmsian texture, take over the first subject at bar 63. Further rhythmic diminution (dotted rhythms) in the upper strings and woodwind at bar 71 counter the inversion, which is now placed in the horns and trombones. After further rhythmic and contrapuntal interplay in the strings (bars 86–96) and a recall of the opening percussive chords (bar 101), there follows a bridge passage (bars 101–112) whose structural position is related to bars 21–25.

At a slightly slower tempo, the second idea is introduced by the clarinets playing in rather mournful parallel major thirds — an effect that is clearly reminiscent of the choral *'O Deutschland, bleiche Mutter'* in the *Präludium*. Ex. 12.18. The texture here is more intimate, though the intricate five-part string writing (bars 131–138 and 144–154) creates great emotional intensity which is reinforced when the trumpet takes over the second idea at bar 156.

Ex.12.18

There is a resurgence of energy at bar 176 initiating a lengthy third section (bars 176–254) based upon some of the rhythmic material heard in the first section (cf. the dotted rhythms), but also adding into the melting pot frenzied semiquaver triplet patterns (e.g. in the upper woodwind and xylophone bars 187–189). A furious accelerando (marked *wild*) is interrupted by a demonic two-note figure from the timpani (bars 253–4) almost reminiscent of the opening of the third movement of Mahler's *Resurrection* Symphony! At bar 255, the first development begins, a passage in 2/4 notable for its sudden augmentation of rhythm (quavers and crotchets replacing semiquavers) and the initial absence of upper strings.

At bar 328, the double development begins, telescoping all the material heard so far, but without recourse to extreme tempo fluctuations. First there is an episode which fragments elements of the introduction and the first subject. A more sustained passage begins at bar 363, where the trumpet inversion of the first subject is heard punctuated by tremolo strings and bare woodwinds. At bar 393, the trumpet is once again pre-eminent, proclaiming the second idea in much fuller scoring than in the first exposition, and combined with the dotted rhythms and semiquaver triplets that dominated the third section. As before, this section is violently curtailed by a nine-bar passage, also marked *wild* (bars 411–419), for full orchestra which leads to the second development and a change of metre from 3/8 to 2/4. This new section (bars 420–557) is initiated by a skittish two-part invention for bassoon and oboe, based on the row and its inversion, and for the most part is notable for its restrained almost chamber-like texture.

At bar 558, the metre once again reverts to 3/8, initiating the recapitulation, which is based almost entirely on the introductory rhythmic figures and the first subject. This builds to an impassioned climax at bar 585 followed by further rhythmic intensification, albeit in a more transparent texture (bars 607–631). A final assault, marked *mit grosser Kraft,* propels the movement to a dramatic and highly dissonant conclusion.

It is questionable how far the 18-bar *Epilog* for soprano, chorus and orchestra, which follows the *Allegro,* achieves a convincing apotheosis for the whole work. Different in style to the rest of the *Deutsche Sinfonie,* it is palpably tonal, centred on A minor and supported by a three-note ostinato on timpani and lower strings. Yet perhaps its modesty of means indicates a strength, for in the uncertain climate of a post-war divided Germany, apotheosis on a grand scale was simply an impossibility.

Throughout this article, I have emphasized the uniqueness of the *Deutsche Sinfonie* within Eisler's overall output. But it could equally well be argued that the work is unique in terms of its historical context[10]. In utilizing the generic term 'symphony' for his masterpiece, Eisler appears to imply some kind of inheritance from the central symphonic tradition that dominated Western music from the time of Haydn and Mozart. But it would be difficult to find precedents for Eisler's work in this repertoire. One can argue that Berlioz's programme symphonies, in particular

[10] The work is unique too as a document of protest against fascism in the 1930s. Other major exiled composers, for example Hindemith, refused to write pieces in direct opposition to the policies of the Third Reich, preferring to retreat into a kind of abstract (some might say escapist) neo-classicism. A more problematic issue, briefly alluded to by Phleps (op.cit. p. 330), is Eisler's use of a diatonically-based serialism, since such a musical language was cultivated by the Schoenberg pupils Paul von Klenau and Winfried Zillig during the Third Reich without encountering protests of 'musical degeneracy' from the regime.

Romeo et Juliette, combine elements of cantata, song, opera and purely orchestral music within the same framework. Likewise, the juxtaposition of vocal and instrumental writing is a central feature of the symphonies of Liszt (*Faust* and *Dante*) and of Mahler (Nos. 2, 3, 4, and 8) Yet these works emanate from a bourgeois tradition — they may in some cases imply social comment, but they never seek to challenge their audience with a call to action.

A more useful parallel may be drawn between Eisler's work and the symphonies of Shostakovich. In the *October* and *May Day* Symphonies, (Nos. 2 and 3) both of which blend purely instrumental and choral writing within a one-movement structure, Shostakovich attempted to match revolutionary sentiments with a revolutionary musical language. But these works lack Eisler's consistency of idiom —the diatonicism of the choral writing appearing at odds with the wild experimentalism of the orchestral sections. When Shostakovich, thirty years later, addressed the idea of revolution in his *Eleventh* (1957) and *Twelfth* (1961) symphonies, his style had matured considerably, yet he reverted to writing purely orchestral music. Through the conscious interweaving of revolutionary songs into the symphonic argument (cf. the third movement of the *Eleventh*), these works may well imply revolutionary sentiment. But in contrast to Eisler's work, they remain essentially programmatic compositions, rooted in nineteenth-century concepts of the symphonic form.[11]

Of all Shostakovich's symphonies, it is the *Thirteenth* (*Babi Yar*), a choral symphony based on poems by Yevgeny Yevtushenko and first performed a year after Eisler's *Deutsche Sinfonie*, which offers the most striking similarities of outlook. Both compositions are provocative documents of protest against oppression. They juxtapose symphonic orchestral music with writing for vocal soloists and chorus. In both, the musical language eschews complexity and remains entirely consistent within its own very defined parameters. The vocal settings are kept deliberately simple so as not to obscure the intelligibility of the text.[12]

---

[11] David Drew Op. Cit.

[12] Shostakovich may well have studied Eisler's work when planning his symphony. In the fourth movement (a setting of Yevtushenko's poem *Fears*), the composer briefly pays a musical tribute to his colleague in a passage which chronicles the Russian people's preparedness to go into battle under shell-fire despite their fear of talking amongst themselves. Shostakovich casts this section of the poem in the form of a defiant march and follows Eisler's example in emphasizing his favourite interval of a minor third.

While force of circumstances has so far prevented Eisler's *Deutsche Sinfonie* from establishing its rightful place at the centre of the twentieth century repertoire, it is to be hoped that perhaps in the 1990s the work's relevance will begin to be fully appreciated. With the rising tide of fascism that has swept through Europe during the past few years, we can ill afford to ignore its evils as so eloquently exposed in this compelling masterpiece.

13

HOLLYWOOD AND HOME: HANNS EISLER'S 'HÖLDERLIN-FRAGMENTE' FOR VOICE AND PIANO

Hanns-Werner Heister

The Context of the *Hollywood Song Book.*

'That is to say, art also changes in tradition. Look, when I returned from the First World War, in 1919, I could never have set a poem like, for example, *An eine Stadt,* because I was fed up with patriotism. The years of emigration, which sharpened the senses, had to come, and also the introspection, the art of remembering. You know, it is a great art, to remember. *You* can't have it because you are younger than me. But once you have been an emigrant for fourteen years, remembering this damned Germany, you get a different view of things. You look back — without sentimentality . . . A stupid composer would have turned all that into sentimental trash. My remembering was "cool, polite, gentle."'

Thus Eisler, in conversation with Hans Bunge on 24 August 1961[1] — almost two decades after the genesis of the six *Hölderlin-Fragmente* which Manfred Grabs[2] dates between May and August 1943:

1	*An die Hoffnung*	To Hope	20 May 1943
2	*Andenken*	Remembrance	3 June 1943
3	*Elegie 1943*	Elegy 1943	10 June 1943
4	*Die Heimat*	Home	21 June 1943
5	*An eine Stadt*	To a City	22 June 1943
6	*Erinnerung*	Memory	2 August 1943

The *Hölderlin Fragments* belong to the *Hollywood Song Book,* planned as a song-collection (and also designated as *The Little Hollywood Song Book*). Eisler began the collection on 30 May 1942 and went on with it until 28 December 1943. It consists of forty-seven songs, a further two 'appended', and a series of unpublished fragmentary aphorisms.[3] The

[1] *Gespräche mit Hans Bunge.* GWE Leipzig 1975, pp. 192–3 [see p. 427 Ed.]

[2] *Handbuch.* See bibliography.

[3] GWE I/16 p. 262.

focal point is poems by Brecht, like those written in exile in Scandinavia [.....] but also some written there and then, especially for Eisler (amongst others the *Hollywood Elegies)*, flanked by poems by Hölderlin, Mörike, Goethe, Pascal, Rimbaud, Eichendorff, Berthold Viertel and Biblical texts.'[4] Alongside the already mentioned *Five Elegies* and the six *Anakreon Fragments*, the *Hölderlin-Fragmente* form a third, relatively closed cycle with the *Song Book*.

Eisler originally numbered the *Hölderlin-Fragmente* from I to VI and also added to the title of each of them *Hollywood Song Book* in brackets. Later, however, he crossed this out; in other words he moved away from the idea of the song-collection. However, the Hölderlin songs form a separate entity through the unifying basis of the texts. No. 2, *Andenken*, Eisler is uncertain about. Here he at first extends the title by a foot-note, *'or the art of thinking back'*. In addition he tries including the song in another idea for a cycle, numbering it *Hollywood Elegy No. 13*, but later rescinds this arrangement. On the whole, however, the *Hölderlin-Fragmente* form a sharply distinct entity through the texts.

Not a completely closed entity, however, for Eisler does not only restrict himself to the art of thinking back and remembering but he thinks ahead too, and envisages, from his exile, a better future in his home-land. In the autograph version of the same second song, he says (later crossed out): *'Preface to the Hollywood Song Book.* In a society which understands and loves such a song book, it will be possible to live safely and well. It is with confidence in such a society that these pieces are written. Hanns Eisler 3 June 1943 (Pacific Palisades). P.S. What can music, alongside so much else, do for the future? It can help to avoid a false richness of tone.'

Hölderlin Texts

Once this future had become the present, Eisler turned once again to Hölderlin. On 15 September 1959 he set another Hölderlin poem: *Um meine Weisheit unbekümmert* (Unconcerned about my wisdom). It is dedicated 'to my wife Steffi', on the occasion of their arrival together in the GDR. The recording by Roswitha Trexler and Jutta Czapski (Wergo 60073; 1975) carries this extra song as No. 7, which now, however, no longer directly belongs to the exile cycle.

---

[4] Fritz Hennenberg: *Das grosse Brecht-Liederbuch*. Berlin GDR 1984, p. 459

[5] GWE I/16 p. 241

Finally, in 1961/62, Eisler reached right back to the *Hölderlin-Fragmente* again in the *Ernste Gesänge for baritone solo and string orchestra* likewise 'dedicated to my wife, Steffi'. The fourth song of the total of seven is nothing other than an orchestration of *An die Hoffnung* where the strings are able to give greater clarity to the canonic counterpoint of the piano part.

Asyl (Refuge), No. 1, forges another link back to exile in the USA from the newly found home in the GDR. The autograph score carries the note: 'Mexico City — Berlin', 1939/1961, but as no sketch has been found in the unpublished work that could be regarded as a starting-point for the *Ernste Gesänge* we may assume that Eisler was referring to a projected work.[6]

The juxtaposition of such diverse constituents makes Eisler's intention all the more significant. Not only does he use Hölderlin texts for the work's opening, the Prelude and Epigraph, but also for No. 6 *Komm ins Offene, Freund*! (Come into the open, friend). He also expressly describes both songs as Hölderlin Fragments in order to emphasize the connection.

At the same time, textually, *Asyl* reveals the new, greater calm or calming. In Hölderlin the poem is called *Mein Eigentum* (My Belongings) — written in Stuttgart in 1800 — and along with much else it articulates the contrast between the man who lives 'secure at home' (Eisler) 'or by his own hearth in his splendid home', and the 'homeless' wanderer. The latter's wish — and Eisler reiterates it significantly — is 'Song, be my kind refuge.' Even this phrase draws on exile music once more, a motif from the end-title music for *The Woman on the Beach*, a film made by Jean Renoir in 1946/47 — one of the countless examples of Eisler's several re-uses of a motive through which he establishes cross-connections between different genres as well as continuities in every radical biographical and idiomatic upheaval.

There are also retrospective lines of connection. In the autograph version of the first song, *An die Hoffnung*, Eisler notes at the end: 'Use this perhaps as extra material for *Goliath* (In the *Singers' War Scene*) (Then set it for strings!)'[8] This refers to an opera project of Brecht and Eisler begun in 1937 in Skobovstrand. Even after the completion of the

[6] Grabs. *'Wir, so gut es gelang, haben das Unsre getan.' Beiträge zur Musikwissenschaft* 15, 1973

[7] Grabs. *Handbuch.* p. 80

[8] Ibid. p. 88

Hölderlin-Fragmente the project still occupied them both. On 6 January 1944 Brecht made a note in his *Arbeitsjournal* – 'frequent talks with Eisler about music (concerning the GOLIATH OPERA) and with Dessau, who is a lot less developed and is inflexible'.[9]

To judge from the outline[10] Brecht and Eisler are concerned here once again with the great theme of a critique of German fascism in the form of an historicizing parable. Scene 3a is called *The Mastersingers of Gad.* Clearly this is an attack on the Nazi Wagner cult and their appropriation of *Die Meistersinger* in particular, which Eisler here links with *Tannhäuser*. (The three crossed out letters could have been the beginning of *'War(tburg)'*. Ex. 13.1

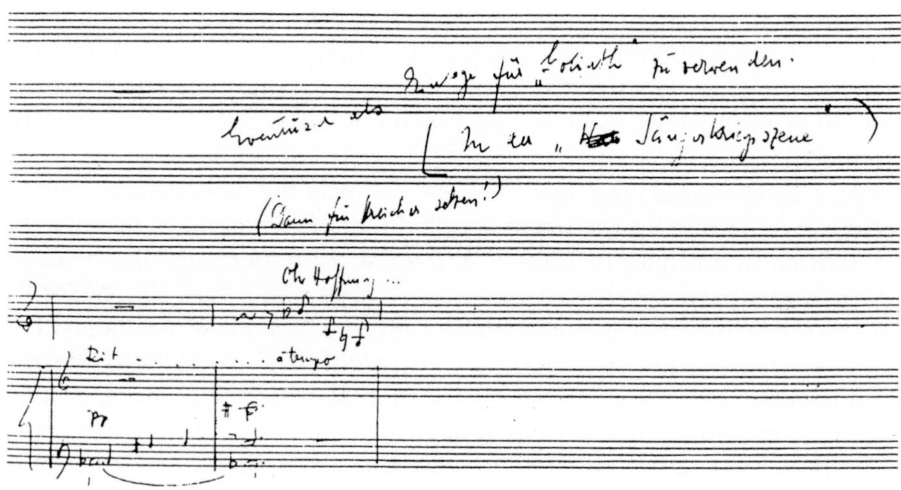

Ex. 13.1

Apart from this Eisler notates two 'bars of prologue'.[11] The piano notation is an exact, transposed inversion of the song opening (in the song the piano comes in on F), i.e., with the intervals 10 – 1– 6. For *Goliath* Eisler really wanted to use a purely instrumental version, without the Hölderlin words.

---

[9] *Brecht Arbeitsjournal* 1938 – 55. Berlin Weimar, No. 701, p. 336

[10] Grabs. *Handbuch.* p. 88.

[11] Ibid.

With a total of eleven texts, Hölderlin was 'the classical poet most frequently set by Eisler'.[12] Eisler saw him as a 'Jacobin'[13] in opposition to the prevailing conservative, nationalistic view. Here he could refer to Georg Lukács, for example, who in 1935 had already written in the Moscow Periodical, *International Literature*: 'For Hölderlin there was no home, neither in nor outside Germany.'[14] A realistic historical prerequisite for the new, progressive assimilation of the elegiac poet, in particular with the suffering at the contradiction between the real and the ideal, was the People's Front, the broadest and most comprehensive possible uniting of all the opponents of the Nazi regime: 'At that time Hölderlin was discovered as the supreme classical poet for the new socialist culture. Under the banner of the anti-fascist united front of the middle class and communists, the unification of cultural heritage and socialism, of Hölderlin and Marx, already insisted on in 1921 by Thomas Mann, was realized'.[15] Mann reiterated his thoughts in 1928 in a different form: 'I said that Germany will only be all right, and will have found itself, once Karl Marx has read Friedrich Hölderlin — a confrontation which is in the process of being arranged. I forgot to add that a one-sided acquaintance would be bound to remain unfruitful'.[16]

It was in an attitude of 'inner emigration' that Paul Hindemith, for example, set Hölderlin in 1933 and 1935.[17] And we understand it as resistance against Nazi nationalism and revulsion to it, when the pianist and composer Gideon Klein (1919–1945), a pupil of Alois Hába, bases one of his two *Madrigals* on a text of Hölderlin in 1943 in Theresienstadt concentration camp — in a Czech translation.[18]

---

[12] Grabs. *'Wir, so gut es gelang.'*

[13] *Gespräche mit Hans Bunge.* 24 August 1961. [see p. 426 Ed.]

[14] Albrecht Dümling. *'Friedrich Hölderlin - vertont von H. Eisler, P. Hindemith, Max Reger,* Munich 1981, p. 12.

[15] Ibid.

[16] Ibid. p. 16.

[17] Ibid. pp. 85 - 91.

[18] See Joza Karas - *Musik in Terezin* 1941 - 1945. New York 1985, p. 23.

Place of Exile - Hollywood

For Eisler himself there were some parallels between his and Hölderlin's situation. Their common denominator is homelessness in the here and now, linked with revulsion and revolt against the reality of the times. 'Like Hölderlin in Germany, Eisler . . . was a stranger too, a fugitive in Hollywood. Both had hope in the future, both produced it for posterity. [. . .] Just as for Hölderlin the retrospective look at Greece represented a utopian contrast to contemporary Germany, so for Eisler, too, the remembering of Germany was at the same time a look forward to the future. With his Hölderlin songs he was aiming both at the contemporary Germany of Hitler and at contemporary Hollywood.' He quoted 'from Germany history and pointed simultaneously at the present — two examples of the German *'Misere'*. In addition to his 'outer emigration', to his opposition to Hitler, there was his revolt against the culture industry in Hollywood.'[19] Exactly like the situation of 'inner emigration', the outward one required discretion in any open expression of political attitudes. (After the end of the war and the Roosevelt era, Eisler was caught up after all in the wheels of McCarthyism). 'The complicated social situation, in which an imperialist state was supposed to stand up for democracy against a fascist dictatorship, although it must have been the object of revolutionary attacks itself, did not license the creation of provocative songs of incitement and struggle.'[20] The openly critical works Eisler wrote for the drawer — to wait there for the hoped-for, better future. He composed the *Hölderlin-Fragmente* in Pacific Palisades near Los Angeles. Materially, because of his work for films, he was better off than most of the artists driven out by Nazism — which, however, did little to lessen his sadness and fury at the lost homeland, or his irritation at the new. Thus he says in passing in the conversation with Bunge (24 August 1961): '. . . I was sitting in Hollywood. Financially I was well off. But it rankled me that these poor Germans are and were such bastards.'[21]

Complementary to the *Hölderlin-Fragmente* is, amongst others, the cycle of *Hollywood Elegies*, called *Fünf Elegien*, to poems by Bertolt Brecht, one in English even, and an additional English one by Eisler himself. No. 2, 'To be performed with gloomy *Schmalz*,' displays a dismissive attitude: 'The town is named after the angels, and every-

---

[19] Dümling. *Hölderlin* p. 96.

[20] Grabs. *'Wir, so gut es gelang.'* p. 52.

[21] [See p. 428 Ed.]

where you meet them. They smell of oil and wear golden pessaries . . .' And Hollywood itself, the main district, is referred to in a grudging, epigrammatic way with a dialectic between major and minor:[22] 'This town has taught me that paradise and hell can be one town. For those without means, paradise is hell.'

Punning fiercely with names and religious-historical references, Joseph Roth writes on 12 August 1934 in the Paris Daily News: 'I came to Hollywood, to *'Hölle-wut'*, [a germanized phonetic spelling of Hollywood meaning 'hell-fury'] to the place where hell rages furiously, that is, where people are the *'Doppelgänger'* of their own shadows. It is the source of all the shades of the world, the Hades that sells its shades for money, the shades of the living and the dead, to all the film-screens of the world. Here all the owners of serviceable shades come together and sell their shades for money and are deemed blessed and holy, according to the significance of their shades [. . . .] This is Hollywood. Hell rages. Here they all frisk about: the producers of shadow players, shadow dealers and make-up technicians, and shadow managers that they call directors, shadow conjurors and shadow lenders. And there are some who sell their own voices to the shade of another who speaks another language.'[23]

The Brecht/Eisler duo, critically self-ironic throughout, catches the ever-present and all powerful commercialization in an image of (intellectual) prosititution:

Elegy I
Beneath the green pepper trees
Musicians are on the streets
In two by two with the writers
Bach's got a 'street' quartet in his bag
Dante wiggles his bony backside

Text Montage as Assimilation of Tradition

In contrast to this present hell, which is at once refuge and exile, distance wins for the time being, if only just. Not only does Eisler's music preserve a certain detachment almost constantly, in spite of a basically friendly attitude which can grow into the loving address of the distant

---

[22] See Wolfgang Hufschmidt's informative analysis *Willst du meinen Liedern dein Leier drehn? Zur Semantik der musikalischen Sprache in Schubert's Winterreise und Eisler's Hollywood Liederbuch.* Esp. pp. 240–244.

[23] J. Roth in *Berliner Saisonbericht. Unbekannte Reportagen und journalistische Arbeiten 1920 - 39.* Ed. Klaus Westermann, Cologne 1984, p. 393.

beloved: even textually, Eisler himself often intervenes in the content and structure, often rigorously and with sustained musical effect, and sweeps away all that is hymn-like, all pathos: 'If I identify myself completely with the text, empathise with it, hover behind it, well, that's dreadful. A composer has to view the text in a way full of contradictions. The tragic element is interpreted by me cheerfully. . . . If ever I'm praised for anything, it will be for resisting the text.'[24]

The general aesthetic and theoretical authorization for this supplies him with a specific view of tradition, of the 'cultural heritage'. Analogously to the dialectical conjunction of *'Volksfront'* and *'Avantgarde'*, he aims at a mediation of history and actuality in which the art of the past is newly evaluated in the light of present experience and selected to meet actual, urgent tasks and goals.

This is the spirit in which, with Ernst Bloch, Eisler in 1938 sketches *Die Kunst zu erben* (Inheriting Art) and, in the sub-title, confronts 'schematic and productive inheritance.'

To this task belongs 'the selection and preparation of classical material suited to such a fight' (meaning the anti-fascist one). 'This, however, commits one further to a thorough critical processing of our historical heritage, in contradistinction to the misuse of it by the Nazis. And in this, the very manner of the method of inheriting, the living relation to the past of the progressive man of today, plays an absolutely decisive part.'[25]

In the *Hölderlin Fragments*, the frequently extreme abbreviation of the original poems is remarkable.

Hölderlin		*Eisler*
I	*An die Hoffnung* (To Hope) 5 verses	 Verses 1 + 2
II	*Andenken* (Remembrance) 5 verses	 Verses 1 + 2 (shortened)
III	*Der Frieden* (Peace) 14 verses	Elegy 1943 1, 2, 7, 8, 9
IV	*Die Heimat* (Home) 2 verses	 2 lines of V.2 shortened
V	*Heidelberg* 8 verses	An eine Stadt (To a town) 1, 2, 3, 5, 8 (5 & 8 shortened)
VI	*Gesang des Deutschen* (Song of the German) 15 verses	Erinnerung (Memory) 1, 2, 4, 6

[24] *Gespräche mit Bunge* p. 192. [see p. 426 Ed.]

[25] *Schriften* 1924 – 1948, p. 407.

The cuts follow one main tendency above all: 'Omitted or severely restricted are depictions of detail, duplicated expressions, thoughts developed too far, allegories, mythical images or descriptions of nature and landscape, in so far as they do not belong directly to the theme of the poem. Anything atmospheric in the text is also repressed because this the music contributes, independently'.[26]

A clear and topical interpretation is supplied too, by the alterations to some of the titles. In *Elegie 1943* the year of composition is given precisely 'in order to relate the 'horrific slaughter' of the poem directly to World War Two; this war, too, had its origins in the excessive claims to power of earlier generations and in rivalries with other European states.'[27]

Through abbreviation as through alteration of title, 'town' takes on a more general application, though Eisler might also be referring here to his home town of Vienna.[28] Finally, the alteration of the title of No. 6 aims at a change in interpretation. Along with the ode *Der Tod fürs Vaterland, Gesang des Deutschen* was 'widely quoted from and set to music'[29] around 1914 as throughout the Nazi period. However, Hölderlin's 'enlightened cosmopolitan patriotism, directed not against foreign countries but against structures of authority in his own country',[30] aims at realizing the ideals of the French Revolution. Eisler takes up these 'Jacobin' perspectives but rejects Hölderlin's solemn appeal to the *polis* as symbol of republic and democracy. With his title alteration he makes it 'clear that he was concerned not with contemporary Germany, the Germany of Hitler, but with one past and destroyed, with Germans not as agents but as sacrifices'[31] — a truly unusual perspective for 1943 that applies not least to the subordinate position of those in exile in the commercial world of Hollywood.

In his invocation of Hope, what interests him above all in his exiled situation is the question; 'Where are you?' He ignores Hölderlin's excursion in search of it *'Im grünen Tale'* (In the green valley) verse 3 line 1, and *'Dort in der Stille'* (There in the calm) verse 3 line 4, together with

---

[26] Grabs. *'Wir, so gut es gelang.'* p. 50.

[27] Dümling. Hölderlin p. 100.

[28] Ibid. p. 102.

[29] Ibid.

[30] Ibid.

[31] Ibid. p. 103.

the anticipation of its appearance. With a plebeian attitude he deletes *'Edle'* (noble) in verse 1 line 3, and with an anti-religious one omits *'und Himmelsmächten'* (and the powers of Heaven) verse 1 line 4; lastly because of its distracting Hollywood associations, the *'Im Busen'* (in the breast) of verse 2 line 4 disappears.

It is not only because they may have been trivialized by over-use by head-teachers and public speakers that Eisler dispenses with the famous last lines of *Andenken: 'Was bleibet aber, stiften die Dichter'* (What remains, however, is supplied by the poets). In spite of the 'writing for the drawer' and the looking to the future, this might well have seemed to him rather illusory and at least, in the framework of the cycle, historically premature.

The anticipated 'actual and imaginary' fulfilment of hope comes only in No. 6 *Erinnerung* — and in a musical way too. Here the omission of the second part (with the exception of No. 5, Eisler always shortens from the end, as if he were a news editor) makes particular sense, since now the 'artist', returned to his homeland and productive there, finally appears: *'Und an den Ufern Sah ich die Städte blühn, ... Die Wissenschaft, wo deine Sonne Milde dem Künstler zum Ernste leuchtet.'* (And on the river banks I saw the towns flourish, ... science, where your sun mildly inspires the artist to seriousness.'

The imperfect tense of *'sah'*, already in Hölderlin suggesting a vision that looks both backwards and forwards, becomes even stronger with Eisler's two-sided character. And, as in ones imagination, so in music, too, (as will be shown), home becomes a present reality. So Dümling is right to generalize: 'At the level of musical expression, too, it is a return to a harmony that would be 'false' as an expression of the present, but which as a memory is at the same time a very Utopia. It is a look back into the future.'[32]

In No. 3 *Elegie*, Eisler's autograph uses the archaic sounding *'schröklichern'* (more dreadful) and this has, correctly, been modernized in the Complete Works edition; but in No. 4 *Die Heimat*, another of Eisler's pseudo-archaisms has survived (verse 1, line 1) *'Froh kehrt der Schiffer heim an hellen* (in Hölderlin *'stillen'*) *Strome.'* (Happy, the sailor returns home to the clear streams.' Grabs[33] points out the morphologically senseless *Strome* in the autograph, which could stem from Eisler's need for a two-syllabled word for his descending falling semitone

[32] Ibid. p. 104.

[33] Grabs. *Werk und Edition.* Berlin 1978, p. 37.

motive. (see Ex. 13.18). However, this cannot justify the alteration in the second verse of *Elegie*, which masks Hölderlin's perfectly clear sense and, syntactically, creates the very sort of obscurity he is often reproached with:

Holderlin	*So gärt' und wuchs und wogte von Jahr zu Jahr* *Rastlos und überschwemmte das bange Land* *Die unerhörte Schlacht, daß weit hüllt* *Dunkel und Bläße das Haupt der Menschen*
Eisler	*So gärt' und wuchs und wogte von Jahr zu Jahr* *Die unerhörte Schlacht, daß weit hüllt in* *Dunkel und Bläße das Haupt der Menschen* *(So seethed and grew and surged from year to year* *Restlessly flooding the frightened land Horrific slaughter* *that (in) darkness and pallor Shrouded the heads of men)*

Only by dispensing with the *'in'*, dispensable also to the musical declamation, is the sense restored.

All in all, however, Eisler's reworking of the text produces the laconic idiom which Brecht was striving for at this time, a brevity and terseness of text formulation as a starting point for that very avoidance of 'false fullness of tone.' It comes closest to the essence of the text to liken Eisler's procedures and his relation to his textual material to those of a librettist. Thus Brecht, too, notes in his work journal for 25 June 1943: 'Eisler has written two marvellous cycles for his *Little Hollywood Song Book,* Anakreon poems and Hölderlin poems. Here we can glimpse a possibility of achieving a chorus in a drama, since from now on the settings are wholly gestic.'[34]

All the same, Brecht, never particularly fussy himself in his dealings with the classics, does seem to have expressed some reservations. Eisler alludes to this in his conversation with Bunge on 26 August 1961, but dismisses the criticism: 'Brecht said to me. . . .: 'It is quite fascinating the way you take the plaster off Hölderlin! You select some lines, set them to music, and somehow it fits.' He was a) appalled (as was my friend Arnold Zweig) — and certainly it is an impudence — but b) both of them were actually in favour of it, because from a poem of Hölderlin's which often has four pages of strophes, I picked out eight lines which were appropriate.[35]

---

[34] *Arbeitsjournal* No. 577, p. 578.

[35] *Gespräche* p. 191 [see p. 426 Ed.]

Eisler characterizes his method of appropriation by saying: 'I wasn't criticizing him, I was quoting him.'[36] What matters to him is dialectical resolution — rejecting, keeping, raising to a higher level — for which he many times uses the image of the *'Fliege im Bernstein'*, (the fly preserved in amber). Brecht sees Eisler's creative realisation of the text as an interpretation: 'His settings are for me what a performance is to a play: he reads the text with enormous precision.'[37]

Verse Metres and Propensities for Prose

What Eisler's presentation of the text disregards, indeed often quite destroys with a considerable lack of care and attentiveness, is the metrical structure of the Hölderlin poem. With the exception of No. 2 of the poems used by Eisler, Hölderlin employs as his model ancient strophic forms — Alcaic for 1, 3, 4 and 6; Asclepiadean for No. 5. (The third familiar verse form, Sapphic, only appears once in Hölderlin; otherwise he confines himself to the other two).[38]

In No. 5, for example, Eisler abbreviates, for his fourth stanza, Hölderlin's fifth in such a way that the metrical regularity of the Asclepiadean verse form is abandoned:

Hölderlin — *Quellen hattest du ihm, hattest dem Flüchtigen*
Eisler — *Du hast dem Flüchtigen kühlenden Schatten geschenkt,*

Kühle Schatten geschenkt, und die Gestade sahn
Und die Gestade sahen

All' ihm nach, und es bebte
Ihm alle nach, und es tönte

Aus den Wellen ihr lieblich Bild.
Aus den Wellen das liebliche Bild.

Hölderlin — *(You had given him spring water, water to the fugitive*
Eisler — *You gave the fugitive cooling shade,*

Given him cool shade, and the shores all gazed
And the shores all gazed

After him and there quivered
After him and there resounded

Out of the waves her fair image.
Out of the waves the fair image.)

---

[36] Ibid.

[37] *Arbeitsjournal* 26 July 1942 No 497, p. 251.

[38] See Gerhard Storz. *Der Versen in der neueren deutschen Dichtung.* Stuttgart 1973, p. 181.

Whereas Eisler here, as in No. 6, preserves at least the outlines of the metric scheme (as in No. 1, too, although interrupted through repetition of the text), in Nos. 3 and 4 he frees it more completely. In No. 4 the Alcaic structure is broken up by repetition of the fourth line in verse one, and in the second verse the metre approaches free rhythm or prose even:

Hölderlin (First version)	*Ihr holden Ufer, die ihr mich auferzogt,* *Stillt ihr der Liebe Leiden? ach gebt ihr mir,* *Ihr Wälder meiner Kindheit! Wann ich* *Komme, die Ruhe noch einmal wieder?*
Eisler	*Ihr holden Ufer, die ihr mich auferzogt,* *ach geb ihr mir, ihr Wälder meiner Kindheit!* *Wann ich wiederkehre,* *die Ruhe noch einmal wieder?*
Eisler	*(You fair shores, who raised me, oh give me,* *you forests of my childhood, when I return,* *peace once more.)*

In the musical declamation of this verse, Eisler's phrasing follows the intended combination of Hölderlin's second and third lines as a sort of *'enjambement'*. The third phrase leads on analogously. In contrast Eisler introduces additional line-breaks with phrases 4 and 5. This emphasizes the metric-melodic extension that is also strengthened by syncopations and the mini-melismatic breaking of syllables on 'ein'-(mal); above all it is determined by the motive, *Ruhe* (peace). Ex. 13.2 (compare Ex. 13.18):

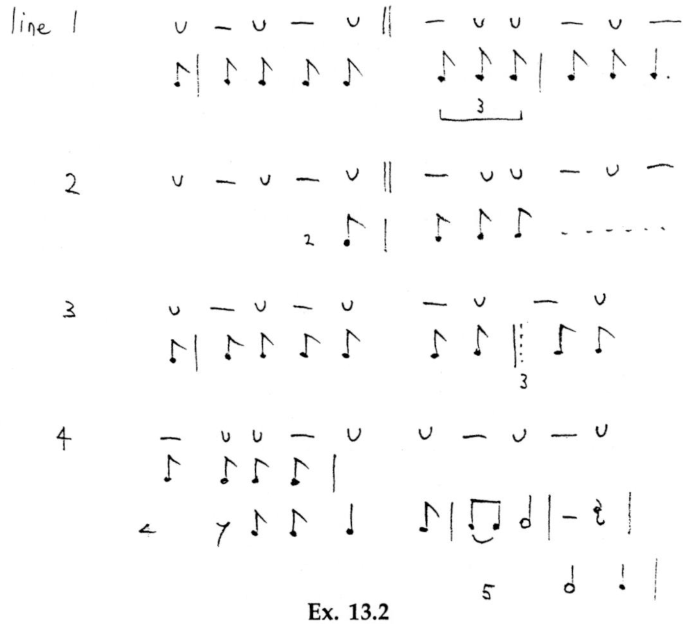

Ex. 13.2

In general it is the specific ode-metre that Eisler destroys; however, in contrast, he often preserves conciliatory structures — most noticeably in No. 5, *An eine Stadt,* which not for nothing, is 'dedicated to Franz Schubert'. Here he adopts the attitude and construction of the classical *Lied,* 'reflected' through his own *Kampflied* tradition.

On the other hand, in No. 2, Eisler brings Hölderlin's free rhythms even closer to traditional verse rhythms and this in spite of the predominantly atonal idiom which in itself really has more of an affinity with musical prose. (See Ex. 13.11)

Even when he is aiming at similar, traditional metric groupings, Eisler still builds in little shocks and deviations. Thus in the last part of No. 2, the key-phrase *'einwiegende Lüfte'* (lulling breezes) leads to a 6/8 rhythm which keeps hovering between two contrasting but complementary chords. Only in lines one and two does Eisler's phrasing alter Hölderlin's line-breaks:

Hölderlin	*An Feiertagen gehn* *Die braunen Frauen daselbst* *Auf seidnen Boden,* *Zur Märzenzeit,*
Eisler	*An Feiertagen* *gehn die braunen Frau'n daselbst* *Auf seidnen Boden,* *Zur Märzenzeit,*

(On holidays, the brown women walk there on silken floors, in March).

The sequence established here of (1 + 1) + 2 bars is at once intersected by a 9/8 bar for the fourth line *'in Märzenzeit'*; this shortens the prescribed two-bar grouping by half a bar (3/8) and produces the sequence $1 + \frac{1}{2} + 2$. Only then does Eisler bring the deviation under control again and composes his lines 6 – 8 as (1 + 1) + (1 + 1) + (1 + 1).

However, he complicates the situation by counterpointing the arrangement of the lines and phrases with a sequence of accompanying chords which deviates from it: Ex. 13.3

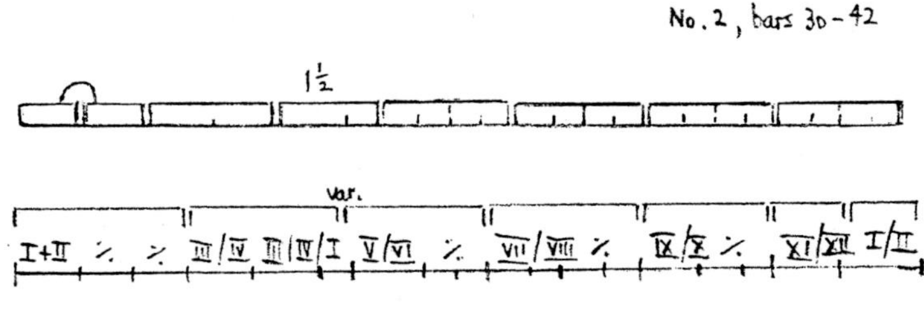

Ex. 13.3

So, at the structural level, too, Eisler both follows the text and at the same time resists it: 'This approach will guarantee optimal comprehensibility of the language; by musical means a counterpoint is added to the text in which the intentions of the text are preserved at a level of musical speech.'[39]

Despite his praise for the 'gestic' settings characteristic of the *Hölderlin-Fragmente* Brecht remained in general sceptical about the eradication of the metrical structure: 'Modern music converts texts into prose even when they are poetry, and then lyricizes the prose. The lyricizing is at the same time a psychologizing. The rhythm is loosened (except in Stravinsky and Bartók). For the epic theatre, this is totally unusable.'[40] At least in his criticism of the 'prosaicizing' tendency of modern music Brecht agrees with Goethe, who criticized a corresponding tendency of (Romantic) literature: 'All poetry should be treated rhythmically! That is my conviction and the fact that people could gradually introduce a poetic prose only shows that they were completely losing sight of the difference between poetry and prose.'[41]

The People's Front and the B-A-C-H Motif

The exile that cut Eisler off from his crucial public, the organised workers' movement, to some extent forced him to revoke his break with the 'bourgeois concert song', which he had made in the twenties. No longer being able to compose in direct, practical involvement with the masses opened up the opportunity to rethink material forgotten or shelved in the earlier 'withdrawal' and to try out something new — great themes, like the concept of the *Deutsche Sinfonie* for instance — as if under laboratory conditions. 'The need to be easily intelligible and directly comprehensible could diminish during the exile period, but of course it was retained and was a necessary aspect of the 'breadth and variety of a realistic way of writing'. (Brecht). What was important now, however, was that the great national subject, the themes of the anti-fascist resistance and the socialist struggles and ideals could not be accomplished with simple means and small-scale forms alone.'[42]

---

[39] Hufschmidt. *'Semantik'* p. 220.

[40] *Arbeitsjournal* 6 November 1944 No. 701, p. 336.

[41] Letter to Schiller, 25 November 1797, quoted in Storz p. 201.

[42] Günter Mayer: *Gesellschaflicher und musikalischer Fortschritt,* in *Beiträge zur Musikwissenschaft 15,* 1974, p. 27.

Certainly the very complexity of the intellectual and compositional procedures widens the traditionally relatively narrow scope of the song with piano accompaniment. Here 'the classical Schubert-type song serves as a model above all: melody dominates of course and indeed at a comfortable pitch that guarantees a comprehensible declamation.'[43] Such modesty and restraint in external matters is compensated for not only by an inner richness but also by the involvement of each individual song in the cyclical grouping. 'In terms of coherence and perspective, individual songs will be too weak to stand alone; only in the cycle can they make their point; and in addition the individual unit can be given further significance by the context of the passage into which it is incorporated.'[44]

Also to be included in the wealth of references is the range of material and means used, as well as methods and procedures. This, as has often been commented on, is true in general of Eisler. According to Georg Knepler, it is 'his astonishing, but quite logical and absolutely successful, attempt to reconcile in his work the apparently irreconcilable, the styles of light music with those of loftier genres, of the modern and the more traditionally based, of a revolutionary stance and an easy-going one, indeed even of elegance.' As the common denominator Knepler proposes the formula: 'the familiar in unfamiliar surroundings.'[45]

For Eisler it is always a question of articulating musically a wealth of ideas; of shaping them precisely and multi-dimensionally in order to give them sense — and this, wherever possible, and in the smallest detail, from the perspective of 'Change the world; it needs it!'

'The basic theme of the cycle,' says Dümling, 'is expounded in the first song, *An die Hoffnung*: the principle of hope as the root of all further development even when set-backs thrust it into the background.'[46]

Eisler sets the key-word itself prominently at the beginning, linked with the invocation. The tempo indication designating both the gesture and manner of performance, intensifies the urgency: '*Zart drängende ♩ (etwas hastig)*' ('Tenderly urgent ♩ (rather hurried)'). The

---

[43] Hennenberg: *Liederbuch* p. 459.

[44] Albrecht Betz. *Hanns Eisler, Political Musician.* Cambridge 1982, pp. 193–4.

[45] George Knepler. *Diskussion mit Eberhardt Klemm* (1965). In Grabs *'Wer war Hanns Eisler?'* Berlin 1983, p. 378.

[46] Dümling op. cit. p. 99. Examples 13.4 and 5 are taken from here.

'expression of thrusting urgency' is at once strengthened by the imitation of the motto in the piano part. Ex. 13.4

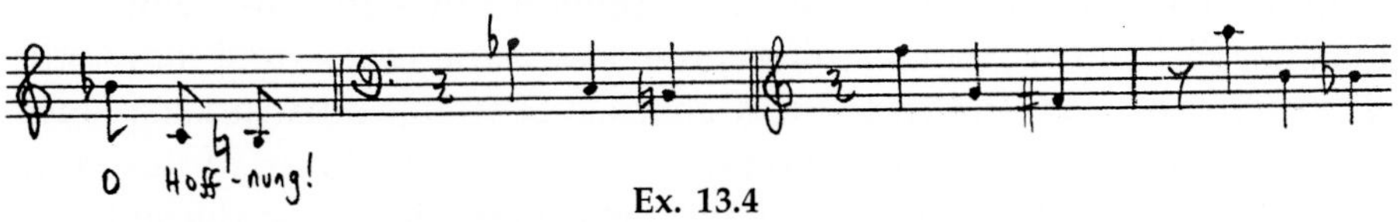

Ex. 13.4

Here, as in the vocal line, by means of developing variation, everything seems always new and different, and yet the same. Ex. 13.5

Ex. 13.5

This reminds us, and not just by chance, of the twelve-note way of thinking in Webern's formulation of it. Admittedly there is no real underlying serial organization here, as far as one can see. But as a background at least, it is unmistakeable. For Eisler is, audibly, endeavouring — in spite of the repetition in the third imitative entry and other small pitch repetitions — to move through the total chromatic in the shortest possible space, as is also suggested by the underlying twelve-note row. Ex. 13.6a and 6b

Ex. 13.6a An die Hoffnung

Ex. 13.6b

B flat as starting point and goal of the imitative entries produces a circular form, and not just an approximate one; on the principle of the 'familiar in unfamiliar surroundings', Eisler also points to connections with a technique which he has used several times in other works, for instance in 'Study on a twelve-note row, *Präludium und Fuge über B-A-C-H'* of 1934. In this the row consists of straightforward sequences of the motto. Eisler's comment on it is sceptical. The choice of this motto 'does not denote a homage to Johann Sebastian Bach, who doesn't need to be honoured in this way. The choice of the motto is much more to be related to the bourgeois mysticism of the workaday musician who often understands no more of Bach than the letters of his name.'[47] (For all that, Schoenberg also makes reference to the motto in his Opus 31).

That Trio was written for pedagogical purposes. In the *Hölderlin Fragmente* such a 'mysticism' acts, in the consciousness of *Volksfront*, as a mediator between the classical heritage and the avant-garde. A structural link is created for this by the minor second which, together with its inversion, the major seventh, is a clear 'code' for atonality. As it does via the code, so it also, within the song, mediates between the predominantly atonal idiom and the built-in tonal elements: 'the minor second stated in the initial phrase combines five major triads and leaps of a sixth.' (see Ex. 13.9 bars 1–3).[48]

From within the intervallic core of falling minor seconds, the motto — used both motivically and semantically as the bearer of the central key-word *Hoffnung* — acts as one of the basic links between the separate songs of the cycle. Even here the connection with B-A-C-H is apparent. In No. 2 it is embedded in the varied sequences of the initial three-note motive. No. 3 begins with a transposed permutation. No. 4, beginning with a series of descending thirds seems to be an exception, but here too, the untransposed code-notes B – A [B flat-A] appear at once in the voice. No. 5 has at the beginning both transposition, in the voice, and permutation, in the piano bass. (See Ex. 13.10b). Finally, in No. 6, the motive at first appears only fragmentarily (the A is included in the piano's varied answer to the voice), but then occurs complete in a transposed permutation. The fact that it begins with the note B flat also completes the circle. Ex. 13.7

---

[47] Eisler. Introduction to the string trio *Präludium und Fuge uber B-A-C-H.*

[48] Karoly Csipak. *Probleme der Volkstümlichkeit bei Hanns Eisler.* Munich and Salzburg 1975, p. 357 n. 508.

Ex. 13.7

'Hope' as a Watch-word, The Motive of 'Home in the Memory'

The organic and chronological links between the individual songs of the cycle are not easy to explain in every detail; the order of the sequence and of composition indicates that a certain development is taking place and that musical thoughts are being successively clarified and defined. It is fairly certain too that Eisler chose and re-worked the poems before writing down the songs, thereby also developing the first thematic ideas. This is supported by such far-reaching structural aspects as may also, with due care, be interpreted organically.

Thus, in another sense even, Eisler is describing an arc from the beginning to the end, from the initial plea to its respective, imagined, anticipated fulfilment. The cycle culminates in fact in a phrygian-plagal F Major final cadence, a familiar and indeed slightly sentimental tonality. (See Ex. 13.22). The beginning of No. 1 thus relates to this tonic as a dominant, as the expression of the still open question. The B flat – C can, together with the E (notes 1, 2 and 6) be interpreted as C7 to the tonic F, whereby the latter, for its part concealed (F – A as notes 4 and 5) is at once anticipated. Moreover F is midway between C and B flat. (See Ex. 13.6a).

Internally, the first song is characterized by dense and complex semantics generated by the words. As usual, (it is the case with all six songs) the vocal line is as a matter of principle declaimed strictly syllabically. The only two deviations from this are for semantic reasons, both, significantly, concerned with words describing physical processes, an area which the language of music approaches more closely than words. So a special emphasis is given to *atmet* (bar 10) with a two-note melisma and *schau-dernde Herz* (bar 17) with the equivalent of a tremolo. In one of the few changes in the version for baritone and strings in the *Ernste Gesänge*, Eisler places the melisma on *-met* rather than *at-* (see Ex. 13.10a), which is no improvement and obscures an internal connection in the cycle (see below).

'Hope' as a musical principle pervades the whole song. Neither the minor second nor the initial exclamation with its falling minor seventh operates purely and simply as a motive. (The falling seventh recurs in a repeated question in bars 6 and 7).[49] The concern is always with a verbal motive and simultaneously a musical one which captures the key-word just like the 'fly in amber'. Moreover, paradoxically enough, the Hope-motive with its falling minor second, the traditional expression of lament, is articulated like an 'In spite of everything!' This fact is achieved by all the phrases, still in a resigned way, being built from descending intervals and having a downwards gesture (apart from the little extension in bar 15).

Elsewhere, Hope appears as a minor third, as in the song *Frühling*, for example, composed on 11 June 1942, a setting of a poem from Brecht's *Steffinische Sammlung*. However, here too the 'fugitive's difficult task' ends with the familiar B-A-C-H motto, transposed and played simultaneously as a cluster. And as in *An die Hoffnung* the chain of major and minor seconds appears in the bass, although for all the seeming similarity of idiom, the orientation is specifically and semantically different. Ex. 13.8

The treatment of the key-word in the piece emphasizes the associations of word and pitch. (For clarity, the orchestral arrangement is used here).[50] Ex. 13.9 Of prime importance is the way words and their meaning are set musically as equivalent or synonymous, for example, with the voice at the beginning with '*Hoffnung*' and its epithet '*holde*'.

---

[49] Dümling op. cit. p. 98.

[50] *Ernste Gesänge*. Breitkopf, Leipzig, 4051. [The transcription from female to male voice and from piano to string orchestra has given rise to further discrepancies. In bar 8, the last note of the first violins is G#, not the original B. The minor seventh seems preferable to a perfect fifth, although the latter interval already exists in the sextuplet group. If Eisler's objective was to avoid bad intonation, he was surely being over-cautious. In bars 10 and 12, the piano bass-line has F# – Eb – Db – C. Eisler's cello F increases the harmonic tension but avoids a clash with the voice part, now at the unison because of the baritone's octave transposition. The D represents a softening of the dissonance with the baritone C, now a minor seventh above the cello. It could be argued that Eisler has effected a small revision of his earlier version rather than just being careless, although he was a very lazy proof-reader. Ed.]

Ex. 13.8 *Frühling*

(Just as here *'holde'* is declaimed with a syncopation, so also is *'wenig'* in bar 9 — iambic instead of trochaic). Since we're concerned with music and not mathematics, certain relationships may not be precise or will be obvious variations, as in the first violins in bar one and onwards. Significant new relationships are specifically created by means of the music, as in the focusing of the question as early as bar 2, in the violas, or the extending of the musical text through the verbal one, as is demonstrated in bar 8, by the first violins, by means of the logic of the four-syllable phrase.

Just as there is an underlying, structural dominant-to-tonic relationship between the beginning and end of the cycle, so, already in this first song, the answer to the clearly-stated question is anticipated, softly and below the surface; the unstilled longing is fulfilled in the musical imagination. In bar 10, there appears, harnessed to the semitone of the *Hoffnung*-motive, a more extended motive of both Hope and Remembering — an anticipation of the main motive of No. 5, there treated sequentially. Christian Siebert outlines its harmonic and motive significance in *An eine Stadt* thus: 'On the one hand, the melodic motive contains a falling major third within a segment of a diatonic scale, thereby implying a major-minor tonality. On the other hand, the succeeding, rising, minor third, which contradicts the implications of the initial notes

Etwas hastig
non legato
Bariton
O Hoff-nung! Hol - de! Gü-tig - ge-schäf-ti - ge! Die du das Haus der Trau-ern-den nicht verschmähst
Geigen
Bratschen
Violoncelli
Kontrabässe

Bariton
und ger - ne die-nend zwischen den Sterblichen wal-test: Wo bist du? Wo
Ggn.
Br.
Vcl.
Kb.
pizz.
gliss.

Ex. 13.9

Bariton
Ggn.
Br.
Vcl.
Kb.
bist du?
We-nig lebt' ich; doch at - met kalt mein A-bend schon. Und
arco
molto
div.
stil - le, den Schat-ten gleich, bin ich schon hier; und schon ge - sangs-los schlummert das schau-dern-de
accel.
Herz.

Ex. 13.9 (cont'd)

and the harmony of their scale, makes possible modulations into distant tonalities. The use of major and minor thirds as the basic substance of the melody suggests mediant relationships which then play a central harmonic role. This motive is also highly significant in its rhythmic structure, both as a formal building block as well as an expressive shape. Finally the harmonization of the first note of the melody as the major seventh of the tonic chord suggests the likely use of expressive dissonance.'[51]

Ex. 13.10a

[51] Siebert: *'Das Kompositorische Schaffen Hanns Eislers.'* Thesis submitted at the *Staatliche Hochschule für Musik* Rheinland Grenzland Institut, Aachen 1982, p. 98 ff.

Ex. 13.10b *An eine Stadt*

Siebert's sketch of the further development of this motive shows the crucial function of the following semitone step, even in the third four-bar phrase, bars 9–12. 'Firstly, the minor third is expanded to a diminished triad on D, which, simultaneous with the use of major thirds, retains a major-key character.' (See Ex. 13.10b, bar 9).

Secondly, by means of the crucial flattening of the G to G flat beneath the sequential treatment of the diminished triad (bars 9 – 11), the phrygian scale is introduced. 'The resulting cross-relations, like all other dissonances, are not for technical and formal purposes alone, but for purposes of expressing meaning. They intensify the harmony and give expression to a sort of astringent backdrop which to some extent poses a hidden question of the text's contented hopefulness.'[52] The B flat in the bass in bar 9 shows how the diminished triad on D relates to the harmonic thinking of bar 1 of *An eine Stadt*.

Both the harmony and the phrasing suggest the tread of a *Kampflied* and other similar chord-sequences, progressions and turns of phrase crop up again and again in these songs of exile in Hollywood, just like in a picture-puzzle, not least as a way of conjuring up the political *Heimat*.

---

52 Ibid. p. 100 ff.

In every song of the cycle, there appears a two-part declaration of love grouped around the core *Hoffnung*-motive, not least on account of this very core. In No. 6, the idea, as a paraphrase of the refrain at the outset and as basis of the concluding second part of the cycle, forms into the motto *'Doch magst du manches Schöne nicht bergen mir* (Yet you may not hide from me much that is beautiful. (Bars 28 ff., see Ex. 13.22)[53] In a situation which is dramatically and semantically analogous, the phrase appears once more, in an interlinked series of sequences in No. 2, at the words *'Geh aber nun, grüße die schöne Garonne und die Gärten von Bordeaux.'* (But go now, greet the fair Garonne and the gardens of Bordeaux).

The phrase is found even in the music for the gloomy text of No. 3, the turning-point of the cycle, analogous to the significance of the year 1943 and the battle of Stalingrad in the middle of the Second World War. It is one of Eisler's frequently used dialectical paradoxes that it should occur at *'die unerhörte Schlacht, daß weit hüllt (in) Dunkel und Bläße das Haupt der Menschen'* (See Ex. 13.15a bars 16–20). So in bar 18, over a chromatic bass, there begins a series of descending seventh chords which, in bar 21, culminates in a seventh-ninth chord on B flat (!).

The phrase occurs in its most veiled form, and with some justification, in No. 4 *Die Heimat*, which, as an elegiac lament, prepares for the contrasting idyll of No. 5. All the same, we find here too the corresponding motto, *'Ihr holden Ufer, die ihr mich auferzogt'*, together with the falling semitone acting as a frame, the characteristic triplet on the third (and last) beat of the bar, the sequential passages, as well as the accompaniment of quasi-tonal chords (here arpeggiated, all justifying the relating of this passage to the motto-phrase). (See Ex. 13.18, bars 16–20).

With this tonal interpretation as a major-minor relationship of the orginally atonal falling semitone motto, Hope, expounded as a lament, returns home as a memory full of hope and anticipation, just as if the motive itself had once more come to its senses.

Wind, River, Women: Motives of Movement signifying a good journey

Like the first song, the second also begins with an upbeat of three syllables in the voice. Similar too is the atonal idiom and swift filling-out of the total chromatic, analogous to twelve-note music, and the contrapuntal 'skills of craftsmanship.' Ex. 13.11 The voice contains

[53] See Dümling op. cit. p. 103 ff.

Ex. 13.11 *Andenken*

already in its first two phrases (bars 1–3) ten different pitches (made up to twelve by the E flat and C in the piano), and returns in a circular way to the B flat starting point more clearly than in No. 1 but ending up one octave lower. 'The interval of a second and the falling third from this 'motto' are used again, not only in the piano interlude but also in the sequential treatment of the thirds motive in the subsequent vocal line ('*Geh aber nun* . . . .')[54] – in which, moreover, the interval of a second is determined by other factors.

The core of the motive corresponds to the key-phrase and has three notes — '*Nordost weht*' (North-East blows). The three syllables are taken up by the piano with motive b, while motives b^{2-6} present, in addition to a rhythmic diminution and an anapaest counterpoint, an intervallic variant. Whereas a^1 and a^2 are immediate variations, by contrast, the identical repetition of b^1 and b^2 stands as a symbol of a natural cycle. The B flat of bar 3, both starting note and goal, already signals, like the delayed, symmetrical perfect fourths (which are linked together with the semitone 'hinge' of the *Hoffnung* motive), arrival at the goal of the '*gute Fahrt*'.

While the wind continues to blow, the instrumental parts simultaneously indicate the goal, the '*Vaterland*', transferred metonymically, as it were, by means of the pitches of '*O heilig Herz*' of No. 6 (cf. No. 6 bar 1, Ex. 13.21). This secret message is wrapped in the sequentially extended 'wind' motive. A further allusion to 'home' is in bar 7, with the opening chord of No. 5, transposed up a semitone, which, expanded by the sharpened ninth, has already prominently appeared in the analogous place in No. 1. (See Ex. 13.10a, bar 9).

The wind continues in the falling thirds, which in bar 7 and 8 get faster by means of both shortened note-values and an accelerando, and abates with the semitone of bar 8.

In spite of the slightly faster tempo, in the following section the motion is calmed by the regular pattern of the accompaniment and the regular, complementary rhythmic shape of the voice part. This is in contrast to the end of No. 1 with its '*leidenschaft*', *accelerando* and *crescendo*. 'The wind which blows us onwards becomes a peaceful, lulling accompaniment,'[55] over which the voice's rhythm suggests the movement of the stream, trees and, at the end, women.

However, Eisler differentiates within the relative unity of this uniform motion. Firstly, widely-spaced broken chords in the piano

[54] Ibid. p. 99.

[55] Ibid. p. 99 ff.

bridge the space between Hölderlin's and his *'hier'* and *'dort'*. Once arrived, the voice moves in oscillating semitones like the gentle ruffling of the wind and waves, in one-bar descending sequences. As a contrapuntist schooled in semantics and in film music,[56] Eisler first takes the voice abruptly up at the words *'tief fällt'* (falls deep), returns it to the same note and only then lowers it a semitone.

In the bass of the piano, a similar process is taking place. Here Eisler first takes up the fourths of *'gute Fahrt'* (bars 5 and 6) and extends them. Just as the nearly symmetrical shape suggests the *'Steg'* (bridge), so the *'scharfen Ufer'* (steep bank) is mirrored in the *crescendo-marcato* and the accented syncopations. Although the top line of the piano virtually doubles the voice, it also contributes something of its own, particularly in bar 18, as it pursues its downward course in semitones like a sort of *passus duriusculus*, its contour of lament and hope providing a counterpoint to the overall idyll. This peaceful scene of memory and hope continues evenly until a new element in this depiction of 'home' enters with the 'brown women'. Ex. 13.12

As a signal of 'home', the piano sounds again the chord of the major third with added sharp seventh, here on A flat and C flat. The identical structure of both chords is obscured by the wide spacing and treatment — because of the perfect fourth in the bass, the harmonic movement is almost like an oscillation between tonic and dominant. Elsewhere, too, Eisler repeatedly creates tonal allusions which, even when triadic chords are used, remain illusions, since they are not pursued to a cadential conclusion. This is especially striking at *'von goldnen Träumen'* (of golden dreams) with the sevenths chords of D and C and the B flat and A major triads (bars 39–41). This strengthens the overall impression, as does the oscillating melody with its unusually frequent melismas, of a dream-like lullaby (*'einwiegend'*).

Eisler sets the *'gehn'* (walk) of the woman to the anapaest rhythm of the diminished *'Nordost'* motive b as an equivalent to the blowing of the wind. The motive's major third is reserved for the *Frau'n* themselves, and then as a reply in a postlude, the piano quotes it twice.

These women of Hölderlin's *Heimat*, which is here a foreign land, obviously French and therefore republican and revolutionary, stand in sharp contrast to the shadowy 'angels' of Hollywood. These also appear, to the accompaniment of a regular syncopated pattern of chromatic sevenths and ninths *'Pfeffer'* chords, in the second of the

[56] See Betz p. 186. 'In the relationship between words and notes Eisler's experiences with the dramaturgical counterpoint of film music have left their mark.'

Ex. 13.12 *Andenken*

Hollywood Elegies, 'to be performed with gloomy *Schmalz*'. Ex. 13.13.

Varied Return

Now, as though for contrast, there is in the grim *Elegie 1943*, 'for the dark times', an allusion verging on a quotation to the above-quoted Hollywood Elegy No. 2 (composed on 9 February 1942, therefore preceding the Hölderlin Elegy). Time signature (3/4), syncopated vocal line, intervallic content, initial augmented triad harmony (admittedly with a different continuation, although analogous rhythmically until the functionally different suspended note at the end), all these are the same. The verbal contexts are:

Brecht	*'füttern sie allmorgenlich die Schreiber . . .'* *(they [the angels] feed the writers every morning)*
Hölderlin	*'dem gärenden Geschlecht die Wünsche nach, und wild ist und verzagt und kalt von Sorgen das Leben.'* (according to their fermenting sexual desires, and life is wild, despairing and cold with cares).

The care-laden, despairing life in exile, as the musical correspondences let us see, is therefore only the other side of the pleasant, but artificial, life. Ex. 13.14

Ex. 13.13 Hollywood Elegy No. 2

Ex. 13.14 *Elegie 1943*

At the beginning Eisler makes the polyphonic textures speak symbolically (similar to the opening of No. 1). 'The use of imitation and variation corresponds to the text's 'transformed return' (*'verwandelt wieder kämen'*). The very first three bars in the piano use the semitone motive in three different rhythmic forms.'[57] In contrast to the element of variation, this moment of reprise emphasizes the basic and unchanging dactylic rhythm. It is supplemented by rhythmically complementary syncopations, heard for the first time in bar 5 on the word *'Wasser'*. Variants of this invade the voice line in bars 13 and 14, and then in bar 19. In bars 18 – 21, it is established as an accompaniment rhythm, then continued even further into the varied return of the opening, bars 22 onwards (See Ex. 13.15a).

The elements of this complex, appear, singly or together, relatively frequently in Eisler as a musical characterization of return — previously one full of pain. So we find in the third Hollywood Elegy chromatic motives, close motivic imitation and, in the final bars, both syncopation and (less consistently and steadily) dactylic rhythms. Here, too, the subject is return.

> *Jeden Morgen mein Brot zu verdienen,*
> *geh ich zum Markt,*
> *Wo Lügen verkauft werden.*
> (Every morning, to earn my bread,
> I go to the market, where lies are sold).

The *Hoffnung* motive is also present, in the voice as a falling sixth (C-E-E flat) and in the piano as a falling semitone (B flat-A) here as a 4 – 3 suspension in an F major triad — *'Hoffnungsvoll reihe ich mich ein unter die Verkäufer'*. (Full of hope, I line up amongst the salesmen.) The similarity even goes so far that here, too, the instrumental interlude and

[57] Dümling op. cit. p. 100.

postlude occupy large areas (in this song even greater than the vocal sections). The reprise of entire sections as a 'reply' or echo[58] belongs to the concept of return, as does the recyling of melodic material.

The *Third Piano Sonata* was composed in July 1943, directly after the *Elegie 1943* and resounds with agitated sadness. In the second theme of the first movement reminders of the elegy-type are heard in the melodic sequences and the chromaticism. In the first theme, Christoph Keller finds parallels and even direct analogies with bars 14–21 of *Elegie 1943*, as well as the same 'attitude, characterized by both grief and calm in the face of the terrible events of the war.'[59] The creative effect of this elegy, radiating out far beyond its place in the cycle, is shown by the fact that Eisler, in the mid-fifties, reached back to the melodic and harmonic formulations of the explanatory third verse, which, on its part, had made use of aspects of the *Kampf* – and *Massenlied*. I refer here to *Horatios Monolog*, which is itself more often found in an instrumental transformation — in the music for the Resnais film *Nuit et Brouillard* and in the prelude to the music for Strittmatter's *Winterschlacht*, i.e., in works which relate also to fascism and the war.

Eisler ingeniously weaves together transformation and repeat, the past and the, at the time even worse, present. The motivic nucleus and starting point is probably not the ideas which appear first in the three-bar prelude, but the one in the vocal line at *'(in) anderen Zorn'* in bar 6, immediately taken up in bar 7, *'in schrecklichern (ver -)'*. Here Eisler has altered the text and introduced the comparative. Just as this fragment of text provides the verbal pattern, so the beginning *'Wie wenn die alten Wasser'* provides the thematic one, which rotates chromatically and gradually rises upwards. Inversions and rhythmic augmentations are imposed upon this. Ex. 13.15a

Bars 4–9 are repeated and varied in 10–15. The interchange between the voice and the top line of the piano shows the similarity between 'just as' and 'so therefore', as well as providing an increase in tension. The procedure, as a process of musical thinking, refers to 'the logical connection; the second strophe provides the solution, the explanation of the water metaphor.'[60]

---

[58] On the musical palindrome see Hufschmidt op. cit. p. 101.

[59] Christoph Keller. *". . . . das weit hüllt in Dunkel und Bläße das Haupt der Menschen," Zum ersten Satz von Hanns Eislers 3. Klaviersonate,* in *Musik, Deutung, Bedeutung. Festschrift für Harry Goldschmidt zum 75. Geburtstag.* Ed. Heister and Lück, Dortmund, p. 88 ff.

[60] Ibid. p. 101.

Ex. 13.15a *Elegie 1943*

On a detailed level, Eisler overlaps vocal and instrumental phrases and creates space for what for the time being might helpfully be called instrumental elaboration and generalization — on the basis of a starting point which is motivically determined by ideas and words. The instrumental reply in the piano postlude expands the complex association of levels of comparison — even *'unerhörte Schlacht'* is of course no longer a metaphor like the image of the Flood, but is still a poetic metonymy for the Second World War. (The explanations of the text relationships in Example 13.15 may clarify some further points). The paradox of Hope as consolation is constantly present (structurally at least because of the semitone step), here even in the deepest misery — and also plainly in the two formulations of bars 4 and 6 and the intervallic character of the ground bass lament, which is an obvious permutation of the B-A-C-H motif. Just as the perfect fifths of *Menschen* (bar 21) and *Leben* (bar 50) are seconded by the Hope motive so at the end of Eisler's *'Dies Irae'*, the advent of better times is also hinted at, albeit still bound up in depression. The harmony, constantly making reference to tonal procedures, culminates, rather abruptly and without an actual cadence, in F major, the cipher chord of *'Heimat'* in the cycle. The suspended B flat sinks, however, through A to the minor third A flat.

Ex. 13.15b *Elegie 1943*

Homecoming Music as Imaginary and Actual Wish-fulfilment

The theme of 'home' is made explicit in the title of the fourth song. Within the overall dramatic shape of the cycle and after the depths of its turning point, *Die Heimat* now approaches its lyrical theme more *actually*, so to speak. Eisler takes up the idea of 'journey' from No. 2 but now links it directly with social activity and his own openly expressed wishes. (At first, in No. 1, hope is only being sought, as yet without any designated concrete goal). At the same time the music draws fulfilment of the wish tangibly nearer.

As in No. 2 (and by suggestion also in the other songs), here the caesuras between the formal sections seem to function like cuts in a film, yet at the same time (especially at bar 10) are determined by a sudden associative inspiration. The first section — '(itself in three parts: a b a^{I}) exposes imitatively the theme of the song and its image of the sailor, i.e., putting to sea and home-coming: the second laments . . . . the sorrowful present, while the third part looks into the future — as a return of the past.'[61] The section from bar 21 therefore functions as both reprise and coda.

Eisler's procedures of *montage* and cross-reference cause the two key sections of this song to become equivalent and therefore, musically, wish and fulfilment of it almost coincide. In method this process of comparison between the happy stranger and the sorrowful *'Ich'* is similar to that in the preceding third song.

The musical starting point is obviously the first phrase, the affirming statement *'Froh kehrt der Schiffer heim'* (Happy, the sailor returns home). On to this is projected the (longer) optative clause *'Wohl möchte ich gern zur Heimat wieder'* (How would I gladly return home.) Only in the final bars is it melodically fully exposed by the piano. In the autograph, the second version shows how Eisler emphasizes the harmonic and chordal aspect more strongly. Ex. 13.16 and 13.17

Eisler varies not only the musical form but also the verbal text — just as he had already altered Hölderlin's original. The nucleus is the melodically descending seventh-ninth chord on F. In No. 5 this chord forms the 'hinge' of the cadence (see Ex. 13.10b, bar 12) and is therefore, like F major, closely associated with 'home'. Here, the tonic is initially missing, but appears, rather concealed, in the first imitative part and then is clearly enunciated at the very end. Chromatic alterations and extensions of the chain of thirds give thematic flexibility to the shape. Ex. 13.18

[61] Ibid. p. 100 f.

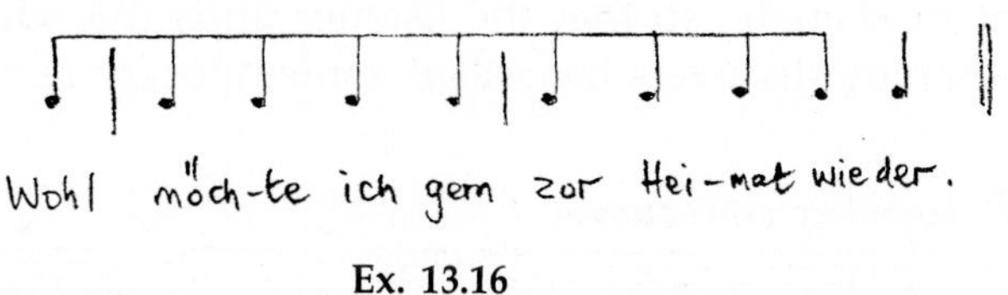

Ex. 13.16

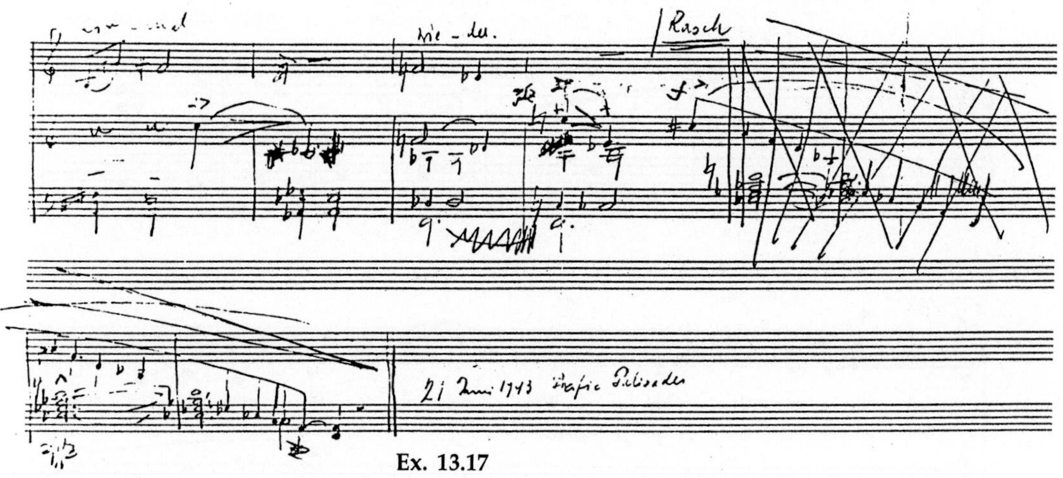

Ex. 13.17

Eisler refers to traditional stylistic gestures, as he has done already in the second song, with its regular accompaniment figures at bars 9 – 15 and from bar 19 for the key-words *Fluss* and *Bach*. Here he does so in the 'remembering' section, bars 16 – 20, this time with an expressly tonal orientation. The falling sixth 'which emphasized the lament of the second part',[62] is inverted to become a rising one. As a major sixth it also determines the ambit of *wiederkehre* (bar 20) and the symmetrical correspondence of *'(noch) einmal'* (bar 22) – while the combination of a segment of major scale (E flat) and downwards movement still preserves the feeling of lament.

Fritz Hennenberg interprets the ending as, harmonically, a kind of alienation. 'The arpeggio is marked out by means of a faster tempo and a *diminuendo* dying away. The harmony of the song precludes any precise analysis because of persistent fluctuations; but the types of chord favoured are familiar from functional harmony. The final dissonance is in fact a gentle spreading out of thirds; at the same time it stands out in a telling way because of a substantially higher level of dissonance. The

[62] Ibid. p. 101.

ending is meant to alienate, so that the listener finds the whole poem alienating and thereby discovers concealed contemporary relevance.'[63]

Ex. 13.18 *Die Heimat*

[63] Hennenberg. '*Zur Dialektik des Schliessens in Liedern von Hanns Eisler*. Berlin 1971, p. 201.

Ex. 13.18 *Die Heimat* (cont'd)

Rondeau in Retrospect

No 5, *An eine Stadt,* seems to provide a tonic answer to the F dominant, gravitating in all essentials towards B flat (major) — that key of all keys which is symbolically so highly charged and therefore emotive. In it, hope is here resolved, made more pointed by allegorizing and movingly fulfilled. (See Ex. 13.10b).

Eisler takes pleasure in portraying the 'lovely image' of home with ever new harmonic twists, mixing the more modern with the old and familiar, the accessible with the surprising. Formally the picture is constructed (as Eisler himself said) as a rondo. In the ABACA scheme, the refrains each contain an instrumental strophe in addition to the vocal one (both the outer sections actually begin with a reprise of the initial four-bar phrase), and the second episode is a clear variant of the first. Already familiar key-words like *Wald, Strom* and *Ufer* reappear and Eisler, like Hölderlin with his image of the bridge over the river, also focuses on a reconciliation between Man and Nature. Musically, Eisler here devises once more a new way of depicting movement — quick repetitions and definite agitation — brought about in verse two and elsewhere by the image of the *Vogel* (bird) and in verse four by the mention of the *Flüchtigen* (fugitive). The quicker tempo contrasts with the almost comfortable and cosy three-four of the refrain. Being so clearly defined and constant, the overall character is different to the floating dream scenes of the second and sixth songs, and contrasts the bright, quick and light with the gloomy, slow writhings of the *'De Profundis'* third song.

Tension tends to be concentrated in the transitions, as at the cadence in bar 37. Here the harmonic and melodic tension arises from the contrast between and combination of the phrygian line in the upper part of the piano left hand and the major-minor tonality created by the falling fifth in the bass. Rhythmically it is created by a quickening of tempo and the appearance of triplets, which evoke onomatopoeically the jolting of the vehicle on the bridge,[64] *'die von Wagens auf und Menschen tönt'* (which resounds with carriages and men). Ex. 13.19a Tension is also created, as in general, by the fusion of the dissonant atonal idiom and the tonal. The tonal references here are to the Schubertian *Lied* and, both in harmony and phrasing, the Eisler *Kampflied.* (Identical in its idiom is the melancholy setting of Brecht's *'Und ich werde nicht mehr sehen — das Land aus dem ich gekommen bin'* composed probably in 1953).

---

[64] Siebert. Op. cit. p. 104 f.

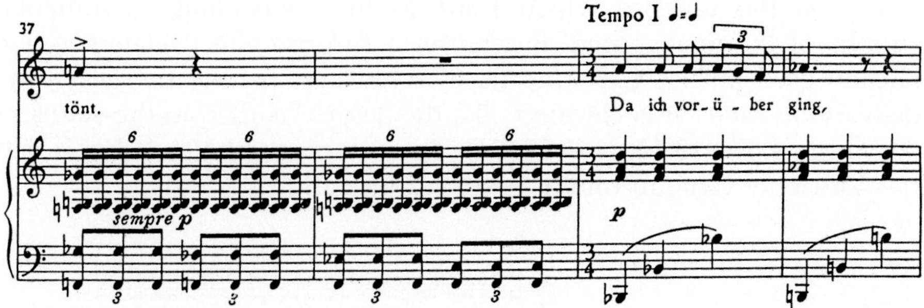

Ex. 13.19a *An eine Stadt*

The second episode also stresses the combination of visual and aural associations. The counterstatement, transposed down a semitone, reflects, mirror-like, the motive whose intervallic span is the semitone step fundamental to the whole of the fifth song, as well as being linked to the triad. Already before this, varied repetitions of the calling third arise, along with turn-motives (bar 53 onwards), a sequence (bars 56–7) and an echo (bars 59–61). Ex. 13.19b

Ex. 13.19b *An eine Stadt*

At the cadence which leads to the concluding instrumental strophe of the final refrain, Eisler uses a surprise effect related to one already used in No. 4. By means of a full bar's pause, he delays the delivery of *'ruhn'*. It is elevated, like the *'wieder'* earlier, to the status of keyword (cf. Ex. 13.18, bars 22–24). The autograph of No. 4 shows that this idea only came to him as a second thought. Ex. 13.20

Ex. 13.20 *An eine Stadt*

The very end of the song brings yet another surprise. Not only does Eisler cadence with the repeatedly varied phrase — 'in which, moreover, the tension of the dominant is palpably weakened by the phrygian line of the top part — towards B flat minor instead of the anticipated major — but follows it, with especial *sforzato* emphasis, with a chord of D flat minor. It seems as though Eisler wishes to warn against trusting ourselves to the sense of security expressed by the cadence.'[65]

Anti-Strophe

The first part of *Erinnerung*, the last of the *Hölderlin-Fragmente*, delays yet again the path to wish-fulfilment. As a part of an anti-fascist and anti-capitalist 'defence of culture', Eisler defends his 'fatherland': Eisler himself said of the song — 'There is a shameless nationalism in it — because, in fact, during my emigration years, I would at times remember Germany — not sentimentally, but through the eyes of

[65] Hennenberg. *'Zur Dialektik'*. p. 201.

Hölderlin, who — as you know — was an early Jacobin.'[66] The concept of unifying the popular front and the *avant-garde,* which in general determines Eisler's production in exile, could at the time be realized only marginally at best, in spite of the absence of a well-defined *avant-garde.* Yet, as a concept, it is in itself worthy of esteem. By the same token, Eisler's attitude, with its anti-cyclical intransigence, as an art of remembrance conscious of the art of the present, is both topical and worthy to be remembered. 'The idea appealed to me at a moment of deepest humiliation for the German people, which unfortunately I belong to, like you. I can't withdraw from it . . . . I wanted to be able to say: "You bastards! But at least I composed something for you". . . . I just wanted some notes to exist. So that the German workers could see: Well, we know this chap — he delivered something. Like the messenger who arrives, gasping for breath and has something to deliver . . . . . Believe me, the idea of delivering, of the messenger that runs and still has to deliver a message, has been the greatest idea that I learned from the workers' movement in my younger years. Having to deliver. Doing something useful which can be delivered.'[67]

Ex. 13.21 *Erinnerung*

[66] *Gespräche.* p. 192. [see p. 426 Ed.]

[67] Ibid. pp. 192–4. [see pp. 429–431 Ed.]

Like an extended, varied reprise, the beginning of No. 6 brings together essential elements from all the previous songs. Most important is the reference to No. 1. Eisler brings Mother Earth, Fatherland, *'Ich'* and other peoples into close relationship with one another, a complex, concentrated abundance of musical ideas. Ex. 13.21

Gradually, step by step, the picture changes. 'Eisler arrives here at an inwardness of expression, such as is seldom to be found elsewhere in his songs. It is an expression of that hope which in the first song seemed still to be lost. In the first section ..... dedicated not to pleasant memories but to the dismal present, a parlando recitative prevails. In the transition over to remembering, the intervallic leap of the upbeat is expanded to an octave, the voice changes more and more to cantabile song, voice and piano merge, the level of dissonance decreases and the tonality becomes clearer and brighter.'[68]

Eisler's music, together with Hölderlin's text, makes the Fatherland, as a place of productive, collective assimilation of 'sun' and 'cities', of society and Nature, home, in the sense outlined by Ernst Bloch at the end of 'The Principle of Hope': 'Once the working, creative man, who overhauls and recasts the realities, comprehends himself as the roots of history and bases what is his, without renunciation or alienation, in actual democracy, then something is generated in the world which shines in the childhood of everyone and in which no-one has yet been — home.'[69]

With the brightness of the major key after all the seriousness, Eisler's *Erinnerung* shines out as both an imaginary and actual appearance of such a home, which is musically called by name in the final and fulfilling passage of thirds. Ex. 13.22

Ex. 13.22 *Erinnerung*

[68] Dümling. Op. cit. p. 104.

[69] Ernst Bloch. *Das Prinzip Hoffnung* (1959). Frankfurt am Main, 1968, Vol 3, p. 1628.

Ex. 13.22 *Erinnerung* (cont'd)

Ex. 13.22 *Erinnerung* (cont'd)

Ex. 13.22 *Erinnerung* (cont'd)

In the last two verses and the postlude, Eisler starts from the central Memory — Home material with its falling semitone A – A flat. He follows this through primarily by means of a combination of developing variation and sequential working. In the example the bars which correspond are placed under each other.

First published in the *Vierteljahresschrift für zeitgenössische Musik* 3/1988. Melos, *Musikverlag B. Schott's Söhne,* Mainz.

14

NOTES ON 'DR. FAUSTUS'

Hanns Eisler

The first draft of the text for my opera *Dr Faustus* was finished on Friday, the 13th of July 1951, and I received the fair copy on Saturday, the 14th of July 1951, in the morning. Yesterday evening, on Sunday the 15th of July, I learned that Arnold Schoenberg had died during the night of the 13th-14th July, at the age of seventy-six.

(With this event a circle has closed in a remarkable way.) I was most profoundly moved. He was my teacher and I try to [. . .] him

Chinese proverb. Schoenberg taught me that one must honour the great teachers and masters.

Late bourgeois music has died with Schoenberg. He was a genius, who followed the path of bourgeois art to the end. Only these can hold their own beside him: Bartók, who through his links with Hungarian folksong, however, occupies a unique and special position not dissimilar to the way that Mussorgsky in the eighties in Russia drew support from Russian folklore and Stravinsky, who at first leant on Russian folklore in a way similar to Bartók; but Stravinsky, through his emigration, lost in the Paris salons all continuity with his tradition and became an elegant, modern composer; his power, his music of the last (10) fifteen years has become more and more empty and cold. (It is remarkable that he is working at the moment on an opera based on an engraving by Hogarth, *The Rake's Progress*. The text is by Auden, the great English poet, who has buried his rebellious youth, his sympathy with the workers' movement, in the Catholic church.)

If I speak of Arnold Schoenberg's death and mention my opera *Dr Faustus*, I have the following reason. In his notable novel *Doktor Faustus*, Thomas Mann invented a character by the name of Leverkühn. This Leverkühn has certain features of Arnold Schoenberg, but also of Stravinsky and Bartók. Thomas Mann has understood splendidly how to capture all the diseases and difficulties of modern music and of musical life as if in a burning glass, and to put in on two legs in the form of Leverkühn. (That Leverkühn also has the disease that killed Hugo Wolf, and bears certain features of Nietzsche, is well known and not unimportant in the context of this observation.)

This Leverkühn makes a pact with the Devil. Thus he is a modern Doctor Faust. His last composition is Doctor Faustus's Voyage to Hell. After the completion of the work he goes mad.

Thomas Mann, who cultivated personal contact with Schoenberg, with Adorno (a philosopher and student of Alban Berg) and with me, described Leverkühn's oratorio 'Doctor Faustus's Lament' in an interesting way. It is a twelve-note composition in the style of Schoenberg. The technical details of this description, which are plausible to an expert, Thomas Mann obtained from Adorno, who for this was labelled a traitor by Schoenberg. Schoenberg felt, on the one hand, honoured that he and his works stood at the centre of the novel. Yet he was also furious that his name does not appear in the book; 'he should at least be named as Leverkühn's teacher'. Schoenberg did not want to be identified with Leverkühn for the simple reason that Thomas Mann concretizes the essence of the pact that Leverkühn makes with the Devil as syphilis, which Leverkühn consciously allows to go untreated because it is well known that the final phase of syphilis stimulates the brain to higher productivity. Leverkühn's Lament of Doctor Faustus goes back to the puppet play. As Thomas Mann finally formulates magnificently, it is the reacceptance of Beethoven's *Ninth Symphony*, the: *'Alle Menschen werden Brüder'*. Thus the pact with the Devil which Leverkühn makes, is as follows: great art, as the Devil maintains, can now only be produced, in this declining society, through complete isolation, loneliness, through complete heartlessness. In music, however, coldness must be constructed. The construction method of the twelve-note system produces a heated cold or a cold heat, just as extreme cold burns like fire.

Thomas Mann is the last great bourgeois humanist. He describes the path that Leverkühn takes with sorrow and concern and equates it with the path taken by the German people up to 1945. In doing so, he equates the icy-hot Lament of Dr. Leverkühn with the lament and the going astray and the crimes of the Hitler regime against humanity and finally the collapse of the Germans under these crimes. Yet Thomas Mann finds in all this darkness of artistic error and artistic education an inspired element: he allows Leverkühn to dream of a new time, when music will again to a certain extent be on first-name terms with the people. For the icy-hot Leverkühn this dream of the future is still unclear. He can neither follow this path, nor does he consider it possible.

Here Leverkühn's dream coincides with Thomas Mann's sceptical humanism, but no longer with Schoenberg's artistic consciousness.

Schoenberg, who was the first to prefigure in music the hysteria and neurosis of the imperialistic era, believed with contrived naivety in divine grace, which enables man to assert himself through great art in the face of time. Schoenberg has always been very confused in these matters. There is a telling anecdote illustrating this point: Drafted into military service in 1915, he was questioned: 'Tell me, are you the famous composer, about whom there has been so much scandal?' Schoenberg answered: 'It's like this: someone *had* to be; no one *wanted* to be; *so I offered myself.'*

This expression is clever, vain, confused and honourable at the same time. Yet Schoenberg is a primeval musician, who got an infinite satisfaction from Viennese songs and Johann Strauss's waltzes, a passionate admirer of Schubert, whose early death he could not lament enough; one of the greatest connoisseurs of the classical legacy. When he was still young, he played chamber music every week, and in fact played exclusively Haydn, Brahms, Mozart, Beethoven, Schubert. He revered Brahms as a great genius of musical construction. He had seen him personally going about the streets of Vienna, and when Alexander von Zemlinsky, later his brother-in-law, showed Brahms his *String Quartet* (in D major), Brahms, who was otherwise uninterested in beginners, began to show interest. He asked after this Schoenberg, and when Zemlinsky reported that Schoenberg at the age of 18 earned his living from menial writing and copying, Brahms, to Zemlinsky's astonishment, offered Schoenberg money so that he could attend the Vienna Conservatory. That was the greatest honour that Schoenberg had ever been paid in his life. Schoenberg refused. For him a little instruction from Zemlinsky, whom he immediately overtook, sufficed; he studied the classical masters with such a profound understanding that he himself soon became a sought-after teacher of harmony and counterpoint and attracted significant talents. The genius of Schoenberg in the theoretical and practical fields is also astonishing.

His brilliance in the field of theory can be characterized as the capacity to see every usual phenomenon as unusual. In practical life (for Schoenberg was also a great man with his hands, a bookbinder, and always had a chest of tools with which he moved from room to room), that meant that he took, for example, a familiar object, to which we had become accustomed, and said, why did one actually make it that way, and not better? He wants to make it better, because one had become accustomed to the old and yet man found satisfaction in the new. Sadly, he had this yearning for innovation, this zeal for progress, striving, and recognition only in the realm of his art, of music, and also, for a brief period, with respect to painting and his handicrafts, his bookbinding, his carpentry. If he had been able to apply this profound insight, this classical attitude of striving, amazement and understanding — 'why isn't that done better?' — to the social realm, he would have become a Marxist. But he had the *petit bourgeois* shyness of social science, of Marxism. Where purity of culture was concerned, he was a *petit bourgeois,* of a kind one finds only rarely. Social science, Marxism, was 'politics' to him, and beneath the artist. 'It's the big men who argue.' And if the workers, as he said in 1918, want to create a new government, he was opposed to it, because, as he said, he had got used to the Habsburgers, and the others would be just upstairs. He said that against me as well, to anger me, and he believed it would be brilliant to fight against the current of revolution; he, the great musical innovator, wanted to remain a conservative in the field of music politics. One of his students, Dr. Polnauer, was at that time, like me, a conductor of workers' choirs. In 1919, Polnauer gave a concert with the Workers' Choral Society in the Hofburg. (I founded the Workers' Choral Society *Karl Liebknecht* in Floridsdorf. We sang wild songs, some of which I composed myself. Polnauer was more moderate.) He, who had a boundless respect for Schoenberg, was so proud of his ability to make the Workers' Choral Society sing well, that he gave Schoenberg two complimentary tickets, with the request that he attend the concert. Schoenberg asked: "Where is this concert?" Polnauer: "In the Hofburg." Schoenberg (scornfully): "You know, Herr Polnauer, I won't go to the Hofburg at your invitation, I'll only go there at the invitation of His Majesty" (in Viennese dialect) and did not come. (His Majesty at that time was the idiot Karl, who had fled to Switzerland; in Hungary he attempted a *putsch.* He was finally sent by the Allies, who thought him too burdensome, to Madeira, where he was done in by cognac.) That was not quite right of Schoenberg. He wanted to provoke us young socialists and communists; for he particularly loved to stimulate his pupils to further achievements in a sharp and genially mocking way.

Also the model of Bach, falsely romanticized, hovered before him. He was Bach, I the head of the Florentine Camerata. He is particularly proud that the majority of his students have not become composers at all. "It is simply unlucky that I have the ability to be able to show how the great masters composed, and thus have put almost all students off composing. Those who have still become composers, have nevertheless learned something substantial from me. At least the insight that they owe everything to Bach, Mozart, Beethoven."

I have disgressed from what actually touched me. I must return to the death of Schoenberg.

His death meant an end. Thomas Mann presents the end of bourgeois music by having Leverkühn-Schoenberg compose the Lament of Dr Faustus according to the puppet play, as it taught the most extreme despair. It cannot go on this way. My opera *Dr Faustus* takes the other path. It should be an opera which is on a first-name basis with the people, which attempts to shape anew the popular elements of the folk play, introduces again the figure of Hanswurst, the people, and in our minds, to a certain extent, rescues the general circumstances of the sixteenth century from the darkness of the models we have of that time.

Schoenberg's death shook me most profoundly. I have learned from him everything that I know. It was not at all easy to learn with him, for there is much one should not learn, and it was difficult to stand up to such a master.

With my opera, I hoped to be able to go a new way, which brings German music out of this dead end and out of its confusion. I can only do that if I do not experiment like my splendid friend Brecht, or indeed provoke and shock, as Brecht likewise does, but rather by coming forward with a mature, rounded, valid achievement; it must be comprehended both by inexperienced ears and by the most experienced, and the text must be grasped by both the least experienced and the most educated. If I succeed, I hope to have made an artistic contribution to the development of German music. The difficulties of this task are enormous. In the text I must guard against the wrong kind of humour, against the so-called colourful 'inspiration' and allusions to our time; but popular humour and allusions must be present. The treatment must be clear and easily grasped, not losing itself down byways nor giving way to certain 'local' charms.

I appear to have hit on the appropriate conception of Faust, and I was much encouraged by the friends to whom I explained it. The musical tasks are no less difficult than the formulation of the text. I have at least twenty-one self-contained numbers to compose, to which are added, however, smaller, less important musical sections. [see p. 257 Ed.]

There must be 6–7 key pieces in this score, which must be composed with extreme care, but must have an immediate effect. How long I will be working on this work, I do not know. One has feelings in which curiosity and timidity are mixed; roughly as one has before climbing high mountains. This example of climbing high mountains is taken from Lenin. I will be having to make use of a technique of mountain climbing similar to that described by Lenin in his parable. The death of Schoenberg is connected in a very curious fashion with my new task, the greatest and most all-embracing which I have yet dared to set myself.

Translated by Karin von Abrams

[The text, dated 16 July 1951, is in a provisional state with numerous alternatives. I have tidied it up somewhat. It appears in *Schriften* 1948–1962 p. 128 ff. Ed.]

LIST OF NUMBERS FOR THE *FAUST* OPERA

Prologue

1 Song of Charon
2 Recitative and Aria – Pluto
Ending with a short chorale by the Seven Deadly Sins

Act One

Faust's Meditation
3 Easter scene (through-composed)
4 Religious test
5 Perlicke, Perlacke
6 The Contract (through-composed)

Act Two

7 Scene with Gretel and a folksong
8 Gretel – Hanswurst
9 Large ensemble (with quartet of negroes)
10 Farewell duet, Grete – Hanswurst

Act Three

11 The Feast (large ensemble with chorus of guilds)
12 Lamentatio No. 1 (secular)
13 Ballet scene in Auerbach's cellar
14 Lamentatio 2 and 3 (one after the other) sacred, fast
(15 Faust – Mephisto, curse)
15 Faust's aria of despair, in the street
16 Beggarwoman – Büttel – Faust (Trio)
17 Hanswurst – Faust (Duet)
18 Chorus – Faust and citizens
19 Faust's death
20 Ritornello (the citizens lament Faust's death)
21 Scene with Hanswurst (who sings the ending)
In front of the curtain – Final song

[This list appears in *Schriften* 1948–1962 pp. 136–137. Ed.]

1. Rudolf and Maria Ida Eisler with their children (from the left) Gerhart, Hanns and Elfriede (Ruth). Vienna, around 1903

2. Eisler in Vienna, around 1920

3. Erik Wirt, Brecht and Eisler at a recording session in Berlin in February 1931

4. Eisler in Prague, November 1937

5. Eisler with the International Brigade in Spain, January 1937

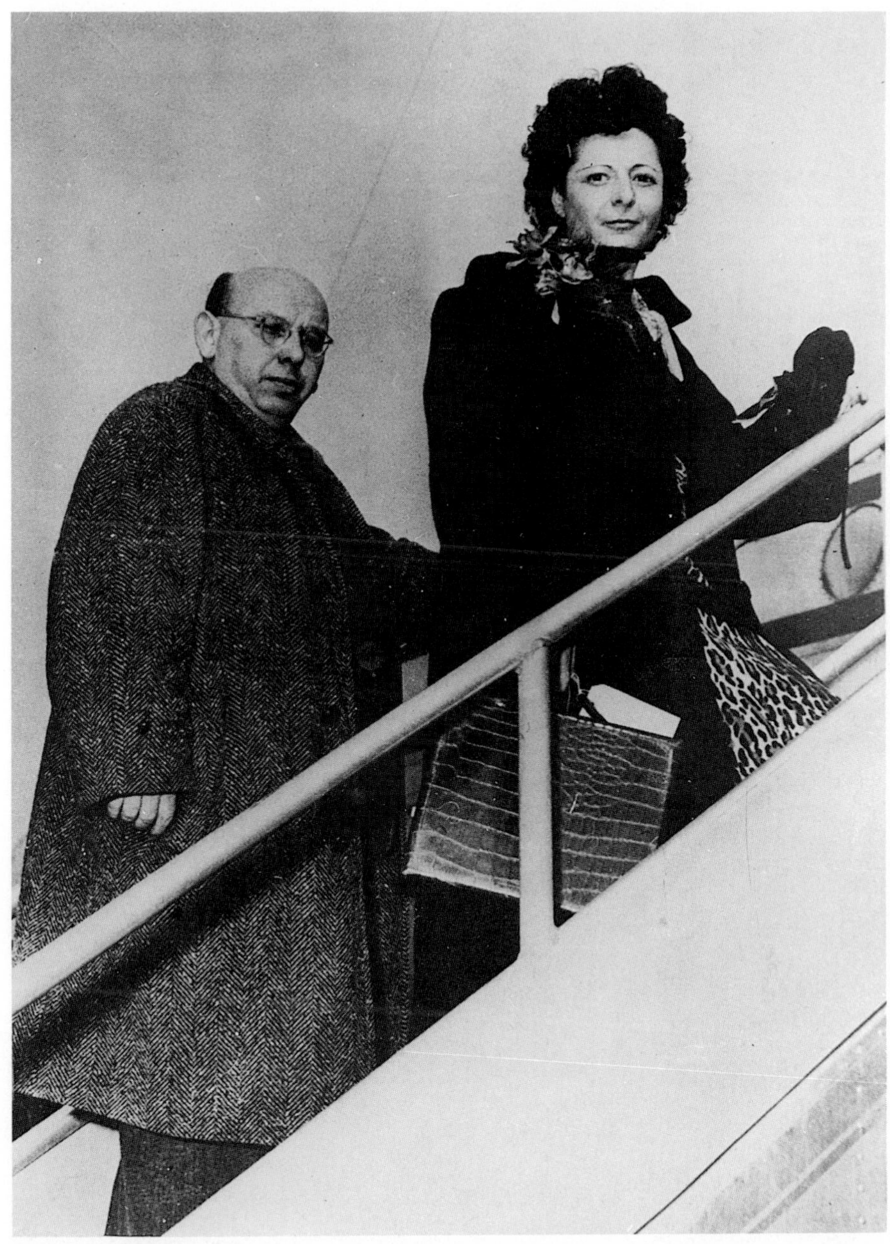

6. Eisler and his wife Lou boarding the plane at New York in 1948

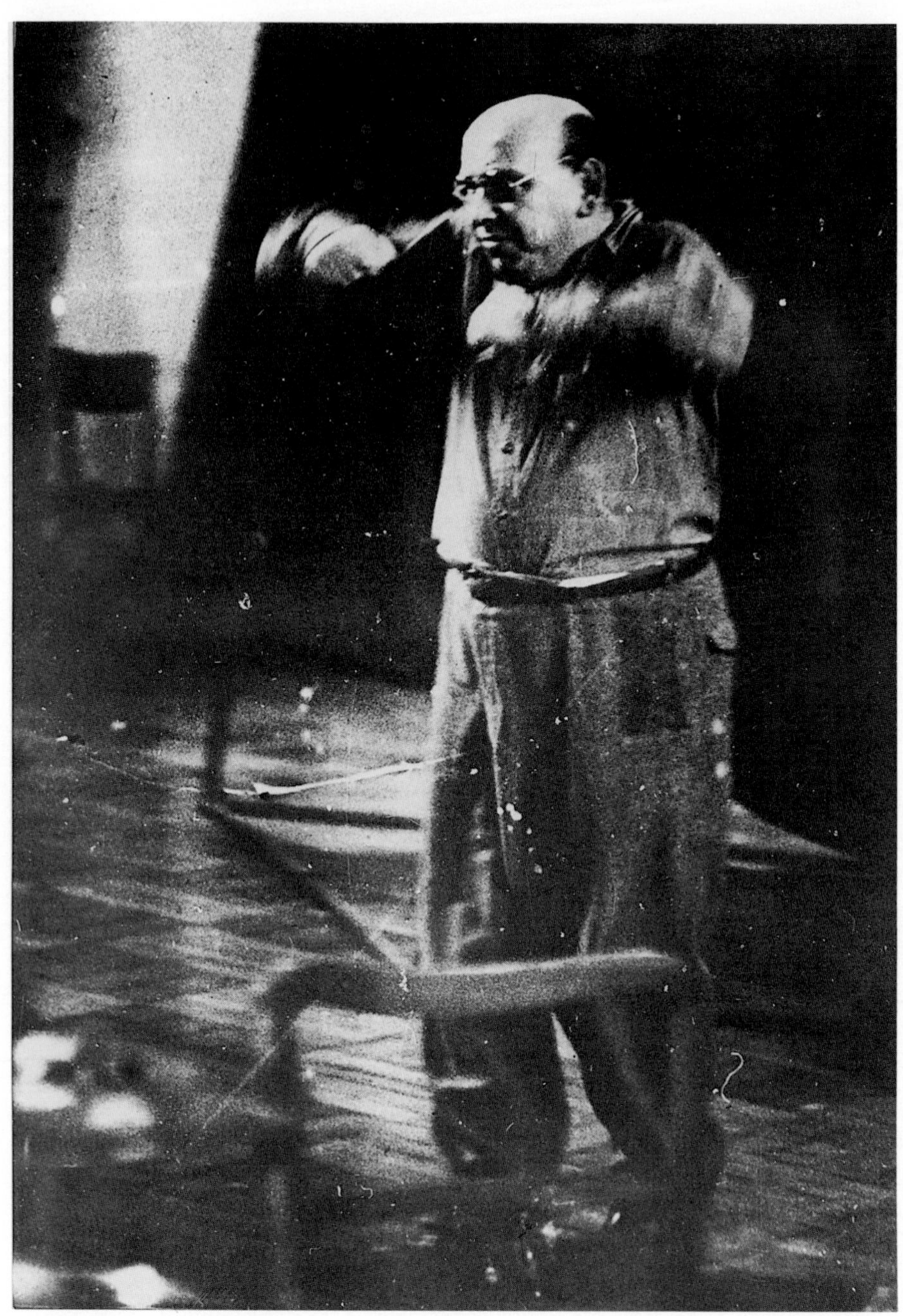

7. At rehearsal in the 1950s

8. In the 1950s

9. Rehearsing the boy trebles for *Galilei* in the 1950s

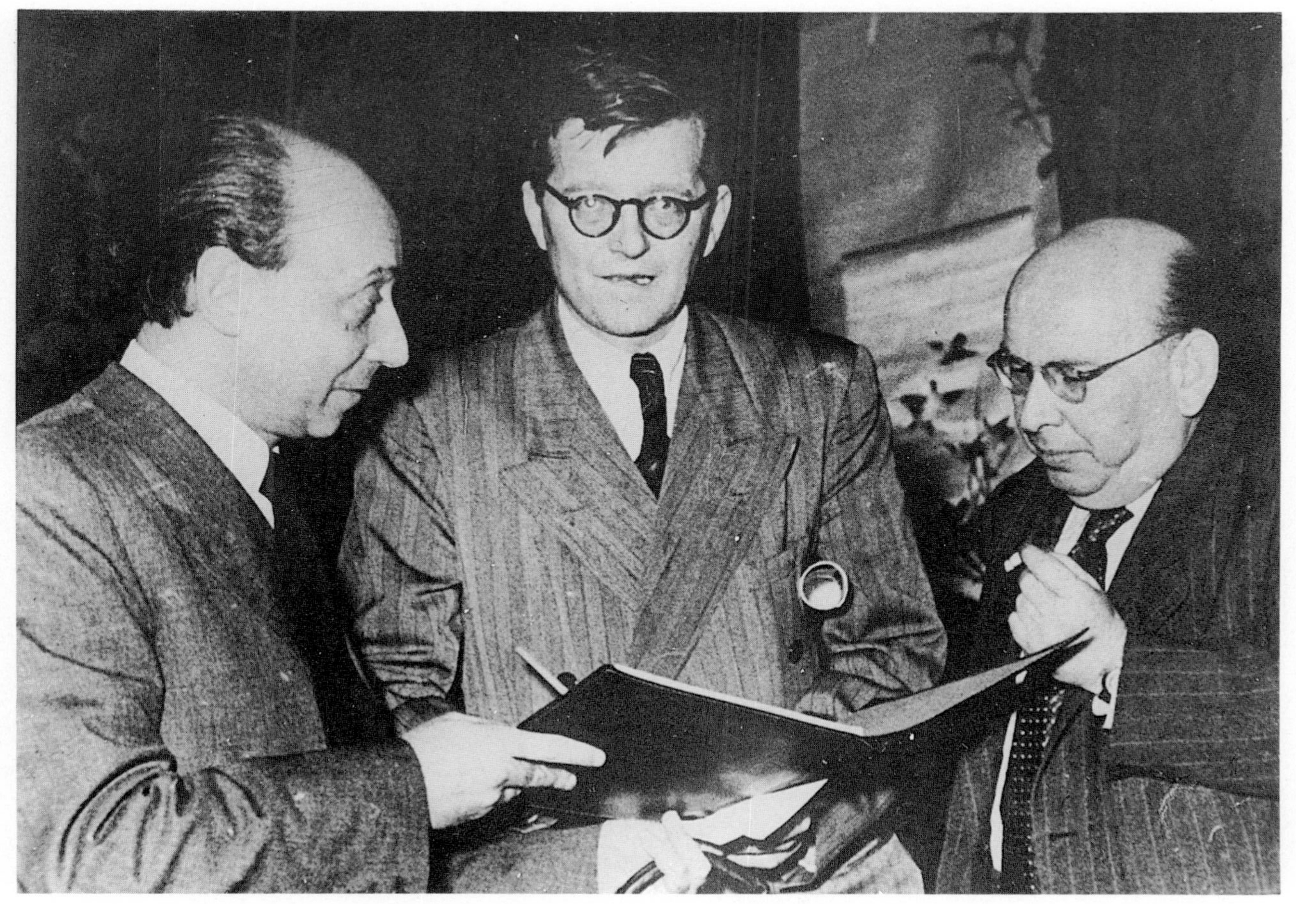

10. At the Peace Congress in Vienna, 1952 with Heinrich Sussmann and Shostakovich

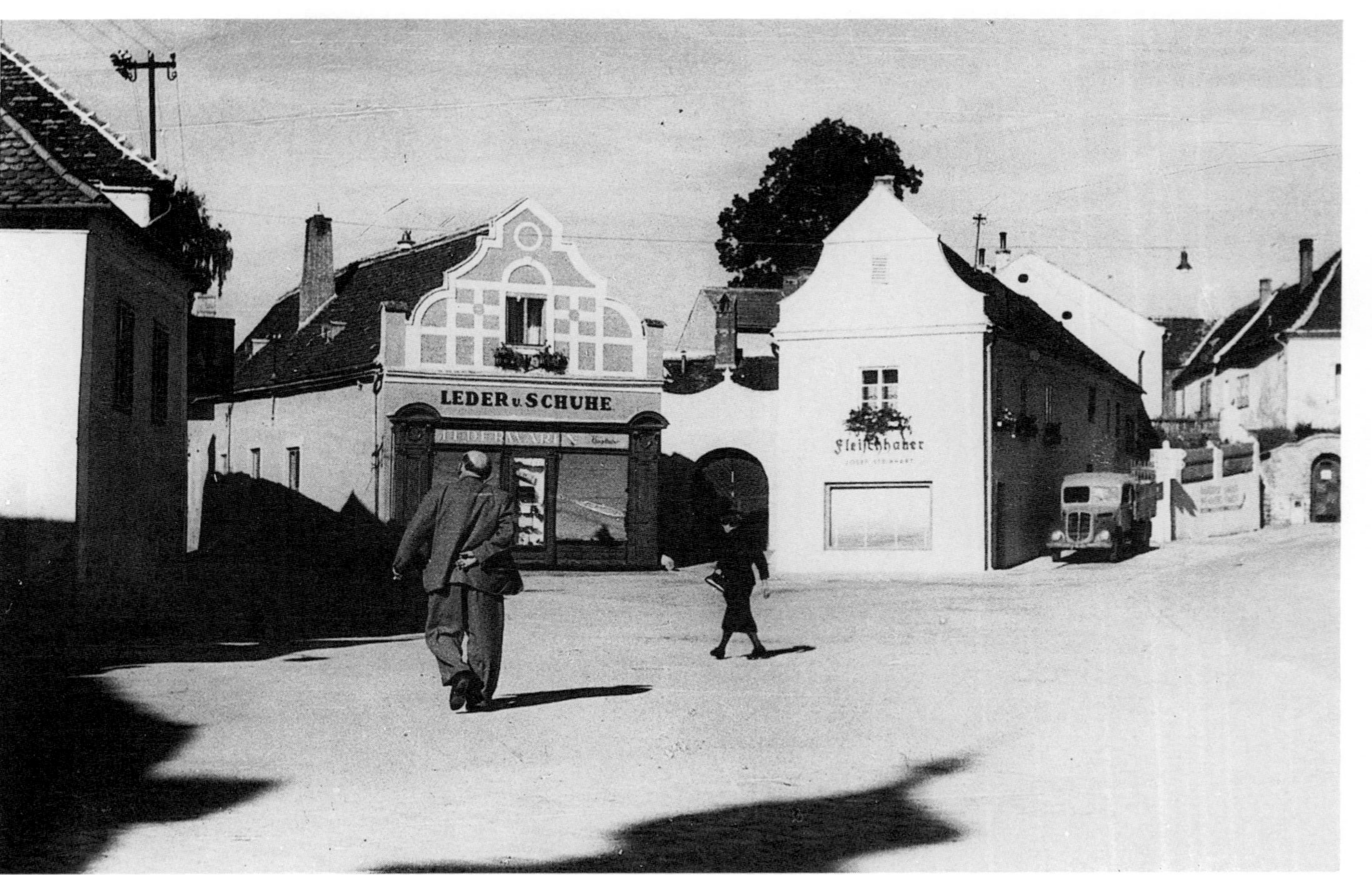

11. In Gars-Thunau (Austria), August 1957

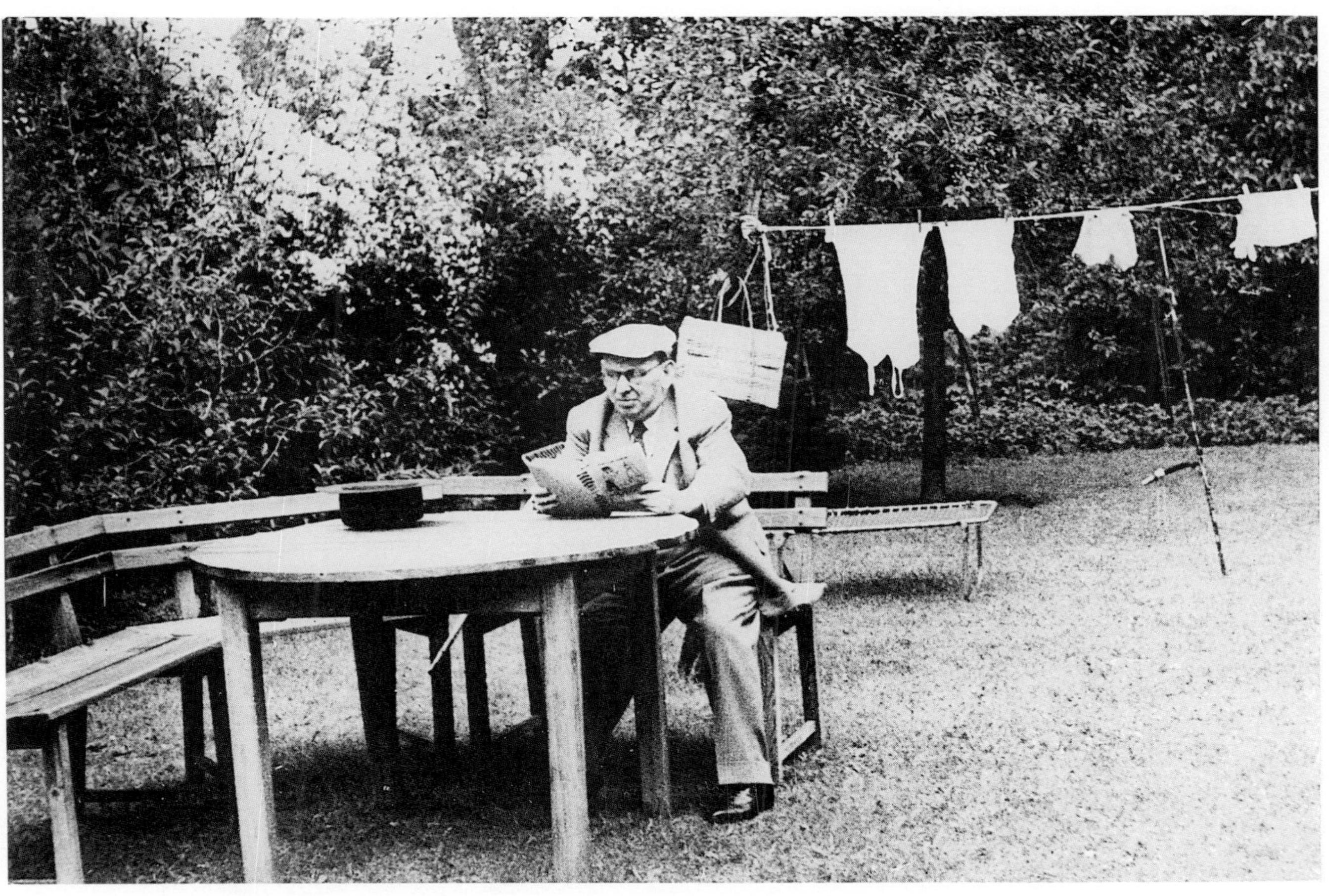

12. In the garden in Pfeilstrasse, Berlin-Niederschönhausen, June 1960

13. Eisler and his wife Steffy, August 1960

14. Eisler in Venice, February 1961

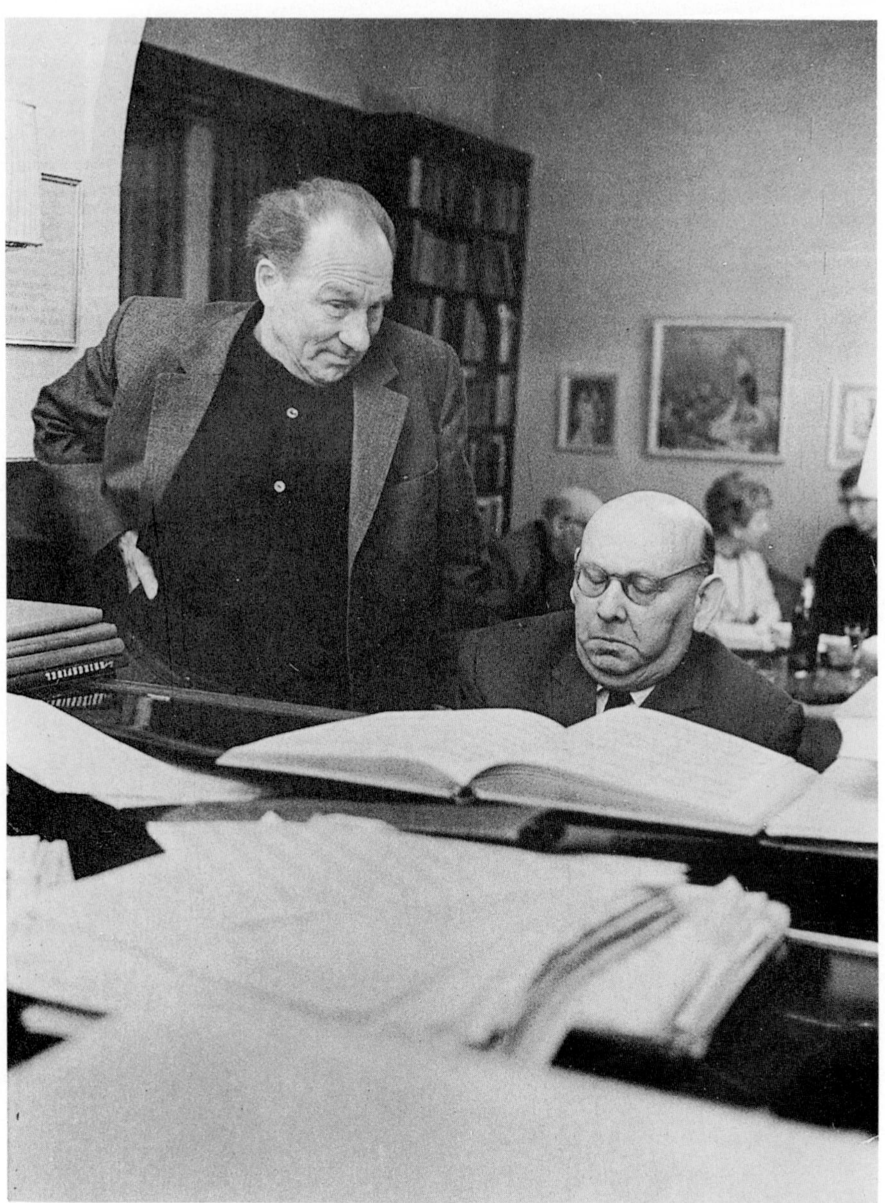

15. With Ernst Busch in 1961

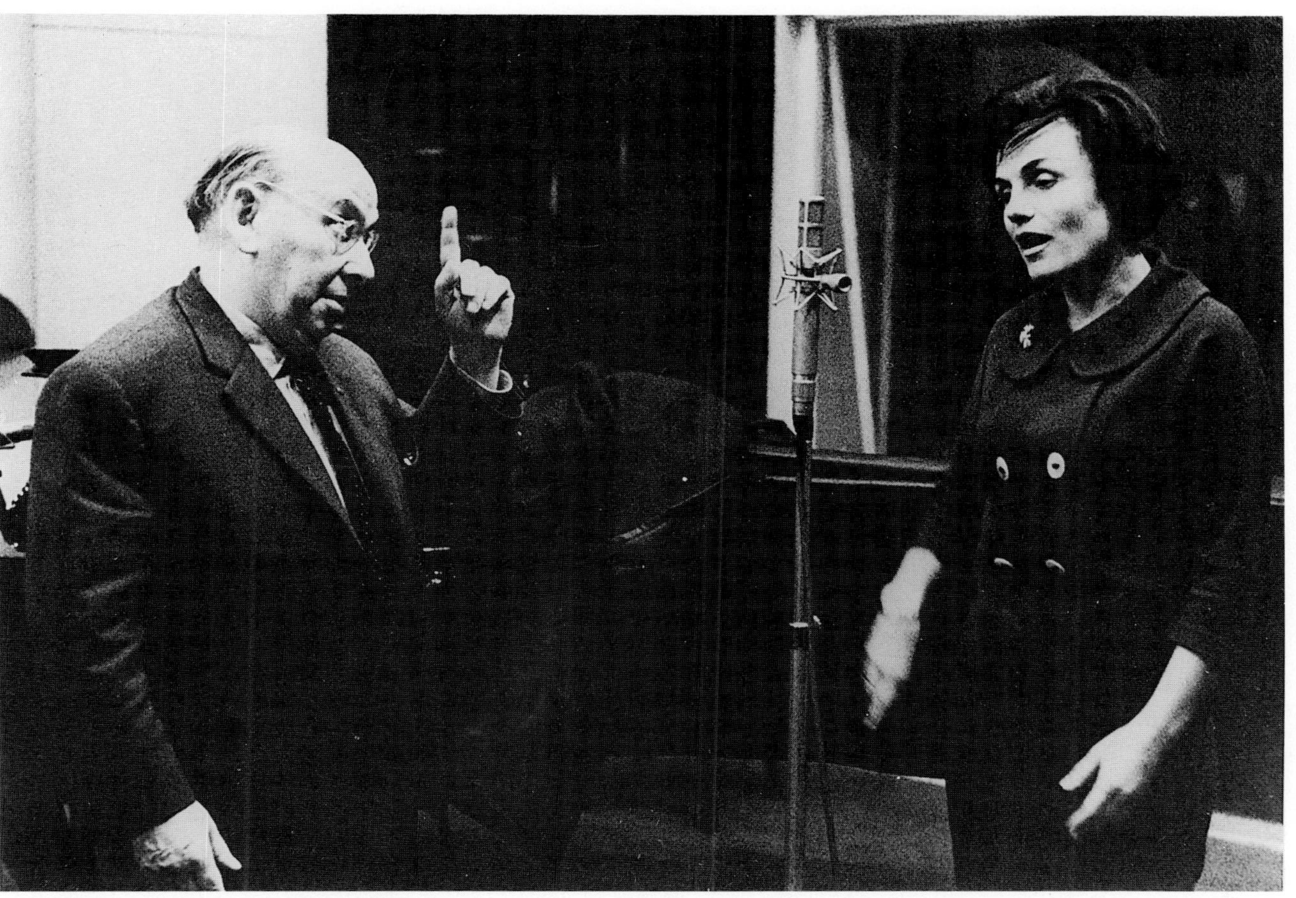

16. Rehearsing with Gisela May in 1961

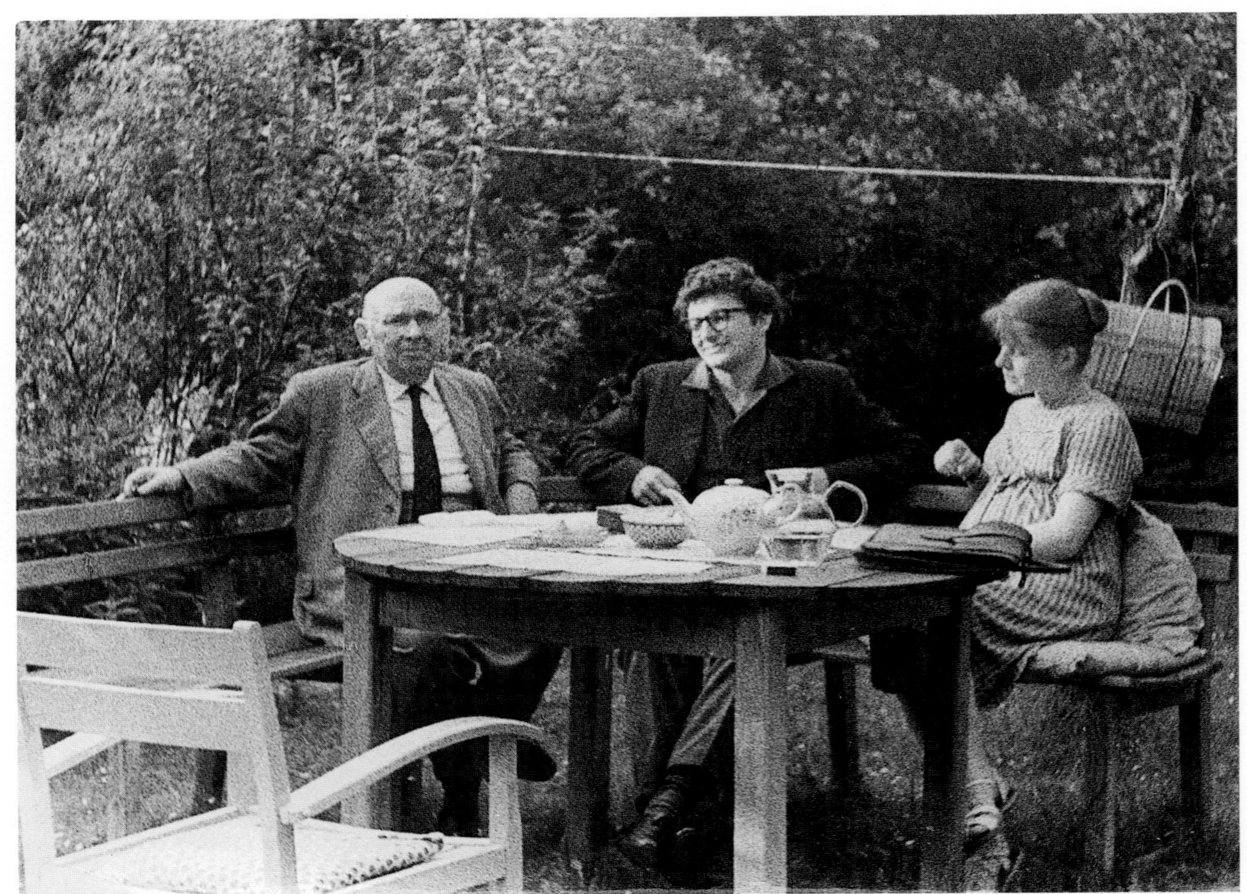

17. In the garden of Eisler's house in Niederschönhausen with David and Rita Blake, June 1961

JOHANN FAUSTUS

An opera libretto

HANNS EISLER

English translation by Peter Palmer

Dramatis Personae

PLUTO
CHARON
AUERHAHN
ASMODI **Pluto's agents**
ZACHARIEL
SEVEN DEADLY SINS
FOUR ATROCITIES

FAUST
WAGNER
KARL
BOY
LAWYER
DOCTOR
TENANT FARMER
BAILIFF
HANSWURST
Parson, Old Woman, Town Councillor and his wife
PEASANTS' CHORUS

GRETE
LORD OF ATLANTA
SECRETARY
SCOWLING FACES (Bodyguard)
ELSA
GENERAL
EXECUTIONER
Lords and Ladies of Atlanta
Staff and Servants
NEGRO SLAVES

COURIER
FISCHER
RECTOR
BEGGARWOMAN
CHILD
VOICE (from on high)
1ST CITIZEN
2ND CITIZEN
STOUT WOMAN

Emperor, German Princes, Captains of the Mercenaries, Captain of the Guard, Guards and Attendants, Chorus of Cobblers, Bakers, Tailors, Peasants, Unchartered Journeymen; Students, Deputation of Nobles

JOHANN FAUSTUS

Prelude

Across the stage runs the river of Hades. In the centre, a landing-stage. Steps lead from this to the door of the Underworld. Charon rows along the river, lands and runs up the steps. He beats on the door with his oar.

PLUTO (*from inside*)
Who dares to intrude
on the contemplations
of Pluto, lord of the Underworld?

CHARON (*beats on the door again with his oar*)
It's me, trusty Charon,
who ferries your dead!
(*He again beats on the door.*)

PLUTO
Let him in,
or else he'll break the door down!
(*The door opens to reveal Pluto.*)

CHARON (*bawling*)
Hey!

PLUTO
What?

CHARON
See here!
(*Hurls his oar to the ground.*)

PLUTO (*contemplating the oar*)
What's up?

CHARON
There's no point to this job.

PLUTO
Why not? what made you
come barging in on me like this?

CHARON
No customers, sir, that's why!
Your folk are slacking
and aren't supplying me with enough great souls.
These Junkers, brokers, merchants, judges —
they don't count and don't pay
and aren't worth the trouble; all they leave behind is a smell.
They're such small fry I've now gone and lost

another three through the chinks in the boat.

PLUTO

I shall summon my agents at once
and give orders
for them to supply you with a great man
who's in good odour,
and has a soul reckoned to be worth more
than thousands put together.

CHARON

High time they did, sir!

PLUTO'S COMMAND

PLUTO

Come here, you crooks of every stripe!
You lousy curs, you bunch of thieves, this way!
You double-dealers, scandalmongers,
corrupting people, spreading intrigue,
copper's narks and low informers,
you renegades: come on!
Sins, big and small, you're to come too,
you greedy dogs and muck-rakers,
and you ferrets,
drop what you're doing
and report this minute
to your lord and master.
(*Pluto's agents flock to him in the course of this speech. Some of them have brown animal's coats, close-cropped hair and tails that wag. Among them is Mephisto, wearing a conventional suit.*)

PLUTO (*surveying them*)

What a sight you are!
And one has to employ such creatures!
(*Sharply*) Auerhahn, Asmodi, Zachariel!
(*The three give a start.*)
There have been complaints about you again.
(*The three try simultaneously to gabble an apology.*)
Quiet!
Auerhahn! How many times must I tell you:
if you go round using your family name,
this firm will go bust.
(*Regards him severely. Auerhahn bows his head in shame.*)
And Zachariel, once again you've been

flaunting the name of Beneckenstein.
(*Zachariel bows his head in shame.*)
And what will your relatives say?
They'll take us to court again,
and you know full well that
in the Supreme Court (*he points upwards*)
I'd lose such a case.
What do you think I gave you an alias for?
(*Silence.*)
Or a shaggy fur coat?
(*Silence.*)
Or a tail?
(*Silence.*)
(*Bellowing:*) What for, Papenburg zu Beneckenstein?

ZACHARIEL (*meekly*)
For wagging, sir!

PLUTO
Then let's see you wagging them!
(*They wag their tails.*)
Our business is in a bad way.
No more earnings,
just a stream of complaints,
one grouse after another!

ZACHARIEL (*raises his hand*)
Sir, it isn't our fault,
it's the fault of the Sins.

PLUTO (*screeching*)
What?

MEPHISTO
An unprecedented state of affairs, sir!

PLUTO (*to Mephisto*)
Fetch the Deadly Sins!
(*Mephisto retires, limping, and introduces the Seven Deadly Sins.*)
What's this I hear? You,
of all fellows the dearest to me, ever-efficient,
you're failing to work!
What's the matter?
(*One of the Deadly Sins raises a hand.*)
Yes, Gluttony?

GLUTTONY
Folk are so badly off,

so desperate to get
a loaf of bread;
they can't afford me any more.

PLUTO

How about you, Lust?

LUST (*in a high-pitched voice*)

A peasant's got
hardly the strength
to satisfy his wife.

PLUTO

You, Anger?

ANGER

I'm out of action.
Princes, Junkers and clerics
have driven me out of the nation.

PLUTO

Pride, Sloth, Envy, Covetousness!
Hasn't one of you got better news?

THE DEADLY SINS (*together*)

No better news!
Anger and sloth, envy, guzzling and love-making,
they've simply driven us out of the nation.

PLUTO

But I have already resorted to
the four terrible Atrocities!
(*Four cloaked figures approach. He registers disgust.*)
Don't you come near me!
Even if I'm forced to use you,
just keep out of my sight!

AUERHAHN (*aside to Mephisto*)

Who are they?

MEPHISTO

Revolting, unnatural vices
that mustn't be named out loud.

AUERHAHN

Whisper them!

MEPHISTO (*whispering*)

The oppression of poor widows and orphans;
the withholding of wages.
(*Auerhahn shudders.*)

PLUTO (*addresses the Atrocities*)

My news is serious:
our boatman refuses to ferry the dead.
It's outrageous of him.
But can you really blame him?
What's this smelly riff-raff you've been dredging up?
I've no time for your small fry.
It's illustrious names that I need, in good odour.
I know:
after the recent troubles you supplied me with lots of them.
But there must be more somewhere.
Where are the country's finest brains,
the thinking, enquiring, the critical minds?
What are they doing?

MEPHISTO

Thinking.

PLUTO (*bellowing*)

What?
(*The Atrocities indicate their perplexity. Pluto addresses all of them*:)
Germany is famous for its scholars.
Give me a scholar, and I assure you
one of those is worth more to me than three cardinals:
more arrogant than a baron,
craftier than a Jesuit,
more corruptible than a judge,
and as coarse as a peasant
if you venture to question his scholarship.
I know of a couple of excellent specimens.
There's one, I'm informed, whose home is in Wittenberg,
a certain Johann Faustus, Doctor in four faculties!
(*Aside to Mephisto*:)
Mephisto, what did he want with four different doctorates —
wasn't he content with one?
Was it zeal, his thirst for knowledge,
a noble mind with lofty aims?

MEPHISTO

No, sir, it was out of despair.

PLUTO

Oh this Germany!
A chap who gets four doctorates out of despair!
I was often in despair,
but never dreamt of that.

What's he up to now?
In the recent troubles, as I recall —
more business involving the peasants, I think —
he took a line we approve of.

MEPHISTO

Doctor Faustus is going through
a great creative crisis,
whereby both intellectual and
physical pleasure is leaving him jaded.
All learning seems shallow to him,
reason repels him.
He craves what he calls a full life.

PLUTOZ

Sounds rather good.
Must have a word with him.

MEPHISTO

Hard to fix!
He keeps trying to escape.

PLUTO

Thus? (*He mimes someone drinking.*)

MEPHISTO

No, thus! (*He mimes someone at prayer.*)
He wants to go back,
back to the (*he stutters*) Faith.

PLUTO

Hm?

MEPHISTO

He's reading the (*after some hesitation*) . . .B-i-b-l-e.

PLUTO

I've nothing against the Bible.
The Book of books contains things that are quite handy
even for our purposes.
Guide his hand when he's browsing,
help him discover those passages
which allude to the vanity of all earthly endeavours.
Such as this passage from Job:
"Man that is born of a woman
is of few days, and full of trouble.

Curtain

***

Act One, Scene 1

Faust's study. The first signs of daybreak.

FAUST

I can't go on like this!
Lethargic and peevish, whatever the work.
I've got all listless and stinking lazy.
When I think how keen I used to be,
leaving my bed as early as three,
to start at the crack of dawn.
How happy I was with my task!
But what's the point now, I ask?
(*Rat noises are heard.*)
That squabbling and scratching
means the rats are scrabbling.
They'd be a threat to a healthy life,
except that the plague is already rife,
princes and Junkers its other face,
source of all our disgrace.
Oh you blind, blinkered Germany!
Beastly way to run things!
What an existence!
And I should put up some resistance.
(*After a pause*:)
I'd be glad to go back.
Possibly I, Doctor in four faculties,
four times despairing of reason and knowledge,
must go back, back to the Faith.
(*He drags a Bible to his desk.*)
Oh, if only the Book of books
could offer some help to this somebody,
who, alas, reads too much.
(*The Bible opens of its own accord.*)
That's odd, it opened just like that.
I'll take it as a sign.
(*He pores over the Bible.*)
The Book of Job — ghastly;
I'd rather not read.
(*Reading*:)
"Man that is born of a woman
is of few days, and full of trouble."

(*Turns the page, goes on reading in a murmur, then stops.*)
But what am I doing this for?
Religion won't help me,
I'm not a child any more.
Whichever way I turn,
there's only black magic to learn.
Although that's dangerous!
(*He goes to his bookshelf.*)

SCENE WITH THE BOOKS

These books of mine!
Where would I be without Gutenberg?
What a job I'd have,
like the princes without their Berthold Schwarz!
Making books and gunpowder:
we Germans are good at that,
but don't enquire
who the books are for —
who the powder's for.
(*Stooping, in a tone of annoyance*:)
Yet again old Wagner
has been putting Luther
next to Thomas Münzer.
Don't belong together.
(*He rearranges the books, opens one by Münzer and reads*:)
"You are going to be sold like cattle.
You may have been vassals before,
but now they will make you no more than slaves.
Stir yourselves and fight the good fight,
whilst you still draw breath.
Look lively, jump to it, and fast!
You will have to make haste,
there's no time to waste."
O Münzer? My noble Münzer!
(*He carefully closes the book and reaches for another.*)
"One must tear the peasants to shreds,
stabbing and strangling,
covertly, openly,
the way that mad dogs must be slaughtered.
To hesitate is a sin.

Therefore, my good sirs,
strike, stab, throttle them all you can!
If it costs you your life, rejoice;
never could a more blessed death be afforded you."
O Luther! My great Luther,
what have you brought upon us!
(*He holds up a book in each hand, showing the audience the titles.*)
One said this and one said that.
But it's too late now to go back.
However much I rack my brains,
O my discordant pair of teachers,
where do we go from here?
(*He carefully returns the books to his bookcase.*)
The sciences!
(*He scans the rows of books.*)
Aha, here's good old Agricola.
(*He opens the book.*)
"De animantibus subterraneis —
On the Creatures of the Underworld.
"Vipers, wood-lice and lizards,
the creature that neither hears nor sees."
How nice to have no eyes or ears!
"Salamanders, hardened in fire."
Their resistance to burning
is what the peasants could have done with.
"Basilisks, endowed with looks that kill."
That'll be their princes.
"Earth-spirits, who are also termed goblins,
seek from the nether world
to make contact
with real human beings."
(*He turns the pages in a bored manner and replaces the book.*)
These sciences are utterly useless.
Now magic!
(*He takes a huge tome and drags it to his desk before opening it.*)
"Nigromantia": see under "black magic".
(*He turns the pages.*)
"Black magic is the ability
to conjure up spirits
in order to
do business with them.

Courage is necessary,
because they are fond of abominable disguises
when they appear.
See under 'de magicis artibus'."
(*Turns the pages.*)
"Magic has its laws and customs."
(*He leans back in his chair.*)
What science can't provide,
perhaps magic will!
Oh to live a life that's great,
where instead of this sorrowful state
I'd realize myself to the full,
growing tall as a tree with a green, sturdy trunk,
however marshy the earth underneath!
If that's the way to stretch me,
who cares if Satan should fetch me!
(*He continues to read in a murmur. Closing the book, he pounds the desk furiously. There is an echoing knock on the door. Loudly:*)
I'm working!
(*The door opens to reveal Wagner.*)

WAGNER

Am I disturbing you?
(*Faust reads.*)
Two students from Cracow University
are asking to be admitted.
(*Faust shakes his head. Exit Wagner.*)

FAUST (*reading from his encyclopaedia*)

"Men tell of a book titled
'Clavicula Salomonis',
which has some excellent formulas
for a simple way in
to the Underworld.
The book is thought to be lost."
(*A knock at the door.*)

WAGNER

Funny.
Those students have vanished, but they left
a pamphlet lying in the anteroom.
(*An enquiring look from Faust. Wagner opens the pamphlet.*)
"Clavicula Salomonis".

FAUST (*ashen-faced*)
I don't want to read it.
(*Wagner lays the pamphlet on the desk.*)
I shall go and take a walk,
ought to meet people more,
it's bad to be always
sitting here by myself.
(*Exit Faust with a nervous glance at the pamphlet.*)

Curtain

***

Act One, Scene 2

THE WALK

In front of the gates of Wittenberg. Karl, a disabled peasant, is beneath a lime-tree. He is stocky, with coarse features, iron-grey hair, blind. The stumps of his arms are supported on sticks. A boy is beside him.

BOY (*begging for alms*)
When Jesus to the garden did go,
then started his bitter woe;
the leaves are in mourning, and the green grass,
for soon he was forgotten by Judas.
They led him into the judge's house,
with sharp weals on his back they brought him out;
scourged with whips and crowned with thorns,
oh, how they put you to scorn.
(*During this song a doctor comes past with a parson. An old woman brings soup for Karl and the boy. She asks the doctor to give her something for her backache. After glancing at her, he plucks a small plant from the meadow and hands it to her. A lawyer appears, gesturing to the two men of learning; evidently they intend to go for a drink. He gives Karl a wide berth.*)

LAWYER (*to the doctor in an undertone, pointing to Karl*)
That chap stood up to being tortured.

DOCTOR (*looking at Karl in disbelief*)
Amazing!

TENANT FARMER (*with a sack slung over his shoulder*)
When you're taking the landlord his rent,
the road drags on.
To make the time go more quickly,

let's think of a good dinner.
There are wonderful dishes
which I have never tasted.
But I'd be happy with something home-made,
if I got it.
(*Dreaming.*)
First a bit of jellied tripe,
followed by liver-sausage,
fried sausage as well, and smoked brawn,
then pease-pudding and some roast pork,
all washed down with brown ale.
A slap-up meal!
(*He trudges on.*)
Before long I shall get to town,
but what's to be done with my landlord?
Until he's bumped off he won't change his ways
in all his born days.
He'll change when he's dead.
(*Sees Karl.*)
A swig for our hero.
(*He gives Karl something to drink.*)
How are you doing
with your "Heia––ohé--and charge"?
(*Karl nods amiably.*)
Alack's the name of the bride,
her groom is called woe betide!
So here we are dressed up in our rags,
feeling how poverty nags.

BAILIFF (*wielding a staff*)
Aren't you aware, you pig,
that the town councillors of Wittenberg
have proscribed and outlawed Thomas Münzer's mob,
and that those who consort with them
will be severely punished?

TENANT FARMER
Don't report me,
I've got quite enough worry. (*Exit.*)

BAILIFF (*pointing at Karl*)
Now he's forced to rely on hand-outs
from all the other poor louts.

(*Exit. This has been observed by a town councillor and his spouse, dressed in their finery. They resume their walk unconcernedly. Enter Faust.*)

BOY

Bow down, tree,
bow down, branch,
from pangs will Judas ne'er be free;
oh, grieve now, leaves and green grass,
mourn for that which has come to pass.
(*Seeing Faust, he raises his hand.*)

FAUST (*recognizing Karl*)

What have they been doing to you, the villains?

KARL

Who's that?

FAUST

It's Hans, from Ried.

KARL

Faust from next door — that Hans?

FAUST

That's right.

KARL

The one who ran away from home?
What have they been doing to *you,* the villains?
(*Faust is silent. To the boy:*)
Examine his face and tell me how he's looking.

BOY

Pasty, as though
he's been holed up indoors for too long.

FAUST

Martin Luther was right:
you ought never to have gone to battle.

KARL

Shut up!
We made a bad job of it,
quarrelling among ourselves.
And too many traitors and cowards.
(*Faust is silent. Karl lowers his voice.*)
Hans, only a blockhead believes those
who say that we're done for.
Believe me, our time will come as surely
as the amen in a prayer.

FAUST

But when?

KARL

They haven't broken our spirit.

Faust

And your body? (*Karl is silent.*)
Karl, I was never against your Münzer,
his books were a tonic,
but to wrangle with the men in power,
that was stupid.

KARL

It was all your Luther's fault,
inciting the bloodthirsty Mansfeld against us,
the pig!

FAUST

And now what, after all the misery and bloodshed?
(*Karl is silent.*)
Here you sit — none the wiser, and begging.

KARL (*in a firm voice*)

Here I sit —- none the wiser, and begging.
(*He beckons.*)
Come closer, old Hans,
my little boy has a song for you.

BOY (*softly, to Faust*)

"Heia, ohé!
Although we've retired from the fray,
our sons will fight better one day."

KARL

He's got a good ear,
ought to be a musician,
it's what we need.
(*Shaking his head, Faust takes some money out of his pocket.*)

FAUST

This is all I've got on me.

BOY (*cheerfully*)

Sevenpence!

KARL

Thank you kindly, Hans.

FAUST

Fare well.
(*He starts to go.*)

KARL

Hans, come back here to your Karl.
Maybe I shouldn't have
called Martin Luther a pig.
He put up a good show
that time in Worms;
but he also campaigned against us,
and I can't forget that.
(*Faust places his hand on Karl's shoulder.*)
Tell me, what's your line of business?

FAUST

Philosophy.

KARL

Then what on earth do you do all day?

FAUST (*with some hesitation*)

I strive for the truth.

KARL

But which truth?
(*He displays the stumps of his arms.*)

FAUST (*quietly*)

You don't signify the truth,
Karl, but misfortune.
What made you go running after Thomas Münzer!

KARL

So you're a philosopher.

FAUST

Some of the philosophers
have been people of courage
and great resolution.
There is the celebrated story
about Archimedes.

KARL

Let's be hearing it.

FAUST

Archimedes, the sage of renown,
lived in Egypt's kingdom.
Alexandria was the great town
where he taught others his wisdom.

The town, it was in fearful straits,
for Huns were knocking at the gates.

Like lions the people stood to defend;
blood ran through the streets from end to end.

And when the Huns surrounded his house,
Archimedes would not come out.
He sat and with a steady hand
wrote equations in the sand.

And when their swords did cleave the air,
he said: "Let no man touch those figures there!"
And from the self-same day he died,
his words were praised on every side.

That, Karl, is what's so noble.
Regardless of the conflicts of the day,
a philosopher strives for the truth.

KARL (*laughs heartily*)
What a fine fellow,
getting himself butchered
with all his stock of knowledge!
(*Faust is nonplussed.*)
And is that your philosophy, Hans?
The Devil take you!
(*Faust makes a sheepish exit.*)

Curtain

***

Act One, Scene 3

A SERVANT IS TAKEN ON

WAGNER
So you're a servant without a master.
We're looking for a servant,
but I shan't engage you
without knowing precisely
who you are and where you come from.

HANSWURST
I'm from the district of Salzburg,
and I worked for the bishop.

WAGNER
What made you run away?

HANSWURST
He wanted to turn me into a soldier.

WAGNER
And did he make you one?
HANSWURST
When he was under siege from the peasants,
he pressed us all into service as soldiers.
WAGNER (*warily*)
What made you come here?
HANSWURST
Folk in the taverns were suddenly saying:
quick, off to the east,
there you will find a new religion
and a new banner.
I hopped it at once and went off to the east.
The banner itself took my fancy, 'twere grand,
its a picture of a wine-glass,
and then the worship! At Communion
the parson's not to guzzle all the wine,
he's to share it with the congregation.
I was quick to appreciate this new kind of ritual.
WAGNER
And now you've fetched up in these parts!
HANSWURST
I hoped to turn a penny in Leipzig.
I'd have liked to work for a butcher,
where there's plenty of sausage,
but the butcher's guild refused to have me.
So I got a job as an apprentice with Fischer,
who came from Ketsch in Swabia;
the guild saw him as another foreigner.
WAGNER
Why didn't you go on working for Fischer?
HANSWURST
On account of his singing.
WAGNER
I can't see why,
it's a Christian practice —
I'll come back to that later, by the way.
HANSWURST
But these were Swabian songs,
and there was one that worried me.
"Fischer," I said,

"yesterday, what were you singing about?"
And he answered:
"Oh, nothing special."
And when I repeated the bit about
setting fire to the thatch,*
he couldn't remember;
and when I asked,
"Fischer, weren't you with the Peasants' League?",
he didn't bother to deny it.
Just looked through me,
and that was the last I ever saw of Fischer;
I'd put the wind up him, likely as not.

WAGNER

So what did you do next?

HANSWURST

Spent time with the students.
Good employment, but
whenever one preached his first sermon
and thundered against the Catholics,
I'd think to myself: what a laugh
if ours was the false religion.

WAGNER

Be warned, when it comes to religion
I'll stand for no mischief — never ever!
You could start in this house from today:
five crowns a year, full board,
and a bonus for holidays;
but there are two things I must ask you
before taking you on.

THE RELIGIOUS TEST

WAGNER

Are you discreet?

HANSWURST

Extremely so, almost dumb.

WAGNER

And are you pious?
(*Hanswurst nods his head.*)

---

* The German line "Drauf und dran, roter Hahn", with its image of a red cock, is a reference to a fire-raising song. Translator's note.

Do you always go to chapel?

HANSWURST

Do I always eat an apple?

WAGNER

I asked if you always went to chapel.

HANSWURST

Surely you've only to look at me
to tell that I'm pious.

WAGNER

If I look at you
I see a bottle-nose, not a prayer-book.
(*Hanswurst shrugs.*)
Luther teaches us that
"not the eye but the ear
possesses the true Christian sense;
an awareness of the invisible."

HANSWURST

Strewth, the invisible!

WAGNER

To show how religious you are,
I want you to sing a chorale.

HANSWURST

But I don't have an ear for music,
no ear at all,
and besides forgetting the words,
it's been so hard to learn the tunes
since Luther went and mucked around with them.

WAGNER

Be warned:
the great Luther was not mucking around;
he has improved the music, made it more Christian.

HANSWURST

But all his tunes sound the same,
all equally solemn and mournful,
like being at a funeral.
That's why I'm glad of our folk-songs,
because there you get so much variety:
some are poignant
because they express sorrow;
other songs are funny
and they make you laugh;

and there are also some that tell a story,
and those are different again.

WAGNER

What a corrupt taste you have.
I think you're a philistine.
But surely you can manage to remember a chorale.
(*Hanswurst paces up and down with a sullen expression, humming to himself. He halts, as though a tune has come back to him, then slaps himself on the head. Wagner registers amazement.*)
He doesn't even know our song of faith!

HANSWURST

The song of faith? I'm word perfect in that.
(*He prepares to sing.*)
"Ein feste Wartburg ist unser Gott,
ein gute Wehr und Waffen."

WAGNER

You rascal, playing on the fact
that our Luther had to shelter in the Wartburg
from his Roman assailants.
Should he have gone burning his fingers
just because of you?

HANSWURST

You've got me wrong, nobody
needs to burn just because of me.

WAGNER

"Ein feste Burg ist unser Gott,
ein gute Wehr und Waffen.
Er hilft uns frei aus aller Not,
die uns jetzt hat betroffen."
Get on with it!

HANSWURST

I've only memorized the start,
but let me sing you a folk-song
on a sacred theme — about Jesus,
and the way that Peter betrayed him.
(*At the word "betrayed" Wagner twitches.*)
It's maybe not as high class
as the Luther hymn,
but it has its merits.

WAGNER

Be warned: in Doctor Faust's household

you are not to use the word "betray",
never ever! Now begin!

HANSWURST

Our Lord, he laid out the supper
with all his disciples.
They went forth into a garden,
and all twelve were joyful.

WAGNER

They weren't joyful, they were mournful.

HANSWURST

In our book they were joyful; that's how
you feel when you're getting some supper.

When their enemies came,
the disciples took to their heels.
One of the foe seized Peter's cloak and exclaimed:
"Bald-pate, you're coming with me."

WAGNER

"Bald-pate"! How can you
presume to call the mighty Peter a bald-pate!

HANSWURST

He didn't have no hair on his pate.

But Peter drew out his broadsword,
trying to rescue his Lord.
His skill with the sword was mean,
not many blows landed clean.

WAGNER

Incorrect. One should say "cleanly" —- not "clean".

HANSWURST (*unrepentant*)

The Lord wagged his finger at Peter:
"Oh, stick your sword in its sheath.
You're an archlotus-eater,
that sword has no teeth."

WAGNER (*bows his head in despair*)

"Archlotus-eater"!

HANSWURST

To Peter it seemed a disgrace
to play no part in the fight.
He went all red and blue in the face,
struck with main and might.

WAGNER (*groaning*)
"Main and might"!

HANSWURST
Malchus was standing nearby,
believed he had nothing to fear.
But then Peter's sword whistled by
and it sliced away his ear.

Malchus began to burst into tears
and he screamed in his pain:
"Lord, the bald-pate has cut off my ear,
please can't you heal it again."
(*Wagner twitches.*)
And Jesus took the severed flesh,
and would have mended it straight.
But Peter, with an angry dash,
begins to remonstrate:

"What was the point of chancing my arm,
if you make me look a chump!"

WAGNER
This song is pure trash!

HANSWURST
"You go and protect this man from harm,
soon as I give him a thump."
(*Enter Faust, who listens in gloom.*)
Pilate sat by the fire,
his chalky face wore a scowl.
Then one of the ruffians, chancing by,
saw Peter and let out a howl.

"Him, he's one of the band,
I saw him in the garden too!"
But Peter lied in his teeth,
bawling: "No, it's not true."

FAUST
What's this lad doing here?

WAGNER
I have, Your Excellency,
engaged him to work in the house.

HANSWURST
Where can I put my things?

FAUST

Give him somewhere to sleep.
(*Hanswurst bows to Faust.*)

HANSWURST (*aside*)

He's awfully pale!
(*To Wagner:*)
How do I get to the kitchen?

Act One, Scene 4

THE FIRST EXPERIMENT

Dumb show: Faust draws the magic square, repeatedly consulting the "Clavicula Salomonis".

DEADLY SINS (*without being seen*)

Fauste!

FAUST (*looking up*)

Who's that?

DEADLY SINS (*like an echo*)

Pride, Covetousness, Envy,
Gluttony, Lust,
Anger and Sloth!

FAUST

Quos ego! That's not enough.
(*The magic square is finished. Faust murmurs incantations. Auerhahn, Asmodi and Zachariel appear.*)
Who are you?

THE THREE

Special agents of Pluto,
the lord of the Underworld,
and now at your service.

FAUST

What are your names?
(*The Three begin to gabble.*)

AUERHAHN

Our names are not important.

ASMODI

What's in a name?

ZACHARIEL

I've four names, but I'm called —
(*Asmodi treads on his foot.*)

FAUST

Quos ego!
(*The Three clap their hands to their mouths.*)
I need servants who are quick to carry out my wishes!
(*Pointing at Auerhahn*)
How quick are you?

AUERHAHN

As quick as the Black Death.

FAUST

That isn't quick enough,
people are still alive.
(*Pointing at Asmodi*)
How quick are you?

ASMODI

As quick as vengeance for treachery.

FAUST

That isn't quick enough,
I'm still alive.

ASMODI

Could that in itself be a form of revenge?

FAUST

So you know all the answers, pig!
(*Pointing at Zachariel*)
How quick are you?

ZACHARIEL

I'm as quick as a man can think.

FAUST

That is quicker than quick,
and yet where the truth is concerned,
men are so slow!
Are there no faster spirits?

AUERHAHN

There's always Mephistopheles.

FAUST

Fetch him here.

THE THREE

You must summon him yourself!
(*They disappear.*)

FAUST

I, Johann Faustus,
Doctor in four faculties,
entreat you, Mephistopheles,
if the swiftest of spirits,
to appear by my magic circle
and to give an account of yourself.
(*Mephisto appears, wearing a conventional suit.*)
You've come looking like a human?

MEPHISTO

Pluto has empowered me
to appear in any shape I choose.

FAUST

How quick are you?

MEPHISTO

As quick as the change from good to evil.

FAUST

I'll settle for that. How speedy that is,
I have learnt, alas, from bitter experience!
Are you prepared to make a pact with me?

MEPHISTO

Of course!

FAUST

No, no, no!
Not so fast, I haven't made up my mind yet.
But I hereby command you
to reappear at midnight tonight.

MEPHISTO

I'll be here the moment you think of me.
(*Exit. Faust falls to the floor. He gets up with an effort.*)

FAUST

I'm exhausted. I shall have to lie down. (*He does so.*)

PEASANTS' CHORUS

When our battle was done
and we lay butchered, outside Frankenhausen,
that life of splendour we've heard of
was finished.
Of Frankenhausen's band, no men
will ever reach three score and ten.
But nor will those who ran away

now live to fight another day.
He who went and asked for quarter
lost his soul in that dread slaughter.

FAUST

Give me air, I'm choking!

Curtain

Act One, Scene 5

BURLESQUE

Dumb show: Hanswurst is sweeping the floor. He notices the magic circle and finds the book on the ground. He opens the book.

HANSWURST

What beautiful letters! (*Spells out a word.*)
"Perlicke".
(*Pluto's agents in devils' form appear around the magic circle.*)
"Perlacke".
(*The devils disappear. Hanswurst looks up.*)
Don't disturb us when we're working,
I'm not having it! "Perlicke".
(*The devils reappear.*)
"Perlacke".
(*They disappear. Hanswurst looks up.*)
Be quiet while I'm studying!
I like the look of these words,
let's go over them again.
"Perlicke".
(*The devils reappear. Hanswurst, without looking up*:)
"Perlacke".
(*They disappear. Hanswurst looks up.*)
Who's making that noise, when I'm reading?
"Perlicke".
(*The devils reappear. Hanswurst quickly looks up and sees them.*)
What's this, then? What do you want?

DEVILS

We're here at your bidding.

HANSWURST

But you look a fine sight, I must say.

DEVILS

We're the devils.

HANSWURST

Ugh, the heck! What do you want?

DEVILS

To wring your neck for you.

HANSWURST

No, I'd hate you to do that.

DEVILS

Leave the circle!

HANSWURST

Just you shove off!

DEVILS

We're staying.

HANSWURST

Why don't you clear off?

DEVILS

We want to pull you to bits.

HANSWURST (*mimics them*)

Pull me to bits?
Then why not get on with it?

DEVILS

We can't get into the circle.

HANSWURST

If you can't get in,
then I can't get out.

DEVILS

Give us your hand.

HANSWURST

What, give it to scoundrels?
You clear off!
(*He sits down. The devils follow suit. He stands up. The devils stand up. He sits down. The devils sit down. Hanswurst reads from the book.*)
"Perlacke".
(*The devils disappear. Hanswurst looks round.*)
Where have they gone?

Aha, what was the word I saw? (*He looks at the book.*)
"Perlicke". (*The devils reappear. Hanswurst gives a shout.*)
We've got them back again! (*He laughs.*)

DEVILS (*shouting*)
Leave the spells alone!

HANSWURST
You bunch of crooks! — "Perlacke"!
(*The devils disappear.*)
I'll teach you a lesson! (*He takes his broom.*)
"Perlicke"!
(*The devils reappear. Hanswurst keeps beating the nearest of them over the head with the broom.*)
"Perlacke"!
(*They disappear. He roars with laughter.*)
"Perlicke"!
(*They reappear.*)
"Perlacke"!
(*They disappear. Hanswurst, faster and faster:*)
"Perlicke" — "Perlacke"!
(*He gives the devils a thrashing.*)

Act One, Scene 6

THE PACT

Faust's study. It strikes twelve o'clock.
Faust listens to the chimes.

MEPHISTO (*offstage*)
In qua forma me vis videre?

FAUST
In what form should you reveal yourself to me?
(*To himself:*)
I must be brave about this. (*Calling out:*)
In the most terrifying form
one could possibly imagine.
(*Mephisto appears in armour, with a helmet and sword.*)
You've come as a soldier?

MEPHISTO
Should I have come as a peasant?

FAUST
Stop it!

MEPHISTO

Tell me the details of the pact
you want me to make with you.

THE NEGOTIATION

FAUST

Point one: to obey me
for twenty-four years and serve me faithfully.

MEPHISTO

Twenty-four years?
Wouldn't half that time be enough?

FAUST

Twenty-four years, assuming
we reckon each year to be three hundred and sixty-five days.

MEPHISTO (*after some thought*)

Right!

FAUST

Point two: you're to provide me
with plenty of money, because I want
to taste every joy the world has to offer.

MEPHISTO

Right!

FAUST

Point three: you're to turn me
into the most charming and handsome of men,
and when I feel like it,
I want to go sailing through the air on my cloak,
wherever I choose,
and at no risk to my person.

MEPHISTO

Right!

FAUST

Point four: you're to teach me
the liberal arts.

MEPHISTO

Name them!

FAUST

The great art of painting,
sublime music,
noble poetry.

MEPHISTO
I can't help you.

FAUST
Are they beyond your powers?
(*Mephisto is silent.*)
I need to be famous. Monarchs
must bow down before me,
hoping to find me in a good temper.
(*He bangs the table.*)
The most vital point in the contract!

MEPHISTO
Thanks to a new art which I shall teach you,
you could learn to make heroes appear,
large as life, and completely convincing.

FAUST (*pondering*)
Men of all ranks need heroes they can look up to. (*Out loud:*)
Excellent!
Heroes shall come and go at my command.
That is the power for which I'm thirsting. (*Aside:*)
If I've gone and lost my honour,
then I need greater, far greater honours!
Point five: you must warn me
of any impending danger.
I'm to meet with no mishaps,
no-one's to touch a hair of my head.

MEPHISTO (*impatiently*)
Right!

FAUST
Throughout those twenty-four years
I want to be in the best of health.

MEPHISTO
But if you're living it up
by gorging, boozing and whoring —
how can you expect good health?
Mind you, I've got my patent remedies for that.
(*He thinks for a while.*)
Faust: having considered the terms of your contract,
I agree to them.

FAUST
Good!

MEPHISTO

And my terms are the following.

FAUST

You want to impose conditions?
Aren't I yours, both body and soul,
as soon as my time expires?

MEPHISTO

Of course, but don't think that only you can
state conditions in such a deal.
(*He bangs on the table.*)
Point one:
you mustn't wash, or comb your hair,
or clean your fingernails.

FAUST

But if I don't, then people will give me a wide berth.

MEPHISTO

Let me take care of that;
everyone's going to regard Faust
as the most attractive man on earth.

FAUST

Right!

MEPHISTO

Point two:
you must never touch a book again
or set foot in a university.

FAUST

But think of my scholarly reputation!

MEPHISTO

People can easily be hoodwinked
into thinking
that Faust is the most industrious of scholars.

FAUST

Right!

MEPHISTO

And point three:
you must renounce love.

FAUST

Renounce love?

MEPHISTO

The most vital point in the contract!

FAUST

I can't love a woman?

MEPHISTO

No!

FAUST

Or my parents?

MEPHISTO

No!

FAUST

Or my friends and colleagues?

MEPHISTO

No!

FAUST

Or my social class?

MEPHISTO

Which class do you mean?
Your fellow professors?

FAUST

No, I despise them. I mean the peasants.

MEPHISTO

Faust, you're deceiving yourself!
Where were you in their darkest hour,
when they were being butchered to death at Frankenhausen?
Those scenes were so ghastly
they almost made the Devil weep.

FAUST (*in a low voice*)

May I love my country?

MEPHISTO

The one the town of Frankenhausen's in?

FAUST

No, that's appalling!
Sucking the blood out of Thomas Münzer!

MEPHISTO (*counting names on his fingers*)

Do you mean Saxony, Anhalt, Mecklenburg,
Hesse, Bavaria, Swabia?
Do you mean Schleiz, Greiz, Lobenstein,
Lauenburg, Ratzeburg, Schwarzburg,
Rudolstadt, Putbus and Lanken?

FAUST

I mean the whole of Germany.

MEPHISTO
The land of princes, Junkers, clerics?

FAUST
No, I despise them.

MEPHISTO
The land of big business, rich merchants
with fat profits?

FAUST
No, they despise me.

MEPHISTO
Do you mean the people?

FAUST (*bows his head. After a pause:*)
May I get married?

MEPHISTO
No!

FAUST
Without love, so they say,
this life is unbearable.
Whom can I love?

MEPHISTO
Yourself!
As you see, our mutual contract
does take love into consideration.
We are simply transposing the idea
from the general to the particular — that is, you.

FAUST
Cut out the dodges,
I used them quite enough in disputations. (*Musing.*)
Besides which, I need a clear conscience.

MEPHISTO
Easy as winking. (*He clicks his fingers.*)
After you've spent a night boozing and whoring,
you'll wake up feeling good and say to yourself
there's no harm in a bit of fun.

FAUST
It wasn't just that I meant.
There's something else I need.

MEPHISTO
What's that?
(*Faust is silent.*)
Speak, Faust!

FAUST

Something's nagging at me,
causing me worry,
sleepless nights.

MEPHISTO

Tell me, Faust!

FAUST

It's war.

MEPHISTO

Which war?
There are many wars, and of different kinds.

FAUST

The war the peasants were fighting.
I just stood on the sidelines.

MEPHISTO

Very smart of you. What else?

FAUST

I am a peasant's son.
(*Mephisto laughs.*)
Don't laugh, you pig!

MEPHISTO

What's gnawing at you, Faust?
You're a Doctor now —
a Doctor four times over.
(*Faust is silent. Mephisto bangs on the table.*)
What is it?

FAUST (*in a low voice*)

You must wipe two songs from my memory.

MEPHISTO

Is that all?
Sing them to me, and you'll forget them at once.

FAUST

I don't want to sing them,
you must guess which they are.

MEPHISTO

There are many songs, and of different kinds.
(*He looks at Faust quizzically.*)
Your first song's the one you heard the Junkers singing.
(*Faust shuts his eyes while Mephisto sings the song.*)

If you want to survive,
young lord of the manor,
just take my advice,
come and follow the banner!
But smartly now and don't linger.

When a peasant's gathering logs,
catch him in a noose,
take away whate'er he's got,
and set his ponies loose.

If he's got no more than tuppence,
tie him! prod him! kick him! punch him!
stab him! flay him! burn him! hang him!
wring his wretched neck!

(*With exorcizing gestures:*)
All over! Forgotten! Sing, nightingale!
(*Faust opens his eyes and runs his hand across his forehead.*)
The other is the one you heard the peasants singing.
(*Mephisto sings with wild gestures, as though charging forward with a spear to the ready. Faust observes him carefully.*)

Heia, ohé! Hei, ohé! Ohé! ohé! ohé! ohé!
Heeeeeeeeeeeeeeee!
Here we go, palace, abbey and crypt,
heia, ohé!
The Holy Bible's our only script,
heia, ohé!
Look lively, and charge . . . .

FAUST (*interrupting*)
I can't bear it, that fearful old song!

MEPHISTO
Fearful? It's quite fearless.
(*Shaking his head, he advances to the footlights.*)
He's a difficult case and needs special treatment.
This may seem a bit uncivil, but I can't help it.
(*He returns to Faust and spits in his face.*)

FAUST
What a vulgar trick!

MEPHISTO
Trick? Have you forgotten?

Faust

Forgotten? Come off it!

Mephisto (*raising his voice*)

Come on, Faust, your two songs!

Faust

I can't remember saying anything to you about a song.

Mephisto

Here's the contract.
We need some blood!
(*He draws blood from Faust's s arm with his cock's plume.*)
Sign here!
(*Faust takes the pen with a trembling hand.*)
You're trembling. Let me guide your hand for you.
(*Mephisto helps him to sign the contract and pockets it.*)
Now, Faust, state your first wish!

Faust

To go away,
somewhere where there aren't any cripples,
and aren't any ruins,
aren't any traitors — somewhere
where nobody knows me.
Away from here!

Mephisto (*standing by a globe*)

Where do you want to go?

Faust

Away!

Mephisto (*turning the globe*)

In the west, across the ocean,
there's a country called Atlanta.
It's both rich and colourful.
Thanks to the new art I shall teach you,
you will achieve great honour.

Faust

And how do we get there?

Mephisto

We'll go by air.
(*He stamps his foot. Auerhahn appears.*)
Auerhahn, we're off to Atlanta.
You're to get Hanswurst over.
(*At his signal Auerhahn disappears. Mephisto turns to face Faust.*)

Don't worry, this won't be dangerous.
(*He spreads a cloak on the floor.*)
Look, your cloak will carry us there.
(*Mephisto takes hold of Faust 's hand and stands on the cloak with him.*)
To Atlanta!

Curtain

PEASANTS' CHORUS
Go on your travels, Faustus!
We shall make this journey too.
In all that you do,
we shall be guiding your hand.
Where you mean to tell lies,
you will utter the truth
against your own will.
We are going to break you.

End of Act One

Act Two, Scene 1

In Atlanta. The Lord of Atlanta's gardens.

GRETE (*shelling black peas into a basket*)
"Though I be far from you,
I'm with you in my dreams
and talk to you;
but when I wake from sleep,
I'm all alone.
All through the night until daybreak,
will this heart be awake
and with my lover.
For you've shown you love me
many times over."
What on earth is that hullabaloo?
HANSWURST (*crashing to the ground*)
My old nag has just thrown me off
in the most peculiar way,
right down from the heavens,
and so here I am, gasping for breath,
because I'm no good as a rider.

GRETE

Who are you?

HANSWURST (*pretending to be dumb*)

Hm, hm.

GRETE

Are you dumb?

HANSWURST

Mm!

GRETE

But you were talking just now,
how is it that you've
lost your voice so suddenly?

HANSWURST

To avoid idle chatter,
but it's no use.
Who are you, foreign darling?

GRETE

Kitchen maid to the Lord of Atlanta.

HANSWURST

A kitchen maid! Tell me,
is the kitchen as nice as you?
(*Grete nods.*)
A beautiful kitchen maid with a beautiful kitchen!
This is ideal — or rather,
as my master would put it,
the utile cum dulce:
the practical combined with the beautiful.

GRETE

Don't talk in that vulgar way!

HANSWURST

Vulgar?
What's so vulgar about a kitchen?
Isn't it a fine place to be, and when you know
that soon there's going to be something to eat,
doesn't it feel great, and eventually,
when all the food's on the table,
are we not looking at something sublime?
Isn't that a blessing
for long-suffering humanity?
Let me tell you, my foreign darling,
that when they're sleeping off a meal, even

the most ferocious of warriors are harmless.
I used to know a titled gentleman
who always said one ought not
to undertake any work between mealtimes,
it only creates discontent.

GRETE

He must be very well off.

HANSWURST

The Devil always craps on the biggest muck-heap.

GRETE

So where is he now, this gentleman?

HANSWURST

Hacked to death he was, by the peasants.
(*Grete laughs.*)
May I ask a delicate question of you,
my foreign darling?
(*Grete nods. Hanswurst, in a whisper:*)
How do I find the kitchen?

GRETE

There's no need to mince words,
I'll see you get something to eat. (*Stepping back:*)
You're a fine sight!
That shirt's all torn, I must mend it for you.
The seam of your trousers has split,
so I'll stitch it up. Handsome
you're not with that nose like a spud,
and you also need a good wash.
But you're a cheerful soul,
and I like it when a man is cheerful.

HANSWURST

What's your name?

GRETE

Grete.

HANSWURST

I'm called Hans with something on the end,
something which is round and not long,
something which goes with mash
and tastes really good; something
without which a man isn't human.

GRETE

I've no idea.

HANSWURST

"Wurst"!

GRETE

How you witter!

HANSWURST

Witter?

GRETE

Witter means to go chattering on
like swallows with their twittering.

HANSWURST

But that's mean, comparing my
chattering with a swallow's.

GRETE

It's a fine bird, Hänschen.

HANSWURST

Don't you say everything's fine,
or I'll start fretting and ask straight out
how long this meal's going to take.
When my belly's been empty three days,
I always say to myself: "That's fine, Hänschen,
a fine old way to let down your body,
you coward, you!"

GRETE

A starving person's no joke.
So shame on your wisecracks!

HANSWURST

I shouldn't have thought about eating,
it always makes me so thirsty.
(*He clutches at his heart.*)
What's happening?
Oh, the old story — feeling faint and giddy.
(*He tries to embrace Grete.*)

DUET

GRETE

If I had a tub of cold water
I would revive you only too fast,
but you will have to stand and droop,
I must go and see to the soup,
and put a stop to idle chatter.

HANSWURST

You can't simply leave me to wilt.

GRETE

I must give my people their dinner,
prepare a hot meal for them,
and finish one or two other jobs;
after that, I want to go to bed.

HANSWURST

To bed?
(*Grete nods.*)
You are trying to poke fun at me!
(*He groans.*)

GRETE

If you are really so unwell,
you ought to get some proper treatment.

HANSWURST

My belly's the seat of this ailment.
It's grumbling like hell.

GRETE

Don't you take advantage of things,
coming here to tug at my heartstrings,
seducing poor creatures like me.

HANSWURST

I'm not pretending!

GRETE

Honest?

HANSWURST (*making the sign of a pledge*)

Honest.

GRETE

Come on, then! It's time we went.
Let's go and find out if the roast
looks quite ready.

HANSWURST

Is it true that people gobble
meat here without bread?

GRETE

When the chicken's on the skewer . . .

HANSWURST

You won't find a chum that's truer.

BOTH

Into the kitchen!

Yes, it's time!
High time to go!
(*During the duet the Lord of Atlanta enters with his secretary and bodyguard. The latter are men with scowling faces. They surround Hanswurst and Grete.*)

Act Two, Scene 2

FIRST SCOWLING FACE
Openly snogging! (*Shouting:*)
The kitchen, quick march!
(*Exit Grete. Hanswurst tries to follow, but stumbles.*)

HANSWURST
Wait for me!

SECOND SCOWLING FACE
Stay where you are! You thought you had it made.

HANSWURST
A poor, defenceless orphan
at the mercy of the cruel elements
is begging for a little refreshment.

THIRD SCOWLING FACE
Why don't you go straight back
where you came from, if you
don't care for this climate?
(*Hanswurst timidly puts out a hand, the palm flat.*)

HANSWURST
I just thought it was raining.

SECOND SCOWLING FACE
Any cash, jewellery,
letters, books or papers?

HANSWURST
All with my master.

SECRETARY
What's your master's name?

HANSWURST
I'm not to tell you that.

FOURTH SCOWLING FACE
Why not?

HANSWURST
Because I'm not allowed to.
(*The scowling men seize him.*)

Let me go! You're pulling my arms off!
(*At a signal from the Lord of Atlanta, the men step back. Hanswurst rubs his arms.*)
Can I tell you by miming it?
(*The Lord of Atlanta nods. Mime: Hanswurst stretches out his hand. He points at it. The Lord of Atlanta nods. Then he half closes the hand and points at it again. The Lord of Atlanta nods again. Then he balls it into a fist.*)

LORD OF ATLANTA
Faust!

HANSWURST
That's my master. (*Rapidly:*)
I didn't give anything away!

LORD OF ATLANTA
Take yourself off to the kitchen,
where you may indulge in a little refreshment.
(*Exit Hanswurst, glancing timidly at the Lord of Atlanta.*)

Act Two, Scene 3

LORD OF ATLANTA
What's the country making of our eminent guest?

SECRETARY
Atlanta is waiting to hear your verdict!

LORD OF ATLANTA
I can't figure him out.

SECRETARY
He is strangely timid, shuns company;
but he has often been seen with your wife.

LORD OF ATLANTA
That's not to go on!
(*The secretary crosses to the scowling group of men, receives a confidential report and reads it out.*)

SECRETARY
He is conversing with her about something
he describes as magic scenes.
If asked to furnish more details,
he becomes reticent;
if caught expressing a contradiction,
he gets angry and yells:
he knows what he's doing, and that's that! (*Looks up.*)

His strange attire
and the individual hair-style
are causing a stir. I'm afraid
it'll be the latest fashion.

LORD OF ATLANTA

Anything that catches on here
gets established world-wide.
(*There is a signal from one of the scowling men.*)
Let's go and eavesdrop.
(*He and his secretary hurry into a summer-house.*)

Act Two, Scene 4

GARDEN SCENE

ELSA

People say that in your country
the birds sing so prettily.
(*Faust nods.*)
They never sing in my garden,
it's as though they had worries.
I have never heard a bird sing up to now.
(*Faust writes something on a piece of paper and tosses it into the breeze; he then raises his hand. The birds in the garden begin to sing. Faust and Elsa listen. It is with some emotion that Faust hears his native birdsong. After a while he signals for it to cease. The birds stop their singing.*)
Is it beautiful in your country?

FAUST

It's grey, not as much colour as here.
But we do possess some good scholars.
Martin Luther teaches at our university.

ELSA

Couldn't you fetch Luther across to Atlanta?
It would be wonderful
to have such a distinguished man over here.

FAUST (*frowning*)

His great task of translating the Bible
takes up nearly all of his time.

ELSA

What does he need to translate the Bible for?
Isn't it all right as it stands?

FAUST

My poor Germany
is all torn and tattered,
a land that's at war with herself.
Tollgates and barriers everywhere,
people can't even travel.
Every patch of soil has its own lord and master,
and each of them has his way of grinding the poor.
Had we a German Bible, a language
in common from north to south, from east to west,
perhaps we could unite.

ELSA

What do you think of our garden?

FAUST

In its abundance it quite transcends
the gardener's art and reminds me of
a jeweller's tray of precious stones and gems.

ELSA

Thank you. (*Faust makes a bow.*)
One shouldn't enthuse over it without
remembering all the hard work that went into it.
It was difficult laying it out. Our negroes
had the job of draining an abominable marsh,
which was horrible work, and quite dangerous
because of the crocodiles.
I don't propose to go into details,
but it cost us a great deal of sacrifice.
We soon realized that to cultivate and maintain it
would call for many more sacrifices.
My poor husband finds it a headache.
(*Faust begins to walk restlessly to and fro.*)
In the cool of the evening, when swarms
of gnats and greenfly start to collect in the air,
he often broods and says:
"Once a marsh, always a marsh,
no matter how lovely it looks."
(*Faust nods in agreement.*)
Yesterday we had to take the whip to
another five blacks; it'll help, but
not for long, because the marsh waters

keep bubbling up again and
producing the weirdest blossoms.

FAUST

In that fungus I see
a light-brown flower which has orange spots on it,
with quivering antennae coming out at the edge.
A strange mixture of lewdness and innocence.
(*He gives Elsa the flower.*)

ELSA

People say we don't have any worries.
Nobody ever mentions the great
responsibility we carry.
Actually I often reproach myself,
accusing myself of failing
to take enough care: my garden could do with
still lovelier blooms and in greater profusion.
(*Faust quickly shields his eyes.*)
What's the matter?

FAUST

It's the harsh light!

ELSA

That's something you have to get used to.

FAUST

It's hard for someone who's fond of the dark.

ELSA

What a strange combination you are
of strength and weakness. The clothes you wear and your
hair-style are also unusual, although that
could well catch on over here. As for the graphic way
you can invest words with a deeper meaning —
amazing. What was it again?
"Someone who's fond of the dark."

FAUST

Let me tell you this much: knowledge
has led me to be contemptuous of everything.
There's so much I've seen and inwardly sifted;
so much that's earned my contempt and disgust.
Men torment one another, and fight over
each other's goods, and think that love only
happens between the sheets. Thus
daylight's hateful, and I love the dark.

Elsa

What a lot you must have gone through!

(She embraces Faust. The Lord of Atlanta and his secretary rush out of the summer-house, followed by their scowling attendants.)

Act Two, Scene 5

THE MAGIC SCENES

Lord of Atlanta *(after an embarrassed pause)*

What are magic scenes?

Faust

It's a new art-form.

Lord of Atlanta

That's ominous. What's new is disturbing.

(One of the scowling men moves forward menacingly. The Lord of Atlanta waves him away.)

Is it to do with painting?

Faust

Possibly.

Lord of Atlanta

The theatre?

Faust

That too.

Lord of Atlanta

With story-telling?

Faust

Yes, I'm sure.

Lord of Atlanta

And music?

Faust

Sometimes.

Lord of Atlanta

And dance?

Faust

Absolutely.

Lord of Atlanta *(shouting)*

What are magic scenes?

Faust

A union of all the arts — the very pinnacle!

(The Lord of Atlanta is speechless with fury.)

ELSA

Remember your liver!
Shall I send for some wine?

LORD OF ATLANTA

Pipe down! (*To Faust:*) Just let me have
a sample or two of this
pinnacle of the arts, and kindly remember
the fact that you're dealing with businessmen.
When it's amateurs, we send them back to where
they came from —
(*Faust raises a hand in protest.*)
but not before they've been allowed a proper hearing.
Our examining boards are made up of
energetic young people who've all been specially trained,
genuine artist-types, with plenty of temperament,
but also willing to persevere. I think
it's useful for you to know that, Faust.
Now show us what you can do, and fast,
because I haven't much time.
(*Negro servants have put out garden chairs. A throng of people has gathered – the lords and ladies of Atlanta with their staff, servants and slaves.*)

FAUST

I must get ready! Where is my secretary?

THE LORD OF ATLANTA'S SECRETARY (*calling*)

Call Doctor Faust's secretary!
(*Others take up the call. Enter Mephisto.. The Atlantan secretary rushes up to him and greets him with a handshake.*)

MEPHISTO

Is your master always in a bad temper?

SECRETARY (*in an undertone*)

His liver plays him up. How's your master?

MEPHISTO

Fit as a fiddle.

LORD OF ATLANTA

We've abolished sorcery in Atlanta;
I despise superstition.
I'm asking for the last time:
what are magic scenes?

MEPHISTO

There's nothing that could be more natural.

My master has acquired his skills in this art
by studying the Opus Mago-caballisticum et theosophicum.
He is improving his mastery through new instruments
which he himself has designed.
(*At a signal from him, Hanswurst produces the instruments. Mephisto gives a demonstration.*)
By means of this metal disc known as a"mirror",
we have succeeded in trapping cosmic rays from the heavens.
Within this box made of electricum metallicum
(*he knocks on it*) . . . they cluster together
and are focused upon a kind of bell. (*He indicates the bell.*)
Its ringing then triggers off phenomena
that we can actually see.

LORD OF ATLANTA

I have followed all that and appreciate
that the whole process is something perfectly natural.
You can get started!

FAUST

What can I show them?

MEPHISTO

Anything but the old versus the new.

FAUST

I don't know the country,
and I don't know the customs.

MEPHISTO

Not good versus bad,
or wrong versus right.
Not fine versus coarse,
or depth versus height.
Don't give us your sorrows,
don't give us your peasants!

FAUST

What, then?

MEPHISTO

Ask them to choose a subject and
show them everything in the
rosiest light!
(*He turns to the Lord of Atlanta.*)
My master requests
that you give him some themes
upon which he will improvise.

LORD OF ATLANTA

Naturally I shall
select my themes from the Bible.

MEPHISTO

A good idea. (*He shudders.*)

SECRETARY (*to a servant*)

The Bible!
(*Others take up the call. Four negro slaves bring a large bible on a velvet cushion, and a lectern upon which they ceremoniously place the book.*)

LORD OF ATLANTA

I have just recently
received this from London; it is the
authorized King John translation.
(*They all doff their hats.*)
Open it!
(*He gestures to Faust, who is hesitating.*)

MEPHISTO

Excuse me, my master has eye-trouble;
his doctor warned him strictly against
so much as touching a book.

LORD OF ATLANTA (*with diffidence*)

I've never made any pretence about it.
I am not a bookworm.
But when it comes to the Book of books!
How often it has revived me in moments of gloom,
how often I have drawn some comfort from it.
As for the actual stories, however,
much of it seems confused and obscure,
contradictory, and sometimes downright absurd.
Take the account of David and Goliath.

SECRETARY (*turns to the relevant passage*)

Goliath fights in heavy armour,
and waving his tarboosh as a warning.
David fights without armour, and using a sling
of the kind peasants use for driving wolves away.
After much to-ing and fro-ing David prevails.

LORD OF ATLANTA (*glancing at his General*)

Like I said, it's absurd!

GENERAL

Sheer propaganda!

Poorly armed troops defeating a well-equipped army!
It's as though my own armoured brigades could be beaten
by any old bunch of peasants using just their cudgels.
I would advise you to censor this story.

SECRETARY

But General, it *is* the Bible!

GENERAL

I must point out to you the very grave danger
of further undermining the morale of our armed forces —
which is already wavering — with such propaganda.

SECRETARY

I'll make enquiries in London
as to whether this story has been garbled through misprints
or perhaps through mistakes in translation.

GENERAL

If London says it was actually
Goliath who prevailed over David,
that should be sufficient.

ELSA

Didn't David have any other
weapon on him apart from his sling?

FAUST

If the cause you're fighting for is just,
you've got a strong weapon.
(*Applause among the ladies. Mephisto gives Faust a kick.*)

LORD OF ATLANTA (*testily*)

Would you say that again?

SECRETARY

He was just saying it must also be asked
who's fighting for whom.

ELSA

For whom was Goliath fighting?

FAUST

For the Philistines.

LORD OF ATLANTA

Who were they?

FAUST

Money-changers and big merchants.

ELSA

And for whom was David fighting?

FAUST (*hesitantly*)
The peasants.
(*Mephisto puts a hand to his forehead.*)

NEGRO SLAVE (*in a high-pitched voice*)
What started the war?

FAUST
The Philistines overran the land of David.

LORD OF ATLANTA
You mean to say the peasants
could think of nothing better to do
than go straight to war?

FAUST
They negotiated first
and then went to war.

ELSA
What a sad world we live in!
War, war, nothing but war!

LORD OF ATLANTA
Enough talk!
(*At his signal, Faust makes a sign to Mephisto. Mephisto signals to Hanswurst, who draws a large circle round the magic instruments. Then he goes up to Faust, helps him on with a cloak and solemnly hands him a hat and stick. Faust steps into the circle. Hanswurst starts the appliances and then rings the bell.*)

MAGIC SCENE NO. 1

Vision: Goliath dances with ponderous, jerky movements. After each series of steps he shakes the tarboosh menacingly.
Vision: David (resembling Faust) raises his sling. The two combatants are shown advancing and retreating. David hits Goliath with a stone from his sling; Goliath sprawls dead on the ground. David takes Goliath's tarboosh and shakes it menacingly. Four negro slaves in chains accompany the action.

NEGRO SLAVES
Goliath, he was the Philistines' slave.
But David, he was a free man.
Goliath took his arms from the Philistines,
but David made his own weapon.
When battle was joined, then David did smite him,
with the help of his trusty sling did he smite him.

Dead is Goliath, the Philistines' slave.
And David was still a free man.
(*The vision fades away. It is a modest success; the lords and ladies clap politely. The applause of their staff, servants and negro slaves is cut off by an abrupt gesture from the Lord of Atlanta. Faust hands Hanswurst his cloak, hat and stick, steps out of the circle and joins Elsa.*)

ELSA

Could you show us that once again?
But without Goliath, just David on his own.
He performs with such exquisite movements.
(*Copying David, she performs a couple of dance steps. Faust looks enquiringly at the Lord of Atlanta, who shakes his head.*)

HANSWURST

Ho! ho!

ONE OF THE SCOWLING FACES

Be quiet back there!

LORD OF ATLANTA (*to Faust*)

My next choice of subject is the story
concerning Joseph and Potiphar's wife.

MEPHISTO

Watch it, Faust! (*Faust nods.*)

SECRETARY (*poring over the bible*)

Young Joseph is loved by Potiphar's wife,
but he does not respond to her love.
Her attempts to force Joseph into loving her
end in a disagreeable scene:
Joseph rushes from her room naked.
This incident causes great excitement
and sets the whole town talking.
Potiphar's wife goes in fear of the
terrible cruelty of her husband,
who is the viceroy of Egypt.
Her favourite slave-girl Naomi suggests cunning.
Her plan is to invite ladies
of high society to eat oranges.
When they have arrived and are
peeling the oranges, chatting,
Joseph is made to join them.
They find him most handsome.
Now the gossips start saying

that every lady of fashion is
pining for Joseph.
(*At a signal from the Lord of Atlanta, Faust makes a sign to Mephisto. Mephisto signals to Hanswurst. Hanswurst helps Faust on with his cloak and solemnly hands him the hat and stick. Faust steps into the magic circle. Hanswurst starts the appliances and then rings the bell.*)

MAGIC SCENE NO. 2

Vision: Potiphar's wife expresses her emotional turmoil in dance. Naomi appears with the female slaves, in chains. A discussion follows. Naomi ushers in the society ladies. They begin peeling oranges in an elegant manner. Naomi fetches in Joseph (resembling Faust), who is bound with a golden chain. The ladies look at Joseph in delight, forgetting about the oranges. They cut their fingers, and the oranges turn red and become blood oranges.

NEGRO SLAVES

Joseph, don't you forget your chain,
golden though it is,
it will always be a chain.
Joseph, don't forget your people,
groaning in their iron chains.
Resist all the beauties,
resist all the beauties of Egypt!
(*Joseph turns away.*)
He has resisted their beauties!
(*The vision fades. Faust gives Hanswurst his cloak, hat and stick, steps out of the circle and rejoins Elsa. The tableau is an enormous success.*)

ELSA

From now on, when I'm eating oranges
I shall always be reminded of the episode
between Potiphar's wife and Joseph.
(*Her graceful observation is applauded; Faust bows to Elsa.*)

GENERAL (*wiping his eyes*)

At "resist all the beauties" I was tickled pink.
(*He splutters into his handkerchief.*)

LORD OF ATLANTA (*to Faust*)

Best of all I liked
the chorus sung by my negro slaves.

That abundance of melody,
that wealth of feeling that grief can produce!
For your third scene I'll have
the chorus of the three men in the fiery furnace.
(*A man dressed in black applauds.*)
Executioner!
How are you feeling today?

EXECUTIONER

Mustn't complain;
except that I can't get any sleep —
it's my gout.

LORD OF ATLANTA

You must train some apprentices.

EXECUTIONER

It's hard finding the talent.
Sometimes you think it's there,
but then it's only the usual glimmering,
hardly worth fostering.

LORD OF ATLANTA

Don't give up too soon, my dear chap.
(*He makes a sign to his secretary.*)

SECRETARY (*turning the pages of the bible*)

The mighty King Nebuchadnezzar,
having subjugated the Jews,
gives orders that they should
renounce their native religion.
Three men refuse. (*To the Lord of Atlanta*:)
Do you want me to read out their names?

LORD OF ATLANTA

No.

SECRETARY

When, even after a number of warnings,
the three behaved stubbornly,
they were thrown into the burning fiery furnace.
But inside the furnace they then struck up a song
which moved the great king very deeply.
He sets them free.

GENERAL

Aha, that's more propaganda.
A group of fanatics singing songs in a furnace
and getting set free, and this general of yours

has to put up with such tosh.
Fat lot of pleasure I get in my job.
Why bother to employ me at all?

HANSWURST

That's what I'd like to know too!

ONE OF THE SCOWLING FACES (*bellowing*)

Be quiet back there!

FAUST (*whispers in Mephisto's ear*)

Can't you do something
to make him choose another subject?

MEPHISTO

Not possible. You've got to
be able to show anything.

FAUST

Yes, but I can't present this
in a traditional style.

MEPHISTO

Oh all right, have it your own way! (*Out loud*:)
In a bold adaptation
of the celebrated legend, my master
will present it afresh.

LORD OF ATLANTA

Proceed.

(*He signals to Faust. Faust makes a sign to Mephisto, who signals to Hanswurst. The latter helps Faust on with his cloak and solemnly hands him the hat and stick. Faust steps into the magic circle. Hanswurst starts the appliances and then rings the bell.*)

MAGIC SCENE NO. 3

Vision: The three men call out: "Rise up, Israel!" An executioner and his two henchmen attempt to silence them. Their mouths are stopped up, and they are brought before the king and his minister. The minister tries to issue a reprimand. They strike up their song again. At a signal from the king, the executioner thrusts them into the fiery furnace. Again they strike up their song. Pointing at the steadfast trio, the negro slaves applaud by rattling the chains on their feet. The three men are burnt to ashes. The lords and ladies laugh and applaud Faust. The negro slaves take up the dead men's song.

NEGRO SLAVES

Rise up, Israel!
Raise yourself above your shame!
(The scowling faces belabour the slaves with heavy leather scourges. The singing breaks off. Faust gives Hanswurst his cloak, hat and stick, steps out of the circle and rejoins Elsa.)

ELSA

You should never have shown us that!
We don't want to know such things,
and we certainly don't want reminding of them.
(She falls into a swoon. Chambermaids bring smelling-salts. While Elsa is recovering, the assembled company demonstrate their concern for her.)

MEPHISTO

Don't say I didn't warn you.

FAUST

But it was all true.
I've seen it for myself; I can't
suppress the truth.
This tongue won't come out with a lie.
O truth, that tastes of wormwood!
O knowledge, my misfortune!

SECRETARY (to the Lord of Atlanta)

An unfortunate subject.
There are, in the Book of books,
lots and lots of nice, agreeable stories.
(*A slave raises his hand. The Lord of Atlanta nods.*)

NEGRO SLAVE

Song of gold, sir.

LORD OF ATLANTA

Gold?

NEGRO SLAVE

Tigers drawing ploughs,
wolves that suckle sheep.
(*He indicates with his hand, calling*:)
Four moons!

LORD OF ATLANTA

This is tommyrot.

HANSWURST

Sir, he means the land of Cockaigne,
but he's forgotten the milk and honey.

SECRETARY

The words of your slave are reminiscent of
the great poet Ovid, who
wrote some verses about the golden age.
How curious — the great Ovid had
the same dream as a humble slave!

ELSA

Perhaps you could recite to us
a few lines by this Ovid?

SECRETARY

They're Latin verses.

LORD OF ATLANTA

Any of you know Latin? (*Silence.*)

FAUST

I'll act as an interpreter.
"Aurea prima sata est aetas, quae vindice nullo,
Sponte sua, sine lege fidem rectumque colebat.
Poena metusque aberant, nec verba minacia fixo
Aere legebantur, nec supplex turba timebat
Iudicis ora sui, sed erant sine vindice."
The golden age was that time when there were people alive who
did what was right because they perceived that they ought to.
Nobody stood in the dock, trembling in front of a judge.
Fear was unheard of.
People lived without fears, secure in their freedom.
(*Huge applause from the gathering, the lords and ladies included. The slaves rattle their chains enthusiastically.*)

LORD OF ATLANTA

Silence!
(*There is complete silence.*)
So you liked it! Do I have to keep on
reminding you of your statutes? Must I
point out time and again that here in Atlanta,
both rich and poor enjoy the same rights
and have the same duties?
I'll give some examples:
one of the laws in our great constitution
prohibits rich and poor equally
from dossing down under the arches.
Another law makes poor and rich
equally free — and I stress the point — free

to buy up a plot of land.
A third does away with class barriers.
Anyone's allowed to call me Oscar,
as long as I say so.
(*He turns to the slaves.*)
Without law and order,
you'd have people stealing the chains
from your legs in the night.

NEGRO SLAVE

But then we'd be free, sir.

LORD OF ATLANTA

Free to starve, dimwit!

FAUST

I'm going to select a colourful composite vision:
The Golden Age in the Garden of Eden.

HANSWURST (*calling*)

Don't forget the honey!
(*The Lord of Atlanta signals to Faust. Faust makes a sign to Mephisto, who signals to Hanswurst. The latter helps Faust on with his cloak and solemnly hands him the hat and stick. Faust steps into the magic circle. Hanswurst starts the appliances and then rings the bell.*)

MAGIC SCENE NO. 4

Vision: Adam and Eve in a colourful landscape, a child at their feet. A group of people, white, black, brown and yellow, are amicably greeting one another. Lion, eagle and bear are peacefully resting together. Sheep are lying with wolves, and deer beside tigers. Hanswurst, taking advantage of Faust's momentary inattention, twiddles some knobs, and food appears.

CHORUS

Fraternity! Equality!

NEGRO SLAVES (*rattling their chains*)

Freedom!
(*A white dove flies up.*)
Peace!
(*The Lord of Atlanta stands grimly in the foreground surrounded by his scowling men, who point in horror at details in the tableau.*)

Curtain

INTERMEZZO ON THE FORESTAGE

MEPHISTO

Where to, Faust?

FAUST

The banquet.

MEPHISTO

Don't go, if you value your life.
(*Faust indicates his surprise.*)
The Lord of Atlanta means to
question you away from the banquet.

FAUST

He's a jealous man.

MEPHISTO

There's also that.

FAUST

What can they prove against me?

MEPHISTO

The fact that you weren't born in Atlanta,
(*an astonished gesture from Faust*)
that you come from Wittenberg,
and that you, as a peasant's son,
have always been working for the peasant's cause,
a secret agent of Münzer's,
here to incite the people of Atlanta
to revolt against their masters.

FAUST

What a foolish lie!

MEPHISTO

They will discover a book in your pocket.
(*He produces it.*)
Do you recognize it?

FAUST

No!

MEPHISTO (*flourishing the book*)

Thomas Münzer's writings!
Don't you remember?

FAUST

No!

MEPHISTO (*reading:*)

"Christ is not the Son of God,
but a man, the people's teacher."

FAUST

That's blasphemy! A capital offence!

MEPHISTO (*goes on reading*:)

"Strive first to obtain enough food and clothing,
then the Kingdom of Heaven
is sure to be yours."

FAUST

How low-minded! Another capital offence!

MEPHISTO (*goes on reading*:)

"All things are to be shared by everyone,
jobs as well as possessions.
To each shall be given his portion
according to need and circumstances."

FAUST

Thumbscrew, rack and gallows!

MEPHISTO (*still reading*:)

"Curb this usury by the great merchant banks."

FAUST

This means I'm done for!

MEPHISTO

To quote his parting words:
"A day of vengeance will surely come upon you!"

FAUST

Can the judges be bribed?

MEPHISTO

Yes, that's chickenfeed! Although these
idiots watch each other so closely that
if one's got more cash than all the others,
they'll promptly put him on trial. There's
nothing more difficult to cope with than
venal idiots who keep checking up on each other.

FAUST

What about your special power?
Don't forget our contract.

MEPHISTO

You needn't worry, Faust.
(*He takes the pact from his pocket and reads aloud from it.*)
"Point two: you must never
touch a book again." Be frank with me!
(*Flourishing the writings of Münzer*)
Have you touched this book?

FAUST (*in a low voice*)
Just the once.

MEPHISTO
I can't give you any more protection
here in Atlanta.

FAUST
I must flee!

MEPHISTO
Yes, this minute!

FAUST
What about Hanswurst?
He knows too much, he's guzzling like mad,
and he's got a girl-friend.
He won't want to shift.
(*Mephisto stamps his foot. Auerhahn appears.*)

MEPHISTO
Auerhahn, Hanswurst must go straight to Wittenberg.
He's only to hear you say the word "trial",
the fat-chops!

AUERHAHN
Wittenberg! (*Exit Auerhahn. Mephisto stamps on the ground and a trapdoor opens. He disappears through the trapdoor with Faust. The curtain rises.*)

Act Two, Scene 6

THE ARREST OF THE ROBBERS

Kitchen garden. Hanswurst is lying on the grass. Grete sits beside him, mending his jerkin.

HANSWURST
I'm fair exhausted.

GRETE
Six sausages, a thick wedge of cheese,
two bottles of wine,
and pastries for afters!

HANSWURST
I shan't be able to eat all that,
it'd be greedy. (*After a pause*:)
Let's have a song.
When I'm full up, I'm fond of a tune.

GRETE

Which tune do you want?

HANSWURST

Whatever you like.

GRETE

Maybe the "Song of the Ring"?

HANSWURST

Not my cup of tea.

GRETE

Or "Far from Home"?

HANSWURST

That's me right now!

GRETE

"To God let us Speed"?

HANSWURST

Too serious.

GRETE

"The Robbers' Arrrest"?

HANSWURST

What's that all about?

GRETE

How two robbers
were planning to steal the Virgin Mary's child.

HANSWURST

Sing it to me!

GRETE (*sings*)

Into the garden did Mary wend,
there she met three slender young men.
The first is Saint Daniel,
then Raphael, then Michael.

HANSWURST

They won't have been mere striplings any longer,
them three, but stout fellows, like peasants
spoiling for a fight, especially Michael.

GRETE

Saint Daniel says: "We'll stay behind,
two knavish thieves have got it in mind
to snatch away — the brazen pair —
your dear little son so sweet and fair."

HANSWURST

Kidnappers!

GRETE

And Mary spoke: "Then guard us right well,
if any man would steal my babe,
see you tie him up to the gate,
and there this thieving knave shall dwell.
Saint Raphael, Saint Michael,
see that you tie him up right well."

HANSWURST

What about something to eat, though?

GRETE

Saint Daniel spoke: "But just behold,
there they both are, this pair so bold.
Both of them all drenched in sweat,
and neither dares to turn his head.
The two of them are firmly bound
to God's own earth, by God's own hand!"

HANSWURST

The Almighty in person!

GRETE

"Let them stand like foolish loons,
until they've counted many moons.
Till they've counted each grain of sand,
the babes unborn in every land."

HANSWURST

It'd take a long time
to count up that far, a whole lifetime,
and even that wouldn't be long enough.

GRETE

Mary delivered them from their plight;
spotless she, whose actions are right.

HANSWURST

She was a dear woman, was Mary.

GRETE

A good mother, steadfast in sorrow.
(*Hanswurst gives her a look.*)
And now I'll fetch you those pastries. (*Exit.*)

Act Two, Scene 7

THE PARTING FROM GRETE

AUERHAHN (*out of breath, tugs Hanswurst by the sleeve*)
I've come to warn you
that they're after you,
mean to question you.

HANSWURST
The couple, no doubt, who
nearly wrenched my arm off.

AUERHAHN
Not two. (*Yelling:*) Hordes of them. I heard
one of them utter the word "mincemeat"
on his way past. You must go straight to Wittenberg.

HANSWURST (*trembling*)
Quick!

AUERHAHN
Slowly!
I'm only taking you under contract.

HANSWURST
What does that involve?

AUERHAHN
This is the deal: I must not only
get you safely back to Wittenberg,
but serve you faithfully for twelve years
and do just as you say.

HANSWURST
Quick now: what do you want in return?

AUERHAHN
I want your soul.

HANSWURST (*gapes in horror*)
You want my soul?
(*Grete brings the pastries. Hanswurst looks at them.*)
All I've got is a tiny little,
greedy sort of soul, but it matters to me
because it helps me enjoy my food.
And you know how much food matters to me.

AUERHAHN
I'll just say"mincemeat"!

HANSWURST (*sits down to eat the pastries*)
Here I sit, I can do naught else!
Just let them come.
AUERHAHN (*to Grete*)
They're after his blood. (*To Hanswurst*:)
Will you be just as firm
when they question you?
HANSWURST (*trembling with the knife in his hand*)
Look at the way I'm shaking
because I'm a coward.
I'll be forced to throw up from sheer worry.
AUERHAHN (*aside*)
If this chap won't budge, Mephisto will be furious.
GRETE (*to Auerhahn*)
What a lather he's in.
I rather like him, because he's amusing,
but now his life is at stake.
AUERHAHN
Hanswurst, your lady-friend has convinced me
you must leave for Wittenberg. There,
however, we shall have some unfinished business to settle.
HANSWURST
I must eat my pastries up and
say my good-byes to my Grete.
(*Auerhahn paces up and down. Hanswurst, to Grete*:)
What a shame I've got to leave you, when I've
got my hands full and travelling's so risky.
But back in Wittenberg, over my bowl of gruel,
I'll be thinking of you. Auerhahn,
go and get me a present for my Grete!
AUERHAHN
What sort of a present?
HANSWURST
I want an embroidered veil,
so as to keep the sun off her.
Also, looking pale will suggest
that she's worrying about me.
(*Auerhahn reaches into the air and presents Hanswurst with an embroidered veil. Hanswurst presents it to Grete.*)
May this gift remind you of your Hänschen,
wittering in his bleak homeland,

instead of with you.

AUERHAHN

Let's be going!

HANSWURST

Wait a minute.
Shouldn't I be asking what lies ahead?
Must I always be anxious about the future?
My dear old mother always used to say: "Hänschen,
aim for something, there's a good boy!"
So I'd like to work for the council, for
in my old age I'll still need to eat, that's for sure!

AUERHAHN (*in horror*)

How can I get you a job with the council?

HANSWURST

Shove off and don't be a pest.

AUERHAHN

Just calm down.
There's always my uncle, Geierhahn:
he's got some pull with the town council.
(*He gazes up at the sky with a meaningful air.*)
I see that a night-watchman has just died,
and the town is desperate
to find a replacement. (*Snapping his fingers*)
We'll make you night-watchman.

HANSWURST

Night-watchman!
That was always my greatest ambition.
Having to keep watch when everyone's sleeping.
Give me some proof you aren't joking.
(*Spitting on his left hand three times, Auerhahn offers his other hand to Hanswurst, who shakes it warmly.*)
This confirms our agreement. (*To Grete:*)
Be honest:
can you live without me,
you child of sorrow?
I can picture you in the lonely kitchen,
stirring the pot by yourself.

GRETE

Take care of yourself!
(*Hanswurst kisses her. In the background a great shadow falls across the stage.*)

AUERHAHN

Here they are!

HANSWURST

Right!
(*They flee.*)

GRETE

There's no stopping the swallows
when it's time to go. It'll take a while
to forget him, my Hänschen.
(*A scowling group of men begin to surround Grete. In a firm voice:*)
Keep away!
(*The circle draws tighter.*)
What's this for?
(*The circle is drawn tighter still.*)
To question me?
(*The circle is now complete.*)
You pigs!

Curtain

End of Act Two

Act Three, Scene 1

WITTENBERG

FAUST

Now that I'm back home, more's the pity,
the country seems as grey and cold as before,
and the old town narrow and cramped
with its dirty streets and alleys.
How glad I was to get away!
Now it's got me in its clutches again.
What can I do?
Looking back on what's happened,
I can hardly call it a treat.
And yet —
Atlanta, your sun shines with infinite splendour!

MEPHISTO

You're still famous, the toast of Atlanta!

FAUST

I'm talked about.

MEPHISTO

The reason's beside the point;
the main thing is, people have heard of you;
for better or worse, you've become a household name.
(*Faust yawns. Two servants bring some wine.*)
We shall have a rare old time here in Wittenberg,
but you must get rid of your servant.

FAUST

You mean Hanswurst?

MEPHISTO

He went and betrayed something.

FAUST

Wagner!
(*Enter Wagner. Faust shouts at him.*)
Wagner,
what made you engage such a blockhead
to work in this house? The chap's idle,
he gossips, and as for his tricks!
These folk should be busy.
Wagner, you're losing your grip!

WAGNER

Your Excellency, I shall give him his notice.

FAUST

That's not good enough,
you're to throw him out of the house.
(*Exit Wagner. Pause.*)
You come across some real characters here in Wittenberg.
When I was crossing the fish market and
grumbling about the smell, one trader said to me:
"It's not my fish that stink, mister, it's me,"
and wanted me to buy some.
What a good salesman, I thought,
choosing the lesser of two evils
and running himself down to boost his wares.
He'd be the loser if you passed him and said:
"What a sweet-smelling fishmonger,
it's only his fish that stink."

MEPHISTO

This place doesn't agree with you,
we must take another trip. (*Standing by the globe*:)
Where do you want to go?

FAUST

Never again will I travel abroad
and try to adapt myself to
foreign customs, accustom myself to the
unfamiliar, oh no!
Here in Wittenberg I intend to become
a great German ideal.
What I want is such extraordinary fame
that mothers nursing their baby sons will sigh:
"I hope he'll be a Faustian character."

MEPHISTO

A greal ideal? Easy as winking!
(*He clicks his fingers.*)
I shall spread the rumour that you've
come back from Atlanta with some wonderful treasures.
All Germany will be invited
to a remarkable exhibition
where Faust, Doctor in four faculties,
will show the people treasures from the
fabulous land of Atlanta.

FAUST

But not just the people. Great men
must bow down before me, hoping to find me
in a good temper.

MEPHISTO

Easy as winking.
(*He clicks his fingers.*)
Trouncing Münzer has cost a great deal of money.
The princes have debts to pay off.
They've got their greedy eyes on the east, where there's
still something left, and they're planning
new forays; but funds are low.
I shall spread the word that you
can provide them with loans in gold from Atlanta.
The Emperor himself will bow down before
a supplier of gold.

FAUST

Whom will you invite?

MEPHISTO (*in meaningful tones*)

The people with the biggest debts.

FAUST

What kind of treasures will there be?

MEPHISTO

Fabulous stuff.
But we shall have to take great care of them
and put things under glass
to stop people touching.
We'll need somebody smart to act as a guide.
Wagner can take on that job.

FAUST

My Wagner's a blockhead, all he's learnt
in this house are one or two catchwords.

MEPHISTO

Don't worry: thanks to the powers
that Pluto has given me,
I can turn your Wagner into a man
of verve, warmth and imagination.

FAUST

Do that, and I shall be the first to applaud!

Curtain

Act Three, Scene 2

THE EXHIBITION

Glass showcases with a great assortment of goods – jewellery, costumes, phials of perfume. In the centre is a large block of gold, with a sign reading "Gold from Atlanta". On the left is a group of natives: four negro slaves who are chained together. In their midst is a young girl wearing a veil. Guards in leather jackets, armed with rapiers and cavalry pistols; attendants.

WAGNER

Everyone is expecting
that in view of this prodigious exhibition,
the princes of the realm will pay their respects
to the explorer,
the great and deserving Faustus. I have prepared for
the festive occasion most thoroughly.
This list contains details
of the noble lords' titles and achievements.
It gives me very special pleasure

to pronounce these great names, and roll them around
on my tongue and savour the taste, like wine.
(*Unrolling the list*)
What power! What grandeur!

FAUST

My secretary will make the introductions.

WAGNER

That cultured gentleman from Italy
was a really excellent tutor;
I could hardly get to sleep that night.
I've never been so excited before —
the sheer weight of ideas has stirred me up and
left my head in a spin. The overwhelming
richness of it all nags me like a disease.
Oh my goodness, this thirst to think and explain!
(*Shouting*:) Find me an audience!
(*Pointing to Wagner, Faust slowly takes off his hat to Mephisto, who acknowledges this with a wave of his hand.*)

COURIER

A letter from the Chief Justice!
(*Mephisto takes the letter and reads it.*)

MEPHISTO (*to Faust, in an undertone*:)

"By threatening them with severe punishment,
we have been able to stop the city companies,
guilds and deputations of peasants
from pestering the noble princes
with complaints and petitions;
but a number of
Münzer's activists have banded together again,
and we fear some disturbances.
The sentry-posts are undermanned."
(*To an armed guard*:)
Take your section to the city gate.

WAGNER (*to the courier*:)

How did the reception go?
Are the princes in a good humour?

MEPHISTO

Were there no incidents?

COURIER

The reception of the princes
by the Chief Justice was a

moving occasion. (*Aside*:) The maids of honour
were singing out of tune again, it's going to be uphill work
to get this modern music established. (*Exit.*)

ATTENDANT (*at the door*)

The guests of honour!

MEPHISTO (*to Faust*:)

Won't you receive them personally
and pay the princes your compliments?

FAUST

No!

(*Mephisto gives him a quizzical look, then crosses the stage to the door. Dumb show.*)

MEPHISTO

His Majesty the Emperor,
Protector of the Roman Empire!

(*Entry of the Emperor. They all bow except Faust. The Emperor appears to ask Mephisto where Faust is. Mephisto points to Faust. The Emperor looks at Faust, who returns the look. The Emperor goes rapidly round the exhibition. After surveying the gold from Atlanta for a short time, he stops in front of Faust and raises his hand. Faust makes a deep bow.*)

The noble princes of Germany
who have suppressed the peasants' revolt.
Ulrich Duke of Swabia, victor at Böpplingen,
Field-Marshal Georg von Frundsberg.
Lord High Steward of Waldburg, victor at Leipheim,
War Commissioner Wilhelm von Fürstenberg.
The Margrave of Bayreuth, victor at Fürth,
the Elector of Saxony,
the Duke of Weimar
and Count von Mansfeld,
the victors at Frankenhausen.

(*An old retainer cries out and faints. Two attendants carry him out.*)

FIRST ATTENDANT

He's too old for a servant.

SECOND ATTENDANT

No, he recognized the cruel Duke;
that man hanged four of his sons.

MEPHISTO

Philip of Hesse.
The Duke of Braunschweig,

victor at Bruchsal and Eppingen.
The Margrave of Brandenburg, victor at Kitzingen.
The Duke of Lothringen, victor at Zabern.
The captains of the mercenaries: Schwend, Beinhaus, Faulstroh, Kummer and Ehrübel.

(*The princes look at Faust, who returns their glances. They go rapidly round the exhibition. After looking at the gold from Atlanta for a short time, they stop in front of Faust and raise their hands. Faust makes a deep bow. The captains of the mercenaries, having glanced at the gold, walk past him.*
Choral scene: The city companies, guilds and peasant deputations with their flags and banners. A group with the placard: "Not Approved by the Guilds". Stamping vigorously, they sing the following.)

COBBLERS

When people have no clogs,
the cobblers go to the dogs.

BAKERS

When people have no bread,
a baker loses his head.

TAILORS

When people can't dress,
a tailor's in a mess.

PEASANTS

When a peasant has no land,
he becomes a firebrand.

UNCHARTERED JOURNEYMEN (*pointing at the guilds*)

They don't have an ounce of sense,
keeping us outside the fence.

ALL

Flour! Leather! Cloth! Membership!

PEASANTS (*louder than the rest*)

Land!

(*Karl, the disabled peasant, appears with his boy at the back of the guilds.*)

CAPTAIN OF THE GUARD (*pointing at Karl*)

That's one of Münzer's gang.

(*Karl is seized by two armed guards. A big, hefty man with black hair standing among the group with the placard intervenes.*)

FISCHER

Take your hands off him!

He held out, when they tortured him!
(*Everyone looks at Karl.*)
Look, you aren't wanted here.
If you want to stay, tell me!
(*The boy leads Karl away. The others watch them go.*)

WAGNER
We have encased the exhibits in fine glass,
touching is not permitted.
I shall now elucidate them for you.
(*Wagner goes upstage.*)

HANSWURST (*detaining Fischer*)
Fischer, what are you doing here?

FISCHER (*sullenly*)
I've come for a look.

HANSWURST
I kept wondering:
where's he got to, old Fischer!
How's life been treating you?

FISCHER
Still shirking, like you used to?

HANSWURST
I've news for you, I've got a proper job.

FISCHER
Who with?

HANSWURST
First I was with the students,
but because we had an argument —
to do with our religion —
I went to Wittenberg.
I studied there with Doctor Faustus,
soon became his favourite pupil
and went abroad with him.
In Atlanta he had to
leave me on my own
because of a girl.

FISCHER
And what's your job?

HANSWURST
When I arrived back in Wittenberg
the townsfolk were ashamed of the fact
that one of the great Fischer's favourite pupils

should go hungry, and they found me a post.

FISCHER

What does the uniform look like?

HANSWURST

A cloak, a lantern and a horn.

FISCHER

A miserable night-watchman!
(*Hanswurst turns away indignantly and mingles with the spectators. Wagner is now heard explaining the exhibits.*)

WAGNER

All these jewels —
a parting gift from the Lord of Atlanta —
are of enormous value. With these,
one could buy up a city
lock, stock and barrel. (*Commotion.*)
Here, we see gold from Atlanta.
My information is that Doctor Faust
is expecting two shiploads.
To alleviate the hardship into which
the criminal peasants' uprising has
plunged us, Faust intends giving them
to the Emperor, as a friendly gesture.
(*Further commotion.*)
Here we see a group of natives.
Observe what noble features they've got,
and they're also renowned for their singing.
The girl in the middle is a traitress.
I daren't tell you what offences she committed,
since there are ladies present.
Her punishment was fair, but dreadful.

HANSWURST (*pointing to the negro slaves*)

Couldn't they give us one of their songs?

WAGNER

Singing is forbidden in the exhibition
for reasons of propriety. (*In an undertone*:)
Still hanging around our Faust?

HANSWURST

Don't tell him.
(*As he goes up to the slaves, he recognizes the embroidered veil. Shouting*:)
What have they done to you, the pigs?

(*He touches a slave, and the body crumbles into dust.*)
Gone, gone, gone!
(*The other slaves dissolve into dust one after the other, Hanswurst is about to hug Grete, but she too crumbles to dust. Shouting*:)
Just dust!
How am I going to remember her,
if she's nothing but dust!

FISCHER (*taking control*)
Mind out! Smash the glass!
(*His associates smash the showcases. As soon as they are touched, the exhibits dissolve into dust, which casts a grey pall over the whole display. Silence.*)
Dust — is that what we're meant to eat?

FAUST
I can explain the whole thing. (*Silence.*)
These treasures must have been
somehow damaged during the voyage.
I shall order some more, some richer ones,
and regale you with a spectacle
unlike anything. . . .
(*A chorus of abuse, consisting of swear-words.*)

MEPHISTO (*striking a classical pose*)
Faust, come to me!
(*He wraps his cloak around Faust. To the chorus*:)
Clear off, you lousy beggars! My Faust
is going to make short work of you.
(*As Fischer makes a rush towards Faust, the guards fire a salvo. The rafters come crashing down. Amid the smoke, sounds of groaning are heard.*)

HANSWURST (*bending over Fischer's body*)
Faust,
now you've gone and killed my friend Fischer!

Curtain

FAUST (*in front of the curtain*)
Brothers, my dear brothers!
Where, after this, is
my mind and my poor soul
to find any peace?
As the hart

pants for water,
so do I gasp.
(*At the end of the lamentation Mephisto's hand protrudes from the curtain and tugs Faust back on the stage.*)

Act Three, Scene 3

RECRIMINATIONS

The banqueting hall of the palace, which shows no traces of damage.

MEPHISTO
What are you moaning for?

FAUST
You started the shooting!

MEPHISTO
What, me? Never!
I've my own methods, they don't include shooting.
I hate noise and tumult, and avoid confrontations.
I'm a master of the art of persuasion.
Shooting I leave to others.

FAUST
You lying toad!
I didn't give the order to fire.

MEPHISTO
Not directly, no.
But you were looking round nervously.
What do mercenaries do when
the boss is looking nervous?
They shoot.
(*Faust is silent.*)
Through your own fault, you've
landed in something ugly
and must leave Wittenberg.
The corpses will have to be buried,
the wounds allowed to heal,
before you can venture to
show your face here again.

FAUST
I won't go.

MEPHISTO
But you'll have to, Faust.

FAUST

No, I'll explain what happened.

MEPHISTO

Folk know what happened.
Give them time to forget.

FAUST

All the dreadful events of the past few years
have taught me a great deal.
I'm seeing things with fresh eyes; even
the familiar characters of classical myth
are taking on new features.
Again I've got this urge to reinterpret.
My views must be heard.
Surround me with people once more;
never in my whole life have I been
so eager for company.

MEPHISTO

People? Easy as winking.
(*He clicks his fingers.*)
We're off to Leipzig.
Curtain

Act Three, Scene 4

FLIGHT INTO CLASSICAL MYTH

Auerbach's cellar. Faust has embarked on a tedious interpretation of the Orpheus legend. The students are racked by gloom and boredom.

Recitative

FAUST

When Orpheus was deprived of
his beloved companion, best of listeners,
sweet Eurydice, he fell silent.
Nature, accustomed to hearing him sing,
grew dispirited.
The Muses implored their favourite son
to make music again.

Aria

Orpheus,
this silence of yours is unbearable.
Refreshing milk no longer pours

from the ewes,
no more honey;
sadly it dies in the comb.
For since you fell silent,
life has lost all its sweetness.
The cattle are groaning in pain
and unwilling to go to pasture.

The mountains have no echo,
the valleys are moaning,
and the Doric wavelets, the brooks
murmur in sorrow.
Roses, you wore your redness in mourning,
anemones also. The people, meantimes,
go forth lamenting aloud.

Who so rash as to seek to play on your flute?
Woe betide him who raises the reed to his lips!
Look all around: since you fell silent,
the tigers have reverted to tigers,
and people, forgetting their gentle customs,
to barbarians.

DRUNKEN STUDENT

Orpheus says nothing,
but he goes on and on and on. (*Laughter.*)

FAUST

Help, Mephisto! The lyrics
are turning to ashes on my tongue.

MEPHISTO (*coming to his rescue*)

To end with, a lively ballet:
Odysseus and the swine.

Vision: Circe the enchantress, Odysseus (resembling Faust) and his companions are seated at a richly embellished table. Circe raises her goblet and drinks to Odysseus, who secretly empties his goblet on the ground. The companions drink and are transformed into swine. They dance the Grand Swine's Gallop.

STUDENTS (*beating enthusiastically on the table with their mugs*)
Onk, onk, onk, onk, onk!

FAUST (*to Wagner*:)

Give them more wine. I want to puke. (*He flees.*)

Curtain

Act Three, Scene 5

FAUST'S PALACE IN WITTENBERG

Wagner is covering a large mirror with a cloth.

DOCTOR
Is he willing to see a doctor?

WAGNER
I don't know, he's a doctor himself.

DOCTOR
What are the symptoms of this strange upset?

WAGNER
During the past week he hasn't slept a wink,
shuffles round the house, groaning.
"Cover the mirrors," he shouts,
"can't stand the sight of myself." Or else
he skulks in a corner, quietly cursing.

DOCTOR
Cursing whom?

WAGNER
Himself. (*The doctor shakes his head.*)
And then at other times he'll go through
the motions of washing his hands. I've seen him
at it for a whole quarter of an hour.

DOCTOR
Does he say anything whilst he's acting like that?

WAGNER
In a whisper I could barely make out,
but it sounded like "blood". Or else
he complains he feels cold and that autumn is coming.

DOCTOR
You should take him for a holiday.
Perhaps the sight of the sea and fresh places
will banish whatever's troubling his brain,
this constant obsession with something that's
robbed him of all his senses.
Don't you think? (*Wagner shakes his head.*)
You'll need to stretch that a bit tighter,
you haven't quite covered the corner.

WAGNER
Careful! It's him!

We'd better get out of the way.
(*Exeunt. Faust enters.*)

FAUST

Younger men are laughing at me,
I'm now the butt of their jokes.
I have drunk the cup of scorn,
and I have tasted contempt.
Why go on any longer?
Whatever may become of me,
I can't sink any lower.
(*A peal of bells.*)
Church bells? Who are they burying?
(*Noise.*)
What's that noise in the streets? Who are they after?
(*Shouts are heard.*) Faust! Faust!
It's me they're after!
(*Faust's servants rush in.*)

MEPHISTO (*in the doorway*)

Don't alarm yourself, Faust,
that turn for the better you wanted so much
has happened. That recognition
of your achievements you dearly desired. . .
(*in a loud voice*)
. . . is coming to you.

FAUST

Who is conferring this honour?

MEPHISTO

Those people in this world who have honours to confer.
(*A deputation of nobles appears.*)

FAUST

Not them! (*Yelling*:) No!
(*He stands motionless.*)

MEPHISTO

The powers behind the trouncing of Münzer
are presenting you with a chain of honour.

LEADER OF THE DEPUTATION

Because, in difficult times,
you always showed great presence of mind,
and because, without much ado,
you helped to cut down the poor,
let all the commonweal

salute you as a great ideal.
Receive from us this chain and medal.
(*He hangs a large chain round Faust's neck.*)

MEPHISTO

The Rector of the University of Leipzig
will now present an honorary doctorate.

RECTOR

Of your bold account of Orpheus
we've a high opinion.
We like to honour the arts —
even, if need be,
forcibly so —
within our dominions.
(*He confers the academic head-dress on Faust.*)

MEPHISTO

The German nation's shining light,
Dr Martinus Luther, has come specially
to congratulate his favourite pupil.
(*The crowd parts to form a lane. Luther embraces Faust, who averts his face.*)

ALL (*pointing at Faust*)

Our great ideal!

Curtain

FAUST IN FRONT OF THE CURTAIN

FAUST

I thought they would hound me to death.
That wasn't the worst of it:
they wanted to honour me.
Let's make a clean breast of it.

CONFESSIO
I was the son of a peasant,
found it hard to abide
that for one bit of mischief my mother
would start to spank my backside.

I ran away to the monks
to learn from their teaching.
But then I heard a lament
and said: That sounds beseeching.

The holy Book was lamenting
that tyrants and men of ill-fame,
those who traded pardons,
only besmirched its fair name.

"The lessons I gave were good,
inscribed in letters of flame;
how could they drive out my truth
and cause me so much shame!

Were the good Lord to return
to our unhappy Earth,
they'd go and arrest him again,
recrucify the man of worth."

And vexed with the monastery life,
I ran away
to where Luther taught,
wanting truth above aught.

For Luther was preaching
against the corruptness of Rome
in German words that rang clear
in even a poor peasant's home.

While learning from Luther's
writing and teaching,
I heard a lament
and said: That sounds beseeching.

Each new-born babe is lamenting
as soon as it glimpses the light,
wails its head off
at so distressing a sight.

On the church door in Wittenberg
Luther's theses were posted.
the peasants did hark to
his mighty protest.

They made their own use of
what Luther had taught,
rose up and rebelled
against ruler and court.

Then was Luther most rueful
they should read him that way,
having proved to them from the Scriptures
that serfs and slaves have no say.

This I could not accept.
I ran away
to where Münzer taught,
wanting truth above aught.

"A pack of vile usurers,
robbers and thieves,"
wrote Thomas Münzer,
"is governing our lives.
So fight the good fight,
put them to flight;
give all you've got,
deliver us from the despot."

In Altstedt the peasants set to,
they ransacked its castle and chapel.
Thomas Münzer looked on,
letting it happen.

This left me aghast,
I escaped from the mire.
But back at Luther's I fell
from the frying-pan into the fire.

For to stave off the princes
Münzer proceeded to act.
His sword was valiant and clean;
I was too slow to react.

Thus read the new order
Münzer preached in Mühlhausen:
those who aren't working shan't eat;
put swords in the hands of the ploughmen!

Luther railed against Münzer,
wrought great malfeasance
by unleashing the dogs
against the poor peasants.

"Go to it, strangle and hang
every rebel, for I say:
nothing on earth is more wicked than
the servant who cannot obey."

O Frankenhausen,
city of doom,
witnessing so much
grief and gloom.

Your streets are spattered
with the blood of the slain;
German dishonour
arose within your domain.

If you don't honour your teacher, it's said,
You're worse than a dog.
But I could stand no longer
the sight of Luther's mug.

After Münzer was beaten,
all stomachs were churning.
Death ravaged the peasants,
strangling and burning.

And hearing their anguish,
I tried to look higher,
to medicine, but only fell
from the frying-pan into the fire.

For no herbs could I find
to cure hunger and blight,
nor dressings and salves
against the chill of the night.

Since I could do naught,
I tried to look higher,
to the practice of law, but fell
from the frying-pan into the fire.

For with princelings against us,
how could justice be sought?
And their judges wouldn't listen
to whate'er I besought.

In growing vexation
I tried to look higher,
but just fell with philosophy
from the frying-pan into the fire.

For all that our thinkers
have ever managed to do
is illuminate miserably
the might of the few.

And when I did see it,
I tried to look higher,
to black magic, but fell —
ah me! — from the frying-pan into the fire.

Doubting my own resources,
I shook hands with those who misuse us.
Now am I sunk lower than the lowest,
my life has been quite useless.

Pledging yourself to your masters
means giving them your blood.
One thing swiftly led to another,
and soon my name was just mud.

So I now go to the wall;
let the same fate befall
any person without
the guts to hold out!

(*A giant hand — it belongs to Mephisto — reaches through the curtain and yanks Faust back from the footlights. He must carry on in his part.*)

Act Three, Scene 6

Mephisto

You great hog, you greedyguts,
never content with what you've got!
Haven't I realized all your dreams?
Aren't you now a great ideal?

FAUST

I can never be an ideal.

MEPHISTO

What can one do to please you!
(*He lunges out with his foot. Faust goes tumbling to the ground. Mephisto helps him to his feet, brushes the dust off his coat and seats him on a chair. Fetching another chair, he sits down right in front of Faust, observing him closely.*)

FAUST

A creature of your type can't appreciate
what I'm going through.
Between "If only I had" and "If only I hadn't"
I falter like a flickering lamp.
Haven't even the strength to spit on myself;
who could be more wretched than I am?

MEPHISTO

A creature of my type can't appreciate
what you're going through?
You're wrong!
For nobody could have
flickered and faltered more than me,
with my power and frailties, between
"If only I had" and "If only I hadn't".

FAUST

You too, Mephisto? (*Pause.*)
Who were you, before you started serving Pluto?

MEPHISTO

I was one of a great host —

FAUST

Name them!

MEPHISTO

I'm not allowed to —
they had me thrown out,
kicked out like a mongrel.

FAUST

Tell me why!

MEPHISTO

I musn't say.

FAUST

Give me a clue.

MEPHISTO

There was something I betrayed.

FAUST (*after a pause*)

And what would you do
in order to rejoin that great host?

MEPHISTO (*rising from his chair*)

If there was a ladder,
a thousand feet high,
and I could climb up it
for just a single moment,
though its rungs were of sharpened knives,
and I had no shoes:
I would climb that ladder.

FAUST (*after a pause*)

Can I still pull round,
or am I done for?

MEPHISTO

Anyone can pull round,
because nobody, Faust,
is done for whilst he's alive.

FAUST

Are there any conditions?

MEPHISTO

One condition.

FAUST

Spell it out!

THE DANCE

Mysteriously and gracefully, Mephisto begins to perform a little dance.

MEPHISTO

If you want to do what's good and fine,
you need one thing only: time.

FAUST

Just time? Then I'm saved.

MEPHISTO

Whichever way you want to hop,
Faustus, your time is up!

FAUST

By tonight half the years will have expired

that we agreed in our pact,
and you dare to suggest that my time is up?

MEPHISTO

Faustus, when you deigned to barter,
you overlooked the peasant's charter.
(*End of the dance.*)

FAUST (*yelling*)

The peasant's charter!

MEPHISTO

When a farmer hires a labourer:
(*gruffly, imitating a peasant*)
come rain or shine, come frost or heat,
twelve hours of work are fit and meet.
Twelve hours set aside for rest
will keep the ploughman at his best.
But me you've worked day and night,
so that your twenty-four years
have been whittled down
to twelve.

FAUST

You're trying to trick me!

MEPHISTO

You've only tricked yourself!

FAUST

Give me one more year.

MEPHISTO

No!

FAUST

One more month!

MEPHISTO

No!

FAUST

One more day!

MEPHISTO

No, I can't! Tonight,
when you hear it strike twelve,
I'll be back for you. (*He disappears.*)

FAUST

Now I'm done for! (*Shouting*:) Wagner!

WAGNER (*rushing in*)

What is it?

FAUST

Renounce the art I taught you! (*Exit.*)

WAGNER

Renounce art? No, never!
Not even if it means rack and ruin!

Curtain

Act Three, Scene 7

AT NIGHT, IN THE STREETS OF WITTENBERG

Bailiff with Hanswurst, who has grown stout

BAILIFF (*bearing a staff*)

Ten at night, and I'm
still patrolling the streets.
The things we're seeing!
People's depravity
has got to such a pitch
that it makes you shudder.
I met this beggarwoman
and gave her a talking-to:
you're to move on, I said,
begging isn't allowed here;
and the next minute
I found her in the street again.
It's no fun to be doing a job like this!
(*Two urchins run past.*)

HANSWURST

Since Münzer was overthrown by the princes,
every child in the district
has seen a man on the gallows.

BAILIFF

It's the peasants' own fault
for getting up in arms!

HANSWURST

My brother-in-law told me
that in Frankenhausen people have
worn down a path to the Schlachtberg,
where they punished Münzer.

BAILIFF

I'm going to stand at another street-corner,

and then it won't be long
before I catch a few more. (*Exit.*)

HANSWURST

That's Faust I can see,
what a nerve the man's got!
(*Enter Faust, looking pale and walking with difficulty.*)
Someone like you shouldn't be
going around without heavy protection,
and the hired guard
ought to be paid double,
because things are that ugly.
Aren't you aware
that the butchers are out to get you?
Only yesterday I heard one of them
saying "mincemeat" again on the way past.
And what for? Because you're a murderer.

FAUST

I'm a sick man.

HANSWURST

Folk like you are always being sick.
How's you good friend the Emperor?
Are you still waiting for your
two shiploads of gold to turn up?

FAUST (*lifting a hand*)

Look at this trembling.

HANSWURST

That's a smart idea, that trembling;
so are those beads of sweat on your brow.
Goes to prove it's an educated person I'm
talking to. But your face could still look
a little bit paler, I think.
Auerhahn, you know, has told me all about
your arrangement with Mephistopheles.
He's soon coming for you, eh?
(*Pointing a finger at Faust*)
And you still owe me my wages!

FAUST (*searching his pockets*)

Here's sevenpence. It's all that's left
of all those great riches I owned.

HANSWURST

Thanks for nothing! That'd suit you fine —

sevenpence instead of five crowns.

FAUST

This coat's made of silk; take it,
and you'll be well rewarded.

HANSWURST

And exchange it for mine, I suppose?
Mixing up clothes like that
will cause a proper old muddle! Mephisto might end up with the wrong person.
Tell you what, Faust.
(*He taps his forehead with his finger.*)
Leave it owing.
(*Exit Hanswurst. The bailiff drives off a beggarwoman and her child.*)

BEGGARWOMAN

Outside town there are too many of us!

FAUST (*aside*)

Perhaps if I were to do a good deed. . .
(*To the bailiff:*)
Why be so rough with her?

BAILIFF (*raising his hat*)

Sir, if I wasn't rough,
they'd tear the coat from your back.

FAUST (*to the beggarwoman*)

Can't you work for a living?

BEGGARWOMAN

After they've hanged my husband
in Frankenhausen,
who's going to give me work?

FAUST (*giving money to the child*)

This is all I've got on me.

CHILD

Sevenpence.

BEGGARWOMAN

Thank you kindly.
(*Exit with her child. It strikes eleven from the church-tower.*)

VOICE

Fauste! Praepare te!

FAUST

I'm to prepare myself?
I can't!

Timor mortis perturbat me! (*Rapidly*:)
The peasants say that by
plucking out an honest man's heart
and putting it in your chest,
damnation can be resisted.
My father lies in this cemetery.
I'll pluck the heart from his breast
and place it in mine. . . .
(*He scrabbles inside his father's grave.*)
Ah, even an honest man's heart
turns to dust.

VOICE

Fauste in aeternum damnatus est.

FAUST

My last moment has come!

FAUST'S LAST WORDS

You people who live after me,
think of Faust and his great retribution,
which followed, limping, yet overwhelmed him.
(*It starts to strike twelve from the church-tower. Faust leans up against a street-lamp. Enter two citizens.*)

FIRST CITIZEN

What's the matter?

SECOND CITIZEN (*calling out*)

A doctor! Is there a doctor?
(*On the eighth stroke Mephisto appears, dressed as a doctor.*)

MEPHISTO

I'm a doctor.
(*Faust lets out a strangled cry.*)
He's in a bad way!
(*He gently lays his hands on Faust's heart. The bell sounds the twelfth stroke from the tower. Faust opens his mouth and dies.*)
Now he's beyond all human assistance.
(*To the audience:*)
Applaudite, amici! Contractum finitum est.
(*Enter two attendants dressed in black and carrying a bier. Mephisto politely doffs his hat. Exit.*)

FIRST CITIZEN

The death of our Faust is

a serious loss for this town.

SECOND CITIZEN

He called himself philosophus philosophorum,
but a lot of people have complained he deceived them.

FIRST CITIZEN

Do you agree with that?

SECOND CITIZEN

For twelve years he never went near our university.

FIRST CITIZEN

It's a well-known fact he became an artist.

SECOND CITIZEN

There's the tale that Faust was a sorcerer
and gobbled up a lad in his household.

FIRST CITIZEN

I can't understand how a chap with your breeding
could listen to such vulgar twaddle.

SECOND CITIZEN

I don't like it when
a scholar turns into an artist.

FIRST CITIZEN

You're biased. People will still be talking
of our Faust in a thousand years from now.
(*They go on their way, still gesticulating.*)

HANSWURST

Now our Faust has been taken;
rightly so, he was a bad egg,
and it'll be a long time before he's forgotten.
(*A window is opened behind him.*)

STOUT WOMAN (*attempting to grab him*)

Rascal, you've been boozing
again, instead of working!
(*Hanswurst slams the window in her face and makes a hasty exit. The bailiff drives Karl, the disabled peasant, and his boy across the stage.*)

FIRST CITIZEN (*looking at Karl*)

One of Münzer's band of ruffians.

SECOND CITIZEN

They've settled his hash all right.

FIRST CITIZEN

What a sight!

SECOND CITIZEN

Quite incorrigible!

BOY

O'er a heath did I wander,
and heard a voice singing,
right wondrous it sounded:
"Go, gloomy night;
come, lovely day!
Peace and joy
and friendliness shall reign."

End

Translator's Note

Eisler's *Johann Faustus* libretto was first published in the German Democratic Republic by Aufbau-Verlag. In 1983 Henschelverlag published a new edition by Hans Bunge. This incorporates a number of changes and revisions which Eisler made after the libretto had gone to press; and it is this edition upon which the present translation is based. In general layout, the English version matches the German. Eisler's use of rhyme — strongly featured in the Act Three *Confessio*, sporadic elsewhere — has been reproduced throughout, a few modifications apart. I have exercised some freedom in my handling of Eisler's fluctuating rhythms. My aim was to create English equivalents, or correspondences: while retaining the basic metrical proportions, I have adjusted the stresses, both in the more conversational sections and in Eisler's artful lyrical set-pieces. Other solutions would have had to be sought, of course, if he had set them to music.

Proper names such as 'Hanswurst' have been left unchanged. The first verse of Luther's hymn *'Ein feste Burg'* (Act One) I thought familiar enough not to require a translation. In Act Three, Scene 4 of the German text, Mephisto announces the tableau of Odysseus, his companions and Circe as that of 'Orpheus' and the swine. I have treated 'Orpheus' as a slip of the pen for Odysseus. On the other hand I have not amended the Lord of Atlanta's reference to the Authorized 'King John' Bible (Act Two, Scene 5). Was this an author's slip, or the character's?

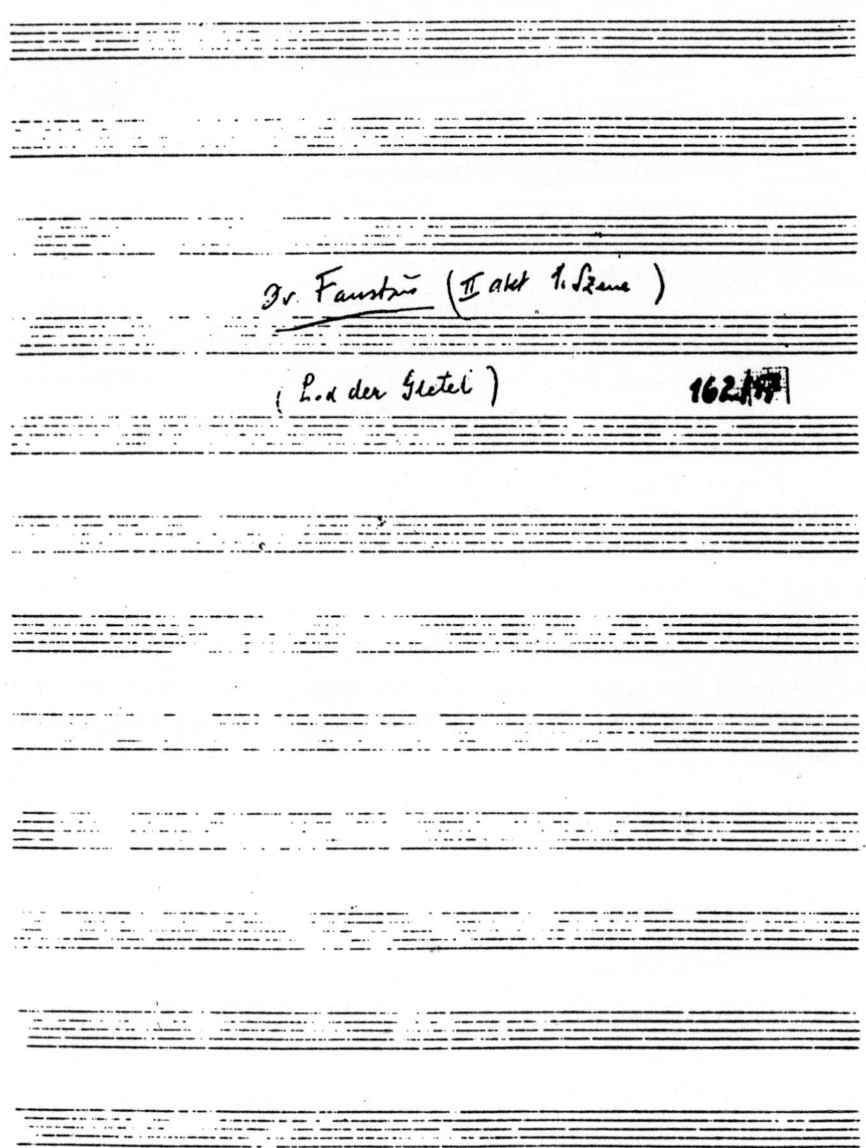

The Publisher apologizes for technical limitations in the following reproduction of original manuscripts.

Ob.
3 Clar
Horn Solo mit Dpf.

Fl.
Horn
Molto Meno
Str.
Vc

Note: It will be observed that Eisler omits verse one in the text of the libretto [Ed.]

15

ON THE 'FAUSTUS' DEBATE

On the risk involved in writing a new 'Faust' for the German public, as undertaken in 1953 by the composer and author Hanns Eisler, and the consequences thereof

Werner Mittenzwei

For a long time the idea of writing a new *Faust* has met with suspicion rather than rejoicing in Germany. And doubly so when it marked somebody's first claim to recognition as a man of letters. In fact, however, Hanns Eisler had already been active in the literary field before he wrote his *Faustus* libretto. Eisler's literary works defy the usual classification. What prompted them were the breadth and richness of his creative imagination — an imagination which transcended any single art form. Anybody trying to grasp Eisler as an author would be quite right to take his music as a starting-point. Eisler's literary style is difficult to sum up, but no less distinctive than his composing style. One of its salient features is the way he marshals and gives artistic unity to a variety of subjects, impressions and perceptions. He developed this approach during the years of the Weimar Republic, the heyday of the literary essay and the feuilleton. It was a period that encouraged vivid phraseology, elegant analysis and arresting conclusions, which would take the form of a punch-line or even a joke. With Eisler, however, all these stylistic resources are combined with the logic of materialist dialectics.

When Eisler wrote his *Faust*, Germany was at the beginning of a new phase in her social and political history. But he did not see the libretto in terms of a contribution to German socialist *literature*. Like many composers before him, he planned to create an opera to a text of his own. So his first job would be that of a literary craftsman — one who had evolved a personal technique for organizing his material. Although not unduly systematic, this technique was both complex and demanding. For Eisler, an artistic procedure always involved a 'partisan' element — which was spontaneous. Behind his technique lay years of experience and a long familiarity with literature. Eisler had acquired it in exile, when he was working over texts by Hölderlin, amongst others, prior to setting them to music. His own special approach to the artistic compilation of literary texts is closely connected with the experience that a composer who was a musical innovator brought to bear on literature. It also depended on the breadth and depth of his reading generally; he needed to have reached 'a certain age' and to have read the classics a number of times first.

Eisler described his *Faustus* as follows in a letter to Bertolt Brecht:

> *The opera will be positively teeming with folk songs, lines from Hans Sachs and traditional material of that nature. This, as you rightly, remark, is vital. I am not a retired schoolmaster hoping to unleash a drama upon an astonished world, but a composer constructing a text and utilizing the available models . . .*[1]

The public got to know *Johann Faustus* as a literary work. Indeed it has a prominent place in the history of German dramatic literature in the nineteen-fifties. But that should not mislead us into regarding and appraising it as drama pure and simple. What Eisler wrote was a libretto, and he constructed it accordingly. (The writer Peter Hacks has gone into this subject in considerable depth. He notes that a libretto looks deceptively like a stage-play, because the events in both are crying out to be staged.) All Eisler wanted was the right text for the opera he was planning. Since he happened to be a real writer and did not go in for such writing as the secret vice of a composer, he produced an exceptionally good text. The paradox is that the merits of a libretto *per se* are not synonymous with literary merit or poetic refinement. Among the essential qualities that Hacks enumerates, two are particularly relevant to Eisler's *Faustus*. First, an opera narrative must be 'as tough as an elephant's hide'. And second, the libretto should be expected to overcome the contradiction between lyricism and drama. An opera which is weighed down by its subject-matter, ideas or ulterior plan will be less than perfect.

In the light of Hacks' comment that 'an opera's durability lies in the durability of its plot', Eisler achieved something, because his opera does have a plot. Everything that happens on stage hinges upon it, and the author's outlook is expressed through a narrative as striking as it is rich in import. But it does not have the toughness of an elephant's hide, nor does it remove the contradiction between lyricism and drama. From

[1] Letter from Eisler to Bertolt Brecht, Ahrenshoop, 27.8.1951. *Sinn und Form*, Eisler issue, Berlin 1964, p. 14.

Eisler's viewpoint it was simply a way of organizing his material. But the new perspective which he brought to bear on this produced all kinds of connotations, resulting in the spiritual tensions that overlie the straightforward story. Intellectually, philosophically, the work rises to the level of great drama. This is not to say that it constitutes a dramatic text. On the other hand it does provide some justification for performing it without the music, and for appraising it as a work in its own right.

I

The fiercest challenge to the classical tradition in literature has come from those artists who admired it the most. Eisler is a prime example. Precisely because he kept returning to the classics, they inspired not only his admiration but also a desire to rethink their noble ideas. Whereas many people know such works only from their schooldays, if at all, Eisler read them again and again, although sometimes in a purely desultory fashion, out of sublime boredom. To even his friend Brecht's surprise, he would read literature as remote from the present as Anacreontic poetry, Voss' *Luise* (a late eighteenth century idyll) and the table-talk of Luther. Since he was a creative artist himself, they elicited his respect. Nonetheless he acknowledged the fact that even in Goethe's masterpieces, there are traces of 'patchwork'. Eisler reflects on his responses to classical literature in the following lines:

> *I have read the classics five times. ... After the First World War I read Goethe differently from before the war. I read him differently again after the revolutionary upheavals in Germany and the takeover of the workers in the Soviet Union. I read him once more during the big capitalist crisis which preceded the upsurge of fascism. When I was in exile I again read him with the greatest enthusiasm, discovering in him a quite new vein of humanity – although I didn't acknowledge this at the time, being occupied with other features of the classics. After 1945, when I was back in Germany, I read Goethe yet again, and once again it was a new experience for me. The glasses with which I was reading him weren't, so to speak, private ones but those of historical developments.*[2]

That Eisler should choose the subject of Faust as the basis of an opera is hardly surprising. Classical literature had helped him to understand both himself and the world around him. And the only real home he had found during his exile was in German literature. Inwardly, Eisler's main incentive for taking up the subject of Faust was that he was so much at home with it.

---

[2] Eisler, Conversations with Hans Bunge ... p. 115ff.

But before he could start work on it, he also needed an external incentive. This came when:

> . . . a puppeteer from the Erzgebirge performed the 'Faust' puppet play at the Academy [of Arts], and I again enjoyed it tremendously. I was amused by the scene where Hanswurst beats the devils over the head with the words *'Perlicke – Perlacke'*. This was after the learned Dr Faust, nervous and wary, had met with the Devil and agreed to the pact with him. It made me want to compose the puppet play.[3]

While studying the pre-Goethean versions of the story in more detail, Eisler came across a passage in the old chap-books where Faust's father, a peasant, warns him against making a pact with the Devil. He urges him to come back home. His son refuses. In the end the father tries to seize hold of him, and with Mephisto's connivance the son kills him by stabbing him. The fact that they were peasants sent Eisler in search of suitable historical 'counterparts'. He found them 'in Thomas Münzer and his peasant revolutionaries, who were the backbone of the German nation at the time.'[4] The association of the old Faust legend with the period of the Peasants' War in Germany gave Eisler a completely new angle on the figure of Faust. It opened up a different view of the world from Goethe's. The time was ripe, it seemed, for a creative dispute with Goethe's *Faust.*

By 13 July 1951 Eisler had finished the first draft of the text. It took him another year to revise it, and on 13 August 1952 he wrote to Brecht that he had completed the work. Aufbau Verlag published it the same year under the title *'Johann Faustus* – an opera'.

There were various reasons, including some highly pragmatic ones, why Eisler drew on the puppet play and the chap-books but not on Goethe's *Faust*. To base an opera libretto on the latter would have been utterly misguided. A poorer, more primitive version would have inevitably resulted. With the pre-Goethean Faust tales, things were different. Here Eisler could at once get to grips with the material, reconsider it and reorganize it. In addition the crude, woodcut-type characterization in the early accounts was very much in keeping with Eisler's aesthetics. He took the puppet play as his principal source. His own narrative sticks basically to the events of the puppet play, from the prelude in the underworld up to Hanswurst's engagement as night watchman. As the location of the 'Magic Scenes' he chose 'Atlanta'

---

[3] 'Die Debatte um Hanns Eislers *"Johann Faustus"*. Hans Bunge, Berlin 1991, p. 139.

[4] Ibid. p. 139.

instead of Parma. And here Eisler was not satisfied with the biblical themes that abound in the different versions of the puppet play. He devised two entirely new episodes: 'Joseph and Potiphar's Wife' and the 'Three Youths in the Fiery Furnace'.

The pre-Goethean Faust tales did create certain problems. The chap-book was not unjustly regarded as originating in 'enemy territory'. Lutherans had used the Faust legend to give fresh substance to the dogma of the existence of the Devil. The image of Faust as a restless, ruthless explorer was intended as a warning, not a shining example. But the Protestant authors did not achieve the desired effect. Although even Luther himself condemned Faust in his table-talk, the deterrent increasingly became the model. Georg Lukács (whose Goethe essays significantly influenced the reception of classical literature after 1945) observed that Goethe had freed the Faust legend from its Protestant, moralistic confinement. He considered Goethe's outlook to be 'immeasurably deeper, far superior to the old versions and therefore in a class of its own'.

Protestant militants, for their part, had tried to counter the Faust image with that of Luther, as 'the honest, unassuming man of God'.[5] What they achieved was to efface the memory of Thomas Münzer as the real alternative to either Luther or Faust. Eisler now proceeded to resuscitate the militancy that the chap-book had sparked off in the common people. It plays a direct part in his version of the legend.

EISLER'S FAUST CHARACTER

Eisler made good use of the pre-Goethean models, but his own conception of Faust went much further. He presents the character to us as follows. Hans Faust, a scholar from a peasant background, is in a state of despair over the thinness and limited usefulness of scientific knowledge. Following in the wake of the massed peasants who are striving for changes, he perceives new opportunities for action. At the crucial moment, however, he cuts himself off from these social forces. Having deluded himself on this point, he looks for other means whereby to convert knowledge into power. He makes a pact with the Devil. This leads to recognition, fame and a talent for exploiting knowledge in unconventional ways. But the Devil gives Faust no control over it. Despite his new opportunities, he keeps thinking back to the earlier idea of revolt. But this no longer sustains him; it destroys him instead. All

[5] See Klaus Völker, *Faust – Ein deutscher Mann . . .*, Berlin 1975, p. 182.

Faust has been granted is virtuosity, not originality — and even the virtuosity is acquired at the expense of an ideal. Faust's art has the power to astonish, but it contains no message of hope. And to Hell with art without hope!

Eisler sets the action at the time of the Peasants' War in 1525 because society was in a state of flux, and Faust perceives the great, over-riding power of science that lay behind it. It is this notion which determines all his actions: it was there from the beginning, and he never loses sight of it. Eisler's Faust is loath to equate his own destiny with the peasants'. Yet he knows that he stands or falls with the peasants, and so *self-betrayal* becomes the main theme. In spite of what experience is teaching him, Faust believes his wits can save him from the situation he has landed himself in. He tries to escape the inexorable consequences with the help of the Devil. The vitality and potential effect of the character and tale derive from the way the positive and negative sides are directly combined — before the final triumph of the negative side.

Notwithstanding the final outcome, Eisler tried to keep Faust suspended between these two poles. He does not depict the actual betrayal so much as the actions which bring it about. Whether this was deliberate policy or a dramaturgic inconsistency does not matter. The point is that Faust is never seen to be stabbing the militant peasants in the back, as it were, and this has a special bearing on the narrative. In the first Act Faust meets Karl, a peasant who was one of the rebels. Here Faust is depicted as a man with a bad conscience who wants to explain himself. As yet he is quite unaware of being a traitor; it is simply that his standpoint has decisively altered. A missed opportunity begins to nag at his mind, but he thinks that with an effort, he can put things right. In this way Faust's self-betrayal starts building up into a living lie. He tries to find another way into the world of science and learning, meanwhile contenting himself with the catchphrase, 'You ought never to have gone to battle!'

If Eisler had already presented Faust as a traitor in the first Act, the meeting with Karl would have had to take a different course. There would have been a head-on clash and Karl would have rejected Faust, because nobody will talk to a traitor. At first, however, Karl's tone is still a conciliatory one: 'Hans, come back here to old Karl!' (I/2). Faust tries to make the scholarly life an excuse for his inaction: 'Detached from the conflicts of the day, a philosopher strives for the truth.' He finds a certain loftiness in this. If Faust had been conceived as a traitor through and through, the events of the drama would have been completely different. A traitor is somebody who has devoted himself to certain ideals in the past but has turned his back on them. But Faust does not make the effort to go against his ideals. On the contrary, he has no desire to abandon them. He wants to pursue them by different means, via what he regards as a third, alternative route. In so doing he betrays himself and ends up on an increasingly treacherous path, being led eventually to open fire on a section of the people. Thus the 'intermediary' power of knowledge he was striving for is turned against his original ideals.

Given the position he was in, Faust was unable to have Luther and Münzer in his pocket simultaneously. Arguing to himself that their teachings stemmed from the same social upheaval, he covers up his own shortcomings by cultivating the delusion that one can be true to both. But this idea is shattered when he is obliged to face reality. So Eisler needed to portray Faust as a 'divided, restless figure with brilliant gifts and ambitious goals', as a man who 'hesitates for a long time' (Brecht). Faust only really becomes a traitor because a wrong path is taking him farther and farther from his original ideas. He can see how he is gradually turning into a different person, and it makes him shudder. Events succeed one another with ominous speed, enabling him to observe his own downfall. When Mephisto tells him that he, Mephisto, is as quick as the transition from good to evil, Faust says he will settle for that. 'I've learnt the hard way, alas, how little it takes . . .' Then he suggests a pact, but when Mephisto promptly agrees, he procrastinates: 'Not so fast, I haven't made up my mind!' (I/4).

Faust believes that with the help of the Devil's pact, he can achieve more through scientific knowledge than through a political commitment to the peasant rebels. He is in fact aware that either solution will be personally ruinous. That is his tragedy. But he will go to any lengths in order to achieve something, whatever the cost. He is seeking not so much to acquire knowledge as to change the course of history. This, in his view, is the only justification for his life, and the only thing that would make it worth emulating. Eisler's Faust is as extravagant as Goethe's in that respect. He not only desires knowledge but also wants to exploit it. He wants to be the sole dispenser of something that can only be truly achieved when everyone is pulling together.

THE PACT WITH MEPHISTO, NOT THE WAGER WITH HIM

Despite the above remarks, there are significant differences between Eisler's treatment of the Faust figure and Goethe's. More than a thirst for knowledge, it is despair which drives Eisler's Faust. His was avowedly to be a 'darker brother' to Goethe's, and there are already signs of it in the libretto. Pluto asks in the prelude why Faust has gained four doctorates — is it because he is so diligent and so eager for knowledge? And Mephisto replies: 'No, sir, it was from despair.' Faust has become disgusted with science, finding it hollow. The peasant disturbances are an opportunity for him to get involved with it again. But after the defeat of the peasants he lapses into his previous despair. Things are even more oppressive than before, because a hope has been frustrated. He cannot go along with the present social order, which is 'brutish'. And science no longer satisfies him.

For Faust, a possible way out of this is to switch from scientific knowledge to art — the art of magic. Magic, he thinks, combines all the arts and should be a means of actually achieving something. This is also why, in his desperate state, he proposes a pact to the Devil. Goethe's Faust, by contrast, makes a wager with the Devil. By using the conditional tense, Goethe gives his Faust more room to manoeuvre. The character does not bow to the inevitable; there is still an option open to him that might turn the tables. As Walter Dietze remarks, Faust and Mephisto are partners to an agreement and in that sense, equals. No longer is the one in thrall to the other. Instead the two are locked in 'a *battle* whose eventual outcome is uncertain.'[6] This is the result of Faust's continual thirst for knowledge. In giving his Faust a quite different slant, Eisler changes the character of the pact as well. Before signing it his Faust has already abandoned the real, objective reasons for scientific pursuits. His inordinate ambition to build up his personality loses momentum. However hard he tries, there is no longer any hope of outsmarting the Devil.

Eisler's Faust simply banks on a pact of relatively long duration. This, he hopes, will see revolutionary changes and give him the influence he is looking for. Everything will sort itself out in time. But there is now no scope for the development of his own personality. He has already started on the downward path to the abyss. He also fails to outsmart the Devil. It is the Devil who outwits Faust, by tricking him out of half the time of their pact.

The options open to Eisler's Faust are based not on his dealing with Mephisto but on his attitude to the peasant rebels. This explains why there is no dramatic duel between Faust and Mephisto. Eisler's Mephisto is something of a two-dimensional figure. That is the price to

---

[6] W. Dietze, 'Tradition, Gegenwart und Zukunft in Goethes *Faust, Der Deutschunterricht*, Berlin 1971, No. 5, p. 277.

be paid for eliminating the wager. There are two traditions in imaginative writing on the subject of the Devil.[7]. One is the 'literary' tradition culminating in Goethe, who created the most wide-ranging drama of this type and made his Mephisto the 'other soul in Faust's breast'. The other is the 'theatrical' tradition, which has always been largely bound up with the puppet play. In this tradition the character simply performs a function; it has been humanized and secularized only insofar as it comes to resemble a diabolical servant. Since Eisler was basing his work on the puppet play, it was the latter tradition he followed, being prepared for the drawbacks. Here his dramaturgy came to his aid, because the epic style that Eisler favoured did not need the cut-and-thrust of a protagonist and antagonist to move the story along.

Eisler's Faust illustrates the cost of gradually descending to treachery. Society is the poorer for it, because of the blow to the advancement of knowledge. But the man responsible is also the loser, for all his talent and ambition. The pact with the Devil does not bring Faust the personal fulfilment he wants. The Devil cannot give him either the authentic creative spark or the ability to achieve changes in the long term. All that Mephisto supplies him with is the satisfaction of being known as an artist, and even this does not last. Not even the Devil can bestow a touch of creative genius, the power to transform people's lives. The magic scenes that Faust stages to general acclaim in Atlanta are no more than masterly imitations. They have no power to change things because their promises cannot be fulfilled.

Here Eisler was polemicizing. Mephisto can only teach Faust the art of conjuring up heroes. He learns how to produce illustrations or models, but they disconcert the powers-that-be only temporarily and do not bring about any real changes. They are all just illusions. Mephisto is a master in Aristotelian poetics and dramaturgy, but not in the radical art that Eisler visualized.

But the best indication of the penalty to be paid for treachery is Faust's loss of the ability to conjure up a utopia. Utopias are only possible for those who are willing to fight, and Faust has repudiated them. Somebody who cuts himself off from the masses can no longer even contemplate the idea of a utopia. Faust has relinquished the motive power for his own development. The constructive aspect of Eisler's text is that it warns us not to think we can try to develop as persons in isolation from the great conflicts of the day. The 'darker brother' to

---

[7] See Peter Schmitt, Faust und die Deutsche Misere. *Erlanger Studien,* Vol. 26, Erlangen 1980, p. 185.

Goethe's Faust makes us aware of a social praxis whereby human beings can rise above misery through their own, mutual efforts.

HANSWURST, THE ANTITHESIS OF FAUST

We have noted how Eisler linked the subject of Faust with the peasants' rebellion. Equally important is the way he linked it with the character of Hanswurst. This largely determined the particular structure and poetic charm of the work. It was Eisler's intention to use the Hanswurst character to point up the popular features of the Faust material. He thought it would give the whole problem of Faust an extra dimension and enable the 'least sophisticated' of people to appreciate the work as much as the best educated. But he was not just harking back to the marionette of the puppet play — far from it. In the old puppet plays the *Kasperle* (clown, buffoon) was purely and simply there to amuse. What Eisler did with this character was to divest it of its abstract quality and give it a completely new function.

In the above respect (and in that respect only), Eisler's approach recalls the young Goethe's. Goethe took a great interest in this particular character. In a farce called *Hans Wurst's Marriage* (1775) he anticipated Eisler by exploiting the puppet figure's crazy antics and its popular appeal. At the same time he gave it an individual sensibility; as Thomas Mann quipped, this Hans Wurst speaks as though he were the author of *Werther*. But the basic philosophy is still the same — 'Do as you like, and just let me be!' Like Goethe, Eisler makes the figure more concrete. Implausible though it may seem, he gives his character the features of a thinker. It can be said of Eisler's Hanswurst that he acts as though he were familiar with the Faust characters in fiction from Marlowe and Goethe onwards. It is as though their fates were helping to determine his standpoint.

To begin with Eisler must have envisaged a much more drastic adaptation of the Hanswurst figure. He even considered presenting him as a positive character by comparison with Faust. But in the event, this was not feasible. 'Certainly Hanswurst is one of the characters most deeply rooted in popular tradition — not unlike Sancho Panza or Leporello — but not a positive character.'[8] On the other hand he is not just devoted to gorging, and this is undoubtedly a plus. As Eisler saw him, Hanswurst represents everybody's right to satisfy his basic needs,

[8] H. Bunge, opus cit., p. 139.

'without which a man isn't human'. To get a sausage to eat may well be his sole object in life, but we must remember that for poor people, even the cheapest form of meat was usually very hard to come by. This figure's priority is something in life that always needs all his energy. Hence it would be fundamentally wrong to regard Hanswurst as embodying the gluttony of vulgar materialism. Eisler illustrated the fact that Hanswurst was concerned with just eating, and not gorging himself, by telling his critics a little story.

> *There was a talented friend of mine who had achieved some renown as an orchestral conductor. It struck me how he went about eating meat in a particularly greedy way. When I asked him about it he said: 'You wouldn't understand this, but I come of Salzburg peasant stock and I've had this terrible craving for meat because I never used to get it.' And he mouthed the word 'meat' over and over again, and his need of it was etched on his face.*[9]

This characterization has a universal quality because it personifies a basic conflict on the global level, namely the food question [*Magenfrage*]. Certainly the question may take an individualistic and commonplace form, but without taking away the dignity which ought to attach to man's elementary needs: eating, drinking, sleeping, somewhere to live, and making love. So there is a positive side to the character of Hanswurst, or the makings of one. But what really turns him into a powerful theatrical figure is the contrast he presents to a positive principle. This confirms the logic of seeing him in association with the figure of Faust.

The drama presents the 'ideological question' [*Ideenfrage*] and the 'food question' [*Magenfrage*] as separate principles, embodied in two essentially different and contrasting figures. Since these two principles depend on one another, they are in fact associated. As a dialectical materialist, Eisler took this as a basis for his dramatic plot and characterization. If he had allied himself with the peasants, his Faust would have been able to combine the two questions. By rejecting such an alliance he forestalls the development of learning along materialist lines.

Consequently the introduction of Hanswurst into the drama takes on a function which is directly linked with the failure of Faust. It confronts Faust with one straightforward aspect of his own self, albeit in a guise that is totally alienated and deformed. To have betrayed the

[9] Ibid. p. 142.

potential development of learning along materialist lines: this is the crime that Hanswurst can tax him with. Whichever camp they stand in, both Hanswurst and Faust are deformed by the failure to unite basic human needs with scientific knowledge.

And so, for all the contrasts between them, Hanswurst and Faust are to meet the same fate. Eisler's narrative derives its consistency from the fact that eventually, both of them are forced to surrender their identity and give up the ghost. Faust loses his creativity, and Hanswurst ends up by losing his comicality. The demolition of the two characters is, so to speak, total. In the end they are virtually indistinguishable. The pact that Faust makes with the Devil does not enable him to do anything truly creative or to achieve personal fulfilment. All that this 'magic art' brings him are fame and applause, and honours which destroy him. Hanswurst, for his part, finally becomes a night watchman. He forfeits both his characteristic wit and his 'permanent dissatisfaction'. In the closing scene he is assailed and abused by a stout woman, and instead of showing his old eloquence he silently throws in the towel. All his individuality has been stamped out. In that sense he is finally no better off than Faust. Faust and Hanswurst illustrate how human capabilities will become stunted if they are isolated from one another.

Eisler concentrates on one basic feature of Hanswurst's character, but he is constantly qualifying it and even, occasionally, correcting it. The Hanswurst we see at the end is not the same as the Hanswurst we see at the start. But at no point does he commit an act of betrayal out of sheer meanness; ultimately he cares about his fellow-men, but he cares even more about food. When faced with a major decision he adopts basically the same policy as Faust and ducks the issue completely. But whereas Faust justifies himself on ideological, philosophical grounds, Hanswurst's only reason is his empty stomach. Where Faust waxes lyrical, Hanswurst is prosaic, but both are steering clear of conflicts. True, they have no desire to be slaves, but neither are they willing to fight for a cause.

Hanswurst's character includes two important features which raise it above the simple Hanswurst of the puppet play. The latter has no pretensions to a soul, whereas Eisler's Hanswurst makes much of the fact that he does have a little one. This 'little soul' is the most that little people can afford to have when nobody has given them much scope or taught them the art of whitewashing. Hanswurst insists on his soul, but not for any high-flown metaphysical reason. It is because he appreciates the link between a good meal and feeling good. 'All I have is a very little, greedy sort of soul, but it matters to me because it helps me to enjoy my food. And you know how much food matters to me' (II/7). Like Faust, he does not mean to stain his conscience but is misled into an act of betrayal imperceptibly. Hanswurst betrays his Grete in the same way that Faust betrays his knowledge.

In another passage Hanswurst says" 'I'm fond of a tune when I'm full' (II/6). Here Eisler is indicating that the character is not just a greedy pig, but this cannot be used constructively. The figure of Hanswurst is a reminder that while none of the world's problems can be solved without considering the 'food question', it does not represent man's fundamental needs in life. A leopard cannot change its spots, yet change them it must — and that is precisely what is beyond Eisler's Hanswurst. But he is not too stupid to grasp the consequences of taking the easy way out. At the end of the drama, he crossly but silently slams the window in the face of the stout woman who is nagging him. This is a kind of acknowledgement that the simple answer was no real answer.

Faust and Hanswurst share a basic flaw, which is their refusal to commit themselves to anything. It is expressed in different and indeed opposing ways; and thus the two characters are opposites. On the one hand we have Germanic high-mindedness, in the shape of Faust. On the other we have German philistinism in the shape of the night watchman. Unlimited idealism is coupled with the humdrum and commonplace. Cowardice has led both characters to squander their opportunities. And Eisler explores this point in a manner which is sufficiently challenging to be both illuminating and of practical benefit to his audience.

WHAT IS THE MORAL OF 'FAUSTUS'?

Eisler asked himself the above question so that he could formulate his primary aim as precisely and clearly as possible. He answered as follows:

> *Anybody who sets his face against his own people and their revolutionary cause, and betrays it by entering into an alliance with their overlords, will literally go to the Devil. He will destroy himself, and deservedly too . . . . Faustus is, like the German people, the pupil of Luther and Münzer, and — again like the German people — he has become embroiled in this mighty struggle; he wavers, going over from Luther to Münzer and then back to Luther; he perceives the true greatness of Münzer too late. After the defeat [of the people] he tries to acquire prestige and power. But once it has been perceived, the revolutionary truth cannot be suppressed, and no matter what Faust does or says, he is expressing the truth he has sold and betrayed. And that is his undoing. After being commended by those who slaughtered the peasants and after being embraced by Luther, he collapses. In his 'Confessio' he turns into a human being, for self-knowledge makes*

> *him human, and so this negative figure also exhibits a positive streak. I thought it possible, in an opera, to show a gloomy little Faust, a Faust who points to himself very worriedly and has regrets. After everything that has happened, I thought, even the great Goethe would not have objected to that.*[10]

As soon as Eisler had finished the libretto, he distributed it among his friends. Copies went to Thomas Mann, Lion Feuchtwanger, Berthold Viertel and Leonhard Frank. Eisler had been greatly impressed by Mann's *Doktor Faustus*, and it seems fair to assume that the novel partly influenced Eisler's choice of subject. He may have felt at the time that a Communist was in duty bound to make an artistic statement with the same material. Both Feuchtwanger and Thomas Mann were quick to react and were unstinting in their praise. It was Mann's normal practice, on such occasions, only to pick out things he could praise, but his reply to Eisler was particularly open and candid. 'The whole thing is provocative all right, and music will probably make it still more so . . . It shows, however, a good, solid German sense of humour, especially in the character of Hanswurst.'[11] When Mann wrote that in its design, the work was 'very new', 'very daring', 'very idiosyncratic', he was really saying that it would be a challenge for its readers and critics. Mann and Feuchtwanger were in agreement on its outstanding literary merits, which surprised even them, although they knew Eisler well. They also confirmed that the work had achieved its intended effect. Feuchtwanger wrote:

> *The effect is very powerful. The reinterpretation of individual episodes in the Faust story is striking, clever, angry, witty. The way it draws on the chap-book, Marlowe and even Lessing as well as Goethe is profound and amusing. The action, loose as it is, hangs together, indeed it doesn't lack suspense. This is a book with meat in it for both the professor and the cook . . .*[12]

After these first reactions at the end of 1952, Eisler had some cause for satisfaction. But the real discussions still lay ahead.

---

[10] Ibid. p. 139ff.

[11] Letter from Thomas Mann to Eisler, 5.11.1952. *Sinn und Form*, Eisler issue, Berlin 1964, p. 247.

[12] Letter from Lion Feuchwanger to Eisler, 10.11.1952. HE Archive, Academy of the Arts, E. Berlin.

II
THE 'FAUSTUS' DEBATE

What first sparked off the debate was an essay by the Austrian author and critic Ernst Fischer which was printed in the last issue for 1952 of the periodical *Sinn und Form*. Since it included some memorable phrases, it had the provocative effect that Thomas Mann had expected the actual libretto to exert. Not that Fischer was more sparing with his praise than Mann and Feuchtwanger. After comparing Eisler's style to the imaginative realism of Breughel's paintings, Fischer concluded:

> *This author has gone back to the purest sources of German poetry . . . He has produced a literary composition [Dichtung] that will hold its own. It may be that Eisler's Doktor Faustus will become what we have lacked for a century: a German national opera.*

The above estimation of Eisler's libretto was fully justified, as time has confirmed. But Fischer's essay was doing Eisler a disservice in as much as it reduced his work to a political tendency which did not square with the ideas it actually contained. The climax to Fischer's exegesis is reached in the following lines:

> *He [Eisler] has had the brilliant idea of combining the theme of Faust with the theme of Münzer, so that Faust's problems stem from his attitude to the Peasants' War. Faust stands for a character who is central to Germany's calamity ('Misere'): the German humanist who flinches from the revolution, endorsing Münzer's ideas while complaining, in his sage but cowardly way, that 'You ought never to have gone to battle!'. At the great moment of decision in the class struggle, he intends to 'stay out of it' at all costs, and events leave him in the position of a turncoat. The German humanist as turncoat.*[13]

'Faust . . . . a character who is central to Germany's calamity' and 'the German humanist as turncoat' were phrases which led to a concentration on those particular points, even before the debate had really got going.

The debate was carried on in newspapers and periodicals, and there were three notable sessions of the Wednesday Society [Mittwoch-Gesellschaft] at the Academy of Arts, East Berlin. There were also additional discussions. Brecht debated the topic with leading members of the Berliner Ensemble (Wiens, Palitzsch, Rülicke, Strittmatter, Djacenko),

---

[13] E. Fischer, 'Doktor Faustus und der deutsche Bauernkrieg' *Sinn und Form*, Berlin 1952, No. 6

and talks went on at the Aufbau Verlag, mainly between Max Schroeder and his colleagues. *Neues Deutschland* published not only the views of its editorial board, which took up a whole page, but also a number of readers' letters. Before the official start of the debate, the April 1953 issue of *Neue Deutsche Literatur* featured a 'Comment on Hanns Eisler's *Johann Faustus* libretto' by a Jena student of German literature, Hans Richter. Leading figures in the arts world were also involved in the controversy. Apart from Brecht and Helene Weigel, they included the poet Johannes R. Becher, the opera director Walter Felsenstein and the novelist Arnold Zweig. Others were Alexander Abusch, Walter Besenbruch, Kay von Brockdorf, Günter Cwojdrak, Hermann Duncker, Rudi Engel, Wilhelm Girnus, Harald Hauser, Oskar Hoffmann, Gustav Just, Heinz Kamnitzer, E.H. Meyer, Kurt Magritz, Hans Rodenberg, Jürgen Rühle and Erich Wendt.

The debate took many forms and was carried on right across the country, but its focal point lay in the Wednesday Society meetings at the Academy on 13 May, 27 May and 10 June 1953. This society had been set up internally to promote an exchange of ideas among Academy members, although numerous guests were always being invited. The name recalls a forum of the Berlin Enlightenment which existed in the late 18th century, and whose members included Friedrich Nicolai and the editors of the *Berlinische Monatsschrift*. One interesting thing about the *Faustus* debate is that some of the participants were already convinced at the time that it was one of the major literary controversies of the century. They compared it with the Sickingen debate carried on by Marx and Engels with Lassalle — an awkward parallel, but this did not bother them. At the third session Arnold Zweig summed up by saying that 'we have had an excellent debate which will make very decent reading in print'.[14] Wilhelm Girnus went even further. At the first session he was already saying:

> *If we proceed in a determined way with this open exchange of opinions, I believe that our discussion of Hanns Eisler's Johann Faustus could be the profoundest aesthetic and philosophical debate of this kind that has ever been held in Germany.*[15]

This was not all that far-fetched, but what enhanced the debate's significance was the way that differing tendencies within Marxist

---

[14] H. Bunge, opus cit., p. 195.

[15] Ibid. p. 64.

aesthetics were confronted with one another and linked with basic political questions of the period. Admittedly the initial politico-aesthetic positions going back to the years of the Weimar Republic and of exile were never directly affected. No illumination was derived from the debate's involvement in artistic plans and political attitudes that went so far back in time. But this may have been just not possible for the participants, either objectively or subjectively.

Anyone who only takes account of the surface arguments, the literary arguments (and the debate proved to be of no significance to Goethe and Faust research), will fail to understand either the ferocity of the debate or the real reasons why the participants took sides as they did. The arguments became separated from the politico-historical basis of the tactical struggles [*Richtungskämpfe*] and entered the broad, abstract domain of German intellectual history. If Marxists who had only just put behind them the rigours of exile and the horrors of the concentration camps were now arguing over Goethe's *Faust* with a quite incomprehensible passion, this was not the passion of a German grammar-school teacher who thought 'his' Goethe was being attacked. What the advocates of the differing Marxist viewpoints were really asking was how to tackle questions of political power in Germany. In the context of politics and the arts, the *Faustus* controversy was reviving and resuming arguments that had been aired at the end of the 1920s. One problem was that for the most part, it was quite impossible to appreciate the full extent to which the aesthetic beliefs of the participants had changed. Political processes, historical and current, lay beneath the literary-aesthetic veneer, but they were seldom discernible. Arnold Zweig commented that despite the high level of the debate, it was taking place in a vacuum, and that Eisler's *Faustus* needed to be discussed in much more concrete terms. By that he meant that the discussion should become involved with the 'problems of Germany as a whole' — with politics which in the GDR of the time were directed towards German unity. The participants were in fact aware that the difficulties of the debate stemmed from the ever-dwindling chances of an 'overall solution for Germany'. This, however, was scarcely evident from the actual debate.

The discussion revolved around the means, methods and opportunities whereby literature and art could figure in Germany's social revolution. This was the real motive for the debate, and not — or not primarily — the German's fondness for their *Faust*. Of course it was also linked with the debates on formalism that Zhdanov had initiated in the Soviet Union, but that kind of argument played less of a role in the

Faustus discussions of the period, even though the political backgrounds overlap. Up to the end of the 1960s, West Germany contributed only sardonic and facile remarks to the debate and never attempted to probe beneath the surface. This was because of her conservatism. She was not interested in shedding light on various ideas of social change by means of literature and art; she only wanted to bolt the doors. It was only the 1968 movement which introduced other viewpoints and put people in touch with scholarly Eisler studies.

THE REBUKE

Before coming to the criticisms of Eisler, we must mention that even his severest critics praised him whole-heartedly on certain points. They were more or less in agreement about the literary quality (which is all the more remarkable because even this point was overlooked for a long time later on). Abusch thought Eisler's narrative 'astonishing for a first-time author'.[16] Hans Rodenberg regarded the whole of *Faustus* as showing a 'skilful use of language' and as an 'astonishingly skilful cabaret piece'.[17] Incidentally, 'astonishing' [*erstaunlich*] was the favourite positive adjective.

Alexander Abusch and Wilhelm Girnus led the opposition to Eisler. This was neither out of personal animosity nor because of the posts they held at the time. Both were prominent literary scholars in the German classical field, and as such, both were constantly mindful of their political roles. In Abusch's view, Eisler's 'main error' was that he had played down, and indeed ignored, the spiritual and poetic significance of Goethe's work for German literature and history. If Faust is living at the time of the Peasants' War, he must be depicted as an 'heroic spiritual figure' engaged in a passionate struggle to combat the German 'calamity'. Eisler read the transcripts of the Wednesday Society discussion at home, and noted in the margin at this point: 'My theme is the Münzer versus Luther conflict.'[18] Eisler was downright shocked that a Marxist like Abusch should accept the German classics without any reservations. Faust, Abusch declared, had always been the major spiritual figure 'in the one-time efforts of the revolutionary bourgeoisie

[16] Ibid. p. 55.

[17] Ibid. p. 80.

[18] Ibid. p. 391.

to know and change the world'.[19] Eisler was bewildered by this — his marginal note reads: 'What was the reason for [German] fascism, and for the defeat?'[20] Abusch took the view that Eisler's *Faustus* was a leftist 'retraction' of Goethe's *Faust.*

Eisler's main adversary, however, was Wilhelm Girnus. Later to be the highly respected editor-in-chief of *Sinn und Form,* Girnus also took charge of the editorial columns in *Neues Deutschland.* Although French writers had substantially influenced his ideas on literature, he was strongly drawn to the German classics. At the time of the controversy he was preoccupied with classical aesthetics, and he gained a degree in the subject after studying with Hans Mayer in Leipzig. The members of the Wednesday Society regarded him as the real expert. He was subsequently to stand by some of his ideas on Goethe and Faust even though the political premises behind the Marxist reading of the classics had altered.

Not only was Girnus extremely displeased with Ernst Fischer's *Sinn und Form* article; he thought he had both a personal and a social duty to attack its philosophy. And it was part of his nature to do so with extraordinary thoroughness. One reason for the violence of his polemics against Eisler was that he thought Fischer's ideas were encapsulated in Eisler's libretto — which was quite untrue. Unlike Brecht, Eisler never dissociated himself from Fischer's theses. Girnus assumed from this that philosophically, he was on the same side of the fence as Fischer.

At all three meetings of the Wednesday Society Girnus was a leading contributor to the debate. As his colleagues saw it, Girnus' opposition to *Faustus* incorporated the main points at issue. These points can be summed up as follows.

1 *Johann Faustus* portrays German history as a calamity [*Misere*];
2 For Eisler, the turncoat is typical of the role played by German humanists;
3 Goethe's Faust came to symbolize a national hero because Goethe regarded the progressively minded nucleus of the German people as typical, despite the negative outlook of the average. What does Eisler think of his assessment?
4 There is no real conflict in *Johann Faustus.* Instead of being contrasted dialectically, as they are in Goethe's drama, Faust and Mephisto simply mirror one another. Hence there is no development either.

---

[19] Ibid. p. 60.

[20] Ibid. p. 391.

5 What does Eisler understand by a creative further development of the classical heritage?
6 What does Eisler think of Ernst Fischer's appraisal of his work in *Sinn und Form?*

Remarkably enough, the question of whether *Johann Faustus* was a work of socialist realism played no part in this intensive discussion. Girnus did raise it right at the end, but only in passing. Eisler replied that the socialist-realist basis went without saying. But, he added, *Faustus* was an opera, and he had yet to discover any principles for writing a socialist-realist opera.[21]

THE SMALL MINORITY OF SUPPORTERS

The impression that the participants in the *Faustus* debate were either completely for or completely against the work arose only later on. Not many people hailed it as something fresh and original. On the whole, East German followers of the arts failed to share the enthusiasm of Thomas Mann and Lion Feuchtwanger. Even those who did not subscribe to the criticisms of Eisler were generally sceptical about his work. The younger generation was very cautious in its arguments and saw no reason to sound enthusiastic. Only Bertolt Brecht, Walter Felsenstein, Arnold Zweig and Hermann Duncker were fully behind Eisler's *Faustus* (give or take the odd criticism). Felsenstein only attended the second session of the Wednesday Society. He surprised those who were there by objecting very sharply to the 'aggressive' and 'personal' tone of the debate. He felt that a solid piece of writing was being beset by accusations that came close to branding the author 'a criminal from the angle of a cultural policy, and a traitor to his country'. Felsenstein distanced himself from any suggestion of that kind. Having made that point clear, he thought he should say that 'I have secured the first performance of this work only on condition that the music for it turns out all right',[22]

Arnold Zweig tried to come up with a practical solution. His suggestion (it did not find much support) was that the libretto had literary potential, but that Eisler would have to agree to rename his hero Knaust. While strongly in favour of the work, Zweig shared the opinion that it was problematic, after Goethe, to write a new *Faust.*

[21] Ibid. p. 209.

[22] Ibid. p. 156ff.

> *All that needs excising is the hero's identity with Faust, because Goethe produced the definitive Faust. We should be clear in our minds from the beginning that once a character has been created on a given imaginative plane, we may run into difficulties if we fall below it.*[23]

At later sessions Zweig persisted in his proposal that Eisler should take someone like the arch-magus Agrippa von Nettesheim as his main dramatic character.

BRECHT'S DEFENCE OF EISLER

Bertolt Brecht put even more energy into supporting his friend's *Faustus* than he sometimes saw fit to display when it came to works of his own. During the controversy with Walter Ulbricht over his *Lukullus* (composed by Paul Dessau, 1950–1), Brecht remained silent. In the case of *Faustus*, however, he took care always to speak up at the right moment. He had already suggested various things whilst the work was in progress, although there was no collaboration of the kind Eisler was used to from Brecht's stage productions. Eisler may have felt that his influence would have been too overwhelming. But he and Brecht must have discussed certain passages in detail. Brecht's papers include the following lines from the work, recorded in his own hand: 'Younger men are laughing at me, and I'm the butt of their jokes. I have drunk in their scorn, and I have tasted their contempt. I can't sink any lower' (III/5).[24]

During the discussions Brecht showed himself to be a shrewd tactician. He wanted not just to give his opinion but to influence the course of the debate. After Abusch's preamble to the first Wednesday Society meeting, Brecht realized how much weight the discussion would carry. So contrary to his usual practice, he took the floor at once.

> *I would propose that we now begin the discussion, but with an eye to the possibility of a further discussion – in two weeks from now at least and four at the most. We have been given a paper which is complete in itself and which puts forward and argues a whole series of ideas. It will surely take time to consider all this material, decide on its main thesis and formulate a reply. The theme is really very important and also very wide-ranging.*[25]

---

[23] Ibid. p. 63.

[24] Reference supplied by Frau Herta Ramthun, Bertolt Brecht Archive, Academy of the Arts, E. Berlin.

[25] H. Bunge, op. cit., p. 51

In his contribution to the debate, Brecht confined himself to pointing out things in the libretto which its critics thought were lacking. For instance, he claimed that there was a strong positive element in Eisler's *Faust*. This character has to be called a traitor, but he could not really carry out his act of treachery. At the end of the first session Brecht again got to his feet and read out the entire (and very long) *Confessio* from the work, despite the fact that everybody knew it. It was Brecht's way of reminding the others that *Faustus* was an important work of literature which merited greater respect, greater attention and better arguments.

Brecht was skilled in dialectical argumentation and used all his subtlety to make people appreciate Eisler's text. In the Berliner Ensemble discussion, Paul Wiens expressed reservations about the Magic Scenes; he disagreed with the way Eisler and Fischer were polemicizing against beauty. Brecht explained this as follows. Eisler, he said, was not against beauty in the scene of Joseph and Potiphar's wife, because it was the wife Joseph was resisting, not her beauty. Indeed Joseph was resisting her in spite of her beauty.

Brecht cultivated the role of a coolly judicious critic who would not indulge in furious quarrels. Only once did he lose his self-control. This was when Walter Besenbruch — a student of aesthetics — invoked the educational function of art and called upon Eisler to remember the German nation's positive energies, and not '*just* root around in the dirt'. Here Brecht could no longer contain himself and burst out: 'That's out of order! I want you to know I protest here and now! I request that you make a note of this protest. That's what people always say when something nasty is exposed: he likes rooting in the dirt.'[26] But he soon apologized for his interruption, adding that there was no harm in losing one's temper occasionally; it happened only too seldom.[27]

Brecht would always gladly concede that what a colleague had to say was a 'very important and interesting point', and even quite 'new'. Nonetheless he stood by his views to the last, without budging one inch. As the debate proceeded, Brecht's propositions were weighed up against Girnus', thus providing a basic framework for the discussions. At the start of the Wednesday Society's last meeting Alexander Abusch, who was presiding, read out Girnus' six theses and Brecht's twelve. Brecht's

---

[26] Ibid. p. 208ff.

[27] Ibid. p. 216.

theses related to what had been said at the meetings. He candidly stated, point by point, where he disagreed with the arguments. Thus he agreed it would be not only a 'serious artistic defect but an ideological one to present Faust as a traitor from the outset, a soul condemned to the flames'. But unlike the article in *Neues Deutschland,* he did not see Eisler's *Faust* in that light. Moreover, he disagreed with Fischer that Eisler's basic idea was that of the 'German humanist as turncoat'. Brecht summed up his thoughts in his twelfth and last thesis:

> *Has Eisler been trying totally to destroy our classical Faust image, to quote Neues Deutschland? Is he killing off, misrepresenting and wiping out a great figure in the German cultural heritage, to quote Abusch? Is he retracting Faust, to quote Abusch again? I don't think so. On re-reading the old chap-book Eisler found a different story from Goethe's and a different central character, who seemed an important one. Important, I grant you, in a different way from the character Goethe invented. To my mind this resulted in a dark twin brother to Faust: a great, brooding figure who can't replace or overshadow his more luminous brother, and wasn't intended to. Rather the luminous brother stands out from the gloomier one and gains in luminosity. That is not an act of vandalism.*[28]

THE ANTITYPE

It was Brecht's contention that Eisler had created an antitype to Goethe's Faust. There was nothing wrong in adopting a new and different approach to one of the great literary creations. But that, said Brecht's interlocutors, was the point in question.

In fact only Walter Felsenstein was fully behind Brecht on this issue. In his view it did not seem to pose any problems. Hence the bald statement:

> *I can't see why there is this assumption that you can't handle the character of Faust in a different way simply because Goethe's use of it produced a work which is part of the national heritage – a work which any enlightened person, anybody with higher aspirations, must pay homage to and can never be without. I'm still waiting for proof that a reworking is a crime against the classical era.*[29]

But even Arnold Zweig was not so sure about this. At all events he did not think such reworkings were sensible, even when undertaken by

---

[28] Ibid. p. 161ff.

[29] Ibid. p. 157.

sensible artisits. That was why he kept putting forward the name of Agrippa von Nettesheim.

Johannes R. Becher, too, thought it was a completely hopeless and hazardous venture. In his *Poetic Confession* he called Eisler's work an imitation of Thomas Mann's *Doktor Faustus*. It was, he wrote, doomed to fail even more miserably than the original, as was predictable, and the only surprising thing is that something like that could happen to such an intelligent, cultured and talented artist'.[30] In the debate his approach to the subject was extremely delicate. He himself had gone in for far too many literary experiments to be in any position to say there was a law against it. When Brecht suggested that rethinking a literary character had been common practice since ancient times, Becher objected:

> *I think, Brecht, to cite the Greek dramatists as an example is a mistake. Euripides took a great deal of flak for rewriting the ancient legends of the gods; you mustn't ignore the fact that he ran up against strong opposition from his critics and didn't simply get away with it.*[31]

But when has a major writer ever let himself be dissuaded from something, despite the risk of critical flak?

It was, however, the opposition which prevailed in the debate. Alexander Abusch voiced it in terms of Goethe's *Faust*:

> *Even for the most advanced bourgeois thinker it is impossible to improve on this, and only a scientific socialism can take on the task of critically developing and redesigning this supremely inspired humanist conception on the part of the bourgeoisie.*[32]

But even the latter proposition met with scepticism from Girnus:

> *In my view it [the conception of Faust] can't be taken any further by going against the existing achievement, the climax of a particular idea, but only by proceeding along the same lines. Perhaps there is somebody who can give Faust a new lease of life. I don't know if there would be much point in it. I would advise any artist against developing the idea further.*[33]

---

[30] Johannes R. Becher, *Poetische Konfession*, Berlin 1954, p. 152.

[31] H. Bunge, op. cit., p. 203.

[32] Ibid. p. 171ff.

[33] Ibid. p. 167.

THE DISCUSSION: A GERMAN SEMINAR

Although it would not be altogether wrong to suppose that the objections to Eisler's *Faustus* were based on a specific view of realism, this would be to simplify the issue. There were also political premises behind the scholarly literary arguments. So the way that the aesthetic ideas were built up may seem very abstract, but it was far from a waste of time. The dilemma was this: in content, the debate was of an entirely political nature, but the form it took was mainly literary. By asking whether it was all right to depict Faust as 'a central character in the calamity of Germany', the debate was immediately involving itself in a topical controversy. As the editor of *Neues Deutschland*, Girnus could not be blamed for his part in this. Girnus further laid down in what ways the 'calamity of Germany' had to be considered as an ideological theorem:

> *Just after 1945 a lot of people were talking about the so-called 'calamity' in Germany's history. To the extent that this was bound up with a concrete historical idea, it had to be connected with the relatively long dominance of reactionary forces .... The denial of progress and the representation of German history as one long calamity is a reactionary, anti-nationalist idea whose object is to destroy the national pride and awareness of the German people.*[34]

This is not the place to consider whether the above statement is really accurate or comprehensive enough. Girnus was certainly right about the fact that the 'calamity' theory was widely favoured between 1945 and the start of the nineteen-fifties. It considerably obstructed not only the advancement of learning but also political developments during that period. The 'calamity' theory had a negative effect because it overemphasized features peculiar to German history, presented setbacks to the forces of progress as a continuous sequence, and established a particular role for German reactionaries.

But did Eisler and Brecht go along with the theory at all? Was it reflected in Eisler's *Faustus*? Brecht was adamant that it only found expression in Ernst Fischer's account of the work. Even though there were things in Brecht's writings which might have been attributed to it, he rejected the theory. He thought that its attitude to history was too passive and fatalistic, not militant enough. Hence his ringing statement: 'It is imperative to start off by acknowledging the thesis that to regard the history of Germany as a complete calamity, ignoring the creative

[34] Ibid. p. 91.

force of the people, is untrue to the facts.[35] This was not just a tactical concession, far from it. On the other hand it was still a possibility that Brecht had seen Eisler's Faust, that 'dark twin brother', in much gloomier terms. During a discussion at the Berliner Ensemble he said:

> *The bourgeoisie can't complain, because it made nothing of Faust — today, Faust survives only in the form of [Heinrich Mann's] Professor Unrat. The bourgeoisie didn't deliver what it promised; nothing really became of it . . . For me, the positive side of the Faust image hasn't even been demolished. But it's never a bad thing for a social class to bear the cost in mind. Here's the image — and here's what it costs.*[36]

Eisler's attitude was slightly different. He defended his militant objective but did not comment on the 'calamity' theory. Nor could Girnus induce him to distance himself from Ernst Fischer. He therefore struck his audience as being particularly stubborn and foolhardy. Privately, however, he examined his position and tried to find an answer to Girnus' questions. He dealt with the 'calamity' idea by saying that *Faustus* was not a philosophy of history and that the idea appeared in the writings of Marx and Engels, with quotations to prove it. His private conclusion was: 'But we still have a national calamity, the division of Germany!' But to infer from this very topical observation that Eisler's critics might have been right after all is to miss the real point. Eisler's work was much too militant, revolutionary and uncompromising for it to be put down to the 'calamity' theory, especially the way Girnus was defining it.

There were various assessments of political events in Germany after 1945. Eisler and Brecht held much the same views on this subject. After their return from exile they found the German proletariat greatly weakened by the horrors of fascism, and also 'being bled', as Brecht put it, by the Western Allies. They regarded the Russians as providing the basic impetus for revolutionary upheaval in Germany, whereas the Germans were even loath to accept 'that an imposed socialism is better than none at all'.[37] Above all, Brecht saw the Germans being placed in a situation where, once again, they were cheating themselves out of a revolution instead of making one. He emphatically supported all the measures taken by the party of the working-class and the government with a view to overturning the prevailing conditions, but he still thought

[35] Brecht, *Schriften zur Literatur und Kunst*, Vol. II, Berlin/Weimar 1966, p. 344.

[36] H. Bunge, op. cit., p. 110.

[37] Brecht, *Arbeitsjournal 1938-1955*, Berlin/Weimar 1977, p. 460.

that first, the Germans would have to be made fully conscious of the crisis they were in.

In both its theoretical and its practical alignment, the cultural policy of the time was significantly influenced by Johannes R. Becher. It differed from the outlook of Eisler and Brecht inasmuch as it was orientated towards mobilizing all the positive energies within the German nation, and towards transforming the nation. This also accounted for the existence of diverse aesthetic conceptions and trends. On the one flank, there was the effort to bring about a change that would lead to a national catharsis. On the other, the contradictions were being radically examined; people in Germany were to be made conscious of the crisis. The purpose of this was, as Marx put it, to add to the 'actual pressure' the 'pressure of awareness' and to make the 'shame even more shameful', so as to make the 'fossilized conditions start hopping about'. The diversity of political motives meant the introduction of diverse aesthetic methods and means into the public arena of the arts and politics.

Some of Eisler's audience looked to him for a Faust who would be a spiritual hero, a passionate fighter against the German calamity. Some of them thought it was a mistake for Faust to be contrasted with Münzer. They quoted a maxim from Part II of Goethe's *Faust*: *'Wer immer strebend sich bemüht, den können wir erlösen'* ('He who is forever striving/can expect to be redeemed'). It was, they thought, nothing less than an expression of Germany's destiny. All this was bound up not with academic, classicist ideals but with the idea that literature could help to transform the consciousness of the German nation. And at the time, this ideology of change was being combined with the concrete political goal of the unity of Germany. What was wanted of Eisler in this situation was a patriotic work that would reflect 'the creative energies of the German people'. Hans Rodenberg implored the Wednesday Society not to accept Eisler's 'renegade of a Doktor Faustus' as the hero of a work 'that seeks to be a national one'. He felt that Eisler had released 'something akin to a Pandora's box . . .'[38]

Brecht took a different view. He thought the attempt to bring about a change in the country by mobilizing everything that was positive about her literature, art and history was misguided. He did not believe that a cultural 'Ideal Homes Exhibition' would result in a revolution across the rest of Germany.

[38] H. Bunge, op. cit., pp. 167-8.

This translation of political issues into literary issues was hardly ever touched on during the debate, let alone examined with regard to its consequences. Only one person steered the discussion round to the real underlying motives, and that was Johannes R. Becher. Until the last session he had mainly kept out of the argument, but suddenly he found himself caught up in the problems that were at the root of it all. How it happened was both curious and touching. After another speaker had appealed rather too loudly to Eisler's political conscience, Becher took the floor. He was, he said, at a loss to understand why Eisler should expound his own viewpoint so badly. While he shared the opinion of Girnus and the others, he wanted to help Eisler a bit. He went on to try and put himself in Eisler's position, starting quite rightly with the period of the Weimar Republic.

> *At one time in his life Eisler perceived something of the German calamity and the vulnerability of the German spirit. He experienced it in the Republic and especially when Hitler came to power.... And what happened in 1933 was that people began to be aware of the most significant manifestations – those who were being oppressed, trampled on and shut up in concentration camps. For Thomas Mann was very prominently involved for a while in dealing with the preconditions of Hitler's rise to power. Nobody would really question that . . .*[39]

For a long time Becher had been assailed and disturbed by such thoughts. Now that he had got going, he was no longer just stating Eisler's position but also voicing his own disappointment:

> *Eisler sees the situation as this. He sees that this German literary uprising from 1934 to 1945, and for a further period subsequently, has met with exceptional obstacles, exceptional setbacks. For when he glances across to West Germany and notes what the attitude of her intelligentsia is, he won't be convinced straightaway that the result is very encouraging . . . He'll be seriously concerned as to whether the intelligentsia, if put to such a test again – not over here now, but in West Germany – won't be a disappointment again. I believe this is his major worry, and he was trying to express it metaphorically.*[40]

By now Becher had really warmed to his theme. Since his return from the Soviet Union, he had used German literature as a means of working out a strategy for a great transformation in Germany. Even so, Eisler's despairing Faust, the harsh criticisms of his friend's work and the

---

[39] Ibid. p. 226

[40] Ibid. p. 226.

over-confidence of his colleagues made him wonder. Perhaps, in mobilizing the positive side of literature, history and art so hastily, they were merely showing off and in danger of getting carried away. In this way Becher's speech took on more and more of the motive force which had inspired Eisler's *Faustus*.

> *I believe — I don't know if this is correct — that 'the calamity' and reaction are not the same .... The term 'calamity' also means the inability to wage a successful fight against reaction .... (To Girnus:) If you ask Eisler how it is that Germany has developed into such a civilized country, he will turn round and ask you this question: How is it, my dear Comrade Girnus, that this splendid, glorious, 'peerless' civilized country has never managed to stage a revolution, and secondly let a Hitler come to power and didn't succeed in getting rid of Hitler, even?* (Although Eisler had not actually asked this question, he had jotted it down privately, in the margin of the transcripts of the speeches of Girnus and Abusch.) *This is extremely important. We thrashed out all these points very thoroughly after we emigrated, some of us to the Soviet Union, where they were of course extremely disappointed with the behaviour of the German intelligentsia, the behaviour of the German workers. That was something we saw for ourselves, and we have become somewhat wary of being dreadfully mistaken again as a result of setting our sights too high .... Even from the viewpoint of terminology, an expression like 'rooting in the dirt' is not legitimate. Because I was deeply concerned about what is going on in the Federal Republic, it would be absolutely possible for me to unleash a barbed satire based on a real passion for my country against what I can only call those arseholes — something purely satirical! I am not obliged as an artist to supplement my satire with anything positive. The intensity of my attack on those people would be a positive thing in itself. As Marx neatly observed, even shame can be a motive for revolution.*[41]

At the end of his speech Becher recalled that he had started it as an explanation of why Eisler was defending himself so badly. He now turned to Eisler and asked: 'Do you think we are just superior to you dialectically?' 'No — rhetorically,' was the reply, to enormous laughter.[42]

The debate was wound up at the third meeting of the Wednesday Society. Afterwards Hanns Eisler was so disheartened that he could not summon up the strength to compose the music for *Johann Faustus*. He went to Vienna for a short time. In Vienna he wrote a letter dated 30 October 1953 to the Central Committee of the SED, the East German Socialist Party:

---

[41] Ibid. p. 227–8.

[42] Ibid. p. 229.

> *It is probably natural for an artistic person to react to outward circumstances in a very sensitive way. You may consider this a weakness, but if I am to be capable of artistic work, I need an atmosphere of goodwill, trust and friendly criticism. Of course it is necessary to criticize, but not in such a way as to destroy any enthusiasm, detract from an artist's stature and undermine his self-confidence as a person. After the attack on Faustus I discovered that I had no longer any desire to go on writing music. The extreme state of depression it left me in is something I had hardly ever experienced. But I have no hope now of finding that vital incentive to write music anywhere else than in the German Democratic Republic . . . . I can visualize a place for me as an artist only in that part of Germany which is laying the foundations of Socialism.*[43]

Translated by Peter Palmer

[43] Ibid. p. 263–4.

16

MUSIC AND POLITICS: THEME AND VARIATIONS

Albrecht Betz

Why, amongst the important names in the history of music, are there so few distinguished composers who can also be apostrophized as significant intellectuals? Hegel would presumably have put the reason for this down to the function of music in the 'System of the Arts', which was to be an 'expression of inwardness' (*Innerlichkeit*), to lend to spiritual states the sensory shape of sound and, thereby, to use forms and materials which are at the furthest remove from the world of real things. The listening-to-within-oneself (*In-sich-Hineinhören*) which occurs when writing music, predisposes the composer, so it might be inferred, far more to an attitude of almost religious reverence, than to one directed outwards, such as is necessary to the intellectual's role as the critical conscience of his time. This demands an involvement with the real conflicts of the actual present, with the social contradictions which are constantly being born out of the political, economic and technical process. The politicization or the autonomy of music? It seems that only in times of crisis is the question of these alternatives posed. It makes the adoption of a position unavoidable.

I

For a dialectical mind like Hanns Eisler's, living in an age so full of catastrophes, it had been since the late twenties both a challenge and an opportunity to combine two extreme positions: that of the most esoteric *avant-garde* of music (The Second Viennese School) and the most exoteric *avant-garde* of politics (the marxist workers' movement). To make creative sparks fly from this mediation of the most heterogeneous elements seemed to him, since his move from Vienna to the Berlin of the Weimar Republic, to be a task he was meant for. That the tensions many times came to breaking point cannot be seen separately from the course of history. The delays in the development towards the socialism which he and his artistic output from then on stood for, the set-backs and detours of a young movement included abortive developments which many times tried his critical patience and solidarity to the limit. It was impossible to foresee, in his lifetime, to what extent the ideals of the October Revolution — universal emancipation, magnanimity and social justice, the abolishing of exploitation — would have turned, seventy years later, into their very opposites. How Eisler would have reacted to the radical events of 1989 we do not know. The return of the old in the guise of the new, of unrestrained liberalism as the *non plus ultra* he might perhaps have understood, with Marx, as the farce after the tragedy.

Atrocities without end, eloquent appeals to human rights alongside ever diminishing *égalité* — how might a radical, modern music which took a stand on such things sound today? What new aesthetic means might be found to display subversive power? What public could be reached instead of the one which, blasé at first performances, seeks only more acoustic stimuli? Eisler's cutting sarcasms were meant in equal measure for the élitist and the commercial music business.

Have we gone back to 1930 again?

II

In Germany the earliest evidence for the application of the attribute 'political' to music is found in Michael Praetorius. It appears (in his *Syntagma musicum* 1614–15) together with epithets like 'profane' and 'free' and is meant to distinguish such music from the realm of the spiritual, from church music. By *musica politica* was meant the non-sacred use of music in the service of the State. This relatively innocent meaning changed little until well into the eighteenth century and it played barely any part in the understanding of music.

Everything changed with the French Revolution. With it a new conception of music was created. For the first time in history, music resulting from political processes was legitimized and was directly used to serve them. *Musique sociale* or *engagée* was an integral part of revolutionary festivities. Its aim was to leave its mark upon social development, instead of being merely subject to it. The reformulation of the concept of music in the writings of the German Romantics seems diametrically opposed to this: music was to be a medium detached from all reality, gateway to and vision of a 'kingdom of the infinite' (E.T.A. Hoffmann) and in no way a mirror of social processes. It was meant to bring back the 'innocence of childhood', 'heal the heart's every fear' (Tieck), instead of involving itself in the mercilessness of the present. Music was to be the bringer of consolation, a place of refuge.

One consequence of the frustrated revolution of 1848 was the polarizing of music aesthetics. To the conservative academicians art and politics were poles apart. 'Political music' was condemned as 'unnatural'. Far from being the actual 'birth-pains of becoming', art should possess 'its own heaven and its own hell'. As it was considered to be committed to a 'universally human' morality, it would find no expression within the domain of fickle politics. A reactionary paedagogical idealism was establishing itself. 'Aesthetically good' music would educate towards what was politically good; 'on the other hand, a seductively bad music, which has a pampering, exaggerated and enervating effect on the spirit of the people, must certainly be called socially destructive, revolutionary' (W.H. Riehl). Seen in this perspective, 'political music' was bound to become a term of opprobrium which branded every hint of actual reality as a violation of music and an incitement of the people.

Progressively the 'New Germans' gathered around Franz Brendel, Liszt and the young Wagner, acknowledged their opposition to this. Music ought not to stand outside the social interests of mankind. In order to remove the division between art and life, the 'politicization' of music was needed. The artist's task was to absorb the ideas and currents of the present and give them expression. How this 'politicization of art' was actually to be understood — as a first step towards an 'aestheticization' of the social — can be deduced from Wagner's road to the Bayreuth Temple of Art. It was a question of an artistic - religious change which would surround life with an art which was anti-realist.

The *Gesamtkunstwerk* had aimed at intoxication, illusion and an overpowering of the public's emotions. To the young, critical generation of composers in the nineteen twenties, all this seemed obsolete, as the over-worked mythology of the *Germanen*, the submission to fate and the search for redemption. They dissociated themselves completely from Wagner's 'world-view art' and its narcotic effect (quoting it satirically, however, when the need arose).

After World War I and the October Revolution, only the debris of the feudal-bourgeois value-system remained. The combination of huge social convulsions and the revolution in the media (radio, gramophone, sound film) compelled young composers to consider how the significance and function of music and, above all, its public were changing. The reluctance to compose only for a social and cultural élite was universal. The change in the relationship between the masses and technology in the big cities, the drives for political and industrial innovation, the view of the present as a time of chaotic transition, the acceleration of the tempo of life and a growing nerviness, all could not leave people's ways of perceiving things untouched. To continue to serve traditional habits of listening would have meant participating in the glorification of what had formerly existed. A cleansing of the emotions left over from late Romanticism was only possible through music by breaking down old habits of listening. Getting rid of the dross of clichés included even musical material itself (contrapuntal forms, harmony, rhythm, instrumentation), as well as the music business with its traditional performance practices (opera, concerts, etc.). In every field, hierarchical classifications, often no longer recognizable, had become like sediment, which in a subtle way emotionally blocked a development towards a more egalitarian democracy. To be sure, these connections were not always immediately obvious. In Hindemith's early works irritation at an all too long prolongation of old musical habits expressed itself in a rebellious sarcasm which even permeated into the performance instructions. Weill made use of jazz and light music in his songs with the well-nigh destructive purpose of producing an attitude of emotional revolt against the *status quo*. Eisler's position was the most radical. Hopes of a revolutionary transformation in Germany led to his developing the concept of 'applied music' (*angewandte Musik*) which, thanks to an unambiguous words-music relationship, made possible precise political statements. The aim of his *'Kampfmusik'* was to help to raise the level of solidarity and of class- and struggle-consciousness of the marxist workers' movement. He shared the hope for a socialist revolution in Germany with countless other intellectuals.

Into this period falls the meeting with Brecht and the beginning of their work together. Both had at their disposal the most advanced developments in the materials of their art and shared the same political perspective. New forms of vocal music, music theatre and film were produced — *Die Massnahme*, *Die Mutter* and *Kuhle Wampe*. Such artistic activity, working *with* the masses, not *for* them, was possible only for a short period during the last years of the Weimar Republic. Later these conditions no longer existed. National Socialism destroyed the revolutionary workers organizations and proletarian counter-culture. Even after their return from exile, in the State Socialism of the GDR, there could be no picking up of the threads because of the bureaucratic disciplining of the arts.

III

Since the beginning of the Weimar Republic, conservative opposition had spoken out vehemently against the radical tendencies of the musical moderns. The proscribing of musical styles and compositional techniques was the equivalent of the defence of the 'German spirit'. Hostility towards intellectuals and anti-semitism were barely concealed. So respected a composer as Hans Pfitzner went so far in his German Nationalist resentment as to denounce atonality as the musical equivalent of Bolshevism and 'Jewish Internationalism'. In the new aesthetic he found a 'symptom of decay' (1920); the danger threatened of a poisoning of the people [*Volkskörpers*]. The biological-mystical overtones should not be ignored in others who swore by 'organic' unity, by the thriving 'community'. Logically, therefore, only tonality was deemed to be natural, 'truly German'. This was argued in the name of national and 'eternally human' values, which were meant to be considered as unpolitical. This allowed leftist and Jewish artists to be excluded under the slogan of 'depoliticization'. The demand for the popular signified for music the renunciation of experiments and shock effects, of structural *montage,* of dissonances, of atonality. A critical-analytical, rational attitude towards musical material was obviously materialistic and therefore un-German. Instead of bestowing piety, harmony, heroism and the preparedness for sacrifice upon musical form, the most that could be expressed with the resources of the new aesthetic (Pfitzner testified to its 'impotence') was 'bloodless' intellectuality and demoralizing individualism. The term which would focus all the invective was ready and waiting — degenerate.

'Degenerate Music' (*Entartete Musik*) was the title of the exhibition which accompanied the *Reichsmusiktage* (Reich-music days) created by one of the National Socialist functionaries in Düsseldorf in 1938. The exhibition was a settling of accounts with the 'chaos-culture' of the Weimar Republic, one year after the Munich exhibition 'Degenerate Art', which had similarly attempted to expose *avant-garde* painting to the philistine outrage of 'healthy public opinion'. Guest of honour in Düsseldorf was, needless to say, Richard Strauss. His *Festival Prelude* formed the upbeat to a speech by Goebbels that climaxed in the proclamation of 'Ten basic principles of German music-making'. The speech included a lot about melody, heart and feeling; most of all, however, about the contrast between 'Jewishness and German music'. Clearly the other main opponent, the workers' movement together with the left intelligentsia, was considered to be already disposed of, so that the aggressive antisemitism could be the dominant feature (which didn't prevent that day from culminating in Beethoven's Ninth — *'Alle Menschen werden Brüder'*!). The centrepiece of the musicological conference which had to supply the theoretical contribution to the Reich-music days was the lecture by Friedrich Blume entitled 'Music and Race'.

For the exhibition, which was aimed at a wide public, its initiator, Hans Severus Ziegler, general director of the Weimar National Theatre, had prepared a cultural-political brochure. The front cover, above the title 'Degenerate Music', presented a caricature of a black saxophonist, grotesquely dressed in top hat and tails i.e., usurping the outfit of the European upper class. On the back there was stuck a rosette with the Star of David, its centre taken by the face of an ape. The animal's gaze was meant to intensify the impression of something dangerous, alien, lurking. The ensemble of associations, to the uncritical observer, was bound to add up to a repellent, Jewish, 'nigger' music.

Ziegler held the decadent 'snobs' responsible for the success of the simultaneously frivolous and sterile degenerate music of the Republic and, in his zeal, hit upon a new formulation – 'de-Germanized' music. The critics, who had promoted the atonal 'forgeries' (*Falschmünzerei*), had also been degenerate. The musical community of the people (*Volksgemeinschaft*) had rejected all this. With 'healthy feeling' (*gesundem Empfinden*) it was holding out for the natural and the elemental, demanding a purification of feeling, insisting on the beautiful, true and sublime. Ziegler had the audacity to maintain that the triad was a specifically 'German element', the core of 'our Aryan tonal system'. He justified his Manichaean picture of world music by appealing to Wagner's article *The Jewish Spirit in Music* (1850).

The attempt of Ziegler and other Nazi ideologues to inject racism into purely musical terminology or to make musical value judgements on the basis of the composer's race – always presented with lofty aplomb from the perspective of furthering the cultural development of the 'community' – makes clear the extent of the aberration reached by the Nazi cultural revolution, taken over and subsidized by the State only a few years after its beginning.

IV

Coming from Vienna, Eisler understood the comprehensive orchestration of musical events in the Third Reich as a psychological preparation for war. From the use of all types of music down to the blatant propaganda, everything seemed to be aimed at producing a collective, increasing of itself, ready both for war and sacrifice. The firm, repeated postulates that a purely *German* music must be achieved and that Germany was the 'pre-ordained land of music in the world' legitimized, when linked together, a claim to leadership that could be carried over into other fields. The imperialism which, still Utopian at first, was directed outwards, was at the same time meant to compensate for the demand of the individual that he renounce the self and dedicate himself to the community and to the established hierarchies. From community singing to musical rallies everything was directed at emotionally welding the masses together into that community of destiny which would follow the Führer. The fact that a comparatively sophisticated opera and concert life, the reserve of the bourgeois public, was kept going well into the war, had little effect on this.

In the autumn of 1935, Eisler travelled to the USA for a concert and lecture tour. He used it to warn about Hitler and his plans for war. He also described the brutality of the regime and its treatment of the opposition. His lecture 'Music and music-politics in fascist Germany' pursued the question of how music serves fascism and what changes it undergoes in the process. He examined individual genres, including light music, folk music, military music, classical and modern music, and analysed the specific misuse of each. Forms long worn-out but still much used because of the authority they possessed in previous ages were being made topical again; the classics were manipulated by being decoratively inserted into party rituals; the blending of the reactionary and the falsely revolutionary; demagogy pervaded everything; and finally there was the constant recourse to the 'intoxication music' (*Rauschmusik*) of Richard Wagner, the German 'myth smith'. All together these elements, for Eisler, resulted in an outrageous disenfranchisement of the listener. Persisting class conflicts, crimes against 'ideological opponents', any scruples about a future war of conquest, all were whitewashed over, or more exactly, shouted down. The use in music of the *Arierparagraph,* (a Nazi law of 1933 excluding non-Aryans from the civil service) Eisler only remarked on mockingly. He seems to have substantially underestimated it. That Mendelssohn's 'Jewish' music for *A Midsummer Night's Dream* was, at the wish of the State cultural authorities, to be replaced by 'German' music, he commented on only as an item of information. The fact itself he could only have considered to be grotesque. (He could not know that in 1935 more than forty composers, among them Werner Egk and Carl Orff, would endorse this requirement). That the race war was only a mask for the class war and in no way the central ideology of the Nazis was an analysis he shared with numerous other intellectuals in exile. It followed that anti-semitism was only an 'instrument' of the ruling classes. It allowed Hitler to behave in an anti-capitalistic way whilst upholding the power of the great monopolies and being in their pockets. Traced back to its socio-economic origins, the Third Reich appeared as an extreme form of bourgeois class domination. Its one real enemy was the organized workers' movement and it was on this that the repression and terror were concentrated in 1933. In contrast, anti-Jewish measures were developed with a gradual increase in intensity – until 1938 they could still be seen as a diversionary tactic, secondary in comparison with the persecution of the 'Marxists'. Hence the apparently clear battle position.

V

From the spirit of all this came, from 1935 on, Eisler's *Deutsche Sinfonie* Op.50, his most extended work and the musical document *par excellence* of the anti-fascist resistance. Its compositional working-out involved an extremely complex set of political relationships. The first question was how, with the catastrophic defeat suffered by the completely unprepared workers' movement and the unleashed Nazi-terror which ranted and raved in the name of the Reich, to express grief at so much sacrifice in such a way as to avoid all resignation or sentimentality? Despair could not be allowed to gain the upper hand. Secondly, the appeal to the powers of opposition, to rebellion and to the solidarity of the persecuted, had to be linked to the protest against the brutality. It was a question of deriving hope from an unbending political stance and not in any way evading the issue by means of a religious solution. Abstract promises of a future triumph were to be avoided – only a stubborn fight offered any prospects. Finally, the usurpation by the Nazis of the word *German* was to be denounced. It is instructive that, at first, Eisler's magnum opus was to have been called *Concentration Camp Symphony*. The change to *German Symphony* in 1938 implied three things: Nazi Germany was a) the country of the concentration camps and b) the country of a hidden but continuous resistance to them. To have come to this position was c) the consequence of the German Calamity *(Deutsche Misere)*, that is to say, the unhappy, because undemocratic, course of German history since the Peasants' War. An expression of the present-day calamity are the concentration camps, both symbolically and absolutely concretely, because the *combination* of capitalism and fascism clearly cannot do without them, causing intimidation, punishment and executions to be everyday occurrences.

Oscillating between oratorio and broadly-planned cantata, using predominantly politically very acerbic texts by Brecht, the *Deutsche Sinfonie* is structured as a large-scale crescendo. Along with the increasingly obvious terror there grows the spirit of rebellion. This development leads out of the lament which follows the *Prelude* (*Largo*) – 'Oh Germany, pale mother, how you are besmirched with the blood of your best sons' – that is, leads out of the intrinsically nationalistically motivated bourgeois war to the international (Marxist) battle slogan, the answer to the real conflict between rich and poor, 'And the class enemy *is* the enemy'.

As a work that lasts a whole evening, Eisler's Op.50 demands large forces — solo voices, speaker, chorus and orchestra. Of the eight vocal movements, those which he wishes especially to emphasize he follows with a purely instrumental movement. Dodecaphonic, modal and *Kampfmusik* elements come together and give to the whole a dark power, severity and dissonance which in no way tolerates compromises with the listener and his need for harmoniousness.

Psychological, and therefore a-political, identification of the self with the singing protagonists is out of the question. The 'heroes' are the nameless intellectuals, workers and peasants who represent their class. As a result the demands on the audience are even further increased.

A performance of the work during the period of exile (for what audience?) was inconceivable for such a monumental work on the grounds of the numbers of performers required alone. So the *Deutsche Sinfonie* was produced as a work of commemoration, for the time 'after Hitler'. It was possible for Eisler to create a great work of radical modernity using the compositional achievements of the Schoenberg School to set Brecht's politically explicit texts in which are crystallized in equal measure the despair and the spirit of revolt of the workers' movement, in a situation virtually without prospects. It was not possible for him to get a performance at that time. From the practical point of view the *Deutsche Sinfonie* had to remain a Utopian *opus*. It retains its place within his *oeuvre* as a great document of a barbaric time against which it bears witness.

The real power outside Nazi Germany on which, if not without sceptical reservations, artists in exile like Brecht and Eisler placed their hopes, was the Soviet Union. In spite of all the deformities, it seemed to represent not only the concrete anti-fascism but the possibilities of the future. Forty years later, the political constellation appeared in a totally different position, as did the relationship of music and politics.

VI

Hardly had the 'End of History' thesis been launched afresh, this time from the USA, than it was massively refuted by the actual course of history. It was 1989; the 'Eastern bloc' was disintegrating, the global changes in East-West power relationships led also to the unification of Germany.

It was the economic decline of the 'real socialist states' and the growing technological gap between them and the West which made their position untenable and the end of the Cold War and the arms race a matter of urgency for them. The ideology which originally mobilised them had lost its strength and the masses refused their loyalty.

It is true that, as a state, the GDR had largely been the henchman and imitator of the Soviet Union, under whose aegis it had arisen and, after forty years, sank. True also that at the end, it was revealed as a thorough-going police-state. However, in the beginning, it had not been seen thus by the representatives of 'the other Germany', those great intellectuals in exile who had had to flee Hitler's Reich. That Eisler and Brecht, Anna Seghers and Ernst Bloch, Arnold Zweig and John Heartfield returned not to West Germany but to the GDR had one central reason. They shared in the anti-fascism declared by the new state to be fundamental to it and were certain that in it lessons of more consequence would be learnt from history than in West Germany. Trust in the anti-fascism of the GDR rested on its being embedded in that oppositional, republican tradition which, in German history, had always been suppressed by conservative forces: it stretches from the Peasants' War of 1525 through the failed revolutions of 1848 and 1918–19 to the opposition to the Third Reich. The fact that this other Germany, always a minority, was not only recognised in the GDR, but that the memory of revolutionary aspirations, the struggles of the oppressed, the spirit of the Enlightenment were being revived and intensively promoted, attracted many in whose eyes *Bürgertum* (the bourgeois world) and social democracy had failed. Was it not that very capitalistic democracy which had directly led, after 1930, to the catastrophe?

For five years now the GDR has been part of the past, an epoch concluded, a further fragment in the history of the formation of the German state, which is so rich in failed experiments. In the face of the non-realization of the utopian socialist project, melancholia beset a proportion of the intelligentsia on both sides of Germany.

Thirty years after Eisler's death in 1962 it is clear how variable the reception of his work, and the musical and theoretical position for which he stood, has proved to be. In a paradoxical way, he was highly revered in the GDR without ever being really influential in a musical environment strongly orientated towards the cultivation of the classical tradition. He was never quite free from the cultural functionary's reservations towards him, the cosmopolitan and the *avant-gardist* of the Schoenberg school. In the *Bundesrepublik*, along with the whole complex of the strongly politically accentuated art of the Weimar Republic,

Eisler's work was given fresh life only by the student revolts of 1968, when to bring up to date the formulating of artistic questions seemed to be the order of the day. With this coincided the slogan, taken over from the 'Prague Spring' — 'Socialism with a human face'. In the West it was a question of finishing the job on anti-fascism, in the East on anti-Stalinism. What was meant by 'facing up to the past' was, by means of a modernized Marxism involving psycho-analysis, to expose and eliminate the reasons for the severe deformities. To stand above such things, above the social conflicts, seemed to have become impossible for the young generation of artists. It was a question of critically appropriating the advanced positions already reached by the Weimar Moderns in order to reach out beyond them. The pleiad of Brecht, Eisler, Piscator, Grosz and Heartfield functioned as a reference point.

However the revolutionary body to which the artist intelligentsia of the twenties could relate, a working class which was at least potentially revolutionary, no longer existed. It had social security, was integrated, had virtual pensioner status. The political establishment in the West did not need, as in the East, to rule with an iron hand. It reacted, in the words of Marcuse, with 'repressive tolerance'. Even explanations of the past were now tolerated, in homeopathic doses.

Gradually the great issues were postponed, diverted to the outside. No longer was there talk of the persistence of inequality and the maximization of profits by the great business concerns in ones own country, but of the problems of the Third World countries and of global ecology. The collapse of the Eastern bloc which allowed large-scale disarmament finally took the wind out of the sails of the opponents of atomic weapons. If it were not for the refugee problem and the difficult assimilation of East Germany into West Germany, the thesis mentioned at the beginning of this section would, wherever possible, be welcomed by a silent majority — the end of history which sees in Western capitalism the best of all worlds.

VIII

What has been the relationship of modern music to politics since then? Does it relate at all? The shock of 1968 did not last long, that much we can say straight away. The attempts of a new vocal music, often by this time using electronic resources, to set political texts and to reach through 'new channels' a public hitherto unapproached, met with a rather limited response. Even the majority of intellectuals did not perceive contemporary serious music as a medium for political subjects and social utopias. Had it distanced itself too far from ingrained habits of listening?

For whatever reason, the second post-war generation of young composers, which began to write in the seventies, soon turned away from politics and from unequivocal statements. What had been the attitude of the first generation?

Directly after 1945 there was a vacuum. It was necessary to get away from the nightmare of the Nazi era, from false pathos and abused emotions, from a music which wanted to overpower its listeners by intoxicating them. The move towards serial composition — Schoenberg and even more, Webern, were the models — meant the re-formulation of musical grammar and syntax. Disillusion, scepticism, asceticism, love of abstraction, all this suddenly had the aura of daring, pioneering achievement; it corresponded to the era's predilection for what was technical and structural. To this was added the discovery of electronic sound generation. So, in the two decades up to 1965, a structural, objective art dominated, which, intent on avoiding all suspicion of ideology, was predominantly instrumental. In his last years, Eisler had foreseen the dangers of this development and sharply criticized it. Integral serialism was bound in the long run to engender a conformist attitude and lead simply to a fetishism about material. To submit oneself compositionally to prescribed parameters and to trust in a mathematical rationale — this went directly against his conviction that music reaches the reason of the listener through his emotions. The capacity for communication, so important for him — 'Music is made by people for people' — seemed to have been completely abandoned.

Exactly this need to communicate (but of course in no way from Eisler's enlightening perspective) is now being claimed as their own by the second post-war generation (those born around 1950). In contrast to the generation of serialists they offer a very private, expressive, lyrical, subjective art. They have travelled so far away from enslavement to dogmas — from a fixation with prescribed structures and from the obligation to develop further the materials and techniques historically arrived at, thereby outdoing in speculative complexity their fathers' generation — that they have landed up with the 'New Simplicity'. Trust in the spontaneous idea, the free, unrestrained fanning out in all sorts of directions, styles and epochs, the uninhibited quoting from the rich store-house of music history, frequently leads into the safe pastures of the traditional, or even the conservative. In many cases it goes way back beyond the Second Viennese School. Instead of epigrammatic brevity, compression of musical thought, terseness achieved by a recognisably controlled compositional technique, there occurs an interminably extended living out of what had been the inspiration of a moment. The talk now is of the rediscovery of direct expression, of a subjective understanding of the world, of basic existence and a belief in music *per se.* Vast orchestral forces are employed to create an often amorphous-sounding product in which the composer clearly allows himself to be led by the intrinsic dynamic of the events – sound, colour, contrast, rhythm and silence. Since the music of all ages and countries is available, as well as the other branches of music, there is a great temptation to set up vast post-modern conglomerates. Anything goes. Schoenberg's statement 'Art comes from having to' (*Kunst kommt von Müssen*) sounds like something from another planet. Yet the manifest confusion and self-indulgence at the beginning of the nineties also signifies a gain in diversity. Presumably, the social constellations of the future, their shapes not yet actually visible, will challenge their people of talent to react – with new compositional methods and new content.

VIII

Phases of stagnation can last a long time but not forever. Eisler was convinced that changed circumstances would also produce the art appropriate to them, and that, conversely, great art has the capacity to register future tremors seismographically, thanks to its capacity to anticipate. As a composer, his apprehensions focussed on the musical illiteracy perpetuated by the music industry. The corrupting of the world of sensations by exposure to a constant stream of sound, the grotesque contradictions between the most modern electronic techniques and the detritus of Romanticism as the musical substance, has markedly increased in the last decades. Eisler ceaselessly repeated that listening must be practised and that acoustic perception needs an education which has to begin as early as possible; not only to create an immunity to contamination by the musical refuse which is pushed around the globe by the dictates of commerce, but because music can be a path to the experiencing of reality, by the cleansing and redefining of perceptions. For Eisler, reality was, in the widest sense, political reality.

17

THOUGHTS ON HANNS EISLER

Harry Goldschmidt

When I call to mind the music of Hanns Eisler — it has been part of my life for almost thirty years — I feel the involuntary need to think in aphorisms. Wherein does this lie? In myself? In his music?

To write a systematic study of the composer Hanns Eisler is, I think, very difficult. One risks building a cage: when it is finished, the bird has flown.

Or might I better compare him, even if no more respectfully, to a chameleon? It seems to me there are two sides to his musical portrait; one steady, like iron, and one continuously changing and fluctuating. The steady, iron-like — that is Hanns Eisler the communist. In the fluctuating one flickers our age of transition.

There is only one sort of universality. A composer can cultivate all the genres of music and still escape from the parochial. That is mere professionalism. Eisler's versatility is different; its mother is the true universality. Because he perceives the whole, he leaves no part out.

Precisely because he perceives the whole, he can be so brief. The memory of two *Lieder* recitals remains unforgettable. In them, in compressed form, was the experience promised by close study of the volumes of *Lieder und Kantaten* — a mosaic, a jigsaw puzzle of sounding pieces from very different periods of his creative life. But in these pieces, song after song, the world, the curving horizons of the modern progressive peoples of our time fit together. In each piece the whole is present. Sometimes the whole becomes so overwhelming that the pieces, in the conciseness of their statement, almost explode.

In accord with the whole is abundance. The abundance of his work is such that in itself it is difficult to grasp (sifting through it will, as one listens, cause considerable difficulties). Yet abundance does not mean over-exuberance. Because he sees the whole, he is a master of omission. Not from paucity of thought, not from poverty of feeling does he work so frugally with notes, but because everything in them is essence. Even in his physiognomy, Eisler plays a dialectical trick on us – his body inclines to corpulence, his music is slim.

Everything about Eisler is dialectical. Only because he loves life so passionately can his music be so unsurpassably corrosive. I know little music which is so scorched as his. But the sick areas are well diagnosed: regularly they are *caries progressiva societatis.* For that reason is Eisler's music so aggressive wherever it is militant. The enemy is recognized, the world must be changed.

A further paradox – Eisler was a pupil of Schoenberg (he has never concealed how much he owes his teacher). Much more than that, he rectified his teacher's 'wrong front'. It was not Schoenberg but he who changed the apocalypse of the world decline into a dawning of a new age. Schoenberg saw his bourgeois world as the whole world. With Eisler it is the other way round – because he did see the whole world, he put the bourgeois world in its proper place. And there it properly stands, condemned to decay.

So, out of Arnold Schoenberg's master class, there emerged the composer who could give the struggling working class the *Solidarity Song*, the *National Hymn* of the GDR and numerous songs for young socialists. So a new, flourishing song could spring out of the mazes of atonality and serialism. So the complicated could again be simple, the true once again beautiful and graceful.

But the simple and the beautiful are also subjected to dialectic. Without their antitheses they are trite and prone to falsehoods. The unnatural, the disintegrating, the loathsome, the loneliness and distress require different expressive resources. This is why Eisler relied on a whole arsenal of diverse 'methods'. How could twelve-note technique be excluded from them? It is a musical cornerstone of that world. But in contrast to his teacher and his teacher's other pupils, Eisler did not use it in a subjective way; only seldom did he identify himself with it. I could name few cases where he availed himself of it uncritically i.e., not as a critic (one example is *Printemps allemand*).[1]

[1] Setting of Karl Kraus's poem *'Nun weiss ich doch, es ist Frühling wieder'*, for voice and piano 1956. [Ed.]

Against this the significant serial works, like the wonderful *Chamber Symphony* or the *Five Orchestral Pieces,* shows us that he followed the logical path from expressionism to critical realism. The extreme tensions of blind subjectivism are objectified, the sparks directed not towards the self but towards the real and bloodily actual enemy — fascism.

Was Eisler's music created only for thinking people? Yes and no! For thinking people it mobilizes feelings, for feeling people it mobilizes thoughts. But here a limitation comes in. Whoever wishes to be lulled by music, whoever requires atmosphere (*Stimmung*) because he is too indolent to think, finds his music either a provocation or simply uncomfortable.

The same limitation applies to thinking. There is professional thinking and there is universal thinking. Professionalism, the rationale of art, is active with Eisler to an admirable degree. But it is not limited in itself. Those who see no more in his music than interesting professionalism will unfortunately never understand him. His professional thinking is integrated into his universal thinking. Almost every song is proof of this. Technical detail, workshop-knowledge, is always of interest in his music, but only as an 'indicator', as a component of a higher intellectual order. To limiting professionalism his universal thinking is no less uncomfortable than it is to passivity of feelings. From this it may result that an Eisler setting (often more than just its text!) has a shocking effect in certain circles, even if people feel loftily exalted about his means.

To these properties belong also Eisler's predilection for adopting the language of the classics. It is true, Bach, Mozart, Schubert and Brahms often show up in his music (we'll leave aside the 'Wagner Question'). Sometimes they are hinted at or clearly quoted melodically and harmonically, sometimes they are elusively woven into the musical texture. Perhaps that is eclecticism? In reality, Eisler refers to the classics no differently to Schoenberg — that is to say, critically. These turns of phrase are just as familiar as they are new. The musical dialectician is in evidence in them from yet another side. The old significance is suspended i.e., simultaneously preserved and eliminated. In the *Grabrede an einen Genossen, der an die Wand gestellt wurde*[2], one hears the

---

[2] 'Speech at the grave of a comrade who was put against the wall' from the music for Brecht's *Lehrstück Die Mutter* 1931. [Ed.]

Golgotha of Bach's Passions, and again, no less movingly, in *Ändere die Welt* (*'Welche Niedrigkeit begingst du nicht, um die Niedrigkeit auszutilgen?'*).[3] For Bach Christian humility and human dignity are still compatible. Eisler's *'ecce homo'* can no longer be separated from the Passion of the fighter. Idealistic thought is superseded and humanistic continuity realistically achieved. And certainly it is not merely 'private' reflectiveness which gives the warm and relaxed charm of a Schubert *Lied* to *Vom Sprengen des Gartens*.[4] For in order that a good Germany might bloom, according to Brecht and Eisler, much trouble, understanding and passion is required and not least charm.[5] Or is the song *Über den Selbstmord* (On Suicide)[6] perhaps to be regarded as an imitation of *Der Doppelgänger*? I think it is much more than that. It is, in fact, a magnificent transferral of Heine and Schubert's terrible Doppelgänger tragedy into the very recent past (1939), a time of no-way-out for everyone, with no star shining in the murky sky. With these resources it would be eclecticism to relapse into the old stance.

The unthinking taking over of old techniques is always anachronistic. It says as little about one's own time as it does about that which is imitated. But here the precise opposite occurs — the old resources and methods take on an unexpected new and topical meaning. The realism of our 'times of transition' has taken possession of them. One thing, though, is striking. Of all the classics to which Eisler makes reference, one is missing — Beethoven! Accident or intention? Were it because of lack of rapport, it would be quite astonishing, for which of the classics made the revolutionary song of the masses more radically his own than Beethoven? Here the common ground becomes clear, and at the same time the difference. Beethoven avails himself of the musical accents of the French Revolution, Eisler of the revolution of the proletariat. Beethoven's heroic pathos is, as Asafiev remarks, the musical language

---

[3] 'Change the world, it needs it. What baseness would you not commit to rid the world of baseness?' From the Brecht-Eisler *Lehrstück Die Massnahme* (The Measures Taken) 1930. [Ed.]

[4] On Sprinkling the Garden. Setting for voice and piano of Brecht's poem. Composed in 1943, the tenth year of exile. [Ed.]

[5] The reference is to the *Kinderlied Anmut sparet nicht noch Mühe* of 1950. 'Don't be sparing with grace (charm), nor with effort, nor with passion or intelligence, so that a decent Germany may flourish like other decent lands? [Ed.]

[6] On Suicide. Composed in 1942. Text by Brecht. *'In diesem Lande und in dieser Zeit dürfte es trübe Abende nicht geben, auch hohe Brükken über die Flüsse. [Ed.]*

of the National Convention. Eisler's revolutionary pathos was forged in the Russian October Revolution and in the class struggles of the German Weimar Republic. So it is Beethoven, who stands the closest to him, whom he can least quote. The revolution has acquired a new quality, the socialist one.

So might this dividing line be only a relative one? Let us hope so! Beethoven's pathos is quintessentially different to that of Eisler. Beethoven's resounds with the vision of the new Man, Eisler's pathos is directed against the old.

One thing is certain; when Eisler 'quotes' the classics, he doesn't imitate them. He refers back to them whenever it seems meaningful. What he does is utterly original; he looks not to the past but to the present, as a leading musician of '*diese Zeit*'. That makes the difference between style and mere mannerism. He, in Goethe's words 'rests on the basis of knowledge, on the essence of things' (*auf den Grundfesten der Erkenntnis, auf dem Wesen der Dinge ruht*). Eisler's method lacks all trace of mannerism; it is style on the highest level. Perhaps it is a manifestation of a 'time of transition'. Such a time is ours. Imperfections will have to be measured by future criteria. For our, for 'this' time, we can, with good conscience, view Hanns Eisler as a master, and not only with regard to his artistic power and vitality and the diversity of his output. The intellectual prerequisite for achievements of this magnitude Goethe saw in the appropriation of the objective world and an innermost accord with it. In Eisler's work, this is richly fulfilled. For that reason it has its place not only in the present but in the future.

First published in *Musik und Gesellschaft* 6, 1958

18

ASK ME MORE ABOUT BRECHT CONVERSATIONS WITH HANS BUNGE: FOUR EXCERPTS

From the Third Conversation – 5 May 1958

B: I'd like to read to you again Brecht's note of 29 July, 1942, from his Working Diary where he is relating a visit which both of you paid to one of Schoenberg's lectures and after that to the Schoenberg family's home.

E: I have a very vivid memory of that lecture, which was superb. Brecht was impressed by the lucidity and logic of a man whose public image – in the world of music, that is – was that of an absolute anarchist. On Thomas Mann, too, the relentless logic and lucidity of Schoenberg's thinking made quite an astonishing impression, one of amazement. There is, in music too, you know, the concept of madness. But to meet such an excellent mind, which is able to lecture so precisely on its subject, and which writes such a strange, extraordinary music, was amazing for Brecht, too. I won't go into details about Schoenberg's lecture, which – by the way – has been edited, among Schoenberg's philosophical and theoretical writings, by Schirmer & Co in New York, I think.[1] One would have to read the lecture to understand Brecht's reaction better. The impression Schoenberg made on Brecht was enormous. I don't know if that becomes evident from the Diary notes. Let me just say, for the record, dear Dr. Bunge, that before taking Brecht to Schoenberg's home I said to him: "Dear friend, I'm taking you to Schoenberg, who is a very strange man. He is a genius. He is likely to talk so much nonsense that you might be rude to him – I know you. On politics he will talk the sort of nonsense only a *petit bourgeois* is able to talk. Of course you know – dialectician that you are – that this is in no way antagonistic to his immense achievements in music."

---

[1] *Style and Idea*. In the summer of 1942 Schoenberg was much occupied with his work for the summer courses at UCLA. It is difficult to know if the text he delivered on 29 July is actually published. According to Brecht's own account, the lecture was about 'Modern composition . . . . . It dealt with the emancipation of the dissonance. The brevity and extreme emotionalism of the first works of his school he explained as the initial struggles and the undeveloped technique.'
[All notes to Chapter 18 are editorial.]

I said: "If you lose control and are rude to Schoenberg, I declare I shall immediately break off relations with you, regardless of our friendship. You must not do that." (I deliberately overdid it to hold Brecht back.) "Otherwise our friendship will be a thing of the past. He is an old and ill teacher" — he was indeed very ill — "and I won't allow you any comment whatsoever. Better not to go. If you want to make his acquaintance I'll take you to him — but no malicious comments!" Brecht often displayed a startling maliciousness, towards foolish people that is! But of course Brecht couldn't fail to notice that this old, bird-like man wasn't a fool but a *petit bourgeois* genius. Also present at this conversation was Helene Weigel, my old friend Helli. It was conducted in precisely that sharp way and accepted by Brecht with a certain satisfaction and respect: Eisler knows how to protect his teacher even before I meet him, so I too will have to behave politely. I have to say, Brecht kept his word. There was not a loud or indecent (*unvornehmes*) — I deliberately use this expression from polite society — word. Brecht listened to Schoenberg with the greatest respect and there was no clash. On the contrary: Schoenberg, who had no idea who Brecht was, observed this odd-looking man with interest — he did look like a mixture of Ignatius of Loyola and a Roman consul in Bavaria, didn't he?

Well, to continue: Schoenberg's home — situated not at Sunset Boulevard as Brecht writes, but at Brentwood (I'm only being pedantic in saying that) — was a real hell. It was a private hell. Even his private life was a twelve-note hell. That is, when a seventy-year-old man has a six-year-old son who is unbearable, though he was a very nice lad (I'm not just saying that, he really was an exceptionally nice boy) . . .
This mess of disorganization in his private life, with small children — Schoenberg's eldest daughter was forty-four years old, his youngest son six. So, these twelve-note family relations, where, for instance, the children of Schoenberg's forty-four-year-old daughter had to address the little man, the six-year-old, as 'uncle', they were hell, and Brecht had a very keen sense of that.

Brecht was deeply impressed by the keenness of Schoenberg's intellect. In *Sinn und Form*[2] I wrote how I encouraged Brecht to write the text of a cantata in honour of Schoenberg's birthday — the seventy-second, I think — for which I wrote the music. I hope I'll find

---

[2] Eisler contributed to the second *Sinn und Form* Brecht *Sonderheft,* Berlin 1957. *Bertolt Brecht und die Musik.* In *Schriften* 1948–1962 p.371 ff.

the sketches — which are entitled 'I learned from a donkey',[3] that is, I hope my dear friend Professor Notowicz[4] will find them. You should read the text of this cantata. Last August I met Frau Schoenberg in Salzburg, but she couldn't remember it. I'm convinced Frau Schoenberg will be able to find this cantata text — unpublished poem, that is — if there is sufficient research.[5] Schoenberg left an immense estate. And now please help me get back to the subject: the lecture at the University — Brecht's behaviour at Schoenberg's home . . . I think it was the first or perhaps the second time he was there, and I was trembling taking him because I didn't want to have my old teacher insulted — Then there is the talk with Schoenberg when I would . . . You know how respectfully I used to do these things. I also used to talk Brecht into completing certain projects. I didn't get far with him either. For instance, that play about the man that used to build his stoves so well, Hans Garbe, Productivity Hero. And when Brecht, shortly before his death, told me about his project on Einstein, again I talked him into it. And the same thing happened when he told me about a third project. That's something I have to put on paper sometime: Mother Germania suckling her sons, the wolves, at her breasts. Helli Weigel was there that time. This one was never written down, I think. But now I've got completely carried away and will have to go back.

B: You were about to recount how you urged Schoenberg on to complete his operas.

E: Well, these operas were never completed. What does a pupil's admonition mean to the master! In the meantime Schoenberg's opera *Moses und Aron*, based on an awful text by Schoenberg himself, has been staged as a fragment, and it made an immense impression, also on Brecht. But the other-work, *Jacob's Ladder*, hasn't even been performed

---

[3] According to Eisler's account of the meeting in the *Sinn und Form* article, Schoenberg told the following story; 'Once I was walking up a hill and, since I have a weak heart, I found the steep path very difficult. But in front of me was a donkey. He didn't go up the steep path but trotted, serpentine, off to the left and right, thereby evening out the incline. So I copied him and can therefore say — I've learnt from a donkey.'

[4] Nathan Notowicz 1911–1968, German musicologist. In 1958 he had held a series of conversations with Eisler. See Bibliography.

[5] The text remains undiscovered.

as a fragment.[6] So we may say that the opera whose completion I urged, has become one of the most imposing fragments in the literature of modern music. I am deeply moved by hearing all this now. As you know, I am not a young man any more; at times I get sentimental. What else is there at the end of that passage?

B: The anecdote about Schoenberg's gloves.

E: Well, let me tell you: Schoenberg in the army — I'm telling this not only for the Brecht Archives, but also for my friend Notowicz —, Schoenberg behaved very strangely in the army.
He was drafted in 1915 and served in a very famous local Viennese regiment, the 2nd *Deutsch- und Hochmeister Regiment*. Somehow, the officers knew he was a well-known musician. But he was considered crazy and the music critics had already treated him abominably. And that's why the colonel — you know what a colonel in the Imperial Army was, don't you? He was a god — the soles of whose shoes we hardly ever saw — had him summoned and said to him: "Tell me, soldier, are you *the* Schoenberg?" Said Schoenberg: "Well, you know . . . Yes Colonel, I am." How dare that mere little colonel . . .? "Nobody wanted to be, somebody had to, so I volunteered."

That is a typical saying of Schoenberg's, which also gives much pleasure to a marxist. Let me add that Schoenberg composed a military march for that regiment which was never played because it was rejected by the band master as too dissonant. I'm sure it will be found in the estate.[7] That's that!

B: What was the impression Brecht made on Schoenberg?

E: Schoenberg said to me: "I know during the Weimar Republic you wrote that *Massnahme* with him, in Berlin. I've never heard it. My students said it wasn't worth anything — without even having attended the performance. They said it wasn't that interesting, and they wouldn't

[6] Eisler and Brecht will doubtless have seen the production of *Moses und Aron* in the West Berlin Charlottenburg Theatre conducted by Scherchen in the fifties. Musically wonderful, dramaturgically and visually embarrassing, it must have confirmed Eisler's view of the work. The first 180 bars of Die Jakobsleiter were conducted by Hans Rosbaud in Hamburg in 1958. The complete fragment was performed in the Grosse Konzertsaal, Vienna in 1961, conducted by Rafael Kubelik.

[7] *Die eiserne Brigade*, march for string quartet and piano, 1916.

listen to it." After that — Schoenberg told me — he violently rebuked one of the students, one of the younger ones, shouting: "How dare you not listen to a work of one of my best students?" So the students who intended to flatter Schoenberg by telling him they wouldn't listen to my works any more, got a terrible telling off. He had no idea about Brecht. I would just repeat to him that he was the greatest German poet of the last fifty years. "Well", Schoenberg just said, "let's hope so."

Gespräche pp 60–64

From the Sixth Conversation — 18 July 1961.

B: Who actually sings your songs "well"

E: We need to talk about genres. In vocal music there are many different genres, types of music. For instance, my Mayakovsky settings[8] are incomparably sung by Busch.[9] There is no one in the world who sings them better. He sings them well because he understands them. Whoever understands how to avoid sentimentality, bombast, pathos and all kinds of stupidity, to recite the text well but nevertheless to sing it, will sing them well. There are some talents. It's no use naming them. Frankly, I see a lot of difficulties in all that. Almost every year one or two volumes of my Collected Works are published. But I am far from seeing singers who could sing them. What can I do? Schubert, too, is being sung appallingly badly. Well, first of all, one should have a good voice, great musicality and something I call 'musical intelligence'. This means, the text has to be sung 'controversially'. To put it absolutely simply, when singing the word 'Springtime' the singer won't indicate Spring by putting emotion in his voice. These are very difficult issues which you may read about in my theoretical works.[10] There is no simple answer to them. Anyway, there will come a singer who isn't stupid. He will sing well, if necessary without much of a voice.

B: Besides your Collected Works there are also records being issued.

---

[8] *Linker Marsch, Lied von Subbotnik, Marsch der Zeit, Regimenter gehn.* All composed in 1957.

[9] Ernst Busch 1900-1980. German actor and singer. Devoted to Busch as he was, Eisler was able to say of him — 'there is no-one who sings flat with such genius.'

[10] Especially the articles 'On Stupidity in Music'. *Schriften* 1948–1962 pp. 338-401. Translated in Hanns Eisler *A Rebel in Music p. 188 ff.*

Let's assume you agree with the production of these records — do you also agree with the interpretations?

E: By no means. Records are issued by the most different singers. I listen to them once. Some of them I think are atrocious, some are excellent. But I feel too tired to concern myself with every bit of nonsense. When the record company engages a singer to sing a song of mine which in performance becomes complete nonsense, I can't help it.

Neither could Brecht concern himself if a play of his was staged in the right or wrong way; not at, say, Greifswald — although he had a huge set-up and could send assistants to Greifswald or to Plauen. I don't have a set-up, I can't go and listen to everyone who sings or records a work of mine. I must say, I reject that altogether.

Mostly, I find records of my works awful and I reject them. But I'm no Don Quixote. I can't reform a whole recording industry according to my taste. I should very much like to do that, but it is not feasible. To give you an example: I prohibited two records because they were badly made. Well, I went to see the people — I had to have a rehearsal, hadn't I — and told them: "Look, dear friends, I wrote *andante con moto* (♩ = 112), and you play it like a tragic *largo*. With this, you ruin the music. Why do you do that? What else do you want me to write in the score to tell you how to get the tempo right? Reading a text that denotes mourning, your mood is turned to mourning. Haven't you really learned that grief can also be sung in a cheerful way, which makes grief even deeper than in this boring way?" Well, dear Dr. Bunge, you see, these are pains which I don't have words to describe. My hopes rest on the next twenty years. That's all I have to say about that.

I can't worry about every performance of a song, symphony or piece of chamber music of mine. Mostly they are badly played and I protest as much as I can, without injuring these impossible singers, conductors and chamber musicians too much, who are really doing their best. Unfortunately, *their* best is not yet *the* best.

B: Which one of those who sing your songs do you prefer?

E: I won't refer to names here — except that of Ernst Busch who really is a singer of genius. The songs for *Sturm* (that is, the songs composed to texts of Mayakovsky) are sung by Busch with such genius, there is no one in East and West to match him. To him I take my hat off. But apart from him I won't refer to anyone by name nor will I suggest anybody else.

What I do suggest is to fight stupidity in music. As you know I am working on an essay — I have already published three chapters-: 'On stupidity in music'. Believe me, that's what matters more than anything to me.

When I attended a concert of workers' choirs in Paris six years ago, I met an old friend of mine from England[11] who had been working for years in the Labour Movement. I said to him afterwards "Do you know, my dear friend, since my youth I've been fighting against stupidity in music, but today I must confess I have been overcome." That is, when I listened to the traditional, stupid singing of superb, well-trained French worker singers.

Which doesn't mean I won't continue fighting against stupidity in music. *So far* I have been conquered. I have really been fighting since my earliest years against this kind of stupidity. Well, one must stick at it. One must not tire of fighting stupidity, and indeed, all bad musical traditions. It's not just up to me. Believe me, none of the famous singers really interprets Schubert or Schumann or Brahms or Hugo Wolf in the right way. The barbarity in musical interpretation is astonishing. I could play records of these famous singers to demonstrate their bad interpretations.

Needless to say, it wouldn't get me anywhere. Neither am I interested in getting anywhere. But it is quite astonishing how even the classics are misunderstood. Schumann becomes *schmaltz*, Schubert — that highly original, nervous composer — becomes a kind of light music — quite astonishing. Even with the best performers. And with symphonic music it's the same. When, for example, a famous conductor who was holding a conducting course here asked me what to teach the pupils I said to him: "Well, show them the way the first two bars of Beethoven's *Eroica* should be played, [Eisler sings] 'shrum, shrum', and then 'tum ti tum ta'. You see?[12] That's how it begins and how it ends. This barbarity in music has been inherited by us from the bourgeoisie. We have to get rid of it. Strangely enough, a lot of our culture-functionaries — especially the inflexible ones — have a high respect for this barbarity, which at times is difficult for me to fight.

---

[11] Most probably Alan Bush.

[12] Not having heard the original tape, I can only assume that the point Eisler is making is clear from his delivery — the contrast between emphatic chords and lyrical cello line.

B: To what extent does the taste of the public determine stupidity in music, that is to say, stupid musical performances?

E: The public is not stupid, the specialists are. My favourite saying is: Everybody is musical, is musically talented. But when music teachers are let loose and teach the child, within four years he will have lost his musicality; which means — something every biologist will assure you of — Man is born musical and loses his musicality only because of a certain way of education. That's a very important statement!

B: What you want to say is that if there were more good performers, the taste of the public could be improved considerably in a relatively short time?

E: That would be a little too utopian. Let me put it this way. If you managed to educate music teachers who in the *Kindergarten* would provide a good musical education for children from four or six years on, then we'd probably get a new audience. If we teach the children! In the socialist system, in the GDR, everything is primarily a matter of education. It is quite unimportant if a gentleman in tails conducts Beethoven's *Ninth Symphony* in this way or the other. What *is* important is the way six-year-old children in Thale, Thuringia, Mecklenburg, in small villages, in collective farms get their musical education. So, our task is not only to educate and to teach, but to teach the teachers! Unfortunately we haven't come so far, in the field of music, that is. For the time being, this would be the most important task.

Just as important also is what is played — or is *not* played — in symphony concerts. But to me it is more important to educate music teachers so as to educate children in the right way, cultivate their ear, their understanding of music. That would be the most important thing.

This is fully appreciated, too, by our state authorities. But the difficulties are great. They can't, all of a sudden, send twenty thousand teachers, who among other things have some knowledge of music, to primary schools, can they? Such are the difficulties, the growing-up difficulties, in the GDR. Don't have any illusions, though. It is not a question of refining the taste of the concert public — rather, it is but *one* of the questions. The main question is laying the foundations of musical education — which begins at the age of six in the *Kindergarten*.

B: Could you please specify that?

E: Cultivating the children's ears, educating their ears towards acquiring a sense of good taste, making them musical. They are musical already, man is born musical – a quality which he unfortunately is deprived of by musical training. The musical education to be practised – there are a lot of practical traditions and examples of how to do that – should not destroy the child's musicality, but encourage it. This can be done straight away.

For example, Brecht could just as well demand that children learn to read and write. I would demand Brecht's public to have read or listened to or watched at least a few classical plays to be able to see what the difference is with Brecht. What is the difference between Wallenstein and Galilei? Wallenstein is terribly irresolute. Wallenstein, in Schiller's presentation, is a kind of Hamlet, a kind of Austrian Hamlet- actually a Weimarian Hamlet. And what is Galilei like? Galilei, too, wavers. Hamlet, also wavers. Wallenstein also wavers. If you, as a literary scholar, really dealt with literature you would have to carry out studies which would help the young generation, just as it happens in my field, really to understand literature (unless we relied only on spontaneous talents). These studies would be very interesting. Unfortunately, nobody does it.

Although I have read something about Brecht in our Republic, something about Schiller, something about Shakespeare, I have never read anything about the connections between these great masters. For instance, about the unsteadiness of a character. A character is represented as unsteady, as developing. There are some great examples of this, but where have they been described? Nowhere.

Now, dear Dr. Bunge, although you in your field, literary studies, didn't carry out the aforesaid necessary studies, you demand it from our primary school music teachers whose job it is, God help them, to teach folksongs at Incy-Wincy-on-the-Unstrut[13] in order to turn the little children into experts on music. Although it is not our aim to make them just experts. What we want, and it is a difficult issue, is for music to enrich man. This is where I hesitate: Do we want our dear comrades from Unstrut to be inspired when a gentleman, a conductor, conducts a Beethoven symphony?

That is certainly something we want – but what is really the task of music? To what extent can it purify dirty feelings? To what extent can it deepen, enrich a man's life? For the didactic side of music is unfortunately not so simple as in literature.

---

[13] *Klein-Winzig an der Unstrut.* Eisler's invention denoting somewhere in the wilds.

All these are issues that haven't even been touched so far. So I suggest that you, after your suggestions to me, show either in a brilliant dissertation or in a small book, for example the unsteadiness, the development of a character in literature. A lot of people will learn a lot: the audience, the writers and the directors. We have an excellent school, the Brecht School. We all saw *'Frau Flinz'*[14] Somehow they are able to perform that, and I must say, quite superbly.

B: Is it more difficult when it comes to music without words?

E: It certainly is. By the way, music without words is not an immanent, but a historical phenomenon. For pure concert music, apart from church sonatas and some kinds of court music, has existed only since the middle of the eighteenth century. It can't be dated exactly, sometime from 1750 on. It was created for people who had a certain interest and pleasure in so-called concert music. 'Pure music' is an utterly crazy expression. Concert music first appeared at courts. Certain church forms were adopted by the courts. They were not secularized until the eighteenth century.

Talking about concert music means talking about bourgeois music. Bourgeois music is independent of chronology. It begins whenever music secularizes itself, makes itself independent from the church. At this point a new curious phenomenon appears — the free-ranging man who expresses himself in music. This is something extremely modern, then, and is still beyond our comprehension.

Having arisen from these circumstances, music cannot easily be adopted by our early forms of socialism. With great pleasure I hear that, here in the GDR, concerts devoted exclusively to Beethoven play to full houses. With displeasure I hear that opera houses playing only Wagner are also sold out. Anyway, we have reached a stage where great numbers of our worker public eagerly attend these events, especially the Beethoven concerts.

To give a quick explanation of that would be asking too much of me. 'Pure listening' — not 'pure music', but 'pure listening' — to abstract music (an idiotic expression, which simply means 'music without words') was quite a new experience during the eighteenth century. What our position on this should now be is not quite clear. What is visible and audible right now is that we can adopt that great heritage, that we have

[14] Comedy by Hermann Baierl. Premiere on 8 May 1961 by the Berliner Ensemble.

adopted it and will continue adopting it. It is difficult for today's music to deal with it.

Look, at the moment I'm writing a symphony for the Leipzig Gewandhaus Orchestra.[15] Believe me, I'm atoning for all my sins — because a) for whom am I writing? For the Gewandhaus Orchestra, those great specialists. b) who will be my listeners? The people of the GDR, who hardly know this tradition of classical music. So I have to offer them something new, skipping over classical music. Believe me, I often sit at my desk in the mornings, holding my head in my hands to solve this task.

I don't want to express *myself* — and would get terribly bored because I have absolutely nothing to express. To produce something practical, useful but also new, and to maintain the standards of my musical thinking — for me that's terribly complicated. The best advice I can give you, dear comrade Bunge, is: Let's not politicize everything! Let's remove some areas of aesthetics and let's not politicize them in so simple-minded a way.

There are remnants from former ages which somehow still survive here, for example the conductor and his eighty musicians dressed in tails. Let's not politicise that. Some of my friends politicize light music in an idiotic manner, judging if something is more American or less American. Believe me, I consider that to be imbecile. Overpoliticizing the arts leads to barbarity in aesthetics. Maybe that is a new proposition. Well, if it's new, it's good.

B: When you say 'politicize' you mean . . .

E: A certain worthless kind of aesthetics, a politicization of aesthetics which leads nowhere. Our young people like to dance boogie-woogie. Politically speaking, we are opposed to that. But on the aesthetic side the young people win because they like to dance it. We don't need this politicizing. As communists and socialists we have such merits that it isn't necessary to politicize every bit of rubbish and to estimate if it corresponds to our ideology. That's idiotic.

B: Those on the other hand who are against dancing boogie-woogie argue that by means of boogie-woogie "several other things sneak in and take possession of our youth".

---

[15] Eisler was working on this at the time of my studies with him. He took pains to conceal from me that progress on it was minimal. The sketches he left are not extensive.

E: Quite right. That's very serious, and as my friends aren't malicious people and won't begrudge young people their way of dancing, they have a sinister feeling that by means of this boogie-woogie — today it's called something else — Americanism steals in. That is completely right. But you can't fight Americanism aesthetically, only politically. Let's educate our young people politically so that they a) dance boogie-woogie and b) are resistant to the political influence of Americanism in the GDR.

I have already said that in two meetings, but, to be honest, without success. It's true the young people were enthusiastic about my being in favour of boogie-woogie, while my friends in the Presidium were against my saying that it should be permitted. But that's how things are. One must not hasten to politicize every aesthetic phenomenon. Maybe, one could give it a Marxist analysis, which is something different. In the difficult situation we were, we are and will be in, cheap aesthetics will implicate us in idiotic contests for which we have neither time, strength nor manpower. For me, it's impossible to talk five hundred apprentices of a big factory out of dancing boogie-woogie and recommend the English waltz instead as the better solution — to give you an example which was told to me. That's nonsense.

Certain kinds of mass hysteria, like American jazz or what certain American religious sects practise, must certainly be prohibited. In this respect I favour police measures. When events end in breaking chairs and stubbing out lighted cigarettes in the palms of girls who collect tickets in the *S-* and *U-Bahn* — all this under the influence of boogie-woogie — of course I'm against it and in favour of prohibition by the police. As regards this I'm a stubborn sergeant-major.
As long as these things don't happen and we are able to keep a check on it, I prefer to regulate it with a certain elegance so as to show we are not unworldly. Look, a Leninist is never unworldly. We just cannot build up every bit of nonsense in the world into a political question. Otherwise, we'd get stuck at the outset.

B: So you think that dancing boogie-woogie doesn't necessarily lead to ecstasy?

E: That may happen, but it doesn't. We can fight boogie-woogie only by politically educating our young people, not just with phraseology but with a real political education! A real young socialist . . .When I was young, in 1919, I used to hop around just like all the others of my age. Maybe you too, dear Dr. Bunge. So that is not the problem. But when people are politically ill-mannered, politically malicious, influenced by the West, and take up against us the attitude of a crook, then boogie-woogie will have its disastrous effects. Let's have good young people! Let's fortify ourselves politically, but not aesthetically! We can't afford to fortify ourselves aesthetically because the American entertainment industry has immense influence everywhere in the world. The American entertainment industry has rendered whole peoples musically illiterate, and continues doing so.

With great pleasure I read that the pop singer Eddie Fisher, the day before yesterday, after he was given a reception by Comrade Furtseva[16] in the Kremlin, sang some pop songs and had great success. The Russians are much more sensible than we are. We can't talk away the attractiveness of American light music with political arguments because, for example, it is "not national". I've heard this objection, too. Neither is the English waltz national. Neither is the waltz German, it's Austrian. Well, if we take to these arguments, it makes no sense at all.

So: no politicizing of questions of aesthetics, but reflecting on what can be done, how the issue could be broadened. But let's not be too hasty! And above all, let's not be arrogant on these issues. We easily are . . . It's a weakness of the great Marxists that in the field of aesthetics we often act foolishly.

Gespräche pp.148–157

From the Eighth Conversation — 24 August 1961.

B: As an example of stupidity in music you recently quoted the setting to music of Goethe's text *'Ich ging im Walde so für mich hin'* [When I was strolling through the woods] by a living composer. Your verdict was very harsh. You yourself set texts by Goethe, Hölderlin and others of the past to music. So I think I am justified in asking: Where does the difference lie?

E: That's a very serious question. Talking about socialist realism means talking about oneself first. Whatever I choose and read is subject to control by myself. And the controllers are my temperament, my talent, my political experience, my intelligence. Of course my understanding of Hölderlin is different from that of a *petit bourgeois*. My understanding of Beethoven, too, is different — and that of Bach. I could play Bach's Mass

[16] The then Minister of Culture of the Soviet Union.

in B minor to you in such a way that you would be surprised at 'what a wonderful piece it is', even according to our interpretation, that is, as a piece of great humanism.

Before setting a poem to music the first thing I do is make a careful choice. Then I shorten it. I only set fragments. Brecht said to me in Hollywood (you will find that in his diary, by the way): "It is quite fascinating the way you take the plaster off Hölderlin! You select some lines, set them to music, and somehow it fits.[17] He was a) appalled (as was my friend Arnold Zweig) — and certainly it is an impudence — but b) both of them were actually in favour of it, because from a poem of Hölderlin's which often has four pages of strophes, I picked out eight lines which were appropriate.

How come a great man of letters or a great poet like Brecht or Arnold Zweig could say to me: "Eisler, you are criticizing Hölderlin!" I wasn't criticizing him, I was quoting him. That's the main thing! And it is an example, too, of stupidity in music. A stupid composer wouldn't do a thing like that. He may have more musicality than me, he may be even more talented than me — but in this he can't beat me.

For example, in those most difficult times of emigration, I set a poem — that is to say, some eight lines — by Hölderlin[18] to music about which Brecht became quite furious and said: "Man, you really are a nationalist!" I deliberately say it in his dialect. (If you like I will play it to you). There is a shameless nationalism in it — because in fact, during my emigration years, I would at times remember Germany — not sentimentally, but through the eyes of Hölderin, who — as you know — was an early Jacobin.

So, intelligence does not only relate to the selection of the texts but also to the way one treats them. If I identify myself completely with the text, empathise with it, hover behind it, well, that's dreadful. A composer has to view a text in a way full of contradictions. The tragic element is interpreted by me cheerfully. I remember how enthusiastic my friend Brecht was when I composed *In Praise of Dialectics*, which has a purely joyful character. If ever I'm praised for anything, it will be for resisting the text. I resisted the contents of the poem and perceived

---

[17] Bunge has pointed out in his editorial notes to the Conversations that no such passage exists in Brecht's Journal and suggests that the introduction Brecht wrote for Eisler's volumes of *Lieder und Kantaten* might be what is referred to: 'He doesn't simply serve up the text, he treats it and gives it something which is essentially Eisler.

[18] *Erinnerung*, the last of the Six *Hölderlin Fragments* 1943. See Chapter 13.

it in my way. That's part of musical intelligence, and he who does not do it is stupid.

B: Which means that whatever has been written, has not been written for eternity but is subject to changes. Whenever you deal with it, it takes on a certain definite meaning which is connected with the time in question.

E: That's a brilliant remark, Dr. Bunge. That is to say, art also changes in tradition. Look, when I returned from the First World War, in 1919, I could never have set a poem like, for example, *An eine Stadt,*[19] because I was fed up with patriotism. The years of emigration, which sharpened the senses, had to come, and also the retrospection, the art of remembering. You know, it is a great art, to remember. *You* can't have it because you are younger than me. But once you have been an emigrant for fourteen years, remembering this damned Germany, you get a different view of things. You look back — without sentimentality. Brecht, too, has written some wonderful things about it. A stupid composer would have turned all that into sentimental trash.

My remembering was "cool, polite, gentle". This "cool, polite, gentle" is already a contradiction in itself. But remembering is also a part of musical intelligence.

B: Is sentimentality in any case and in any form to be condemned?

E: Yes, but not sentiment. The Germans — as you know well — are an unhappy people. We are just sentimental and brutal. We have but two horrible categories: either we exterminate people, gas Jews and send our young people against Russian tanks — or we are sentimental, singing: *Ich weiß nicht was soll es bedeuten* . . . For my part I would change that line into: "I know very well what it means . . .". That is the "national defect" which is not national but can be explained by means of the method of production in Germany. This country was industrialized very early. The industrial revolution began in the first third of the nineteenth century. It had certain shortcomings: that the central power never got a look-in, as had France under Henri IV or England under Elizabeth I. As you know, Germany was not able to bring about national unification until after the war of 1871 when it was imposed from above, by Prussia. A lousy unification, that. Marx, in his writings on the war against Napoleon III, announced his demands, hoping that through unification

[19] Number Five of the Hölderlin Fragments

a bigger house for the German workers could be built — which would mean not a particularistic but a national workers' movement. I enjoy remembering this proposition of Marx. For me that's colossal. So these serious defects have nothing to do with nationalism, race or anything like that.

But we still have these defects today. How long was Germany united? From 1871 to 1945. You will agree: it's a disgrace! Yes, who has, has. That's all we have. For a nation — to use a big word — that's somewhat little. But it's not a national question but one of economy. Today, again we are divided. And I say it openly — we deserve it. And yet the Germans have Karl Marx, Friedrich Engels, Karl Liebknecht, Rosa Luxemburg — I am not talking about poets and artists etc., that is, the blossom of culture.

During my emigration years I wrote a song which made Brecht go pale and say: "How can you compose something like that!" That was about the time of Stalingrad. I am ready to sing it to you so that you may see that, in a time when you were very nationalist, dear Dr. Bunge, I was as nationalist as you were — only in a different way. This poem is a fragment from Hölderlin. I wrote it in 1944[20] — at a time when nobody would give a damn for us Germans. You, dear Dr. Bunge, were in a prisoner-of-war camp in the Soviet Union, I think, while I was sitting in Hollywood. Financially, I was well off. But it rankled me that these poor Germans are and were such bastards. They were bastards.
I'll read the poem now, a very famous one:[21]

Erinnerung.
O heilig Herz der Völker, o Vaterland!
Allduldend, gleich der schweigenden Mutter Erd',
Und allverkannt, wenn schon aus deiner
Tiefe die Fremden ihr Bestes haben.
Sie ernten den Gedanken, den Geist von dir,
Sie pflücken gern die Traube, doch höhnen sie
Dich, ungestalte Rebe, da du
Schwankend den Boden und wild umirrst.
Doch magst du manches Schöne nicht bergen mir.
Oft stand ich, überschauend das sanfte Grün,
Den weiten Garten, hoch in deinen
Lüften auf hellem Gebirg', und sah dich.
Und an den Ufern sah ich die Städte blüh'n,
Die edlen, wo der Fleiß in der Werkstatt schweigt,
Die Wissenschaft, wo deine Sonne
Milde dem Künstler zum Ernste leuchtet.

[20] On 2 August 1943 in Pacific Palisades, California.

[21] Of Hölderlin's fifteen quatrains Eisler uses the first, second, fourth and sixth.

Remembrance.
O holy heart of peoples, O Fatherland!
All-suffering like silent Mother Earth,
Misjudged by all when strangers
take from your depth their best.
They harvest your thoughts, your spirit,
readily they pick the grape, but jeer
at you, misshapen vine, as you
creep over the ground staggering and wild.
But many a beauty you would not hide from me.
Often I stood overlooking the gentle green,
the wide garden, high in your air
on a bright mountain, and saw you.
And on the river banks I saw the towns flourish,
noble ones, in whose workshops diligence silently prevails,
I saw science, where your sun
mildly inspires the artist to seriousness.

When I played that to Brecht (you'll find it in his Journal), he was appalled by my nationalism. The idea appealed to me at a moment of deepest humiliation for the German people, which unfortunately I belong to, like you. I can't withdraw from it. I have to admit, it was completely tactless to compose something like that. When the Russians had reached the Oder I said: "They harvest your thoughts, your spirit, readily they pick the grape, yet jeer at you, misshapen vine!" — it's bad taste to compose something like that. I composed it. Do you know why? It's part of the dialectic of the artist. I said to myself that when I got back, I wanted to be able to say:"You bastards! But at least I composed something for you!" What do you think? Is it too severe?

B: No. There is a similar text by Brecht . . .[22]

E: Yes, he wrote that later. Now, this is no slandering of my friend Brecht: when Brecht saw me setting Hölderlin to music — this is not the only one; I set about twenty poems by Hölderlin — he said, savouring his words enthusiastically: ". . . *wo deine Sonne milde dem Künstler zum Ernste leuchtet*". Brecht was totally transported. He had never read this poem before. Brecht was transported, although he said: "Hanns, you are a nationalist!"

B: Your demands on the audience for understanding dialectics are enormous.

[22] The reference is to Brecht's poem *Über Deutschland* of 1940

E: My demands on the intelligence of the artist are enormous. Imagine: me, an old communist, living in America; watching tank battles; watching you, dear Bunge, sacrificing yourself for a wrong cause — and me composing a poem for the glorification of Germany. You must admit: if there is dialectic, then this is it. Would you admit that?

B: Yes, I would. Even more examples are coming to my mind. During those dark years of emigration you wrote the *Deutsche Symphonie* — for how many choral singers?

E: Four hundred people — a hopeless undertaking.

B: A symphony, that is, which — if anywhere — you could perform only in the Staatsoper of the GDR.[23]

E: Yes, but Bertolt Brecht, too, wrote a play like the *Chalk Circle* that could be staged only when the proletarians have power. In short: we wrote for the dictatorship of the proletariat, in the form we call today the *German Democratic Republic*. But is that a reason to praise ourselves? No! I tell you: we had no choice. We can only turn to the bourgeoisie or to our working class, which raised us. You remember that famous poem of Brecht's: " . . . and with pleasure will I go to school again . . ." We are pupils of the working class. We just couldn't do otherwise.

There's no merit in that, no virtue, no courage either — it's nothing. Pupils follow their master. That's all I have to say.

B: You simply wanted to survive.

E: Not even that. I wanted to hand down something.

B: Isn't that the same thing?

E: It is. What I wanted to say was: Imagine I had been struck down by an accident twenty years ago. I just wanted some notes to exist. So that the German workers could see: Well, we know this chap — he delivered something. Like the messenger who arrives, gasping for breath and has something to deliver. I had nothing more in mind. Fame is a secondary thing — which in my position I won't be able to achieve. What would I do with it, anyway? But to deliver something — that's at least

[23] The premiere took place there on 24 April 1959.

something I can do. Believe me: The idea of delivering, of the messenger that runs and still has to deliver a message, has been the greatest idea which I learned from the workers' movement in my younger years. Having to deliver! Doing something useful which can be delivered. Do you think I could sing the song to you now? I'm very hoarse already. Let's try it. *Erinnerung*, fragment from Hölderlin, composed in 1944' (Eisler sings the song, then listens to the recording) That singing is unacceptable, bawled out like at one of those national associations, like *'In Treue fest . . .'*[24]

B: I protest!

E: Dear Bunge, it is eleven o'clock at night now. I'm so eager to talk with you that I'm ready to deliver this hoarse, bawling affair in the hope that one day it will be understood. I would like to add a few afterthoughts: It is well known that the early Christians could meet only illegally. Thus, many rumours about the real nature of Christianity came into being. To what extent even fervent believers were subject to misunderstandings can be seen from a graffito on the Palatine representing Jesus crucified with a donkey's head, while an inscription underneath says: "Alexandros prays to his god." This Alexandros is believed to have been a North African or Egyptian mercenary who transferred the animal-headed Egyptian gods to Christian belief, which he did not know but which appealed to him.

Likewise during a general strike in the Borinage in Belgium, I watched coal miners demonstrating and carrying a portrait of Marx, badly painted by an amateur. He looked like a malicious miner with a black complexion. And he didn't differ much from the strikers. History has to be understood in the same way. These comparisons are very useful. It is not easy to understand them. You haven't got wisdom ready-made in a bag. You have to work hard to earn it. Class struggle may appear in the most different forms, and it is our task to be involved in the struggles, to recognise their different forms and to take part in them. Telling this story of the Borinage brings early feudalism to my mind, an era which made completely different demands on its people.

For instance, a knight . . . and now I'm quoting in English: "A knight was supposed to enjoy music, poetry and dancing and to be an adept of the 'gay science'". Raoul de Houdenc wrote that in 1230. We communists have to take up this proposition, to alienate it and to

[24] Eisler ironically invents a bit of text for a Nazi-style rallying song.

formulate it anew. Under socialism it is not enough for the new man to have this — that's a very primitive way of putting it — but he must have much more. The new, though, comes only from the old. Brecht has already said the same thing:[25]

Am Grunde der Moldau wandern die Steine,
es liegen drei Kaiser begraben in Prag,
Das Große bleibt groß nicht und klein nicht das Kleine
Die Nacht hat zwölf Stunden, dann kommt schon der Tag.

Stones roll on Moldau's ground,
three emperors lie buried in Prague.
Great remains not great, and small not small.
Twelve hours has the night, then day will come.

Let's not forget that. Because the danger for all of us, as we strive and struggle for the new, is of forgetting the old; the old, critical things which we know about. That sounds banal — unfortunately it's the truth.

Gespräche pp 191–197

From the Eleventh Conversation — 6 November 1961

E: As you know, for about twenty or thirty years it has been my practice to arrange verses by great poets for my needs. Especially from Hölderlin, who over-writes (*überschreibt*) — which, by the way, was Schiller's reproach: Hölderlin's profusion — I pick what I find readable today. That is, I read Hölderlin with the eyes of 1961. I'm going to read you some lines which I assembled from Hölderlin. The original poem is called *Der Gang aufs Land* (Stroll in the countryside). You will find it in the second volume of the *Kleine Stuttgarter Ausgabe.*

I advise you to read the original, afterwards. I won't recite the original because of lack of time. My *montage* reads as follows:

Komm! ins Offene, Freund! zwar glänzt ein Weniges heute
Nur herunter und eng schließet der Himmel uns ein.
Weder die Berge sind noch aufgegangen des Waldes
Gipfel lacht uns und leer ruht vom Gesange die Luft.
Trüb ist es heut, es schlummern die Gäng und die Gassen und fast will
Mir es scheinen, es sei, als in der bleiernen Zeit.

---

[25] *The Song of the Moldau* from Brecht's *Sveyk in the Second World War* which was first performed in Warsaw on 17 January 1957. Eisler's score is extensive.

Dennoch gelinget der Wunsch, Wissende zweifeln an einer
Stunde nicht. Denn nichts Mächtiges ist unser Singen.
Zum Leben aber gehört es, was wir wollen.
Kommen doch auch der segenbringenden Schwalben
Immer einige noch, ehe der Sommer, ins Land.

Come! into the open, friend! There is but little brightness today
from up yonder, and heaven encircles us tightly.
Neither have the mountains arisen nor are the forest's
tops visible, and empty rests of song the air.
Gloomy is the day, lanes and alleys slumber;
it almost seems to me
like a leaden age.
The wish, though, is fulfilled, the knowing ones won't
doubt because of *one* moment. For nothing powerful is our singing.
It's part of life, though, what we will.
For there are always several of those beneficial swallows
which arrive here before the summer comes.

These few lines I extracted from a rather lengthy poem, and I'm looking forward with pleasure to the thunderstorm of the literary historians. But, as I have said before, Brecht, for example, considered the 'deplastering' *(Entgipsung')* of Hölderlin and the re-reading from today's point-of-view very useful.

But I see you have some more remarks which we can deal with right now. This was but an interlude''Reading Hölderlin on a gloomy day in November''.

B: I would like to ask a question as regards that. Do you follow any principles in compiling such a selection and *montage*?

E: Curiously enough, there are no principles. It is not a scientific method but an artistic one. Which means, you read a poem and try — without being a barbarian — to assemble whatever seems important to you today.

It becomes obvious — when you read the poem again — that it expresses great doubt. But this doubt, as the poet has it, means that the knowing one — or, as Hölderlin says: the orthodox, the true believer — won't doubt just because of one moment. That's a great thought. It means that a communist who may be in a bad mood for a while won't take this moment to be the general situation, but will just call it a moment of bad temper.[26] This seemed to me a truly poetical notion,

[26] In his note, Bunge makes the point that here and later, Eisler's interpretation is of his *montage*, not of the original.

which should be preserved in the music — I shall compose it — because otherwise it will get lost.

As I've often said before: The task of music is to preserve, like a fly in amber, such poetical notions and images lest they get lost. For, who is going to read *Der Gang aufs Land*, dedicated to Landauer, by Hölderlin in the second volume if not comrade Eisler when he hasn't anything to do? Another thought is the *Komm! ins Offene, Freund!* — Come! into the open, friend — a beautiful phrase with lots of meaning. Transferred to prose its meaning would be": 'Let's come to the point!' — which is"empty rests of song the air". That too, was the state of the composer who at that very moment wasn't composing. Also "gloomy is the day". It seems "to be like a leaden age". This is one of those phrases of genius we find only in Hölderlin. It reminds us of Ovid's *Metamorphoses:* the iron age, the golden age. Hölderlin is talking about the leaden age. 'Lead' here means the non-shining, the suppressing, the dull — things that appeal to one during a gloomy moment. Further down: "the wish, though, is fulfilled, the knowing ones" — that's what I say; Hölderlin has: *true believers* — "won't doubt because of *one* moment". I have already explained that.

To me, especially to us, who not only believe in the social function of art but have practised it, it seems wonderful to sing the praises of antagonism."For nothing powerful is our singing. It's part of life, though, what we will." That's a great proposition which contains the positive as well as the negative. Of course every artist — the musician, too — believes that his work is of decisive importance for the whole of society. But Hölderlin says: "For nothing powerful is our singing. It's part of life, though, what we will." — which is much more concrete, joyful, better than a somewhat vague naivety which believes that through one song the whole world can be redeemed. On the other hand — as you know — songs like the *Marseillaise* and the *International* have played an enormous part in world history. So this singing has to be shown from both sides. I show the other side of singing.

Finally, there is also a coquettish attitude in the poem which is especially amusing: "For there are always several of those beneficial swallows which arrive here before the summer comes". This is the coquettish attitude of the artist saying: of course he is far ahead, and he brings the summer — the yet unrecognized summer — like swallows who arrive too early. That early swallows may freeze to death, is another thing. But this coquetry of Hölderlin's and the beauty of the coquetry — or, if you want to avoid the word, a certain kind of melancholy in this coming early — should be preserved, too, like a fly in amber. Look, this is — if you like — a small contribution to my working method when I compose songs. Whatever I said was squeezed out of me by your questions. These thoughts didn't come to my mind while I was reading the poem. On the contrary, I selected the verses according to their poetical beauty. But to me the poetically beautiful is only the useful, the intellectually useful. This is an instinctive process which I tried to explain after your inquiry.

B: Your explanation belongs to our old subject "On stupidity in music" . . .

E: Correct.

B: . . . while you were now giving a positive example of how an old and partly antiquated text can be rendered useful today.

E: If you read critically. That's very difficult. It demands a great deal of practice, also a certain age, I have to say. It needs — I'm telling you a commonplace — a certain experience of life. And of course not the experience of life of a *petit bourgeois,* but that of an old communist. He has to know precisely what is at stake, what he can say and for what use his words are. In this case [i.e. Hölderlin's poem] the words will be useful for the enrichment of a socialist listener.

From many points-of-view something is displayed which is usually called "prevailing mood", that is, autumn. Autumn, too, is socialised, as it were. I socialize autumn. To a bourgeois this must sound like terrible vandalism. But curiously enough, the socialization of autumn . . . an awful expression. But let's put it this way: I can't abandon my social view, even when autumn is coming. It functions there, too — as a reflex.

Once we have got used to thinking and feeling in this way, it can enrich our emotional life and thus cleanse it and promote it towards reason. After listening to my autumn song one wouldn't fall for autumn that easily. Well, maybe I'm saying this in a somewhat pretentious way. A lot of people will continue falling for autumn — but not me. And I try as much as is in my power to prevent people from falling for autumn — yellow leaves falling, early morning mist — but to make them look at it with pleasure, as it's very beautiful, and with enrichment. You're quite right. In normal music — that is, when we talk about great poems set by composers — you won't find these moments. Of course, you find colossal, grand moments. I remember a song by Brahms *Auf einem*

Friedhof — the poem is by Storm, I think[27] — where the poet goes into a cemetery — very beautifully composed by Brahms. It was a rainy day, he had been to the cemetery, had looked at many graves. The final thought, then, is: On all graves there was the word 'Recuperated.' (*Genesen*) That is a Protestant, pietistic attitude which has made me sick since my youth. Because I don't believe death to be recuperation, but the end.

When I was on holiday in Thuringia I visited a small village cemetery. There was a sign at the entrance saying:"We are but guests on earth". That's a famous quotation from the Bible. This saying made me very angry that day as it was raining, as I remember; it was a dull day. I said to myself: So where is the landlord then? And — I said — all that just to be a guest? A despicable humiliation which only religion can offer us.[28] This saying annoyed me very much.

Let's see what we have: Brahms' song *Auf einem Kirchhof* — my memory of the small graves in a village cemetery in Thuringia, with that inscription 'We are but guests on earth' — my protest against that — and this autumnal reflection, for Hölderlin's poem is about an autumn day. Don't think these are artistic principles. There is nothing behind it but the man — there are hundreds of millions, or at least there should be — to whom dialectical materialism has really become his second nature, who looks at a flower and finds it beautiful, and finds other things in it too. So these are not sophisticated attitudes but completely natural behaviour. It's like your drinking coffee or going for walks.

B: So it is a question of attitude, and one rather based on principles because this method . . .

E: The word 'principle' bothers me. A question of attitude. I can't look at the world other than I do.

B: I don't insist on the word 'principles'. What I meant was a practical attitude which results from the philosophy of dialectical materialism.

E: Correct. And *this* way — you know — autumn is twice as beautiful. Leaves are of a better yellow than they are for the metaphysician, and

---

[27] From *Fünf Lieder* Op. 105. Text by Detlev von Liliencron.

[28] The German transcription reads — *'so etwas an Niedrigerkeit Kann uns nur die Religion geben.'* As Bunge says, this beautiful expression may have been just a slip of the tongue.

grief is more moving than for the blockhead who pursues religiosity. The decay and rotting of autumn are more impressive and thought-provoking than they are for the poetical fool. So, that means that to the dialectical materialist the beauty of nature shines brighter, its characteristics — spring, autumn, summer, winter — are more significant by far, indeed may even be elevated to a general situation, a general sensation. So, sensation is not abolished, not replaced by something which blatherers call "cool thinking" — as if there were such a thing — it's not degraded to cool thinking. On the contrary. Autumn blossoms [sic] much more gloriously to me than to the metaphysician, and only then achieves its actual meaning. If you ask me if this puts me into a better mood — a private question — I say: no! The better mood, though, is not a question of art but of private feeling.

B: Is the process really as naive as it presents itself now? Is this *montage* a chance product? Did it come into being because you happened to take a volume of Hölderlin from the shelf? Could you have written the poem — as you assembled it — by yourself?

E: Well, I'm not a poet . . .

B: My question is naughty. Hölderlin represents reality with a poetical image, and the explanations you gave of your *montage* were also poetic. What is the essence of this poetical explanation?

E: I had already been infected by Hölderlin. You can only describe poetry poetically. So, above all I should say: the term 'naive' may be important in art — not only with Schiller ("On naive and sentimental poetry") but with Brecht it is important. But in spite of that, with this question of naive, I can't actually get started with it any more. Because a higher consciousness, which Marxists have, abolishes the term 'naive' in the following way. Actually, naive is only the uncorrupted eye, which apprehends stimuli, sensations, situations as they actually are. Naivety today, for Marxists, would mean a pre-thought (*Vordenken*). Before thinking arrives, the object has to be contemplated. To that extent, 'naive' is right. First I have to look carefully at a tree before I can describe it. Looking is naive. In the same way as wondering is the origin of philosophy — think of Greek philosophy.

Now, you have to discriminate very carefully between things like 'naive' and 'intellectual'. I think, these are basically opposites. One can say: 'naive-unnaive'. If I look at a tree unnaively, it would mean looking at a tree in order to see something. That wouldn't be naive. That would be in the first place inartistic and unscientific. If you like, Einstein was the most naive physicist of all times. He looked at things as if no one had looked at them before. He saw physical processes in a naive way. In this case there *is* naivety. But one has to purge the concept of naivety before one can operate with it. So I suggest you now repeat the word 'naive' in your sense.

B: You interpreted Hölderlin's verse *Komm! ins Offene, Freund*! as meaning 'Let's come to the point!' Is there a factual explanation why you assembled the poem this way?

E: No.

B: What relations are there to our present reality?

E: Well, they are extremely simple and — if you like — naive ones, again. When I was reading Hölderlin it was a gloomy afternoon. There is nothing more to it than that. I didn't have it in mind to read Hölderlin when I woke up early and in the morning was working on something completely different. But in the afternoon, at four o'clock, when I had nothing to do, I took down a volume of Hölderlin to pass the time. And when I was leafing through it, I found this poem. That isn't a naive process, but a chance one, which plays a certain role in the arts. With minor works; the major ones have to be planned.

But poetry especially often has something spontaneous and haphazard, I should even say — the literary historians may cross themselves — something partisan-like. One finds something. In the literary forest I find a poem. Mostly I find them by accident. Even when I wanted to set a poem of Brecht's, I used to find it somewhere, at a certain time, being in a certain mood. This partisan-like feature of the composer, in small forms, which don't demand much planning, is important for the producing process.

B: I'm afraid people won't be satisfied with an explanation as simple as that. Someone learning about your poetic *montage* on 6 November, 1961, may ponder about the connections and become a victim of speculations because he thinks you had certain reasons for your interest, especially today, in this poem of Hölderlin's. Do I assume too much in thinking that?

E: No, you are not going too far. May I say — we're in the same boat — that's a typically German question, as you try, with a certain pedantry, so esteemed by us Germans, we're so thorough — to find a system where none exists. I just have to look out of my window to see that it is autumn. Or to have a walk in my garden, which I avoid because it bores me after a short while. The fallen leaves, too, bore me.
By the way: In one of my volumes you will find: *Buckower Elegie*. I had visited Brecht out there at Buckow, wrote a text and set it to music. I had even become a poet, something rare with me — and I should do it as seldom as possible because I am no poet — and gave a description of falling leaves. I called it *Preussischen Herbst,* and there is the line: "The trees, always stripped of . . ." I don't know the exact words, one would have to look it up.[29] Brecht found it very funny.

It's called *L'automne prussien.* I even chose a French title. Now, that's a classical method of alienation: the observer in Brecht's garden watches the autumn and describes it as *L'automne prussien.* Brecht, too, considered it extremely curious and funny.

Well, these are the simple reactions to everyday life which one is subject to. If I had taken a different book, Mörike, for example, I probably wouldn't have found anything. I like reading poetry. It's part of my profession. So, every now and then when I've nothing to do, I take out a volume of poetry. I have to describe it in this low-key way, Dr. Bunge, otherwise you with your outstanding talent will create a enormous literary theory of the composer, the composition and the words — which unfortunately will be wrong. Because there is this

---

[29] *Wenn der Mond von den Wolken verdeckt wird,*
Scheint er doch im Wasser.
Das ist die Schönheit in diesen gewaltigen Zeiten.
Die Wildenten schreien in Röhricht.
Mein Freund hat keine Flinte.
Da ist kein Lärm, da ist Ruhe.
Preussischer Herbst, die Bäume beraubt schon
Aber noch immer fallen die Blätter.

When the moon is concealed by the clouds,
Yet it shines in the water.
That is the beauty in these violent times.
The wild ducks cry in the reeds.
My friend has no gun.
There is no noise, there is calm.
Prussian autumn, the trees already bare,
But still the leaves keep falling.

partisan-like feature. You will find that in politics, too. Let's not completely abolish the spontaneous, partisan-like — it may even go as far as the anarchistic. As long as it is restrained.

Gespräche pp 218–225
Translated by Wolfgang Pick

19

HANNS EISLER THE THINKER

Georg Knepler

Only a few decades have passed since Hanns Eisler was composing, thinking, making his mark on the world. And yet the circumstances in which he did so appear so distant that it is as if whole worlds separate us from them.

Now one can certainly be affected by Eisler's music without knowing the conditions under which it was composed, nor what he was thinking at the time. In this respect, it is no different from the music of other significant composers.

But Eisler reacted with rare intensity, precision and awareness to the circumstances around him. I refer not only to contemporary events — although there was no shortage of earth-shattering events during Eisler's lifetime — but also to the possibilities and opportunities for mankind to propose an alternative to its wars, its misery and its ignorance, whilst avoiding the word 'utopia', which Eisler certainly would not have considered valid. For that reason something important is lost when one does not know or does not consider in what sense Eisler wished his music to be related to mankind and to the world. It was one of his fundamental beliefs that the composer had to consider more than just his compositional method.

The beginning of Eisler's career as a composer promised a great deal. He was just twenty-one years old when Arnold Schoenberg accepted him into his master class in the autumn of 1919, and encouraged him, as we know, not merely in musical ways. Amongst dozens of musicians who counted themselves his students, Schoenberg spoke only Eisler's name in the same breath with those of Alban Berg and Anton von Webern. He knew that these three were the most important composers to emerge from his circle. Before he was thirty years old, Hanns Eisler was assured of a brilliant career as a composer; he was considered one of the hopes of contemporary music.

Yet this career led into a world threatened by human catastrophes. As a soldier, Eisler only just survived the First World War; he was drafted in 1916, at the age of eighteen. He and others had witnessed with horror that 'marketplaces could become battlefields, and then turn again into the former' — the phrase was formulated by Karl Kraus, the great satirist and poet, whose work Eisler knew and valued. Countless people saw at the time that the bourgeois world (*Bürgerwelt* — also a notion coined by Karl Kraus at that time) possessed, even in theoretical terms, not a single concept which could be used to avoid catastrophic transactions in the future, or to overcome need, misery and ignorance. It is one of many forgotten (or suppressed) facts, that after the First World War hundreds of millions of workers and peasants — not only in Europe, but also in China and in India — looked to revolutionary Russia. And many of the cleverest and most imaginative intellectuals throughout the world had some sympathy for Communism — or at any rate an understanding of it.

In this situation Hanns Eisler took a step which literally changed completely his thoughts and actions, his way of living, his way of composing — his entire life. In the mid-twenties, with the acuteness and logic which distinguished his thinking at all times, he drew his theoretical conclusions and translated them with equal consistency into practical steps. Eisler considered bourgeois musical life to be sterile. For him the concert hall and the opera house were suspect, being too far removed from everyday reality. He challenged his composer colleagues to abstain from 'an age . . . of bombastic symphonic music, played-out chamber music and esoteric songs', to discover 'real people, everyday life.'

It was inevitable that such profound changes in Eisler's conception of the world and of music would also affect his relationship with his revered teacher. It so happens that an exchange of letters between Schoenberg and Eisler from the year 1926 has for the most part been preserved, and from this the argument can be reconstructed. It is among the most instructive documents of contemporary musical history. It not only reveals far-reaching problems, but also shows the noblest side of both men. They do not play down the profound differences between their respective outlooks, but express them with a rare incisiveness, without thereby overlooking or denying the esteem in which they held one another. Schoenberg did not consider Eisler's concern for questions of humanity dishonest. He himself had also attempted, with the aid of the written word, to involve himself in issues concerning human existence — in 1917 with an outline plan for achieving and ensuring peace, and in 1947 with the essay *Menschenrechte* (Human Rights). Admittedly, he thought that an artist should above all articulate himself in artistic terms, and there are indications that Schoenberg's *Männer-*

chöre Opus 35 (1929–30) and also his *Moses und Aron* (1930–32) are related to the disagreement with Eisler. The sentence with which Schoenberg concluded his correspondence with Eisler — and which ushered in an estrangement and distance between the two which was to last for years —, is amongst the most beautiful one can imagine: 'And if I can help you in any way, you well know that it would be a fresh injustice on your part not to tell me. — Best regards.!

Eisler, for his part, saw before him a path which appeared not to cross nor even to intersect with that of Schoenberg, his students, his school, his conceptual world, his way of composing or his public. And yet his high regard for Schoenberg was not affected by this. Even in difficult times, Eisler did not deny it, and it persisted throughout his life.

Inherent in Eisler's position, however, was also that illusion which contributed to the failure to reach his objective, for which there was no alternative. His setting himself apart from bourgeois musical life, the separation from everything 'modern', the appropriation of reason to himself alone, implied the vice of impatient revolutionaries: forgetting that in many questions the other person can also be right and that one can err oneself.

Eisler determined on a new audience, on new forms of contact with that audience and a new way of writing, in order to bring his music closer to them. He allied himself with the most active and revolutionary-minded section of the workers' movement. Although he himself was not a member of any party, throughout his life he was close to the German and Soviet Communists.

Attempts have been made to show that Eisler's music suffered as a result of this — or that some of his works must be placed in a subordinate category relative to others —, because it originated from an impulse which was politically motivated. This overlooks the problematic nature of the music of our century and particularly the nature of the Eisler problem. Any and every distinction made between 'political' and 'non-political' pieces in his work makes use of inadequate intellectual categories of thought. If one understands 'political' (according to an old definition which arose at the time of the European Enlightenment) to mean that which should serve the public good — and Eisler understood the concept in this sense only — then every note that he wrote is political.

But naturally he considered and differentiated very precisely the responsiveness and responsive capacity of his various listeners and attempted to keep the different functions of music separate. 'Music for listening', as he occasionally termed it, had to follow different laws to 'applied music', in other words music intended for films or for the theatre. With equal care he thought through the necessities and possibilities which he had to work out when he wrote for workers' meetings or for demonstrations — political music in the narrower sense of the word. Compositional means had to be found — and Eisler did find them — which made the music accessible without being banal, without making use of exhausted, corrupted musical forms. Actually, works like the *Solidaritätslied* (1931) or the *Einheitsfrontlied* (1934) or completely different again, the music for *Die Massnahme* (1930) or for Gorky and Brecht's *Die Mutter* (1931) are truly amongst the most original and individual pieces of their time, completely 'intrinsic Eisler' ('*des Eislers*'), as Brecht put it.

Eisler's music is tied to historical situations in the most profound way possible through the attempt to react to them not merely meditatively, but rather to participate in shaping them in an active and even interventionist manner. Behind this lies the conviction that music can reach deeper into life than people, including composers, know. As Eisler rightly believed, knowledge of the power of music has entered into old myths. In our present time, however, musicians have distanced themselves too much from the true interests of mankind — which are, at bottom, of a quite simple nature. And those who listen to music have forgotten, or have never learned, how to listen to music. A very complex mechanism operates here, one which is difficult to penetrate and yet is responsive to analysis. Composers should learn to understand it, should recognize what people need and find ways of formulating it in their music.

During the first phase of his creative work, which lasted until Hitler's assumption of power, Eisler held fast to this position, quite obviously without any doubt of its correctness.

Something different can be seen in Eisler's intellectual position during the period of enforced exile. During this time, too, he naturally worked primarily as a composer, as an accompanist when his songs were performed, and as a conductor of his own works, above all in Spain during the civil war against Franco's fascist armies. But he was also a theorist, a participant in conferences and seminars, in gatherings with friends and colleagues in Czechoslovakia and in Austria, in France, several times in the Soviet Union and in Denmark with Brecht. It was only during his stays in the USA, between 1935 and 1948, that Eisler first met people who lived and worked under completely different conditions to those prevalent in Germany before Hitler or in the early years of the Soviet Union.

It is very probable that during this time Eisler had an ear relatively open to the opinions of people who were not on the side of Communism, perhaps even to the music of composers who did not meet his high standards, and yet were to be taken seriously as people and as allies in the fight against Hitler's barbarism. We need not conceal the fact that (later too, in Germany) Eisler's natural amiability towards his colleagues occasionally collided with his aversion to their music, which he considered 'stupid'. He handled such conflicts with bravura, readily shielding himself behind sarcastic politeness.

Much of the film music from the period of exile was intended, above all, to help him earn a living, yet nevertheless exhibits thorough craftsmanship. But the majority of the compositions were written mindful of a Germany and a Europe after Hitler. And there they had, and continue to have, their effect. Again and again he consciously put to the test new compositional means. Characteristic of these pieces are, for example, the *Deutsche Symphonie*, planned and executed in large part during the time of exile, the great *oeuvre* of songs and cantatas from these years, the *Woodbury-Liederbüchlein*, and much else.

The most highly differentiated period — and in many respects the most difficult — was Eisler's last great phase of creativity and work, which began with the end of the Second World War, was to last for seventeen years, and was closely linked to the German Democratic Republic.

During this time Eisler recognized and assimilated the fact that capitalism was not the only ideology mired in a profound crisis. He saw signs of crisis in the workers' movement, in the Soviet Union and in the young socialist countries. I recall a saying of Eisler's from the fifties. 'If you want a different Soviet Union,' he said, 'you'll have to paint it on the wall . . .'.

Eisler not only experienced with active sympathy the prehistory, the early history and the development of the German Democratic Republic; he attempted to contribute critically to the form it took, and not only with his compositions of the most various kinds. It is part of his tragedy — and not only his — that these loyal and (as it later emerged) necessary criticisms found less and less audience. Indeed, though officially honoured and respected, he was neglected as a composer — his great works were performed less and less frequently — and as a theorist he was increasingly ineffective. One of the most shameful chapters in the cultural history of the GDR — the criticism, pursued in extended conferences and repeated articles in the press, of the text of his opera *Johann Faustus*, published in 1952 — had embittered him, almost made him lose heart; he suffered for this. But until his death he did not give up hope that the socialistic countries would learn to translate into practice the theories and principles to which they were committed.

Hanns Eisler did not delude himself that he had a self-sufficient theory of music, nor even one concerning the transition from capitalism to socialism. But he sought with active intelligence, great knowledge and untiring attentiveness, to intervene, warning, criticizing and correcting, whenever he saw only too clearly that matters were not in good hands. He not only took into account the contradictions within his own conceptions. Made aware of them, he in fact valued them as a spur to new insights. For this reason he considered suspect the insights of others which were presented as 'eternal'. It was not only political renewal that interested him; he understood very well that the further development of science and technology would also change people, their lives and their music — and he was not thinking of the refinement of weapons, nor of destructive over-production in a world plagued by hunger, disease and ignorance.

If one considers Eisler's work from the point of view of whether the solution of human problems to which his work was devoted has succeeded, one comes to a bitter conclusion. Only a brief historical moment after his death, the German Democratic Republic — he happily called it names, in which ironic distance resonated equally with his acknowledged ties to it, as in: 'our dear GDR' —, hardly more than a quarter-century after his death, the dear GDR has collapsed in shame.

The enormous difficulties of establishing a social order which constitutes an alternative to capitalism, and is equal to capitalism's hostile powers, were too great for the leading politicians of the GDR. Thus the unification of the two parts of Germany was determined by the interests of powerful financial and industrial groups and accordingly ushered in by conservative politicians who, for their part, saw their opportunity in hastily arranged elections which were promoted with deceitful promises. As these lines are written, the representatives of capital are attempting to occupy as many leading positions as possible, as if they had conquered the country in a war. Whatever might stand in the way of their profit must be brutally destroyed. Every possible source of competition must disappear, including those in the scientific and artistic fields, as well as every possible alternative to the profit economy, including those in the heads of thinking people. Not only must everything disappear that truly should not and cannot be saved from the remains of the GDR, but also — and precisely — whatever, in spite of everything, is worth preserving or capable of reconstruction: arrangements and concepts which, however deficient, served the social security of people, the solidarity, the hope of a life in which man is a helper of other men, to use Brecht's words.

Thus a situation has arisen which in its characteristic measures, events, attitudes, verbal formulations is compellingly reminiscent of the times in which Hanns Eisler wrote his most provocative pieces. It is too early to say whether and how this tragic parallelism of history will manifest itself in the musical life of Germany. We can affirm, however, that this situation does help us to understand Eisler's mental world and creative processes, and that what for some people appeared to have only historical interest has now unexpectedly become reality.

Eisler loved to adapt himself, in his musical concepts, to what he readily termed 'the naive aspect of Marxism': that every person has the right to live free of worry and fear, that among human rights is the right to work, that there should not be some people feasting, while some are starving. And he well knew that these 'naivities' were the foundation and prerequisite of Marx's precise analyses and philosophical conclusions.

The *Lied des Händlers,* from the *Massnahme,* composed in 1930 and hence over sixty years old, is the song of a merchant whose colonial principles have now also become reality in Germany. Naturally the profiteers of today do not say what Brecht and Eisler had their prototype of the exploiter sing, to cheeky jazz rhythms: Ex. 19.1

Ex. 19.1 *Die Massnahme. Song von der Ware*

Weiß ich, was ein Mensch ist,
Weiß ich, wer das weiß?
Ich weiß nicht, was ein Mensch ist,
Ich kenne nur seinen Preis.
[Do I know what a man is,
Do I know who knows it?
I don't know what a man is,
I know only his price.]

The *Stempellied* (1929) parodies a line of poetry which people in Germany know from school: '*Wer hat dich, du schöner Wald, aufgebaut so hoch da droben?* (You beautiful forest, who has built you so high up there?') Today, when roughly half the population of the former GDR is either unemployed, suffers insecure working conditions, is pushed into premature retirement, or in some other way is forced out of the normal patterns of work, and when this is a new event in Europe, the bitter irony of the *Stempellied*, so 'beautiful' to sing, will be understood only too well:

Wer hat dich, du kleiner Mann,
Abgebaut so hoch da droben?
[You little man, who has
Sacked you so high up there?]

No doubt one will also understand anew the sarcasm of *Einkäufe* (Shopping), a text which Tucholsky had written as long ago as 1919 and which Eisler set to music in the style of a *chanson* in 1956. Reflecting on what one could give little Michel on the first birthday of the first German Republic, the singer advises his uncles and aunts:

Doch schenkt ihm keine Reaktion!
Die hat er schon. Die hat er schon!
[But don't give him any reaction!
He's got that already. He's got that already!]

'*Diese Welt wolln wir uns mal von nah besehn*!' (We wanna look at this world close up for once!) When I first heard this line, sung in a grand arrangement by a four-part mixed chorus, to a melody like the *Marseillaise* — conducted, incidentally, by Anton von Webern in the *Grosse Musikvereinssaal* in Vienna —, it must have been 1929. The piece is called: *Auf den Strassen zu singen* (To be sung in the streets), for mixed voices and several side drums. Again today politics are being made on the streets of the former GDR, and it looks as though Eisler's Opus 15 will also be rediscovered. As early as 1929, Eisler wrote a *Gesang der*

Besiegten (Song of the Defeated), with his own words. The first line runs: 'Let us not lose heart in these dark times'; this has taken on new meaning. And the now-famous lines from the *Lob der Dialektik* in *Die Mutter* have retained their old meaning:

Wer noch lebt, sage nicht: niemals!
Das Sichere ist nicht sicher
So, wie es ist, bleibt es nicht.
Wenn die Herrschenden gesprochen haben
Werden die Beherrschten sprechen.
Wer wagt zu sagen: niemals?
[Whoever is still alive, don't say: never!
What is certain is not certain
As it is now, it will not remain.
When the conquerors have spoken,
The conquered will speak.
Who dares to say: never?]

The macabre way in which works from one of Eisler's early creative phases become topical and useful once again confirms that his musical impulses reacted to crimes within human society which are long-lived. If today he had to view his work critically, he would have every reason to feel himself justified. He would have to set a question mark only by those of his pieces which formulate the solution:

Arbeiter, Bauern, nehmt die Gewehre,
Nehmt die Gewehre zu Hand!
[Workers, peasants, take your weapons,
Take your weapons in hand!]

Incidentally, the considerations set out here are no mere intellectual game. Eisler's final work confirms that his thoughts revolved around possible defeats, future struggles, around despair and new hope.

His last work speaks a clear language — *Ernste Gesänge* (Serious Songs) after texts by Hölderlin, Viertel, Leopardi, Richter and Hermlin, for baritone solo and string orchestra. The *Ernste Gesänge* were composed during the last year of Eisler's life, 1961–62. Two of the six songs are (at least in outline) of an older date. That Eisler reflected much about the selection, number and sequence of the poems is verified; that intimations of death also played a part is clear from the content; that he had not ceased to think politically (in the sense defined above), is clear from the inclusion of a poem with the title *XX. Parteitag* (20th Party Conference), that is, of the Communist Party of the Soviet Union, at which the crimes of Stalin were uncovered. The *Ernste Gesänge* are a testimony.

It is one of those works which makes it clear that Eisler had taken issue seriously with Schoenberg, without subordinating himself to his teacher. We are dealing with a work of the most complex simplicity, very characteristic of Eisler's later style. In it are some of the most beautiful verses in the German language, among them Hölderlin's wonderful lines:

> *Möge der Zimmermann vom Gipfel des Dach's den Spruch tun;*
> *Wir, so gut es gelang, haben das Unsre getan.*
> *[Let the carpenter speak his piece from the peak of the roof;*
> *We, as best we could, have done our part.]*

The work concludes with words by Stephan Hermlin, in which Eisler, contrary to his custom, presents the key word three times:

> *Künftigen Glückes gewiß, gewiß, gewiß.*
> *[Certain, certain, certain of future happiness.]*

The fifth song, after a poem by Helmut Richter, the one referring to the 20th Party Conference, closes with the motto that encapsulates the aim — not 'utopian' — of Eisler's entire work: Ex. 19.2

> *I hold you enclosed in my arms.*
> *Hope has sprouted like a seed.*
> *Will the dream now be fulfilled of those*
> *Who gave their life for barely imagined happiness:*
> *To live without fear.*

Translated by Karin von Abrams.

Ex. 19.2 *Ernste Gesänge.* No. 5 *XX. Parteitag*

20

RECOLLECTIONS

David Blake

In 1964 I was invited to contribute to the special volume of the East Berlin periodical *Sinn und Form* dedicated to Eisler. I had to put my mind to the task only two years after his death and wrote a mixture of personal reminiscences and musical analysis and comment. Today, some thirty years on, another death has taken place, that of the GDR. As with any bereavement, the loss takes time to sink in. There are, I'm sure, countless thousands of former GDR citizens who, still, wake in the morning and say 'I don't believe it.' For the many dedicated, sincere communists who, like the rest of the world, do not mourn that awful, stupid, blinkered and corrupt government, the loss of the entire country, of even the hope of making it better, has been cataclysmic. Other contributors to this book have inevitably made reference to European events and developments since 1989. It is because of these changes that I decided to broaden the scope of these reminiscences to include a little more about life in East Berlin during the year of my study there. I regret very much not having kept a detailed diary at the time. I might have guessed that the experience would be of unusual interest as well as of crucial importance to my personal development.

Twice in my life I have been looked at aghast by a travel official with the words 'Why do you want to go there?' (The second was in Miami en route to Haiti in 1974). The man at Liverpool Street Station was disbelieving as he helped me and my wife (six days married) to load our trunk. The expression of the customs official at *Berlin-Ostbahnhof* (now *Hauptbahnhof*) when we arrived at eight o'clock on a Saturday night without visas was not just incredulous but panic-stricken. The police, who could have issued a forty-eight hour visa, had gone home. Fortunately I had a list of phone numbers of people to contact (not for this purpose, though!) kindly provided by Alan Bush. I showed this to the not at all unfriendly official who immediately caught sight of the name of Ernst Hermann Meyer, the distinguished composer and former Eisler pupil, but rather better known publicly as a member of the Party Central Committee. We spent the next three days at his house, during which time he arranged a government stipendium for me, thereby nicely supplementing my Mendelssohn Scholarship. The bureaucratic problem of what to call me was also solved by my becoming Eisler's *Meisterschüler* at the *Deutsche Akademie der Künste* of East Berlin.

I was under no illusions about Eisler's reasons for accepting me as a private pupil — after a serious heart attack earlier in the year, he was not teaching at the *Akademie*. I was there on the recommendation of Alan Bush and because of Eisler's wish to be diplomatically positive. It certainly wasn't on the basis of my existing compositions; these were quickly disposed of. (I know now from my own experience how hard it is to be interested in a new pupil's old works). Our unexpected arrival found Eisler away in Salzburg and so we were installed in a mildly depressing first floor guest house in *Wilhelm-Pieck-Straße,* whilst the problem of where we were to live for the next year was confronted. At that time I had heard only one work by Eisler, the Quintet *Fourteen Ways of Describing Rain.* Apart from an obvious curiosity to know more, I reasoned that the more I knew about him, the more I would benefit from his teaching. As an undergraduate I had been very interested in the Schoenberg School and knew of his connection with it, but the 'Karl Marx of music' side was new territory. I therefore spent a lot of time in the *Akademie* library reading his scores and listening to records and tapes. Our first meeting was friendly and encouraging and I was set the standard Schoenberg-Eisler task of writing variations. Life over the next three weeks consisted of attempts to write a theme which satisfied him, studying in the library and searching for somewhere in East Berlin to eat decently.

To a pair of political naives, Berlin was bewildering, fascinating, and just a little scary. So many aspects of the GDR were quite different even to someone who had seen Hamburg in 1953 and Cologne, Koblenz and Frankfurt in 1958. Any list would start with the large number of ruins remaining from the war, the vast spaces of *Karl-Marx-Platz,* the monumental architecture of *Stalinallee* (soon to become *Frankfurterallee),* the minimal traffic, the socialist slogans which replaced the commercial advertisements of the West, the lack of luxury or even convenience goods, the limitations on what food could be bought and the stink of brown coal. It would continue with the excellent and amazingly cheap transport system, the rich and stimulating artistic life — the two opera houses (one with Felsenstein), the orchestras, chamber concerts, the *Berliner Ensemble* and *Deutsches Theater* presenting theatrical productions of a brilliance and imaginativeness I had never imagined existed — the museums and the never-ceasing political debate. Only days after our arrival the State celebrated its eleventh anniversary. *Unter den Linden* and *Karl-Marx-Platz* were turned into one enormous fairground and market. Huge numbers of people swarmed about, taking in the various entertainments, the singing of the much revered Paul Robeson, choirs, folk groups, buskers, and eating a lot of *Wurst.* Spirits seemed good although life under the Ulbricht regime was, it has to be said, on the Spartan side especially in the winter. Any relief from the pork available from the local shops had to be sought from the HO store in central *Alexanderplatz,* vegetables were limited, butter shortages occurred and fruit was scarce. (The frozen raspberries from Bulgaria were delicious). After a month, accommodation was found, not by the State machinery but by personal contacts. We occupied two rooms in a crumbling flat rented by a Russian lady who was very charming to us. Our accounts of Britain fuelled her passionate anti-Communism and after our occasional trips across the nearby checkpoint to West Berlin for oranges, real coffee and decent chocolate, she warbled rapturously about the 'golden West.'

So, in our little bohemian pad, with hired piano and essential bits of borrowed furniture, a pattern of life established itself. Eisler was still convalescing from his illness — no alcohol, no sugar, little work and regular afternoon naps. Lessons were fixed from one to the next and worked out at about three per fortnight. No fees! His house was only a half-mile walk away and I would arrive around 4.30 for tea. I had produced about ten themes for variations and to prevent my utter despair he rather grudgingly accepted the tenth and let me proceed. The exercise, clearly stemming from the Schoenbergian principle of perpetual variation, was to derive all material from the theme in the strictest possible way. We sat on opposite sides of the round table in the room which served as study and living room (the house was quite small) and he would read through what I had brought in silence. (How this looked to me can be seen from the cover of this book.) After a while he'd say '*Ja; nicht schlecht*' and go over to the piano. He'd then, in a way that was painful and at first mind-numbing, play the piece very slowly and disjointedly, banging out notes and chords again and again, singing some of the lines in a sort of atonal groan. Periodically he'd look at me sitting beside him and say — 'Is this what you mean?' On the first few occasions I resented this, because I absolutely did not mean my piece to be an a-rhythmic, martellato, disconnected row. Soon I came to understand how he was, in this heartless way, testing the harmony, the counterpoint and the intervallic tensions. Other factors came later. To some extent I adopted this method back home when I tried things out on the piano. It certainly focusses the ear and successfully destroys music which relies overmuch on timbre for its interest! I was being trained in *thematische Arbeit*, logical motivic relationships, the functional connection between the counterpoint and harmony and structural thinking. When my week's work had been partially (sometimes totally) demolished, scribbled on, joked about and suggestions made for the next day's task, he would open a volume of Beethoven sonatas and play fragments of this or that one, contrasting *Kopfthemen* with *Periodenthemen*, drawing attention to phrase construction, transition passages, motivic working and so on. We spent a couple of sessions on the Thirty-two variations in C minor. His analysis of these, published in Notowicz' volume of conversations with him, was famous and I knew I was receiving some of what he had received from Schoenberg. Another favourite was the *Variations on a theme of Schumann Op.9* by Brahms, once again an inherited predeliction. More rarely, we looked at twentieth century music, some Schoenberg, some Eisler, but the classics were our models. This didn't mean that I was writing pastiche or even tonally. My music was actually getting more chromatic and less and less tonally orientated, a process somehow encouraged and facilitated by the disciplined motivic thinking required of me. But the tonal models remained relevant with respect to the structuring of the periods, the manipulation of the tensions and the psychological timing. The *Variations for piano,* my acknowledged Opus 1 was finished in November 1960. Eight variations and a finale remained from the many that I wrote. I had some trouble with the Coda and asked his advice. I watched him scribble on my manuscript a possible way of arriving at the final cadence, identifying so completely with what was my problem that his own creative imagination was awakened. This is radically different to a teacher's correction of Palestrina counterpoint exercises or Bach chorale harmonisations. It is the identification with the pupil's own originality and *particular* problems. I didn't adopt every aspect of what he sketched but the rhythmic diminution (penultimate line of Ex. 20.1) seemed then a brilliant condensation and summing up, and still does.

I copied it out neatly and asked him what he thought. 'It's not bad. By all means play it — but to your friends.' In spite of that, I'm quite proud of it. The transformation from my earlier music (which had won me the Mendelssohn award) to these very intense and dense six minutes now astonishes me.

So much of what I wrote during those months did not survive — other pieces for piano, a scherzo for orchestra, two movements for string quartet. The nine-minute *Andante* for string quartet I had written without supervision. Eisler had sprung on me the news that he was

Ex. 20.1 David Blake. *Variations for piano.* Final page of sketch with Eisler's suggestions.

going to Switzerland for about six weeks to avoid the sub-zero Berlin temperatures. Somewhat blithely, I thought, he proposed that, as soon as he was settled in a hotel there, my wife and I should join him so that teaching could continue. Worried at the expense this would mean, I sat in freezing Berlin working at my melancholy *Andante,* waiting for the summons. It came fairly soon, from the *Casa Tamaro:* 'This Ascona is not suitable for a lengthy stay. Much too dear! I'll return to Berlin at the end of February.' He suggested I send him my latest work, but it was hardly worth it as there were only two weeks to wait. On his return from a trip which had included Florence and Venice, I took him the new piece, which I had tested and tried, played and replayed. I got the usual 'not bad' and we went to the piano. Half-an-hour later he had convinced me that what I had laboured over for three weeks was worthless, lacking substance and sinew, mere mood-music. Having so deflated and depressed me, he still sent me off determined to do better rather than too discouraged to want to work. Eisler's previous *Meisterschüler* studied with him for four years or so and had been put through the full process, including species counterpoint. Although I had done the music tripos at Cambridge, I'm sure that would have happened to me too. With only one year available however, he allowed me to compose freely and made no stylistic suggestions. He did once chide me for something which was too much like Shostakovich. He also queried my wish to write a string quartet — very few people listened to them. My quartet proved to be the only other composition to survive from that year. It's a big four-movement piece and I was unable to complete the finale before having to return to London. I sent it to him some months later and his comments on the last movement had their usual perspicacity. Ex. 20.2

Early on in our relationship Eisler made it clear that his instruction of me would be purely musical. He had no desire to talk politics or have any other sort of influence on me. I said that I wanted to take the opportunity to learn in every way I could and that it would be a shame if I couldn't ask him questions about a whole range of things which concerned me. He readily conceded this, and with pleasure and relief, I think, and over the months, after the actual lesson, we chatted, sometimes for more than an hour. His wife Stephanie usually joined us. She, too, was a musician, had led an eventful life and had much to contribute as we ranged widely over literature, politics and music. Eisler used a mixture of German and English to teach me. His English, with an American twang, was of course rather good and he enjoyed the opportunity to use it again. That was fine by me but I had to concentrate when, for difficult bits, he relapsed into German and just as quickly back again.

It must be remembered that the Berlin wall was not built until August 1961. The exchange rate was 11.40 DM to the pound and currency speculation was the norm. It was possible in a *Wechselstube* of West Berlin to change one West mark for four and a half East marks. This explained why the most expensive seats at the opera were occupied by large numbers of American servicemen, the senior officers often ostentationsly dressed in full evening uniform. I gradually came to understand the reasons for the frequent hostile looks on the trains and buses and the

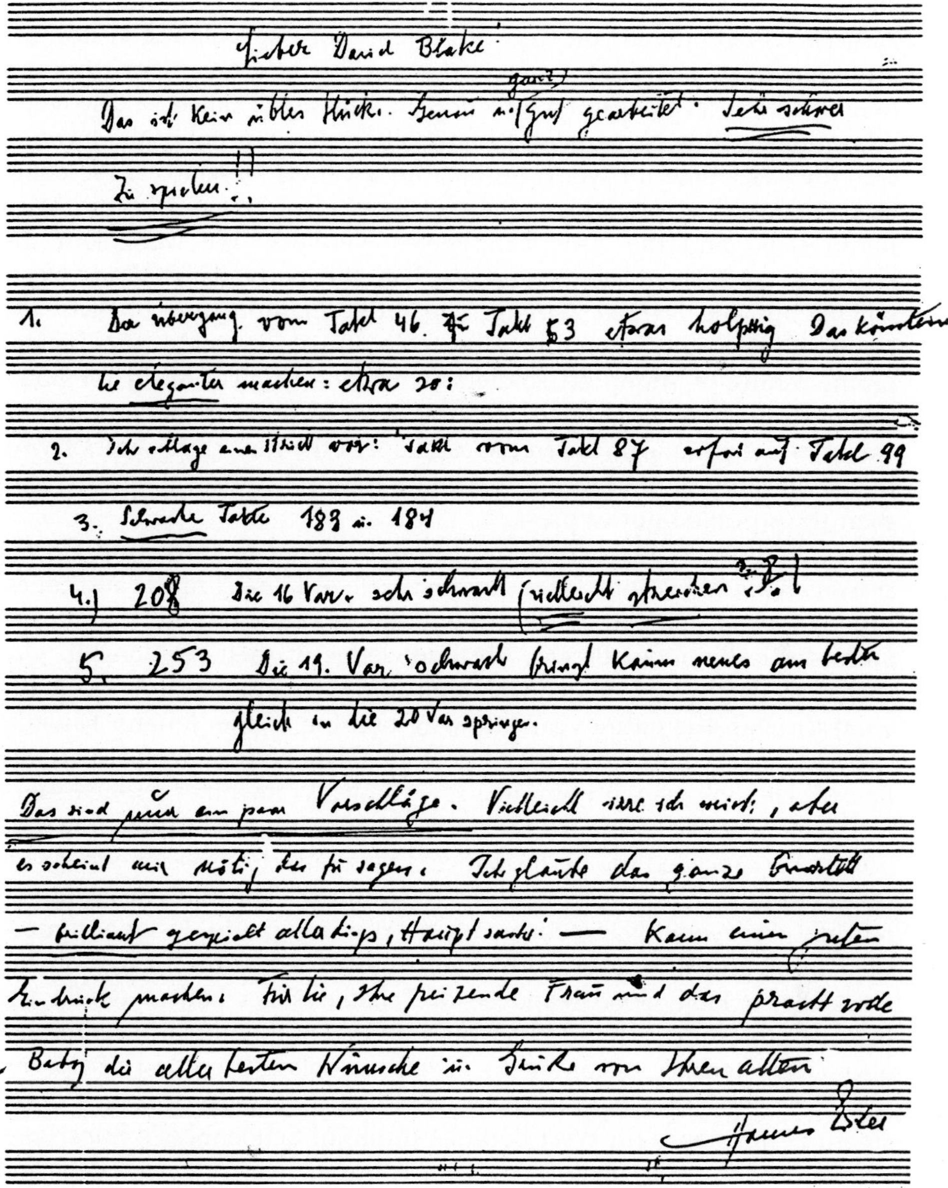
Lieber David Blake!

Das ist kein übles Stück. Genau und (ganz) gut gearbeitet. Sehr schwer zu spielen!!

1. Der Übergang vom Takt 46 zu Takt 53 etwas holprig. Das könnten Sie eleganter machen: etwa 28:
2. Ich schlage einen Strich vor: Takt vom Takt 87 sofort auf Takt 99
3. Schwache Takte 183 u. 184
4.) 208 Die 16 Var. sehr schwach (vielleicht streichen??)
5. 253 Die 19. Var. schwach bringt keine neues am besten gleich in die 20 Var springen.

Das sind nur ein paar Vorschläge. Vielleicht irre ich mich, aber es scheint mir nötig das zu sagen. Ich glaube das ganze Quartett — brilliant gespielt allerdings, Hauptsache! — kann einen guten Eindruck machen. Für Sie, Ihre reizende Frau und das prachtvolle Baby die allerbesten Wünsche u. Grüße von Ihrem alten

Hanns Eisler

Dear David Blake!

This is not a bad piece. Precisely and quite well executed. *Very hard to play*!!

1. The transition from bar 46 to bar 53 somewhat clumsy. You could make it *more elegant:* about 28:
2. I suggest a cut: [bar] from bar 87 direct to bar 99
3. *Weak* bars 183 and 184
4. 208 The 16 var. very weak (*perhaps bowed*??)
5. 253 The 19 var. weak provides nothing new best to jump straight into the 20 var.

These are just a few suggestions. Perhaps I'm wrong, but it seemed to me necessary to make them. I think the whole quartet - brilliantly played of course, essential! — could make a good impression. To you, your charming wife and beautiful baby, very best wishes and greetings from your old Hanns Eisler

Ex. 20.2 Eisler's comments on *String Quartet No. 1* 1962 by David Blake

surly attitudes of waiters and shopkeepers. When you produced an *Ausweis* which proved you were a resident, not a speculating visitor, the attitude changed. Indeed we received very friendly treatment from our neighbours, local tradesmen, our doctor, although I failed to discover a relaxed, amenable bureaucrat. What really began our political education was the availability of world news from a variety of sources. We could listen to three interpretations of a world event from the GDR radio, West Berlin radio and the American Forces Network. We were sent the Guardian and The Listener and we had the party daily *Neues Deutschland* and the *Berliner Zeitung.* The subtle manipulation of facts, the interpretative slant even in respectable British journals, the blatant brainwashing of American soldiers (what does NATO mean for you?) demonstrated that what I had been told was the province of communism was also a technique of the free West. I spent the next thirty years trying to convince my mother that it was more harmful to read the Daily Mail than the so-called gutter press.

Early on, I was struggling through *Mutter Courage*, and *On the specific in music* by Zofia Lissa, my first taste of marxist music aesthetics. Eisler laughed sympathetically about the second of these, but talked enthusiastically about Brecht. My knowledge of their relationship was then very patchy so I missed the opportunity to probe deeply. I actually went through the entire year knowing nothing of the 'Johann Faustus' debacle, so my view of Eisler's role in GDR society was also badly flawed. He took me with him to a few things. I remember a rehearsal of his *Kleine Sinfonie* where the trumpeters had not brought their waa-waa mutes. He cancelled the performance. I went also to a session where his music for the film *Globke* was being dubbed. The film incorporated recently discovered Nazi footage of the Warsaw ghetto. Eisler accompanied these ghastly scenes with a soft, muted fugue for strings on the basis that a Hollywood response of Tchaikovskian pathos would not only be grotesquely stupid but would obliterate the horror. I remember also a very formal session at the *Akademie*, when the guest of honour was Hermann Scherchen. In the concert hall we listened to a tape of his recent performance (in West Berlin, I think) of Schoenberg's *Erwartung*. The reception was polite. Afterwards Eisler was very excited and voluble. Only much later did I understand how important an occasion for him this was, part of the ongoing defence in the GDR of his old 'twelve-note formalist' teacher. As with *Moses und Aron* (which Scherchen was conducting in West Berlin at this time) Eisler abhorred the text and loved the music. He was sure that Schoenberg's most significant and original works were those of the period from around 1907 to 1912.

Another event in the *Akademie* which amused and annoyed me very much was a recital by a visiting French pianist who played Ravel's *Valses nobles et sentimentales.* I suspected, as I listened, that no one in the hall knew the piece. This was confirmed by the tumultuous applause after the last climax which denied us the entire *épilogue.* The poor pianist couldn't bear to shame her hosts by playing it afterwards.

Many other experiences from that year remain very vivid — the Felsenstein productions at the Komische Oper of Janácek's *Vixen* and Offenbach's *Bluebeard,* Brecht's *Galileo* with Busch, *Mother Courage* with Weigel, and an absolutely hair-raising production of *Arturo Ui* with Schall as Hitler; many concerts by the excellent orchestras. Once, after Mahler's Fifth, Ernst Hermann Meyer enthused radiantly. I said my favourite was the Ninth. Ah, but the Fifth ends so vitally, so positively! It's what we need!

Not all performances were wonderful. It was often difficult to cast operas and indifferent singers from West Germany were sometimes necessary. I remember a performance of *Tristan,* ravishingly played by the orchestra, in which the inadequately voiced protagonists exhibited painful desperation at Wagner's demands. My wife begged to be taken home even before the Act 3 Prelude.

Probably because I was married, I didn't socialise with other students. Regrettably, I had very little contact with other young composers although I met many older people. Our close and enduring friendship with Georg and Florence Knepler began — after Eisler's death, without his knowing it, Georg became my replacement guru. The experience with Eisler was a memorable one because I entirely subscribed to his musical standpoint as far as the *'humanistiche, bürgerliche Musiktradition'* was concerned and was also made aware for the first time in an inspiring and exciting way of the revolutionary, proletarian line of music culture.

Since 1961 the value for today of the German symphonic tradition has been challenged not only on an aesthetic level (which was quite inevitable and proper) but also on a technical level. Problems are only recognizable as such against a body of accepted fact and a commonly held, proven set of values. Thirty years ago a man in his sixties could feel strong and sure in his knowledge of the classical tradition and could teach its techniques with unshakeable faith in their value and significance. Like *his* teacher Eisler taught a compositional technique based on the works of Bach, Mozart, Beethoven and Brahms. I am aware that in my own case, strenuous exercises in techniques of thematic development and preoccupation with phrase construction, variation, motivic unity and so on, during a crucial stage of the formation of my musical personality led to an unconscious acceptance of many of the concomitant aesthetic values of the style. Eisler's knowledge of French music, for instance, seemed to be scanty by comparison with his profound understanding of Austro-German music and his relative unconcern with this other music reflected his lack of intellectual and emotional involvement with it. He kept his enormous vitality and intellectual curiosity right up until his death. But my experience was that this curiosity was not brought to bear on the New Music and he sometimes professed bewilderment at certain recent developments. In saying this, I mean in no way to diminish him. I merely wish to show that a teacher can only teach what he knows and understands.

In retrospect, Eisler seems to me to have been not merely a good teacher, but a great one. The imaginative level at which he taught was a measure of the intellectual stature of the man. He had the ability to demolish a piece and yet leave one in a state of determination and hope for the next day's labours. This was because in my experience he was never at a loss for a solution to a musical problem — if a passage was *etwas holprig* he found ways of making it *eleganter*; if a transition was weak, he could strengthen it; he was alive to the slightest hint of *Melodisierung* and helped to eradicate it. Thus during a lesson one learnt specific things and was left in a stronger position technically for the avoidance or solving of similar problems in the future. I want to stress the *specific* nature of his teaching and contrast it with the situation today, when technical criteria are in such a state of flux that comments and criticism can mostly only be generalized.

To be in the presence of a great intellect is a strangely unambiguous experience. It is well known that Eisler was a master of the art of self-contradiction, using non-sequitur, change of tack and playing devil's advocate in a brilliantly ironic way in an attempt to look at a problem from every angle, to expose it fully to the gaze of his interlocutor. For an ordinary person to take part in this, let alone keep up with the pace and fully appreciate the wide range of references which his enormous reading threw out, was wonderfully stimulating, and exhausting.

The effect of the whole year has been lasting. To some extent Eisler sits on my shoulder as I compose. When in doubt I conjure him up to help clarify my thinking and decide whether to reject something. He helps me guard against bombast, excessive length, 'melodizing', weak transitions. He wags his finger at ideas for certain pieces — is it necessary, is it useful? My interest in and love for his music has not waned. I am still thrilled by *Der zerrissene Rock* in *Die Mutter*, delighted by the wit of the suites and moved by so many of the songs. I rate his Opus one more highly than Berg's and would much rather listen to *Palmström* than *Pierrot*.

I went back to the GDR several times. I have been to Berlin twice since its demise. On both occasions, I have felt confused and unable to come to terms with what has happened. I left Berlin in 1961 feeling that, for all its problems, the GDR was a hopeful place, that society could actually change, that the human lot could improve. The disappointment is bitter. Observing the manic determination with which attempts are made to eradicate almost entirely everything the GDR stood for, not just ideologically and politically, but academically and artistically, seems to me not only madness, but extremely dangerous, breeding as it does resentment, hatred and bigotry which will reap its own rewards. One must hope that as the initial fervour and malice abates, that a sense of balance will return and a reasoned assessment can take place of what deserves to be salvaged from the GDR's forty years of existence.

Man is a product of society. He is continually pushed and driven by what concerns it. Let us take care that our social objectives are the correct ones and that the urge towards what is general, broad and binding is guided in the right direction.

Hanns Eisler
26 August 1962

CHRONOLOGY OF EISLER'S LIFE

1898 Born 6 July, Leipzig. Son of Rudolf Eisler 1873–1926, Austrian philosopher and Marie Eisler née Fischer 1875–1929. Sister Elfriede b. 1895, brother Gerhart b. 1897.

1901 The family moves to Vienna.

1904 Eisler begins school.

1908 Attends *Staatsgymnasium No. 2.*

1909 First untutored attempts at composition.

1916 Serves in Hungarian regiment of the Austrian army. Wounded several times.

1917 First extant compositions.

1918 Composes numerous songs. Demobilized from the army in November.

1919 Short period of study at the New Viennese Conservatory with Karl Weigl. Begins studies with Schoenberg in the autumn.

1920 Conducts the *Stahlklang* choir of the Siemens-Schuckert factory in Floridsdorf. Marries Charlotte Demant on 31 August. Accompanies Schoenberg to Holland. Proofreads for Universal Edition.

1921 Conductor of the *Karl Liebknecht* Workers' Choir. Teaches at the *Verein für volkstümliche Musikpflege*. Begins his *Wiener Tagebuch* on 27 August.

1922 Taught by Webern during Schoenberg's absence in the summer.

1923 First performance of the Piano Sonata Op.1 on 10 April in Prague by Eduard Steuermann. His studies with Schoenberg end.

1924 Publication of the first article on Eisler in *Musikblätter des Anbruch* by Erwin Ratz.

1925 Awarded *Künstlerpreis* of Vienna. First articles published. He moves to Berlin.

1926 Controversy with Schoenberg. Applies for membership of the German Communist Party. Rudolf Eisler dies on 14 December.

1927 First reviews for *Die rote Fahne* ('On the 100th anniversary of Beethoven's death'). Begins collaboration with the agitprop group The Red Megaphone.

1928 Lectures at the Marxist Workers' School (MASCH). Composes first Brecht setting *Ballade vom Soldaten*. Georg Eisler born.
1929 First meeting with Ernst Busch. Eisler's mother dies.
1930 First visit to the Soviet Union. Premiere of *Die Massnahme*.
1931 Leads a study group on dialectical materialism and music. Gives lecture in Düsseldorf 'The builders of a new music culture'. Composes music for the films *Niemandsland* and *Kuhle Wampe*, which includes the *Solidarity Song*.
1932 First performance of *Die Mutter*. Committee member of the International Music Bureau.
1933 Beginning of exile. Travels to Czechoslovakia, Paris and London.
1934 Meets up with Brecht in Denmark. Begins work on music for *Die Rundköpfe und die Spitzköpfe*. Composes the *United Front Song*.
1935 Lecture and concert tour in the USA in aid of Saar refugees. Premiere of *Kleine Sinfonie* in London by the BBC conducted Ansermet. Organizes first Workers' Music and Song Olympiad in Strasbourg. President of the International Music Bureau. Lectures at the New School for Social Research in New York. First plans for the *Deutsche Sinfonie*.
1936 Returns to Europe. Attends ISCM Festival in Barcelona. In London with Brecht and Richard Tauber. First performance of *Die Rundköpfe* in Copenhagen.
1937 In Spain with the International Brigade. Collaborates with Ernst Bloch in Prague. Marries Louise Jolesch née von Gosztonyi.
1938 Moves to the USA. Holds post as lecturer at the New School for Social Research.
1939 Visa expires and Eisler goes to Mexico City as guest professor at the State Conservatory.
1940 Begins the Film Music project with grant from Rockefeller Foundation.
1941 Composes several film scores and uses the music for orchestral and chamber works.
1942 Moves to Hollywood. Collaborates again with Brecht. Renews contacts with Schoenberg. Begins Hollywood Songbook. Writes *Composing for the Films* with Adorno.
1943 Anacreon and Hölderlin Fragments. Begins music for *Schweyk*.
1944 Receives Oscar for his music to *Hangmen also Die* (Wexley/Lang).
1945 In New York with Brecht. *Furcht und Elend des dritten Reiches*.
1946 Music for *Leben des Galilei*. The campaign against communist infiltration of the USA begins.
1947 Hearings of the House Committee for Un-American Activities.

Eisler and Brecht summoned before it. International campaign on Eisler's behalf. Solidarity concert for him in Los Angeles.

1948 Eisler deported from USA. Farewell concert of his music in New York. Flies to Prague via London. Contributes to Second International Congress of Composers and Music Critics in Prague. Visits Berlin.

1949 Moves to Berlin. Sets Becher poem which becomes national anthem of the GDR.

1950 Member of the Academy of Arts and teaches composition. Professor at the Hochschule für Musik (later the Hanns Eisler Hochschule). Chamber works performed at ISCM in Brussels.

1951 Plans a Faust opera.

1952 Libretto *Johann Faustus* published. Wide-ranging debate begins.

1953 Three 'Faust Discussions' held in the Academy of Arts. Spends several months in Vienna.

1954 Returns to Berlin. First volume of *Lieder und Kantaten* published. Gives lecture on Schoenberg at the Academy.

1955 Divorced from Lou Eisler. Visits Paris.

1956 Jean-Vigo prize for music to *Nuit et brouillard*. Composes songs for *Schweyk*. Brecht dies.

1957 Premiere of *Schweyk* in Warsaw.

1958 Marries Stephanie Zucker-Schilling (née Peschl). Receives National Prize, First Class, of the GDR. Sixtieth birthday celebrations.

1959 Premiere of *Deutsche Sinfonie* in Berlin.

1960 Visits Vienna. Suffers heart attack.

1961 In Lyons and Paris for French production of *Schweyk*.

1962 Visits London for performance of *Deutsche Sinfonie* by BBC. Completes *Ernste Gesänge*. Dies on 6 September in Berlin.

CHRONOLOGICAL LIST OF MAIN WORKS WITH TEXT REFERENCES

1917 *Dumpfe Trommel und berauschtes Gong* — two songs (tenor and soprano) 12, 16
Galgenlieder — six Morgenstern settings 12–14
1918 *Die Mausefalle* (Morgenstern) for voice, violin and piano 14
Lass aller Spannung der Freude (Tagore) for voice and piano 17
Gesang des Abgeschiedenen for alto and chamber orchestra 16
Wenn es einmal so ganz stille wäre (Rilke) for voice and string trio 17
1919 *Dunkler Tropfe* (Morgenstern) for voice and piano 17
1920 *Zwei Lieder* (*Bitte an den Hund, Rondell*) for voice and piano 20
1921 *Ich hab die Nacht geträumet* for voice and piano (*Volksliedbearbeitungen*) 17
1922 *Sechs Lieder* Op.2 20–24
1923 Piano Sonata Op.1 2, 11, 17, 21, 24–27, 467
Divertimento for wind quintet Op.4 21, 27, 40
Klavierstücke Op.3 21, 24, 27
1924 *Palmström* (Morgenstern) Op.5 4, 12, 29–39, 41, 463
Duo Op.7 for violin and cello 40
1925 *Drei Männerchöre* (after Heine) Op.10 53
Piano Sonata No.2 Op.6 40–44
Klavierstücke Op.8 45–49, 105–8, 111
1926 *Tagebuch des Hanns Eisler* Op.9 4, 50–52, 79
Lustige Ecke 57, 61
1927 *Zeitungsausschnitte* Op.11 3–4, 8, 52–61, 136
Film music to *Opus III* (Ruttmann)
1928 *Vier Stücke* for mixed chorus Op.13 8, 54
Zwei Männerchöre Op.14
Ballade vom Soldaten (Brecht) 8, 79, 468
Auf den Strassen zu singen Op.15 448
1929 *Kominternlied*
Zwei Männerchöre Op.17
Tempo der Zeit (Weber) cantata

Music for *Der Kaufmann von Berlin* (Mehring) 79
Stempellied; Der rote Wedding 448
1930 *Zwei Stücke* for mixed chorus Op.21
Die Massnahme (Brecht) 74, 79–89, 149, 396, 410, 416, 444, 447, 468
Der heimliche Aufmarsch
Sechs Balladen Op.18
Vier Balladen Op.22
Suite No.1 for orchestra Op.23 183
1931 Film music to *Niemandsland* (Trivas) (Suite No. 2) 468
Die Mutter (Brecht) 74, 84, 85, 100, 149, 396, 409, 444, 449, 463, 468
Film music to *Kuhle Wampe* (Brecht) (Suite No. 3) inc. 396, 468
Solidaritätslied 408, 444, 468
1932 *Kalifornische Ballade* — radio play (Ottwalt)
Kleine Sinfonie Op.29 182, 460, 468
Suite No.4 Op.30 (from music for the film *Die Jugend hat das Wort* — Ivens)
Klavierstücke für Kinder
Sieben Klavierstücke Op.32
O Fallada, da du hangest (Brecht)
Vier Wiegenlieder fur Arbeitermütter
1933 Film music to *Dans les rues* (Trivas) (Suite No. 5)
Film music to *Le grand jeu* (Feyder) (Suite No.6)
1934 *Die Rundköpfe und die Spitzköpfe (Brecht)* 56, 91–102, 468 (inc. *Lied von der belebenden Wirkung des Geldes*)
1935 *Lenin* (*Requiem*) 84
1936 *Gegen den Krieg* for small chorus 85
1937 Nine Chamber Cantatas 129
Zwei Elegien
Violin Sonata (*Die Reisesonate*) 36
1938 String Quartet 103–132
Film music *400 Millionen*
1939 *Lieder aus Svenborger Gedichte VI*
Deutsche Sinfonie 78, 85, 181–202, 217, 400–1, 430, 445, 468, 469
Nonet No. 1
1940 Film music *The Children's Camp* — Septet No. 1 148, 149
Film music *White Flood* — Chamber Symphony 149, 182, 409
Funf Orchesterstücke (*400 Millionen* — Ivens) 409
1941 Film music *The Forgotten Village* (Steinbeck) — Nonet No. 2
Variations for piano

CHRONOLOGICAL LIST OF MAIN WRITINGS

1924 Arnold Schoenberg the musical reactionary.
1925 Must the music lover know something about music theory?
1927 Ludwig von Beethoven. On the 100th anniversary of his death.
On modern music.
On the bourgeois concert business.
1928 The new religiosity in music.
On the situation in modern music.
1931 The builders of a new music culture.
1932 On the crisis in bourgeois music.
1933 The materialistic basis of kitsch.
1934 History of the German Workers' Movement from 1848.
1935 Music and music-politics in fascist Germany.
On the position of the modern composer.
1942 Composing for the Films (with Adorno).
1947 Fantasia in G-men.
1951 Letter to West Germany.
1952 On the 125th anniversary of Beethoven's death.
Johann Faustus — libretto.
1954 Arnold Schoenberg.
1958 On stupidity in music.

LIST OF CONTRIBUTORS

Karin von Abrams Born in Portland, Oregon and educated at the University of California (Santa Cruz), University College London and Kings College London, where she also taught for three years. She has been a full-time translator and writer since 1983, though she took a two-year 'sabbatical' to work on the magazine Opera Now (where she became Managing Editor). Her translation *A Voice from Germany*, a volume of speeches by the German President Richard von Weizsäcker, was published by Weidenfeld & Nicholson in 1986.

Márta Batári Born in Debrecen, Hungary, 1953, studied at the Zoltan Kodaly Conservatory, Debrecen, then at the Hochschule für Musik, Dortmund. János Maróthy's wife since 1982. A singer and a musicologist, they have jointly produced what they call Analytic Music Performances for University courses, musicological conferences and popularizing programmes in Hungary and abroad and a series of joint publications on musical behaviour.

Albrecht Betz German scholar, born in Korbach, 1943. For many years a lecturer at the University of the Sorbonne, Paris, he is now Professor of German Studies at the University of Aachen. His publications include *Ästhetik und Politik – Heinrich Heines Prosa,* 1971; *Exil et engagement – Les intellectuels allemands et la France 1930–1940* and *Hanns Eisler, Musik einer Zeit, die sich eben bildet,* 1976 published in English as *Hanns Eisler, Political Musician,* 1982.

David Blake Born London, 1936. The only British pupil of Eisler. Professor of Music at the University of York. Compositions include the operas *Toussaint* and *The Plumber's Gift,* the cantatas *Lumina* (Pound), *From the Mattress Grave* (Heine), *In praise of Krishna* (Bengali texts), *The Bones of Chuang Tzu* (Chang Heng/Waley), *Rise Dove* (Césaire), two concertos, three string quartets, two septets, several works for chorus and much else.

Georg Eisler Son of Hanns Eisler. Born in Vienna, 1926. Spent childhood and early youth in Manchester. Distinguished painter with numerous exhibitions in major galleries including *Musée d'art Moderne,* Paris, Uffizi, British Museum, Venice, Biennale, Albertina.

Fiona Elliott Born in Scotland. Completed Ph.D on Eichendorff at Edinburgh University, where she now lectures in the Department of German. Translator of texts on German music, art and contemporary literature.

Harry Goldschmidt Born in Basel, 1910, died Berlin 1986. Professor of Music at the GDR *Hochschule für Musik* from 1950–55, then a freelance musicologist with special interest in Beethoven and Schubert.

Hanns-Werner Heister Born Plochingen/Neckar, 1946. Germany. Studied musicology in Berlin. Since 1971 freelance writer. Publications include *Musikwissenschaft als Sozialwissenschaft* (1972), *Das Konzert, Theorie einer Kulturform* (1983). Contributor to Contemporary Musical Thought, Routledge 1992.

Tim Howell Born in Kent, 1956. Completed DPhil thesis on Sibelius at Southampton University, published by Garland Press. Lecturer in Music at University of York since 1986. Contributor to Music Analysis and Music and Letters. Editor of Part III, The Structure of Music in Companion to Musical Thought, Routledge 1992.

Eberhardt Klemm Born 1929, died Berlin 1990. Distinguished GDR musicologist and Director of the Eisler Archive from 1985. Writer on diverse subjects including Mahler, Ives, Satie, Cage and Reich. Editor of Berlioz' *Memoirs,* Schindler's *Beethoven,* Schoenberg's *Harmonielehre,* the piano works of Debussy.

Georg Knepler Born in Vienna, 1906. Studied musicology with Guido Adler and piano with Steuermann. Accompanied Karl Kraus. Spent war years in London, returning to Berlin to be founder director of GDR *Hochschule für Musik.* From 1959 was Professor of Musicology at the Humboldt University and Chief Editor of the *Beiträge zur Musikwissenschaft.* Books include *Musikgeschichte des 19ten Jahrhunderts* 1961, *Geschichte als Weg zum Musikverständnis* 1977, *Karl Kraus liest Offenbach* 1984 and *Wolfgang Amadé Mozart,* English edition CUP 1994.

Erik Levi Born in 1949. Senior Lecturer in Music at Royal Holloway College University of London. An active broadcaster, performer and journalist, he is the author of *'Music in the Third Reich'* published by Macmillan 1994

János Maróthy Born in Budapest, 1925. DPhil in aesthetics from Budapest University, under Lukács. Professor of Aesthetics in Faculty of Philosophy, Budapest. Books include *Music of the Bourgeois, Music of the Proletarian,* English version 1974, *Music and Man* 1980; with Márta Batari, *Musical Infinite* 1986.

Günter Mayer Born in Berlin, 1930. Studied philosophy, aesthetics and musicology at Humboldt University, Berlin. Since 1959 has taught there. Professor since 1980. Publications include *Weltbild – Notenbild* 1978 and numerous articles on diverse subjects. Editor of three volumes of Eisler's writings.

Werner Mittenzwei Born in Limburg, 1927. Professor of Literary Theory. Director of the *Zentralinstitut für Literaturgeschichte* at the Berlin *Akademie der Wissenschaft* 1969–73. Books include *Brecht's Verhältnis zur Tradition* 1972, *Das Leben der Bertolt Brecht oder der Umgang mit den Welträtseln* 1986.

Peter Palmer Born in Nottingham, 1945. Read modern languages at Cambridge before studying stagecraft at the Zurich Opera Centre. Freelance journalist and translator. Has completed an introduction to the twentieth-century Swiss composer Othmar Schoeck (to be published by Toccata Press). Translator of Bloch's *Essays on the philosophy of music.*

Wolfgang Pick Born in Germany, 1941. Studied architecture in Berlin and English and Latin Philology in Hamburg. Lives in Corfu. Teaches at the Ionian University and is a freelance translator.

Gerd Rienäcker Born in Göttingen, 1939. Studied musicology at the Berlin Humboldt University. Taught there from 1967. Professor of theory and the history of music theatre 1988. Publications on Bach's Passions and cantatas, Handel, Gluck, Wagner, Brecht, Berg and Eisler.

John Willett Born in London, 1917. Educated at Winchester and Oxford. After the war he worked for the Manchester Guardian and the Times Literary Supplement. The most distinguished British Brecht scholar, his publications and translations are numerous and include *The Theatre of Bertolt Brecht* 1959, *The New Sobriety* 1978 and *Brecht in Context 1984*. He is a collaborator with Ralph Manheim on the edition in English of Brecht's complete works.

BIBLIOGRAPHY

Primary Sources

Hanns Eisler. *Collected Works*
Edition established by Nathan Notowicz. Editors Stephanie Eisler and Manfred Grabs. *Deutscher Verlag für Musik,* Leipzig 1968. [EGW].

Series 1 *Vocal Music*

1 *Die Massnahme*
2 *Die Mutter*
3 *Kalifornische Ballade*
4 *Die Rundköpfe und die Spitzköpfe*
5 *Höllenangst*
6 *Schweyk im zweiten Weltkrieg*
7 Theatre Music (*Der Kaufmann von Berlin — Dantons Tod — Kamrad Kasper* — Draw the Fires — No More Peace — *Furcht und Elend des dritten Reiches — Leben des Galilei*
8 Theatre Music (Volpone — Lysistrata — Hamlet — *Katzgraben — Theaterg'schichten — Der Held der westlichen Welt — Tage der Kommune — Die Gesichte der Simone Machard* — Lofter — *Wilhelm Tell*)
9 *Palmström — Tagebuch des Hanns Eisler — Tempo der Zeit*
10 Chamber Cantatas. Edited by Manfred Grabs. 1982
11 *Deutsche Symphonie*
12 Lenin — *Mitte des Jahrhunderts — Bilder aus der Kriegsfibel*
13 *Rhapsodie — Das Vorbild — Die Teppichweber von Kujan-Bulak — Ernste Gesänge*
14 *A cappella* choruses
15 Early *Lieder*
16 *Lieder* for voice and piano. Edited by Manfred Grabs. 1976
17 *Kampflieder, Songs* and *Chansons* for voice (or chorus ad lib.) and piano
18 *Neue deutsche Volkslieder, Chansons, Lieder* for children and young people. Edited by Nathan Notowicz. 1968.

19 Tucholsky *Chansons*
20 *Lieder* with ensemble
21 *Lieder* with orchestra
22 Arrangements with piano of 20 and 21
23 Versions with piano of theatre music songs
24 Arrangements with piano of theatre music songs
25 Supplement (Arrangements etc.)

Series 2 *Instrumental Music*
1 Suites for orchestra Nos. 1 and 2
2 Suites for orchestra Nos. 3 and 4
3 Suites for orchestra Nos. 5 and 6
Edited by Eberhardt Klemm. 1977
4 *Winterschlacht*-Suite — *Puntila*-Suite — *Tage der Kommune*-Suite — *Sturm*-Suite
5 *Kleine Sinfonie — Fünf Orchesterstücke — Thema mit Variationen — Scherzo mit Solo-violine*
6 *Kammer-Symphonie*
7 Nonets Nos. 1 and 2
8 Septets Nos. 1 and 2
9 Chamber Music
10 Piano Music
11 Supplement (Arrangements etc.)

Series 3 *Writings and Documents*
1 Music and Politics. Writings 1924–48
Edited by Günter Mayer. 1973
2 Music and Politics. Writings 1948–62
Edited by Günter Mayer. 1982
3 Music and Politics. Addenda
Edited by Günter Mayer. 1983
4 Composition for the Films
Edited by Eberhardt Klemm. 1977
5 Poetical writings
6 Letters
7 Conversations with Hans Bunge. *Fragen Sie mehr über Brecht.* Transcribed, with commentary by Hans Bunge. 1975
8 Dialogues (Conversations and interviews)
9 Documents 1898–1948
10 Documents 1948–1962

Other editions of selected works

Lieder und Kantaten 10 volumes
Breitkopf und Härtel, Leipzig. 1955–66
Selected Songs 5 volumes Deutscher Verlag für Musik, Leipzig. 1973
Single Works Opp. 1–21, Opp. 60–65
Universal Edition, Vienna. 1924–73
Johann Faustus (libretto) Aufbau Verlag, Berlin. 1952
New edition edited by Hans Bunge with essay by Werner Mittenzwei
Henschelverlag, Berlin. 1983
Reden und Aufsätze
Edited by Winfried Höntsch Reclam Verlag, Leipzig. 1961
Materialen zu einer Dialektik der Musik
Edited by Manfred Grabs. Reclam Verlag, Leipzig, 1973
Composing for the Films OUP, New York
Dennis Dobson, London. 1947
Hanns Eisler A Rebel in Music
Selected writings edited by Manfred Grabs
Seven Seas Books, Berlin. 1978
Bunge, Hans. *Fragen Sie mehr über Brecht, Hanns Eisler im Gespräch*
Rogner und Bernard, Munich. 1970
Notowicz, Nathan. *Wir reden hier nicht von Napoleon. Wir reden von Ihnen! Gespräche mit Hanns Eisler und Gerhart Eisler*
Transcribed and edited by Jürgen Elsner
Verlag Neue Musik, Berlin 1971

Bibliographies

Notowicz/Elsner. *Hanns Eisler. Quellennachweise.*
Deutscher Verlag, Leipzig. 1961
Klemm, Eberhardt. *Hanns Eisler. Chronologisches Verzeichnis der Kompositionen.* Kulturbund der DDR, Berlin. 1973
Grabs, Manfred. *Hanns Eisler. Ein Handbuch. Kompositionen-Schriften-Literatur* Deutscher Verlag, Leipzig. 1984

Special issues of periodicals

Sinn und Form Hanns Eisler Sonderheft.
Rütten und Loening, Berlin. 1964
Musik und Gesellschaft. Zum 60. Geburtstag Hanns Eislers. Juni 1958
Henschel Verlag, Berlin

Musik und Gesellschaft. 20. Todestag von Hanns Eisler. September 1982
Henschel Verlag, Berlin
Das Argument – Hanns Eisler. AS5 Berlin. 1975
Beiträge zur Musikwissenschaft. Hanns Eisler 1989–1962. Heft 1/2 1973
Verlag Neue Musik, Berlin
Arbeitshefte – Akademie der Künste der DDR, Berlin
Nr. 19 *Hanns Eisler heute.* 1974
Nr. 28 *Hanns Eisler – Werk und Edition. Eine Dokumentation von Manfred Grabs.* 1978

Books

Adorno, Theodor W. *Philosophy of Modern Music*
Trans. Mitchell and Bloomster
Sheed and Ward, London. 1948

Albert, Claudia *Das schwierige Handwerk des Hoffens – Hanns Eislers 'Hollywooder Liederbuch' (1942–43)*
J.B. Metzlersche Verlag, Stuttgart. 1991

Betz, Albrecht *Hanns Eisler – Political Musician*
Trans. Bill Hopkins
Cambridge University Press 1982

Brecht, Bertolt *Gesammelte Gedichte* 4 vols.
Suhrkamp Verlag, Frankfurt am Main. 1967
Poems 1913–1956
Ed. Willett and Manheim
Eyre Methuen, London. 1976
Die Massnahme. Kritische Ausgabe
Ed. Steinweg
Suhrkamp Verlag, Frankfurt am Main. 1972
Translated as *The Decision* by John Willett. 1987.
Unpublished
Letters 1913–1956
Trans. Manheim Methuen, London. 1990
Arbeitsjournal Berlin-Weimar (no date)
Working Journal
Trans. Willett Methuen, London. 1993
Brecht on Theatre
Trans. Willett. Methuen, London. 1964
Theses on the Faustus Debate. Brecht's Works – Zur Literatur und Kunst

Brockhaus, Heinz Alfred
Hanns Eisler Breitkopf und Härtel, Leipzig. 1961

Bunge, Hans *Die Debatte um Hanns Eislers 'Johann Faustus'. Eine Dokumentation* Basis Druck, Berlin. 1991

Döblin, Alfred *Berlin Alexanderplatz* Trans. Eugene Jolas Penguin Books 1978

Dümling, Albrecht *Lasst euch nicht verführen. Brecht und die Musik* Kindler Verlag, Munich. 1985

Eisler, Georg *Skizzen* Compress Verlag, Vienna. 1990

Elsner, Jürgen *Zur vokalsolistischen Vortragsweise der Kampfmusik Hanns Eisler* Deutscher Verlag, Leipzig. 1971

Feuchtwanger, Leon *Success* Martin Secker, London. 1930
Die Geschwister Oppermann. 1933

Goethe, Johann Wolfgang von
Urfaust
Faust

Goldschmidt, Harry *Um die Sache der Musik* Reclam Verlag, Leipzig. 1970

Grabs, Manfred ed. *Wer war Hanns Eisler* Verlag das europäische Buch, Berlin. 1983

Hašek, Jaroslav *The Good Soldier Sveyk* Trans. Cecil Parrott Penguin Books. 1974

Hennenberg, Fritz *Hanns Eisler* Bibliographisches Institut, Leipzig. 1986

Ivens, Joris *The Camera and I* Seven Seas Books, Berlin. 1969

Klemm, Eberhardt *Hanns Eisler für Sie porträtiert* Deutscher Verlag, Leipzig. 1973

Knepler, Georg *Geschichte als Weg zum Musikverständnis* Reclam Verlag, Leipzig. 1977

Lyon, James K *Bertolt Brecht in America* Methuen, London. 1982

Lucchesi, Joachim and Schull, Ronald
Musik bei Brecht Henschel Verlag, Berlin 1988

Mann, Thomas *Doctor Faustus*
Trans. H.T. Lowe-Porter 1949
Genesis of a Novel 1949

Mayer, Günter *Weltbild – Notenbild – Zur Dialektik des musikalischen Materials*
Reclam Verlag, Leipzig. 1978

Mittenzwei, Werner *Das Leben des Bertolt Brecht*
Aufbau-Verlag, Berlin. 1986

Morgenstern, Christian
Alle Galgenlieder
Insel Verlag, Frankfurt am Main. 1947

Paddison, Max *Adorno's Aesthetics of Music*
Cambridge University Press 1993

Phleps, Thomas *Hanns Eislers Deutsche Sinfonie Ein Beitrag zur Ästhetik des Widerstands*
Bärenreiter, Kassel. 1988

Piscator, Erwin *The Political Theatre*
Trans. Hugh Rorrison.
Eyre Methuen, London. 1980

Schebera, Jürgen *Hanns Eisler im USA Exil*
Akademie Verlag, Berlin. 1978
Hanns Eisler Eine Bildbiographie
Henschel Verlag, Berlin. 1981

Schoenberg, Arnold *Harmonielehre (Theory of Harmony)*
Trans. Roy E. Carter
Faber and Faber, London. 1978
Style and Idea
Ed. Leonard Stein. Trans. Leo Black
Faber and Faber, London. 1975
Selected Letters
Ed. Erwin Stein. Trans. Wilkins and Kaiser
Faber and Faber, London. 1964

Stuckenschmidt, H.H. — *Arnold Schoenberg His life and work* Calder London 1977

Traven, Bruno — *The Cotton Pickers* Allison and Busby, London. 1979

Willett, John — *The Theatre of Bertolt Brecht* Methuen, London. 1959
Brecht in Context Methuen, London. 1984
The New Sobriety: Art and Politics in the Weimar Period 1917–33 Thames and Hudson, London. 1978

Articles

Blake, David — Mein Lehrer Hanns Eisler *Sinn und Form Eisler Sonderheft,* Berlin. 1964
Hanns Eisler *The Listener.* 15 September 1966

Dahlaus, Carl — Thesen über engagierte Musik *Studien für Wertungforschung* 3, Graz. 1972

Dessau, Paul and Goldmann, Friedrich — Versuch einer Analyse zu Hanns Eislers Kantate *Die Teppichweber von Kujan-Bulak* *Sinn und Form Eisler Sonderheft,* Berlin. 1964

Drew, David — Eisler and the Polemic Symphony *The Listener.* 15 September 1962
Eisler and Austrian Music *Tempo.* June and September 1987
From the other side: reflections on the Bloch centenary. Introduction to Ernst Bloch's *Essays on the Philosophy of Music.* Cambridge University Press. 1985

Dümling, Albrecht — Schöenberg und sein Schüler Hanns Eisler. Ein dokumentarischer Abriss. *Arbeitshefte 24 – Arnold Schönberg* Akademie der Künste der DDR, Berlin. 1976
Zur Funktion der Reihentechnikin Eislers Deutscher Sinfonie from *Berichte über Internationalen Musikwissenschaftlichen Kongress Bayreuth* 1981, Bärenreiter 1984

Eisler-Fischer, Louise — Faust in der DDR. Dokumente
Neues Forum, Vienna. October 1969

Fischer, Ernst — Eisler und die Literatur
Sinn und Form Eisler Sonderheft. 1964

Grabs, Manfred — Film- und Bühnenmusik im sinfonischen Werk Hanns Eislers.
Sammelbände zur Musikgeschichte der DDR Vol. 1. Berlin 1969

Zum Frühwerk
Arbeitshefte 19 Hanns Eisler heute
Akademie der Künste der DDR, Berlin. 1974

"Wir, so gut es gelang, haben das Unsre getan." Zur Aussage der Hölderlin — Vertonungen Hanns Eisler.
Beiträge zur Musikwissenschaft XV/1–2, Berlin 1973

Goehr, Alexander — Untitled article in *Sinn und Form Eisler Sonderheft*, pp. 344–7. English original, dated 1964, unpublished

Haug, Wolfgang — Hans Faust und Hans Wurst in Eislers Version der Faust-Sage *Das Argument* AS5, Berlin 1975

Hennenberg, Fritz — Zur Dialektik des Schliessens in Liedern von Hanns Eisler *Sammelbände zur Musikgeschichte der DDR* Vol. 2, Berlin. 1971

Klemm, Eberhardt — Bemerkungen zur Zwölftontechnik bei Eisler und Schönberg *Sinn und Form*. 1964 Vol. 5

Knepler, Georg — '. . . was des Eislers ist'
Beiträge zur Musikwissenschaft, Berlin. 1973 Vol 1/2

Mayer, Günter and Knepler, Georg

Hätten sich Georg Lukacs und Hanns Eisler in der Mitte des Tunnels getroffen?
Dialog und Kontroverse mit Georg Lukacs
Ed. W. Mittenzwei, Leipzig. 1975

Planchon, Roger — Hanns Eisler à Lyon
Théâtre populaire, Paris 1961
German version in *Sinn und Form* 15/1. 1963

Rittig, Julia — Hanns Eislers Frühe Lieder in ihrer Zeit — Eine Bestandsaufnahme.
Diplomarbeit — Humboldt Musikwissentschaftliches Institut, Berlin. 1991. Unpublished

Szeskus, Reinhard — Bemerkungen zu Eislers Deutsche Sinfonie
Musik und Gesellschaft, Berlin. 1973

INDEX